Entrepreneurship

An international introduction

Dafna Kariv

Routledge
Taylor & Francis Group

LONDON AND NEW YORK

First published 2011
by Routledge
2 Park Square, Milton Park, Abingdon, Oxon OX14 4RN

Simultaneously published in the USA and Canada
by Routledge
270 Madison Ave, New York, NY 10016

Routledge is an imprint of the Taylor & Francis Group, an informa business

Typeset in Perpetua and Bell Gothic by
Keystroke, Station Road, Codsall, Wolverhampton
Printed and bound in Great Britain by
CPI Antony Rowe, Chippenham, Wiltshire

British Library Cataloguing in Publication Data
A catalogue record for this book is available from the British Library

Library of Congress Cataloguing in Publication Data
Kariv, Dafna.
   Entrepreneurship: an international introduction / Dafna Kariv.
      p.cm.
   Includes bibliographical references and index.
   1. Entrepreneurship. I. Title.
   HB615.K367 2011
   658.4'21—dc22   2010031383

ISBN: 978–0–415–56119–8 (hbk)
ISBN: 978–0–415–56120–4 (pbk)
ISBN: 978–0–203–83193–9 (ebk)

This book is dedicated to my father, Dan Barel. His memory and his inspiration will always be special to me, touching upon all aspects of my life.

Contents

CONTENTS

List of case studies

AT A GLANCE

List of illustrations

LIST OF ILLUSTRATIONS

List of tables

Foreword

Preparing for entrepreneurial practice

Louis Jacques Filion
Professor and Head of the Chair of Entrepreneurship, HEC, University of Montreal, Montreal, Canada

These days, new venture creation plays an essential role in renewing the economic and social fabric. In most societies, new ventures are regarded as the main contributors of innovation, creating jobs and providing added value. The wealth of a nation depends on its ability to generate innovation, and most of that innovation is the product of new ventures.

Not only has the number of new ventures increased, but the range of entrepreneurial prospects has also grown. However, in spreading its wings, the world of entrepreneurship has also become more complex. Every day, new ventures are launched in emerging sectors, with new entrepreneurial models as their basis. Until now, we have been used to preparing venture creators for the more traditional manufacturing and service sectors. Today, though, growing numbers of entrepreneurs can be found in the social and philanthropic fields, as well as in the technological, cultural, artistic and entertainment sectors.

Organizations – along with all the other elements of our society – are becoming more complex, and that complexity has generated a rapidly growing set of potential opportunities. Most venture creators must now be able to define existing, emerging and latent needs that reflect not only market development, but also the more sophisticated levels of education to which people aspire, and the technology-based environments in which they live. In addition, they need to be able to devise ways of defining the boundaries of these new, emerging sectors.

Increasingly, these new ventures, regardless of where they are situated, tend to focus on the global market; in fact, the number of firms operating globally from the time of inception doubles every year.

Today's venture creators and entrepreneurs are much more highly qualified and have more sophisticated learning cultures than ever before, with the result that anyone who may be considering entrepreneurship as a future career path needs a complete and well-developed overview of their target field.

Dafna Kariv is a well-known specialist in the field of entrepreneurship. She has written a book that will appeal to a broad range of readers. The book has been designed to present a structured approach to the learning required in preparation for entrepreneurial practice and venture creation in today's global environment.

More than 70 entrepreneurs from 45 countries were interviewed for this book. Readers will find more than 20 very different case studies that will inspire them to construct their own mental models of the entrepreneurs they wish to become, and what they wish to accomplish. In the jungle of increasingly specialized literature, here is a book that not only provides an overview of the subject, but also proposes avenues for readers to explore its various aspects in more depth.

Dafna Kariv's book is both complete and well documented, and its readers will find the expertise and inspiration they need to bring their dreams to fruition.

Acknowledgments

This is my first published book, the outcome of much thought, eagerness, inspiration and determination. Its publication would not have been possible without the enthusiastic effort and support provided by a number of individuals to whom I owe a debt of gratitude. First, my heartfelt thanks go to Terry Clague, Sharon Golan and Alexander Krause of Routledge for commissioning the book and for guiding me through the fascinating publication process. Their comments, ideas and noteworthy professional and practical assistance, as well as their constant support, helped me shape the book and raise it to the highest level.

Special thanks are due to my beloved and supportive family: my husband, Raanan, for his remarkable faith in me and for supporting me unfailingly throughout my career; my children, Tomer, Ofir, and Shir, for always making me smile and for their loving patience and encouragement. I hope that one day they will read this book and understand why I spent so much time in front of my computer. Thank you, my dear family, for being a constant source of strength for me throughout the entire writing process.

I am honored to have the opportunity to express my gratitude to Professor Louis Jacques Filion, Head of the Rogers – J.A. Bombardier Chair of Entrepreneurship, HEC, Montreal, Canada, who inspired and motivated me to write the book, for having greatly influenced my thinking and for opening my eyes through his comments and ideas.

I would like to thank all of the entrepreneurs that I interviewed for generously spending hours sharing their entrepreneurial stories with me, and for providing a robust foundation for this book's concepts.

I am grateful to the College of Management, Academic Studies, Rishon Lezion, Israel and to the School of Business Administration at the College of Management, for providing financial support and technical input for the work on which this book is based.

I offer my grateful thanks to Ms. Camille Vainstein, for her help in editing the manuscript, and in reading, commenting on and assisting in clarifying sections of its various drafts. I am indebted to Ms. Revital Alteberger, research assistant, who contributed substantially to the book's organization and formulation in the final stages of its preparation.

Dafna Kariv
February 2011

Introduction

WHO SHOULD READ THIS BOOK?

This book is targeted to students at academic institutions in entrepreneurship programs and at small-business management and business schools, their teaching staff, and researchers in entrepreneurship and small business. Most important, this book is for entrepreneurs and future entrepreneurs, be they students or people who are still engaged in corporate jobs. It provides a foundation for those who want a wider overview of what starting a business means and involves, by introducing the entrepreneurial business phases in different countries, cultures and sectors of industry, as well as at different levels of success.

The book includes a broad introduction to the field of entrepreneurship in order to familiarize the readers with the most well-established terms, concepts and models derived from research in the field that has contributed to this area with its robust academic and practical perspective. Each chapter includes references for the readers' convenience, to expand upon their knowledge on the different topics discussed and analyzed in this book.

Most importantly, the book is enriched with a range of case studies of active, real-world entrepreneurs from different countries based on their narratives. These case studies are introduced in every chapter, followed by questions for discussion to allow students and entrepreneurs of diverse backgrounds to learn from others' previous experiences. The wide range of case studies was chosen to enable almost any entrepreneur to identify with the stories by spotting similarities to his/her personal or business's characteristics. As such, the reader will more easily understand how entrepreneurial concepts can be applied to real business situations encountered in his/her entrepreneurial realm. The case studies, contributed by entrepreneurs from around the world, were collected by the author, who personally conducted all interviews face-to-face, and over the telephone and Skype.

An annotated list of internet resources is introduced at the end of some chapters, including sites that offer useful reference information for the book's topics, thus encouraging their implementation. The list does not attempt to cover all of the websites and internet resources relevant to entrepreneurs, but rather to give the readers examples of such resources, which may assist them in their search for others.

ENTREPRENEURSHIP IN A GLOBAL CONTEXT

Entrepreneurship is the predominant form of business organization: statistics from the Global Entrepreneurship Monitor (GEM) indicate that roughly 60–90 per cent of businesses worldwide are entrepreneurial. In most countries, entrepreneurship is emerging as the major factor paving the way for economic development, by having a synergistic impact through job creation, innovation, helping to increase female, ethnic and minority participation in the workforce and alleviating local poverty in inner cities and suburban areas (Kariv et al. 2009; Kariv, Menzeis and Brenner 2010).

Many books have been published to guide budding entrepreneurs in launching businesses, familiarize individuals with the entrepreneurial realm, and introduce entrepreneurial thinking, spirit and know-how to potential and active entrepreneurs. Most of them portray local economies; alternatively, they focus on the US economy, which tends to surface in most books as the point of reference for a discussion on entrepeneurship in many other economies. This book, however, embraces diversity, and is specifically targeted to expose the differences between countries and cultures, as well as the core topics in entrepreneurship. There is a need to reveal the realities of the various entrepreneurial cultures and economies around the world, and to bring diversity in entrepreneurship to the forefront of research and practice, especially because books presenting such a broad perspective are scarce. This dearth led to the writing of this book, in order to provide a platform for discussions on the main issues of entrepreneurship through multifaceted and multicultural lenses.

As such, one of this book's more important aspects lies in its broad international coverage of activities involved in launching and managing a successful venture. Core activities of entrepreneurs, be they from Canada, Israel, Great Britain, Malaysia, Australia, Kenya, the United States, China, or elsewhere, are illustrated and discussed as case studies and 'at-a-glance' anecdotal stories. The success stories of entrepreneurs[1] from twenty-two countries, covering all continents, are presented: each one emphasizes a different aspect of entrepreneurial activity, while together they provide an overview of the global phenomenon of entrepreneurship.

Specifically, this book traces the entrepreneurial path with different case studies, which are the stories of entrepreneurs from different countries and cultures, possessing different backgrounds and human capital (age, educational level, entrepreneurial experience), having diverse motivations to become entrepreneurs, and influenced by different environmental and cultural determinants. Their businesses are from various sectors of industry, in different phases of development, and varied in terms of their success experiences. For example, this book illustrates the complexities of the *environment's effects* on the entrepreneur and the entrepreneurial business by presenting the case of Baby-Dalózó, which offers a catalogue, a magazine and a website for baby products in Hungary; the *entrepreneurial culture* is introduced in the story of Shlomi and Osnat Zingler, the Israeli franchisors of Leonidas Belgian Chocolates, who demonstrate a pure entrepreneurial spirit in their daily routines; *innovation* in the entrepreneurial context is presented by Speak-ing-4-u, Australia, which was launched as a most innovative idea and business in 1980, before widespread use of the internet for marketing; *building a concept in marketing* is demonstrated by Fai Yang, the owner of e-HK.Flowers, Hong Kong, specializing in web-sourcing for delivery and shipment of specialized flower bouquets, and *mentorship* is explored by tracing the road taken by Rutujit Jindal, an active university professor in India who works independently as a paid mentor, and the very different story of Paterina Cammarata, of Verona, Italy, the new owner and CEO of Consiglio, a family enterprise that provides counseling and mentoring services for the business sector in Italy. These are just a few examples of the book's concept: through this variation, the book attempts to identify the core essence of entrepreneurship that emerges in any entrepreneurial business.

The book's overall perspective is practical, built upon a background of the main theoretical models and concepts in entrepreneurship – its ideas and recommendations therefore stem from both practice and theory.

BASIC THEORETICAL MODELS IN ENTREPRENEURSHIP AT A GLANCE: A RESEARCH EVOLUTIONARY PERSPECTIVE

Entrepreneurship is the world's oldest profession, known as a popular employment feature of the pre-industrial revolution era, which persisted throughout the 100-year industrial revolution and has been expanding ever since. A major explanation for entrepreneurship's steadfast persistence through the years is its ability to change and re-change form, renew itself, adjust to the demands of a particular time and place, and reinvent itself through the development of economic, technological, social and regulatory conditions. Today, the entrepreneurial society is still expanding but it is also continually transforming and redefining itself, such that the market and society as a whole can no longer imagine a world in which entrepreneurship would not exist.

A quick overview of the evolution of entrepreneurship illustrates how far we have come and enables us to envision future developments in the entrepreneurial realm (Churchill et al. 1987; Gavron, Cowling and Westall 1998; Schoonhoven and Romanelli 2001; Von Bargen, Freedman and Pages 2003).

The evolution of research into entrepreneurship began in 1730, when Richard Cantillon, a Parisian banker and economist, introduced the term *entrepreneur* (literally, 'undertaker' in French). His pioneer *Essai sur la Nature du Commerce en General* presented his first definition of entrepreneurship as self-employment of any kind. He stated that entrepreneurs buy at certain prices in the present and sell at uncertain prices in the future. The entrepreneur is a bearer of uncertainty, he concluded. Following this, the French Jean Baptiste Say (1880), inspired by Adam Smith's economic theories, joined a group of *laissez-faire* economists known as the *idéologues*, who sought to relaunch the spirit of enlightenment in republican France. Say emphasized the essential nature of entrepreneurship to society as a whole, and defined the entrepreneur as the agent who unites all means of production and who finds in the value of products, the re-establishment of the entire capital he/she employs, and the value of the wages, interest, and rent he/she pays, as well as profits belonging only to him or her. Taking this a step further by focusing on the 'central figure' of the system, Frank Knight (1921), the American economist founder of the Chicago school and author of the book *Risk, Uncertainly and Profit*, added the entrepreneur's attempt to predict and act upon changes within markets, and emphasized the entrepreneur's role in bearing the uncertainty of market dynamics. In the long run, Knight stressed, entrepreneurs are required to perform fundamental managerial functions, such as direction and control.

Joseph Schumpeter (1934), the Austrian economist and political scientist, argued that perfect competition would not eliminate profits due to uncertainty, and he was the first to emphasize the role of innovation in the entrepreneurial realm. In his first book, *Theory of Economic Development* (1911), his popular book *Capitalism, Socialism and Democracy* (1942), and others, Schumpeter equated entrepreneurship with the concept of innovation applied to a business context. Schumpeter said that the entrepreneur is the innovator who implements change in the marketplace by creating new combinations. These new combinations can take on several forms: the introduction of a new good or quality thereof; the introduction of a new method of production; the opening of a new market; the conquest of a new supply source of new materials or parts; getting a new organization off the ground. As such, the entrepreneur moves the market away from equilibrium. In contrast to Knight, Schumpeter consired managers of already established businesses to be non-entrepreneurs.

Penrose (1959) in *The Theory of the Growth of the Firm* (see Penrose 1959; Pitelis 2005) and her colleagues Barney (1991a, b), Mahoney and Pandian (1992) and Wernerfelt (1984), all from a resource-based perspective, asserted that entrepreneurial activity involves identifying opportunities within the economic system. Like Schumpeter, they argued that managerial capacities differ from entrepreneurial capacities. Later on, the American economist Harvey Leibenstein (1979) claimed that the entrepreneur fills market deficiencies through input-completing activities. Entrepreneurship involves activities necessary to create or run an enterprise where not all markets are well established or clearly defined and/or in which relevant parts of the production function are not completely known. Israel Kirzner (1973, 1979) stressed that the entrepreneur recognizes and acts upon market opportunities, and that an entrepreneur is essentially an arbitrageur. In contrast to Schumpeter's view, the entrepreneur moves the market toward equilibrium.

In the 1950s, following the work of Arthur Cole, attention shifted away from economic functions to more personal analyses of individual entrepreneurs. During this phase of development in the field, many researchers attempted to discover common character traits that might help distinguish entrepreneurs from non-entrepreneurs, including the former's alleged 'need for achievement', a proclivity for risk-taking, an internal locus of control, and even one's place in the family birth order (Hornaday et al. 1985).

Prof. Louis Jacques Filion, in his research report (1997) 'From entrepreneurship to entreprenology', presents and discusses the trends in the field's development.

NATIONAL CULTURE AND ENTREPRENEURSHIP

Cultures are powerful phenomena. They can shape behavior at the individual level and affect institutions at the national level. However, research in entrepreneurship has revealed that some cultures 'produce' higher levels of entrepreneurial activity, in terms of innovation, opportunity recognition and exploitation, creativity, proactivity, search for business support, and actualization of the business plan (Busenitz and Lau 1996; Lindsay 2005).

Researchers in various disciplines are intrigued by the relationship between culture and levels of entrepreneurial activity, and agree on the considerable and vast effect of culture on entrepreneurship.

This book aims to demonstrate different cultures in the entrepreneurial realm (e.g., entrepreneurs from different countries or different sectors of industry), using different institutionalized assistance for their businesses, of different genders and ages. These parameters, among others, represent the differentiation between entrepreneurs as influenced by national culture, business culture, gender-related culture and generation-based culture. Although cultural influences are powerful, it is this book's objective to purify entrepreneurship and reveal its core attributes, i.e., an innovative individual who launches a business can be Indian or Israeli, man or woman, baby boomer or Generation Y; he/she is still an entrepreneur.

Culture is an inherent construct of entrepreneurship and has significant effects on: (1) institutional profiles (e.g., cognitive, regulatory and normative dimensions); (2) behavioral dimensions with respect to business implementation styles, business plans, management styles, and (3) beliefs (e.g., entrepreneurs' interpretation of the environment, the economic-structural determinants, potential customers' preferences). Yet, some concepts lie at the heart of entrepreneurship and cross-cultural variation, such as innovative ideas, visionary businesses, opportunity exploitation, and creative processes. These are considered the constructs of entrepreneurship, its genetic material so to speak, and they represent the collective meaning of entrepreneurship.

Culture is defined in many studies as a set of shared values, beliefs and expected behaviors embedded in the values that shape national institutions (e.g., social, educational, political and technological systems), all of which then reflect and reinforce national values and beliefs (see Figure 1). A country, community, or institution's culture is mirrored in many aspects of entrepreneurial life because these cultures reflect the degree to which individuals consider entrepreneurial behaviors and characteristics (e.g., innovativeness, risk-taking, creativity, proactiveness, etc.) as desirable or beneficial. As such, processes such as problem-solving, thinking outside the box, coping in vague situations, information-seeking, team management and opportunity identification will also be affected by the culture in terms of the levels to which they are applied, the way they are conducted, and the results that they achieve (Hofstede 1980b; Shane 1992, 1993; Davidsson 1995; Busenitz and Lau 1997; Busenitz, Gomez and Spencer 2000; Makino and Neupert 2000; Mitchell et al. 2000; Mueller and Thomas 2001; Hayton, George and Zahra 2002).

Many studies on the microperspectives of entrepreneurship have been skewed toward cultural values and entrepreneurial behavior stemming from Hofstede's (1980a, 1980b) taxonomy of significant cultural dimensions for explaining behaviors, preferences and beliefs of people in the organization (discussed later on in this book). These studies have stressed the notion that the effects of culture on entrepreneursip consist of either boosting or blocking entrepreneurial behavior, for example, by introducing, via various means (media, schools, teaching material, higher education, books, business orientation), the notion that some characteristics and behaviors (e.g., innovation, creativity, independent thinking) are attractive and rewarding, thereby prompting individuals to choose entrepreneurship as their preferred path. This, however, is not enough to foster entrepreneurship: countries supporting such characteristics should echo the national, entrepreneurial culture and facilitate engagement in entrepreneurship by establishing national-based support systems for innovative businesses: financial support schemes, fiscal incentives, social security systems, labor market regulation, bankruptcy legislation, media involvement, and educational institutions (e.g., financial support for studying technological programs in schools and in higher education; programs and training courses for entrepreneurs). Such national activities will be reflected in a growing number of entrepreneurial businesses at the national level.

In their instructive chapter, Zahra and George (2002) provide a categorization of international entrepreneurship definitions into: businesses engaged in the international arena (McDougall 1989; Tiessen and Merrilees 1999), businesses that seek to gain significant competitive advantage from the use of resources and sale of outputs in multiple countries (Oviatt and McDougall 1994; Zahra, Ireland and Hitt 2000), or through a combination of innovative, proactive, and risk-seeking behavior that crosses national borders (Shane 1993; McDougall and Oviatt 2000). In all cases, an

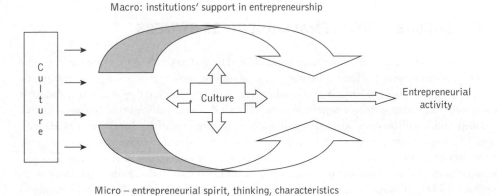

Figure 1 The 'retro–verso' relationship of culture and entrepreneurial activity

understanding of national cultures and hence national markets, especially entrepreneurial markets, is warranted.

At the microlevel, entrepreneurial-based characteristics and behaviors are the driving forces behind national institutions' establishment of means at the national level to facilitate the entrance into entrepreneurship of those individuals who choose it.

Studies investigating the behavioral dimensions of entrepreneurship have found differences in motivation to enter into entrepreneurship, management style, entrepreneurial behavior and the meaning of success and high-performing businesses for individuals coming from different cultures. For example, there are individuals who choose entrepreneurship because of a need for approval, perceived instrumentality of wealth or a need for personal development, reflecting the entrepreneurial spirit of their national culture. For others, coming from countries with lower levels of entrepreneurial spirit, the reasons for choosing entrepreneurship are: 'I have no other choice,' 'I cannot work for someone else,' 'I have been unemployed for a while now.' This clearly shows the effects of culture on entrepreneurial activity from both macro- and microperspectives (Hofstede 1980a, 1980b; Scheinberg and MacMillan 1988; Mitchell et al. 2000; Shane and Venkataraman 2000; Mueller and Thomas 2001; Hayton, George and Zahra 2002; Shane 2003; Young, Dimitratos and Dana 2003; Köllinger, Minniti and Schade 2007).

Culture is a most important topic to the emerging transnationalistic patterns in entrepreneurship. Acknowledging that culture affects entrepreneurial behaviors will ease communication between entrepreneurs of different cultures and countries. Many entrepreneurs develop cross-national relationships (e.g., in strategic cooperations, joint ventures, acquisitions or entry mode into new markets), and/or maintain cross-cultural inter-firm relationships with employees and clients, suppliers and investors, and such relationships need to be effectively managed. A more thorough knowledge and awareness of cultures has become one of the major building blocks in ongoing entrepreneurial business activities, as such knowledge can be turned into a vehicle for learning new skills, fostering new ideas, reducing risk, and facilitating effective resource-sharing with people and businesses from different cultures. For example, finding foreign investors is much easier when the entrepreneur understands what the prospective investor emphasizes in a potential beneficial investment, while understanding the cultural orientations and values of target clients may enable a determination of how to penetrate the different markets, how to structure a business plan or how to make the pitch (Kogut and Singh 1988; Shane 1994; Steensma et al. 2000).

This book aims to acquaint its readers with a wide spectrum of cultural variation and to show how such variation 'paints' entrepreneurship in different colors, thereby promoting its multiplicity.

ENTREPRENEURS VERSUS SMALL-BUSINESS OWNERS

For many entrepreneurs, the launching stage is manifested by the establishment of a small business: most entrepreneurs cannot afford a bigger business, some prefer controlling the business's processes in a smaller business format, while others minimize risk by starting small. Yet, although there is overlap between entrepreneurial and small businesses, the distinction between entrepreneurship and small-business ownership is quite apparent: small-business owners are not necessarily entrepreneurs, even when entrepreneurs are small-business owners (Carland et al. 1984; Stewart et al. 1998; Miles, Covin and Heeley 2000; Runyan, Droge and Swinney 2008).

The definition of entrepreneurship ranges from 'Schumpeterian' individuals – the innovators (Schumpeter 1934), to those demonstrating an initiative-oriented, inventive behavior; individuals that behave proactively to achieve a business goal, individuals with a personal value orientation (Gasse 1982), those who are ambitious, growth-oriented, restless (Carland et al. 1984; Gundry and Welsch

2001; Sexton et al. 1997), competitive (Covin and Slevin 1991), visonary (Filion 2002, 2004), and endeavor to lead and be influential in their environments. As such, entrepreneurs find ways to make exchanges in which the stakeholders see how they will benefit from cooperating in return for whatever the corporate entrepreneur needs by influencing and leading (Cohen 2002; Vecchio 2003).

Distinguishing them from small-business owners, entrepreneurs are portrayed as exhibiting a higher propensity for risk, being more motivated to perform research and development (R&D) in their businesses, to create new technology and to use and/or create networks to advance their business's goals (Schumpeter 1934; Vesper 1980; Miller and Friesen 1983; Covin and Slevin 1989; Lumpkin and Dess 1996). Moreover, unlike small-business owners, entrepreneurs strive to create value through creativity and innovation, by exploiting unexplored or undiscovered niches in the market and establishing a sustainable hallmark for their products and ideas (Carland et al. 1984; Brush and Chaganti 1998; Cooper 1993; Cooper and Artz 1995; Stewart and Roth 2001; Runyan, Droge and Swinney 2008).

For the most part, small-business owners actively manage their businesses; this is a unique and quite distinctive endeavor, because such businesses are fragile in terms of market penetration and survival. Unlike entrepreneurs, their main goal is to obtain money from the business, since initially they perceive it as a primary source of income, rather than a place for self-fulfillment or for establishing a sustainable hallmark. Therefore, small-business owners are likely to be risk-averse and to want to keep their business at a controllable level, thereby achieving long-term stability in a particular 'comfort zone' and reaching 'acceptable' business performance levels, rather than taking the entrepreneurial approach of maximizing their business performance or influencing the marketplace. Studies show that small-business owners have less of a preference for innovation than entrepreneurs and do not engage in new business practices or strategies to advance their business performance; similarly, they are less focused on innovation of their products and technologies (Vesper 1980; Carland et al. 1984; Stewart et al. 1998; Stewart and Roth 2001).

This book spotlights entrepreneurs, and draws their exclusive portrait by tracing the hub of entrepreneurial characteristics and behaviors, as exhibited by entrepreneurs from different places and cultures.

ENTREPRENEURSHIP TODAY

Today's definitions of entrepreneurship are diverse and the topics investigated within this framework are varied. The following are the main areas in research and practice:

- *New venture creation* – highlighting the reasons for venture creation, motivations, environmental characteristics and the importance of the context, personal and psychological characteristics of entrepreneurs, managerial characteristics of entrepreneurs versus managers (McClelland 1961; Gartner 1985).
- *Emerging organizations* – focusing on the resources for newly founded firms (Bird 1988; Katz and Gartner 1988).
- *Joint ventures and international research* – referring to entrepreneurial firms' collaborations, including franchises, as well as to country-wide and cross-cultural studies (Johanson and Vahlne 1977; Hornaday et al. 1985; Hamel 1991; Lane and Lubatkin 1998).
- *Entrepreneurship and economy* – focusing on growth rates, longevity of newly founded firms, venture capital and financing start-ups (Baumol 1968; Bates 1990; Porter 1998).
- *The push–pull theory* – or its interpretation in the opportunity-based versus necessity-based conceptualization of entrepreneurship – provides an important point of departure for the development of entrepreneurship theory vis-à-vis economic considerations.

The *opportunity-based* conceptualization of entrepreneurship was developed by Howard Stevenson and collaborators, echoing Kirzner's (1973) classical definition regarding alertness to opportunity – defining entrepreneurship as a process by which individuals pursue opportunities without regard to the resources they currently control; thus opportunity is considered the bridge that connects the unfulfilled market's needs and the solution that might satisfy those needs (Stevenson and Jarillo 1990).

The *necessity-oriented* approach, on the other hand, addresses starting a business because no better alternative to earning a living exists: it is a matter of survival, and it is more strongly associated with developing economies than with developed ones (Timmons et al. 1987; Timmons 1999). Studies on Latin America and Africa address this basic approach in exploring entrepreneurship.

Broadly, new ventures founded by opportunity entrepreneurs are considered to have much stronger positive long-run effects on the economy in terms of employment, innovation, and growth than start-ups initiated by necessity entrepreneurs.

- *New venture performance* – referring to the firms and their performance implications and the fit between the firm and the environment (Stuart and Abetti 1987; Naman and Slevin 1993; Lumpkin and Dess 1996), as well as demographic studies of business start-up growth and survival.
- *Organizational learning and the resource-based view* – focusing, among other things, on entrepreneurial education and research (Levitt and March 1988; Barney 1991a, 1991b; Conner 1991).
- *Social networks* – highlighting the importance and effects of social networks on entrepreneurial dynamics and success (Granovetter 1973; Larson 1992; Uzzi 1997); inward and outward networking and transnational networking.
- *Entrepreneurial culture* – exploring the unique culture of entrepreneurship (Hofstede 1980a, 1980b, 1980c; Shane 1993, 1994; Mitchell et al. 2000; Hayton, George and Zahra 2002).

Other interests, such as *high-technology ventures*, *incubators* and *spin-offs*, as well as *case studies*, are also part of entrepreneurship research.

In summary, throughout the evolution of entrepreneurship research, entrepreneurs have often been considered those who bear risk while pursuing opportunities, and have often been associated with creative and innovative actions. Entrepreneurs also take on a managerial role in their activities, but routine management of an ongoing operation is not considered to be entrepreneurship. In this sense, entrepreneurial activity is fleeting: an individual may perform an entrepreneurial function in creating an organization, but later is relegated to the role of managing it without performing any entrepreneurial function. Following this, many small-business owners would not be considered entrepreneurs.

THE BOOK'S APPROACH

This book traces the entrepreneurial process through the theoretical building blocks of entre-preneurship, i.e., from the resource-based, process-oriented and output-oriented perspectives. In addition to grounding the theoretical fundamentals of entrepreneurship, these can also be translated into entrepreneurial practices for the conception and initiation of a successful new venture in the marketplace.

The book has been organized to follow the logical progression of starting a new entrepreneurial venture so that by the end of the book, students will have a complete and comprehensive understanding of 'how to start and operate an entrepreneurial business'. The topics presented and discussed in Part I focus on the resources of the entrepreneur and entrepreneurial business – the resource-based approach to entrepreneurship, introduced in this book through the general question 'who is the entrepreneur?' The resource-based approach in this context can be viewed as a continuing search for competitive advantage in the creation, acquisition, utilization and management of a business through valuable, rare, inimitable, or non-substitutable business resources (Barney 1991a), such as tangible and intangible assets, skills, competencies and learning mechanisms. In this book's context, the focus is trained on the entrepreneur's motivation, human capital, psychological characteristics and creativity, and on education and training for entrepreneurs

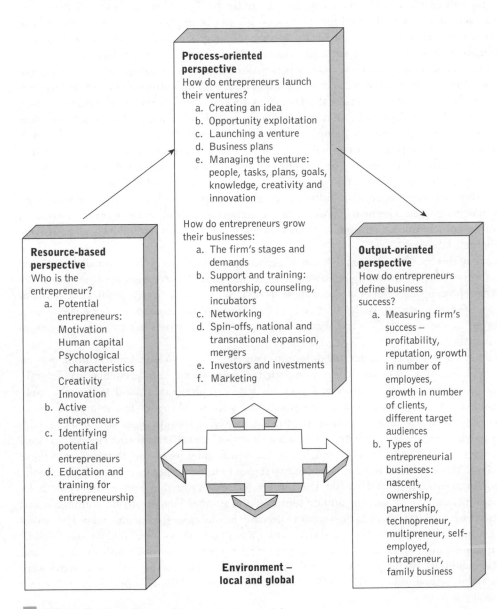

Figure 2 *The book's model: the entrepreneurial process*

– all resources which are fundamental determinants of the business's performance (Barney 1991a; Teece, Pisano and Shuen 1997) and that are perceived to provide a sustainable competitive advantage to entrepreneurial businesses (Lado, Boyd and Wright 1992). Students and entrepreneurs who read this book can learn how to enhance their entrepreneurship-relevant capabilities toward fostering their business's sustainable competitive advantage.

This perspective is followed, in Part II, by the process-oriented perspective, which presents the entrepreneurial venture's creation from the creativity and innovation that spark entrepreneurial ideas, to exploiting opportunities, testing a business concept in the marketplace, and implementing the concept through managing the entrepreneurial business, including marketing, finance and managing sustainable growth. In reading this part of the book, students and entrepreneurs will become acquainted with the multiple processes that can be applied by entrepreneurs to run successful ventures, as well as identifying the specific advantages and weaknesses of these processes in different business and environmental situations. The focus on the process enables adopting some techniques and strategies, as well as creating personalized strategies to manage the entrepreneurial business. Part III is oriented to entrepreneurial outputs, of both the entrepreneur and the business. This part includes a discussion on the business's success through the measurement lenses: evaluating the business's profitability, reputation, and growth levels, among other things, will allow students and entrepreneurs to adopt and/or create standards to monitor their business performance and use processes that will enhance their business success accordingly. One other main output of the entrepreneurial path is reflected in the types of entrepreneurial businesses that entrepreneurs choose: by finding the best fit for his or her entrepreneurial avenue (e.g., ownership, partnership, technopreneurship, multipreneurship, entrepreneurship from the home (e.g., mompreneurship), entrepreneurship with family members as in family businesses) among others, the entrepreneur ensures a self-fulfilling experience and consequently, an enduring and satisfying entrepreneurial career.

In one of this book's more unique features, seventy-one interviews were personally conducted by the author, in person and by telephone and/or Skype, with entrepreneurs from forty-five countries spanning all continents. From these interviews, twenty-two case studies and six at-a-glance cases are presented. With a few exceptions,[2] details of the business and/or entrepreneur appearing in the case study were changed to protect the interviewee's privacy and ensure confidentiality.

Tracking down entrepreneurs in different countries for interviews for this book was an extremely complex task: the journey included chasing down entrepreneurs via federal/governmental and private centers and agencies for entrepreneurs around the world, web, professional and private networks, recommendations from colleagues in the area of entrepreneurship from academic institutions worldwide, as well as from professionals working with entrepreneurs around the world; there were a few 'walk-ins', that is, entrepreneurs who had heard about our search for interviewees through word of mouth and were willing to take part in those interviews. The interviews were executed in two stages: first, the author introduced herself to the entrepreneur by e-mail and sought the entrepreneur's permission and willingness to be interviewed; upon approval, the author sent a one-page questionnaire to be completed and returned by e-mail. This allowed the author to prepare the questions for the interview. Interviews were executed via telephone, Skype and face to face, and all interviews were conducted in English[3] – even though most of the interviewees and the author were not native English speakers – and lasted around thirty to forty minutes. Of the included case studies, some of the interviews were conducted in several sittings and by different means to obtain additional information.

NOTES

1 Some personal and/or business details of the entrepreneurs have been altered in order to protect their privacy. Only those entrepreneurs who specifically asked to be presented by their real names and details, and signed a contract to that effect, are presented accordingly. Many details are imaginary and any similarities to other existing businesses is random.

2 In a few cases, we were asked, and agreed, to present the exact details of the business: formal letters to this effect were prepared and signed by the entrepreneurs.

3 Except for the interview with the Israeli entrepreneurs, which was conducted in Hebrew.

REFERENCES

Barney, J.B. (1991a) 'Firm resources and sustained competitive advantage', *Journal of Management*, 17: 99–120.

Barney, J.B. (1991b) 'The resource-based view of strategy: origins, implications, and prospects', *Special Theory Forum in Journal of Management*, 17: 97–211.

Bates, T. (1990) 'Entrepreneur human capital inputs and small business longevity', *Review of Economics and Statistics*, 72: 551–9.

Baumol, W.J. (1968) 'Entrepreneurship in economic theory', *American Economic Review*, 58: 64–71.

Bird, B. (1988) 'Implementing entrepreneurial ideas: the case for intention', *Academy of Management Review*, 13: 442–53.

Brush, C. and Chaganti, R. (1998) 'Businesses without glamour? An analysis of resources on performance by size and age in small service and retail firms', *Journal of Business Venturing*, 14: 233–57.

Busenitz, L.W. and Lau, C.M. (1997) 'A cross-cultural cognitive model of new venture creation', *Entrepreneurship Theory and Practice*, 20: 25–39.

Busenitz, L.W., Gomez, C. and Spencer, J.W. (2000) Country institutional profiles: unlocking entrepreneurial phenomena', *Academy of Management Journal*, 43: 994–1003.

Carland, J.W., Hoy, F., Boulton W.R. and Carland, J.A. (1984) 'Differentiating entrepreneurs from small business owners: a conceptualization', *Academy of Management Review*, 9: 354–9.

Churchill N.C., Homaday, J.A., Kirchhoff, B.A., Krasner, O.J. and Vesper, K.H. (1987) *Frontiers of Entrepreneurship Research, 1987*, Wellesley, MA: Babson College Center for Entrepreneurship Studies.

Cohen, A.R. (2002) 'Mainstreaming corporate entrepreneurship: leadership at every level of organizations', *Babson Entrepreneurial Review*, October: 5–15.

Conner, K.R. (1991) 'A historical comparison of resource-based theory and five schools of thought within industrial organization economics: do we have a new theory of the firm?', *Journal of Management*, 17: 121–54.

Cooper, A.C. (1993) 'Challenges in predicting new firm performance', *Journal of Business Venturing* 8: 241–53.

Cooper, A.C. and Artz, A. (1995) 'Determinants of satisfaction for entrepreneurs', *Journal of Business Venturing*, 19: 439–57.

Covin, J.G. and Slevin, D.P. (1989) 'Strategic management of small firms in hostile and benign environments', *Strategic Management Journal*, 10: 75–87.

Covin, J.G. and Slevin, D.P. (1991) 'A conceptual model of entrepreneurship as firm behavior', *Entrepreneurship Theory and Practice*, 16: 7–25.

Davidsson, P. (1995) 'Culture, structure and regional levels of entrepreneurship', *Entrepreneurship and Regional Development*, 7: 41–62.

Filion, L.J. (1997) 'From entrepreneurship to entreprenology', *Journal of Best Papers*, 42nd World Conference, International Council for Small Business, San Francisco, 176–92.

Filion, L.J. (2002) 'Elements for an entrepreneurial metamodel', in N.F. Krueger (ed.) *Critical Perspectives on Business and Management*, vol. IV, London: Routledge.

Filion, L.J. (2004) 'Operators and visionaries: differences in the entrepreneurial and managerial systems of two types of entrepreneurs', *International Journal of Entrepreneurship and Small Business*, 1: 35–55.

Gartner, W.B. (1985) 'A conceptual framework for describing the phenomenon of new venture creation', *Academy of Management Review*, 10: 696–706.

Gasse, Y. (1982) 'Elaborations on the psychology of the entrepreneur', in C.A. Kent, D.L. Sexton and K.H. Vesper (eds) *Encyclopedia of Entrepreneurship*, Englewood Cliffs, NJ: Prentice-Hall, 57–71.

Gavron, R., Cowling, M. and Westall, A. (1998) *Entrepreneurial Society*, London: Institute for Public Policy Research.

Granovetter, M.S. (1973) 'The strength of weak ties', *American Journal of Sociology*, 78: 1360–80.

Gundry, L.K. and Welsch, H.P. (2001) 'The ambitious entrepreneur: high growth strategies of women-owned enterprises', *Journal of Business Venturing*, 16: 453–70.

Hamel, G. (1991) 'Competition for competence and inter-partner learning within international strategic alliances', *Strategic Management Journal*, 12: 83–103.

Hayton, J.C., George, G. and Zahra, S. (2002) 'National culture and entrepreneurship: a review of behavioral research', *Entrepreneurship Theory and Practice*, 26: 33–52.

Hofstede, G. (1980a) 'Culture and organizations', *International Studies of Management and Organization*, 10: 15–41.

Hofstede, G. (1980b) *Culture's Consequences: International Differences in Work Related Values*, Beverly Hills, CA: Sage Publications.

Hofstede, G. (1980c) 'Motivation, leadership, and organization: do American theories apply abroad?', *Organizational Dynamics*, 9: 42–63.

Hornaday, J.A., Shils, E.B., Timmons, J.A. and Vesper, K.H. (1985) *Frontiers of Entrepreneurship Research, 1985*, Wellesley, MA: Babson College Center for Entrepreneurship Studies.

Johanson, J. and Vahlne, J.E. (1977) 'The internationalization process of the firm: a model of knowledge development and increasing foreign market commitments', *Journal of International Business Studies*, 8: 23–32.

Kariv, D., Menzeis, T. and Brenner, G. (2010) 'Business success among visible and non visible ethnic entrepreneurs: a look at the effects of unemployment, co-ethnic involvement and human capital', in Special Issue of 'Ethnicity, Cultural Diversity and Entrepreneurship', *Global Business and Economics Review*, 12: 115–50.

Kariv, D., Menzeis, T., Brenner, G. and Filion, L.J. (2009) 'Ethnic entrepreneurs in Canada: transnational networking and business success', *Entrepreneurship and Regional Development*, 21: 239–64.

Katz, J. and Gartner, W.B. (1988) 'Properties of emerging organizations', *Academy of Management Review*, 13: 429–41.

Kirzner, I. (1973) *Competition and Entrepreneurship*, Chicago: University of Chicago Press.

Kirzner, I. (1979) *Perception, Opportunity and Profit*, Chicago: University of Chicago Press.

Knight, F.H. (1921) *Risk, uncertainty and profit*, Boston, MA: Hart, Schaffner & Marx; Houghton Mifflin Co.

Kogut, B. and Singh, H. (1988) 'The effect of national culture on the choice of entry mode', *Journal of International Business Studies*, 19: 411–32.

Köllinger, P., Minniti, M. and Schade, C. (2007) 'I think I can, I think I can: overconfidence and entrepreneurial behavior', *Journal of Economic Psychology*, 28: 502–27.

Lado, A., Boyd, N. and Wright, P. (1992) 'A competency-based model of sustainable competitive advantage: toward a conceptual integration', *Journal of Management*, 18: 77–91.

Lane, P.J. and Lubatkin, M. (1998) 'Relative absorptive capacity and interorganizational learning', *Strategic Management Journal*, 19: 461–77.

Larson, A. (1992) 'Network dyads in entrepreneurial settings: a study of the governance of exchange relationships', *Administrative Science Quarterly*, 37: 76–104.

Leibenstein, H. (1979) 'A branch of economics is missing: micro-Micro theory', *Journal of Economic Literature*, 17: 477–502.

Levitt, B. and March, J.G. (1988) 'Organizational learning', *Annual Review of Sociology*, 14: 319–40.

Lindsay, N.J. (2005) 'Toward a cultural model of indigenous entrepreneurial attitude', *Academy of Marketing Science Review*: 1–15.

Lumpkin, G.T. and Dess, G.G. (1996) 'Clarifying the entrepreneurial orientation construct and linking it to performance', *Academy of Management Review*, 21: 135–72.

Mahoney, J.T. and Pandian, J.R. (1992) 'The resource-based view within the conversation of strategic management', *Strategic Management Journal*, 13: 363–80.

Makino, S. and Neupert, K.E. (2000) 'National culture, transaction costs, and the choice between joint venture and wholly owned subsidiary', *Journal of International Business Studies*, 31: 705–13.

McClelland, D.N. (1961) *The Achieving Society*, Princeton, NJ: Van Nostrand.

McDougall, P.P. (1989) 'International versus domestic entrepreneurship: new venture strategic behavior and industry structure', *Journal of Business Venturing*, 4: 387–400.

McDougall, P.P. and Oviatt, B.M. (2000) 'International entrepreneurship: the intersection of two paths', *Academy of Management Journal*, 43: 902–8.

Miles, M.P., Covin, J.G. and Heeley, M.B. (2000) 'The relationship between environmental dynamism and small firm structure, strategy, and performance', *Journal of Marketing Theory and Practice*, 8: 63–75.

Miller, D. and Friesen, P.H. (1983) 'Successful and unsuccessful phases of the corporate life cycle', *Organization Studies*, 4: 339–56.

Miller, D. and Friesen, P.H. (1984) 'A longitudinal study of the corporate life cycle', *Management Science*, 30: 1161–82.

Mitchell, R.K., Smith, B., Seawright, K.W. and Morse, E.A. (2000) Cross-cultural cognitions and the venture creation decision', *Academy of Management Journal*, 43: 974–93.

Mueller, S.L. and Thomas, A.S. (2001) 'Culture and entrepreneurial potential: a nine country study of locus of control and innovativeness', *Journal of Business Venturing*, 16: 51–75.

Naman, J.L. and Slevin, D.P. (1993) 'Entrepreneurship and the concept of fit: a model and empirical tests', *Strategic Management Journal*, 14: 137–53.

Oviatt, B.M. and McDougall, P.P. (1994) 'Toward a theory of international new ventures', *Journal of International Business Studies*, 25: 45–64.

Penrose, E. (1959) *The Theory of the Growth of the Firm*, Oxford: Blackwell.

Pitelis, C. (2005) 'Edith Penrose, organisational economics and business strategy: an assessment and extension', *Managerial and Decision Economics*, 26: 67–82.

Porter, M.E. (1998) *The Competitive Advantage of Nations*, Basingstoke, UK: Macmillan Press.

Runyan, R., Droge, C. and Swinney, J. (2008) 'Entrepreneurial orientation versus small business orientation: what are their relationships to firm performance?', *Journal of Small Business Management*, 46: 567–89.

Scheinberg, S. and MacMillan, I.C. (1988) 'An 11 country study of motivations to start a business', in B. Kirchoff, W. Long, W. McMullan, K.H. Vesper and W. Wetzel (eds) *Frontiers of Entrepreneurship Research*, Wellesley, MA: Babson College; 669–684.

Schoonhoven, C.B. and Romanelli, E. (2001) *The Entrepreneurship Dynamic in Industry Evolution: Origins of Entrepreneurship and the Evolution of Industries*, Stanford, CA: Stanford University Press.

Schumpeter, J.A. (1911) *Theorie der wirtschaftlichen Entwicklung: Eine Untersuchung über Unternehmergewinn, Kapital, Kredit, Zins, und den Konjunturzyklus,* Leipzig: Duncker & Humblot.

Schumpeter, J.A. (1912) *The Theory of Economic Development*, trans. R. Opie (1934), Cambridge, MA: Harvard University Press.

Schumpeter, J.A. (1934) *Theory of Economic Development*, Cambridge, MA: Harvard University Press.

Schumpeter, J.A. (1942) *Capitalism, Socialism and Democracy*, New York: Harper.

Sexton, D.L., Upton, N.B., Wacholtz, L.E. and McDougall, P.P. (1997) 'Learning needs of growth-oriented entrepreneurs', *Journal of Business Venturing*, 12: 1–8.

Shane, S. (1992) 'Why do some societies invent more than others?', *Journal of Business Venturing*, 7: 29–46.

Shane, S. (1993) 'Cultural influences on national rates of innovation', *Journal of Business Venturing*, 8: 59–73.

Shane, S. (1994) 'Cultural values and the championing process', *Entrepreneurship Theory and Practice*, 18: 25–41.

Shane, S. (2003) *A General Theory of Entrepreneurship: the Individual–Opportunity Nexus*, Northampton, MA: Edward Elgar.

Shane, S. and Venkataraman, S. (2000) 'The promise of enterpreneurship as a field of research', *Academy of Management Review*, 25: 217–26.

Steensma, K., Marino, L., Weaver, M. and Dickson, P. (2000) 'The influence of national culture in the formation of technology alliances by entrepreneurial firms', *Academy of Management Journal*, 43: 951–73.

Stevenson, H.H. and Jarillo, J.C. (1990) 'A paradigm of entrepreneurship: entrepreneurial management', *Strategic Management Journal*, 11: 17–27.

Stewart, W. and Roth, P. (2001) 'Risk propensity differences between entrepreneurs and managers: a meta-analytic review', *Journal of Applied Psychology*, 86: 145–53.

Stewart, W.H., Watson, W., Carland, J.C. and Carland, J. (1998) 'A proclivity for entrepreneurship: a comparison of entrepreneurs, small business owners, and corporate managers', *Journal of Business Venturing*, 14: 189–214.

Stuart, R. and Abetti, P.A. (1987) 'Start-up ventures: towards the prediction of initial success', *Journal of Business Venturing*, 2: 215–30.

Teece, D.J., Pisano, G. and Shuen, A. (1997) 'Dynamic capabilities and strategic management', *Strategic Management Journal*, 18: 509–33.

Tiessen, J.H. and Merrilees, B. (1999) 'An entrepreneurial model of SME internationalization: evidence from six cases', in R. Wright and A. Rugman (eds) *Research in Global Strategic Management*, vol. 7, Greenwich, CT: JAI Press, 131–54.

Timmons, J.A. (1999) *New Venture Creation: Entrepreneurship for the twenty-first Century*, Boston, MA: Irwin/McGraw-Hill.

Timmons, J.A., Muzyka, D.F., Stevenson, H.H. and Bygrave, W.D. (1987) 'Opportunity recognition: the core of entrepreneurship', in N.C. Churchill, J.A. Hornaday, B.A. Kirchhoff, O.J. Krasner and K.H. Vesper (eds) *Frontiers of Entrepreneurship Research*, Babson Park, MA: Babson College, 109–23.

Uzzi, B. (1997) 'Social structure and competition in interfirm networks: the paradox of embeddedness', *Administrative Science Quarterly*, 42: 35–67.

Vecchio, R.P. (2003) 'Entrepreneurship and leadership: common trends and common threads', *Human Resource Management Review*, 13: 303–27.

Vesper, K.H. (1980) 'New venture planning', *Journal of Business Strategy*, 1: 73–5.

Von Bargen, P., Freedman, D. and Pages, E.R. (2003) 'The rise of the entrepreneurial society', *Economic Development Quarterly*, 17: 315–24.

Wernerfelt, B. (1984) 'A resource-based view of the firm', *Strategic Management Journal*, 5: 171–80.

Young, S., Dimitratos, P. and Dana, L.P. (2003) 'International entrepreneurship research: what scope for international business theories?', *Journal of International Entrepreneurship*, 1, 31–42.

Zahra, S. and George, G. (2002) 'International entrepreneurship: the current status of the field and future research agenda', in M.A. Hitt, R.D. Ireland, S.M. Camp and D.L. Sexton (eds) *Strategic Entrepreneurship: Creating an Integrated Mindset*, Oxford: Blackwell, 255–88.

Zahra, S.A., Ireland, D.R. and Hitt, M.A. (2000) 'International expansion by new venture firms: international diversity, mode of market entry, technological learning and performance', *Academy of Management Journal*, 43: 925–50.

Part I

The resource-based perspective in the entrepreneurial course

Chapter 1

The environment and entrepreneurship

OBJECTIVES

After studying this chapter you will be able to:

■ Identify the key features of the environment in which the business will operate in order to plan how to use the advantages and minimize the disadvantages for the business it brings in;

■ Deepen the knowledge on each of the environment's dimensions: economic, sociocultural, political and legislative, technological, ecological and operational.

■ Recognize the market's main features and outline the business's suitability and potential competitive advantage accordingly.

■ Understand the role of market – and the environment – analyses for establishing valuable advantage right at the pre-launch stage.

■ Conduct research on the market and the environment in which the business is planned to operate.

■ Adjust the business's planned products and/or services based on the data gathered from the environment's analysis.

The first step in successfully putting an idea into practice is deciding upon the main industry or area of operation. Many products and services may be suitable for, or adaptable to, filling important needs of different industries and sectors. For example, a company for consultancy in marketing nanotechnological materials, a company conducting R&D of software programs for special-needs children, or a company providing management outsourcing services for agro-industry may each adapt its product to suit various different industries connected with the hi-tech sector, the special-education sector, or the agricultural sector, respectively. Entrepreneurs should determine which sector is best for their envisioned product and/or service, and in which sector their businesses will profit the most. A market analysis may be helpful in making the best decision (Rodie and Martin 2001).

THE MARKET ANALYSIS

The market is the general arena of potential exchange of products and services. Prior to launching a business, the potential entrepreneur must familiarize him or herself with the local market and the specific sectors and industries relevant to the planned venture. The entrepreneur should assess the feasibility of penetration of his or her products or services into the market by assessing two main dimensions:

- The number of active customers for the products/services.
- The volume of sales for the products/services.

Both dimensions should be assessed for a specified time period and in a defined geographical area. Then, information and data on the market, such as the characteristics of the target clients' purchasing habits, saturation levels, etc., must be ascertained (Hanssens 1980; Schwienbacher 2007).

For example, in order to launch a business that sells cars, information about the following should be gathered:

- Client preferences, tastes and attitudes (e.g., family vehicles, hatchbacks, sports cars, etc.).
- Market evolution (e.g., in the past five years, more women have been buying family cars than have men).
- Division of sales of different car types (e.g., family, luxury–family, sports–family, etc.).
- The market's saturation level.

The best way to gather such information is through *market segmentation*. Turning to the previous example, in many countries the element of safety has become the most important feature, and potential customers are willing to pay more money for cars with newer and better safety technologies. Acknowledging this, the entrepreneur wishing to launch a business for selling cars should focus on safety (complementary accessories or new technologies for greater safety). However, entrepreneurs should be aware that each segment of the potential buyers may be looking for different safety-related features in their cars: families will look for safety devices in the back seats, where the children sit, while young drivers will look for safety in the braking system or the engine, and businessmen who use their cars for hours on end will look for safe tires and anti-corrosion accessories. Entrepreneurs have to assess their prospective market according to the different needs and demands of their potential customers, and market segmentation enables overall coverage of the market and identification of consumers' needs, as well as of competitors' activities and market trends.

Three major principles guide market segmentation:

- *Geographic segmentation:* the number of businesses dealing with the proposed product/industry/sector, etc.; volume of sales, turnover, mergers, etc., in a bounded geographic area. For example, the number of businesses in e-marketing in the region of Paris, France.
- *Demographic segmentation*: the general characteristics of the owners of new ventures, such as gender, age, nationality, language spoken, education and specialization. For example, what is the profile of entrepreneurs who develop children's computer games? Do they have academic certification, are they specialists in computer-related programs, are they educators or former teachers, are they young entrepreneurs (i.e., in the age-range of their customers)?
- *Psychological segmentation:* customers' main motivation for purchasing the proposed product (e.g., economic, prestige, comfort, trendiness; customer loyalty to a specific product, trade-

mark or company; sensitivity to publicity and marketing, such as promotion, quality, price, quality of service, etc.).

USES OF MARKET SEGMENTATION

Table 1.1 illustrates the market analysis and utilization of the information collected in order to implement an innovative idea, in this case 'social spa-ing'. Social spa-ing is a new concept offering a total spa experience (holistic treatments, therapies, healing rituals, and so on) along with a *different* place where people can interact informally. Its target clientele comprises business people, and it is planned as a calm, relaxing environment for business meetings, negotiations, workplace celebrations, and conferences. The social spa-ing concept is based on the underlying philosophy that a venue that is likely to balance the senses will have a favorable impact on individuals' business performances: negotiations will be more positive and constructive, meetings will be more productive, and so on.

Such an innovative idea is usually risky, and the entrepreneur wishing to develop a venture based on this concept must gather the relevant data in order to assess the potential success and profitability of such a place. The data should be collected for each of the market's three segments – geographic, demographic, and psychological – on the basis of which the entrepreneur can consider whether to launch a venture built on this concept or not (Gustavsen, Finne and Oscarsson 2001).

THE ENVIRONMENT

An analysis of the environment is one of the most important elements in weighing whether to launch a venture, in that it helps determine *if*, *when* and *how* to launch the business. Environment is a multifaceted entity that comprises different types of sub-environments – economic, sociocultural, technological, etc. – and understanding the importance of analyzing the environment prior to launching a business is therefore critical. Each sub-environment is characterized by distinct local conditions. Thus launching an elegant restaurant in a business area of one of San Francisco's outlying neighborhoods is different from launching one in the business area of a small town in, for example, Minnesota: both the cost-effectiveness of opening such a restaurant and its odds for survival are dependent on the sub-environment (Gartner 1985; Dubini 1989; Doh and Pearce 2004).

The dimensions of the environment that should be examined in the elaboration of the venture-creation process are:

- Economic.
- Sociocultural.
- Political and legislative.
- Technological.
- Ecological.
- Operational.

The economic environment of a new business is the main factor determining its chances of survival; it is therefore the most relevant and concrete dimension. Studying the pertinent data and information and the particulars of the local economic environment will facilitate penetration into

Table 1.1 Characteristics of the market for spa-ing

Inquiries	Market for the specific product	Characteristics		
		Business	Owner	Customer
Actual demand for the product	Emerging; popular among couples and tourists	Most spas are located along beaches close to the peninsula; 40% increase in number of spas in Halifax area in past five years; spa size is usually medium; about 20% end in closure	Traditional spas are owned mostly by ethnic newcomers (mostly Asian nationalities) who specialize in holistic treatments and therapies, and in healing rituals to rejuvenate and balance the senses	Clients are mostly couples aged twenty to thirty-five years and tourists from Europe; Canadians come only from July to September
Evolution (mergers, expansion, closures, etc.)	Expansions	Intense development in past five years along with high rates of closure, especially of traditional spas and those of non- or less than deluxe standard; most spa expansions are in the deluxe range	Owners of deluxe spas have a 'high-tech' attitude, favor technological solutions; offer a neat, high-tech atmosphere; they want to make fast money; spas owned by ethnic Asian nationality entrepreneurs represent most of the closures	Clients of hi-tech companies tend to have their lunch breaks in spas (especially deluxe spas)
Competitors and new businesses	Increasing by differentiating themselves; innovative spas targeting specific clientele (business people; women and mothers, etc.) appear	Innovative, subject-oriented; clubs offering treatments plus sports facilities; aimed at different customers, etc.	Investors view spas as an investment rather than as the realization of a lifelong dream	Customers are not loyal to a specific spa or specific treatments; they shop around and thus encourage competition
Saturation point (very low, low, medium, high, very high)	Medium	—	Medium. New spas are launched in the Halifax area at an average rate of one every two years	Low. Customers are willing to spend money on spa treatments
Potential demand for the product (forecast)	High rates of new spas	Content-oriented, with a focus on recreation, or specializing in health-related activities (cardiovascular, weight training and workout room, etc.)	Indigenous entrepreneurs; franchisers of successful chains around Canada	Businessmen — to refresh and energize; for negotiation meetings

the market of the product(s), and of the venture itself. The data, numbers and facts that are important to acquire during the realization stage include gross national product (GNP), gross national income (GNI) and net national product (NNP). Other factors that are important to acknowledge in the process of realizing the venture are: trends in the local market such as the phase and rate of economic development; the degree of employment growth or decline; recession; economic wealth ('the bubble') or poverty; economic crises ('the bubble bursts'); inflation; American dollar fluctuations in the stock market; taxation and political fiscal and monetary regulations, etc. The data may be found in the published files of the different countries' National Bureau of Statistics, in various national publications, in OECD publications,[1] in Global Entrepreneurship Monitor (GEM) publications,[2] in the publications of national academic institutions, and from professors and researchers in the relevant fields (Lumpkin and Dess 1996).

The sociocultural environment constitutes the sub-environment of potential customers for specific products and/or services. Entrepreneurs should acquire information about the potential customers' profiles in terms of their demographic and social characteristics, i.e., gender, age, ethnicity, economic status, familial status, and who the main consumers of the product are (adults, families, children). Such information enables the entrepreneur to adjust the products, services or complementary services to the potential consumers' needs. For example, in a shop for women's fashion, where most of the potential clients will be women, including mothers, a nursery where children will be taken care of while their mothers shop is a complementary service that is very relevant to the business's goals: such a service can only be planned by tracking the potential clients' characteristics.

Other social and cultural sub-environments are also very relevant to entrepreneurs. For example, in countries with emerging environmental and ecological movements, entrepreneurs planning new businesses are constrained to carefully consider the acquisition and use of environmentally friendly machinery, and to adjust their infrastructure to the nascent cultural attitudes. This is especially important for today's younger global entrepreneurs and for those planning to launch their business simultaneously in several countries. Lack of familiarity with prevailing attitudes such as 'clean technology' or the 'green revolution', which have a major impact on consumers' state of mind, and failure to take them into consideration, means risking the success of the businesses. Entrepreneurs should pre-plan and adopt protection programs, efficient use of fuels, conservative water- and paper-consumption practices, pollution diffusion, and other environmentally friendly solutions relevant to their business.

The political and legislative environments. Just as any game begins with the recognition and acceptance of its rules, and the understanding that the game cannot be played without rules, so too there are rules for the process of venture creation. Entrepreneurs cannot 'start the game', i.e., launch a business venture, before familiarizing themselves with the rules that the business is constrained to follow. International, local and municipal rules relevant to venture creation exist everywhere: some are obligatory and others are normative; some are concrete, understandable and easy to apply, while others are vague and complicated to follow; some might mitigate or contradict one another; others are new rules that have to be implemented at once or within a given time. In all cases, the rules must be recognized and understood by the new venture founder prior to launching the business.

Entrepreneurs should realize that many of the rules that have to be followed are actually for their own benefit: these include, for example, regulations regarding patent property, R&D infrastructure safeguards, various regulations regarding funding and investments, non-discriminatory recruiting procedures, and others (Spencer, Murtha and Lenway 2005).

The technological environment. In this era of the internet, CDRoms, high-tech robotics, sophisticated materials, fabrication, and innovative distribution techniques, entrepreneurs of new ventures should follow the technological developments characterizing the environment. Ongoing updates and a profound familiarity with innovations in the professional area of the business's main product(s) are essential. Consumers keep up and move along with the times, and they expect the businesses they are dealing with to not only move ahead but also to enlighten them, and to guide them as to which of the updated products should be purchased.

Entrepreneurs must follow R&D progress in order to forecast their products' long-term feasibility and profitability. However, businesses should not consider only the technological environment; clients' demands for technological improvements in the goods or services they are buying are important factors in their interactions with suppliers. Taking the previous example of social spa-ing, even a spa that offers the best massage treatments but lacks the most technologically up-to-date equipment such as sophisticated rain showers, steam rooms, and advanced complementary facilities will be less attractive to important potential clients, who will opt for the newest, most innovative and most 'in' products in the technological context (Naman and Slevin 1993; Shane and Ulrich 2004).

The ecological environment. Nature, the climate and environmental factors have become focal points in the entrepreneurial realm. Ecological considerations regarding where and when to launch a venture (Carroll and Khessina 2005), and global preservation approaches are emerging almost everywhere. Al Gore's documentary on global warming, *An Inconvenient Truth* (2006), is but one illustration of the 'taking action' or 'proactive' atmosphere in which everyone, but especially businesses, need to calculate their specific impact on global ecology. Entrepreneurial businesses should acknowledge these trends: they should support and preserve clean environments by applying processes that sustain natural ecosystems and that conserve and protect natural resources, and, in general, implement practices that reduce the footprint of development (Carroll and Khessina 2005; Kariv and Kirschenbaum 2007a, b).

The operational environment. Familiarity with one's direct and indirect competitors prior to launching a new business is extremely important as it allows the entrepreneur to deal most effectively with the competition, either by finding a different niche than that of the competitors or by competing on such factors as price, quality of service and range of expertise.

The direct competitors are individuals or companies that offer similar or identical products and/or services which answer the same customer needs and demands. For example, when examining where to locate a private dental clinic, the entrepreneur should know how many dental clinics are already active in the given area, and what specific expertise they offer (e.g., emergency treatment, preventive, restorative or cosmetic treatments, treatments for adults, seniors or children, etc.). The entrepreneur should also find out how successful the competitors are in terms of size, client diversity, reputation, marketing and advertising.

Indirect competitors are companies or businesses that offer parallel or similar products or services that respond to similar client needs or demands. For example, establishing a new bakery in an area where restaurants and coffee shops abound will undoubtedly lead to tough competition since the clients have an array of alternative possible sources of baked goods (D'Souza and McDougall 1989; Waldersee, Griffiths and Lai 2003).

The entrepreneur should thus analyze the following aspects of the proposed operational environment:

- Existence of active direct and indirect local competitors.
- Number of competitors.
- Types of products and services provided by the competitors.
- Prices of products and services provided by the competitors.
- Present and potential clientele.

- Number and types of employees needed.
- Location of existing and proposed businesses.
- Strengths and weaknesses of existing businesses.
- Potential of attracting clients.

CLIENTELE

Entrepreneurs are well advised to launch their businesses with some clients already identified or secured. To this end, they should apply at least some of the market-segmentation techniques used by entrepreneurs prior to launching their ventures, and identify the consumers most likely to use their products/services, and their characteristics. After identifying these, they may approach the people with the identified profiles and/or modify their products/services so that they will be attractive to the target clientele. The inquiries that should be investigated cover three broad areas (Table 1.2).

More specifically, entrepreneurs should use the '4-W' technique to ascertain *where*, *when*, *why* and *how* people buy products similar to theirs. This inquiry should include such questions as:

- What main need or demand do the new products/services answer?
- What do clients expect from the product (durability, reliability, etc.)?
- Why would clients buy the planned product/service (it is a basic necessity, e.g., groceries or stationery; the entrepreneur is known as an expert in his or her field; the business is a franchise with a known reputation)?
- How much would clients be ready to spend for the planned product or service?
- Is the product/service dependent on a particular season of the year?
- Is the market for the planned products/services stable?
- Is the demand for the product/service influenced by publicity, discount offers, etc.?
- Who or what has the greatest impact on decisions to purchase the products and/or services – the buyer him or herself, family members, work colleagues, the social circle, the surrounding lifestyle?

Table 1.2 *Market segmentation*

Geography

- *Where* are most of the clients for the planned products/services located (suburbs, inner city, business areas)?
- *Where* is the demand for the planned products/services highest?

Demography

- *Who* is buying or using similar products/services (men, women, children, families)?
- *What* are the lifestyles, status and income levels of the clients?

Psychology

- *What* is the motivation to buy the product or use the service?
- *Who* or *what* influences this motivation?
- *How much* money are the intended clients ready to spend for the planned products/services?

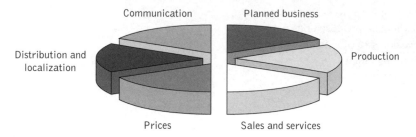

Figure 1.1 *The main topics in market research*

The topics that are associated with the information gathered from the '4-W' technique are presented in Figure 1.1. Information to answer the above-listed questions can be gathered in one of two ways: an independent research survey, or engagement of a specialist to carry out such a survey. The first option allows for more control of the search process by the entrepreneur, as well as ongoing adaptations to his or her specific needs. Such hands-on management of the search for information also promotes a more intensive and in-depth study of the strengths, constraints and limitations of the market. This is the least expensive option, but it is usually time-consuming.

The internet can and should be exploited in order to access facts and general knowledge on entrepreneurship, and there are several sites that provide such information.[3] Other sources may also be utilized: economics journals, academic journals on economics, trade or professional publications, which have a more practical perspective and periodicals dealing with ongoing market matters, statistical data published by the particular country's bureau of statistics, university libraries, and centers for entrepreneurs. It is also important to communicate with active entrepreneurs, to interact with potential clients (asking questions, analyzing their replies), and to experience similar products and services provided by future competitors.

Engaging a specialist or company that provides data and market analyses can facilitate the information-gathering process and provide evidence-based support for decision-making. Not only are such specialists usually more experienced in such procedures, they are also very well networked and have access to otherwise less accessible databases (Chrisman, Chua and Steier 2002).

SUMMARY

Prior to launching a venture, entrepreneurs should conduct research on both the market and the environment in which they are planning to operate. They must have a thorough grasp of their potential clients' behaviors regarding similar products and/or services and be aware of the major trends in terms of the active clients' profiles and their motivation for purchasing the product to be offered. Thorough familiarity with the market is a valuable advantage at the pre-launch stage in either preparing a marketing plan that will attract clients already engaged with existing businesses (e.g., one that will attract people having dental treatments in one clinic to a new clinic that is planned for launch in the same area), or to adjust the products or services of the planned business so that it will attract a different target clientele or answer different needs than those provided by the existing businesses (e.g., the new dental clinic can offer a twenty-four-hour emergency switchboard or employ experts in dental treatments not available in the specific area).

CASE STUDY 1.1   Baby-Dalózó, Hungary

Baby-Dalózó provides a relatively unique service in Hungary: it offers a catalogue, a magazine and a website for baby products, equipment and services to both retail stores and individuals.

Aggie Molnár, a thirty-three-year-old entrepreneur, launched Baby-Dalózó three years ago when her first daughter, Mara, was born and she found it difficult to locate a place where she could buy both the equipment and the varied products needed for the new infant. Aggie Molnár and her husband were even more frustrated when they realized that the shops they found were either very expensive or did not carry some of the products they asked for: 'In one shop there were beds and baby carriages, but no toys or baby clothes for newborns. So we went to a different shop where they told us that they had baby clothes but did not have any guidance books for new parents. We were going from one shop to another, and in each one there was always something lacking,' says Molnár.

The manager of one of the baby stores told Molnár and her husband that he buys most of the store's merchandise according to market demand as he is never sure if merchandise that is not in demand will be sold and does not want to keep unsold stock in the store. He also remarked that although he had been in the business for about thirty years, he himself had no idea who the best manufacturers for baby products were. Molnár did not pay attention to the man's remark at the time, but when Mara was about eight months old, she decided to quit her job, and the store owner's words came back to her: she decided to launch a business. Her idea was to gather information about baby products and equipment and put them all into a catalogue that would be distributed to a broad range of suppliers and consumers; she envisioned a database, updated monthly, that would include a list of suppliers and buyers of products and equipment for infants, with prices and sales, recommendations, and many other details that might ease the entire process. Using personal savings, she started working from home.

Molnár expected that it would be relatively easy to penetrate the market, since it was necessary only to present the new idea to suppliers, free of charge (at first), in order to produce the first catalogue. To her surprise, not a single business owner was willing to include the name of his or her business in the catalogue. She was aware that marketing and advertising were at a very early stage in Hungary at that time, and that most baby supplies were acquired in neighborhood stores or by finding other sources, usually by chance. She was convinced this was neither the most economical nor the most satisfying way of outfitting the new baby. Although she was disappointed in her failure to produce the catalogue, Molnár launched a company – with great concern but much support from her husband. Founding a catalogue for businesses producing and selling baby products and equipment was an innovative concept, but she felt that, although it would entail a certain amount of consumer education, the Hungarian market was ripe for such a new idea. Molnár says that most of the people with whom she and her husband discussed her idea suggested that she consider going into a different business.

Molnár began by conducting a market survey, by telephoning companies in order to find those that might suit the catalogue. Most were very suspicious about her proposed service, particularly about the 'free-of-charge' advertising and distribution of the catalogue. After three months, supplier response was still very limited, and she decided on a different strategy. At her husband's suggestion, she posted the catalogue on the internet. She arranged it both by types of products and equipment and by suppliers, in alphabetical order. Going on to the internet obliged Aggie Molnár to be more creative and dynamic; she hired a young graphics student to design the catalogue, making it both user-friendly and attractive.

By going on the Web, Molnár's concept gradually penetrated the market, and the catalogue's range of advertisers expanded. She believes that the internet made her services more visible; the products and services were categorized and well organized, the photographs of the equipment and products were attractively displayed, and it was easy to contact the companies that advertised on the website. Both manufacturers and store owners benefited from the catalogue; their sales increased, and requests to advertise in Baby-Dalózó increased as well. Molnár's marketing concept was based on a one-month, commitment-free trial in advertising; businesses wishing to continue advertising once the month was up had to pay. Requests to advertise in the Baby-Dalózó catalogue also increased, and some links she had been trying to establish several months earlier, to manufacturers outside Hungary, began to become active: Romanian, Moldavian, Italian, Polish and French manufacturers of baby products and equipment started to advertise in the Baby-Dalózó internet catalogue.

'The problem of penetrating the market with a familiar, expected product or service versus an innovative concept is always there; I could have waited for a while and started this business after someone else had introduced the concept. It might have been easier; my husband and I spent a lot of money at the beginning of my business, with no returns. The competitors we face now had a smoother path. However, I am glad that I was the founder of such an idea in Hungary. If you research your environment very carefully, you always find some open-minded people who are prepared for a different concept. This is how you create your own niche,' says Molnár.

'At first, sales were fairly poor, as I had expected; still it was disappointing and somehow frightening. I couldn't guarantee that things would get better, although I had a strong intuitive feeling that they would. In order to target my potential clients, I used many techniques simultaneously; besides the market research, which helped me segment my potential clients and sort their products and services, I was constantly looking for companies that were active in the market. I mainly used the internet for this, but I also used my contacts to find such companies; finding the companies was relatively easy, but getting them to cooperate was very difficult. I personally contacted each one of them and presented myself and my new concept. I was trying to emphasize the win–win aspect of the situation, of cooperating together on such a project, as well as to show them the potential avenues of our cooperation. Some of those companies that I contacted acknowledged the potential of such a project and agreed to advertise through our catalogue; but I couldn't be sure how much they trusted that it would enhance their sales. I was persistent in looking for different companies that were active in the market, and that suited the catalogue and could benefit from it. It was a lot of work, and sometimes frustrating; there were many refusals, but there was also correspondingly positive feedback from those that had been advertising in Baby-Dalózó.'

After a while, the range and number of companies advertising in Baby-Dalózó expanded. Baby-Dalózó continues to grow in terms of sales, number of companies advertising in the catalogue, product innovation, product diversity, number of employees, and more. But Aggie Molnár says that her satisfaction comes mostly from product innovation: 'I've had very positive feedback from relatives and friends on the use they make of the catalogue as individuals, so I launched a different

magazine – one that targets parents and pregnant women. It provides lists of stores and manufacturers, but has many other sections, such as an interactive blog where parents can communicate
with each other, a recommendation-of-the-day section; a "beautiful baby of the month" contest,
and much more.'

QUESTIONS FOR DISCUSSION

1   Identify the different environments that Aggie Molnár worked in, from pre-launch to the present.
2   What are the main relationships between the sociocultural and technological sub-environments
    that Baby-Dalózó is active in?
3   What was Aggie Molnár's main focus while launching her company? Can you analyze the
    motives that led her to focus especially on this particular aspect?
4   With Hungary now rapidly entering the internet era, how would you suggest that Aggie Molnár
    proceed with her services?

NOTES

1   At www.oecd.org/.
2   At www.gemconsortium.org/.
3   The sites, in alphabetical order, are: ADI, the African Development Institute, dedicated to fostering
    and promoting the human and material development of Africa, www.africainstitute.com/about.html;
    ASES, an international entrepreneurship network, focused around the Asia-Pacific region, that
    helps foster a new generation of entrepreneurs ready to innovate in the ever-changing global
    markets, www.asesinternational.org/mission.htm; CIE, the Center for Innovation and Enterprise
    in Africa, www.ifc.org; CORDIS, Community Research and Development Information Service on
    European Research and Innovation activities, http://cordis.europa.eu/en/home.html; EBAN, a
    European angel network promoting the exchange of experiences and good practice and the role of
    business angels and their networks near public authorities, http://www.eban.org/; Eureka, a network
    for market-oriented R&D, www.eureka.be/home.do; GEM, Global Entrepreneurship Monitor,
    www.gemconsortium.org/; for each country, government websites for entrepreneurship or SMEs;
    IFC, Private Enterprise Partnership for Africa, to stimulate private-sector growth, promote
    sustainable private-sector investment in developing countries, helping to reduce poverty and improve
    people's lives, www.ifc.org/about; International Council for Small Business, www.icsb.org/; IRC
    network, supporting innovation and transnational technological cooperation in Europe,
    www.innovationrelay.net; local authority for SMEs, microbusinesses; local Ministry of Trade,
    Industry, Employment, per country, per region.

REFERENCES

Carroll, G.R. and Khessina, O.M. (2005) 'The ecology of entrepreneurship', in S.A. Alvarez, R. Agarwal
    and O. Sorenson (eds) *Handbook of Entrepreneurship Research: Disciplinary Perspectives*
    (*International Handbook Series on Entrepreneurship*), New York: Springer.

Chrisman, J.J., Chua, J.H. and Steier, L.P. (2002) 'The influence of national culture and family involvement on entrepreneurial perceptions and performance at the state level', *Entrepreneurship Theory and Practice*, 26: 113–31.

Doh, J.P. and Pearce, J.A. (2004) 'Corporate entrepreneurship and real options in transitional policy environments: theory development', *Journal of Management Studies*, 41: 645–64.

D'Souza, D.E. and McDougall, P.P. (1989) 'Third World Joint Venturing: a strategic option for the smaller firm', *Entrepreneurship Theory and Practice*, 13: 19–35.

Dubini, P. (1989) 'The influence of motivations and environment on business start-ups: some hints for public policies', *Journal of Business Venturing*, 4: 11–27.

Gartner, W.B. (1985) 'A conceptual framework for describing the phenomenon of new venture creation', *Academy of Management Review*, 10: 696–706.

Gustavsen, B., Finne, H. and Oscarsson, B. (2001) *Creating Connectedness – The Role of Social Research in Innovation Policy*, Amsterdam: John Benjamins Publisher.

Hanssens, D. (1980) 'Market response, competitive behavior, and time series analysis', *Journal of Marketing Research*, 17: 470–86.

Kariv, D. and Kirschenbaum, A. (2007a) 'Collective spatial perceptions of men and women commuters: linking space, jobs and activity', *Journal of Human Ecology*, 22: 71–82.

Kariv, D. and Kirschenbaum, A. (2007b) 'Linking space and labor markets: towards an alternative conceptualization of labor market behavior', *Journal of Social Science*, 15: 187–95.

Lumpkin, G.T. and Dess, G. (1996) 'Clarifying the entrepreneurial orientation construct and linking it to performance', *Academy of Management Review*, 21: 135–72.

Naman, J. and Slevin, D. (1993) 'Entrepreneurship and the concept of fit: a model and empirical tests', *Strategic Management Journal*, 14: 137–53.

Rodie, A.R. and Martin, C.L. (2001) 'Competing in the service sector: the entrepreneurial challenge', *International Journal of Entrepreneurial Behaviour and Research*, 7: 5–21.

Schwienbacher, A. (2007) 'A theoretical analysis of optimal financing strategies for different types of capital-constrained entrepreneurs', *Journal of Business Venturing*, 22: 753–81.

Shane, S.A. and Ulrich, K. (2004) 'Technological innovation, product development, and entrepreneurship in management science', *Management Science*, 50: 133–44.

Spencer, J.W., Murtha, T.P. and Lenway, S. (2005) 'How governments matter to new industry creation', *Academy of Management Review*, 30: 321–37.

Waldersee, R., Griffiths, A. and Lai, J. (2003) 'Predicting organizational change success: matching organization type, change type and capabilities', *Journal of Applied Management and Entrepreneurship*, 8: 66–81.

Chapter 2

The entrepreneurial culture

OBJECTIVES

After studying this chapter you will be able to:

- Recognize the versatility of the concept of entrepreneurial culture.
- Characterize the different types of entrepreneurial cultures in the context of their ecosystems.
- Recognize that entrepreneurial culture is molded within entrepreneurship, throughout its course from the pre-launch stage to the established stages of the business.
- Acknowledge that an entrepreneurial culture is shaped and affected by different internal and external business factors.
- Describe the different facets through which entrepreneurial culture may present itself (e.g., the entrepreneur's behavior, the business idea, the business plan, the business atmosphere, the team's creativity, among others).
- Identify the most important factors in an entrepreneurial culture that lead to accomplishing a business's goals, and target a business toward adopting the cultural factors that are relevant to it.
- Implement the most relevant factors to the business in order to stimulate an entrepreneurial culture in the business.

WHAT IS ENTREPRENEURIAL CULTURE?

Entrepreneurial culture is a multifaceted concept. Broadly speaking, rather than a job or a livelihood, entrepreneurship is a mindset and a lifestyle, and it is much more than just including 'we are entrepreneurs' in a mission statement. The entrepreneurial culture is an inherent entity steeped within and directly affected by the environment in which an entrepreneurial venture exists. It is based on values and norms that guide the general activities and processes of the venture, and it activates the development of new, entrepreneurial-oriented values and norms for use in that same venture. As such, an entrepreneurial culture enables the business to be dynamic and adaptable by inventing and reinventing its internal activities and processes.

In addition to the more obvious effects, such as sociocultural environment, the presence of potential entrepreneurs, or the stage of development of the local economy, the development of an entrepreneurial culture is stimulated by several main sources (Figure 2.1): the industry's innovation culture, in terms of level of technological innovation, innovation spirit and tolerance toward innovative processes; the founder's spirit, including his or her drive to create, innovate, take risks; employees' innovative and entrepreneurial spirit – it is very difficult to manage a team toward innovation, creativity or opportunity identification when the team lacks entrepreneurial spirit. Both country and global cultures have significant, independent impacts on the business culture, in terms of inventions, new development and encouragement to develop products or services to satisfy current or potential needs; the local market's culture, which may differ from the country's or industry's culture, refers to the customers' willingness and preparedness to purchase innovation and to the suppliers' willingness to supply it.

Researchers of entrepreneurship (Kirzner 1997; Ács and Audretsch 2003) argue that an entrepreneurial culture develops when there is an absence or lack of knowledge and information in the environment on specific topics, there is room in the market economy for the growth or establishment of businesses, and there is demand for certain services and products. Such a phenomenon of environmental disequilibrium is conducive to the development of an entrepreneurial culture. One of the main signs of an entrepreneurial culture is the proliferation of startups in the business environment.

From a microperspective, the cultural characteristics of entrepreneurs that lead to entrepreneurial 'venture-ism', creativity, risk-taking, and independence are crucial in determining the entrepreneurial culture within the local environment. The entrepreneur's talents, accumulated

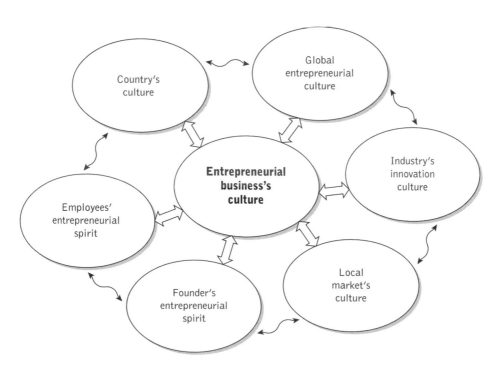

Figure 2.1 *The main influences on entrepreneurial business culture*

knowledge and specific characteristics, which Leibenstein (1968) calls 'input-completing capacity', constitutes another layer in the development of the entrepreneurial culture. The entrepreneur applies this capacity, extends the production function, and thus broadens the existing set of inputs. The presence of spinoffs, different entrepreneurial projects, innovations and inventions developed in ventures, represent, at least in part, the role that entrepreneurs play in the entrepreneurial culture and its outcomes.[1]

In addition to the surrounding entrepreneurial culture, each business venture also creates, or develops, its own culture. This culture is affected not only by the particular characteristics of the entrepreneur, but by the stage of the business: at the launching stage, it is characterized by a vague, less focused, restless and creative-innovative energy, while in the later stages of development it is characterized by an emphasis on maintenance and quality, although at these stages as well, innovative ideas are examined and implemented if considered worthy (Hofstede 1980a, b, c, 1983a, b, 1984, 2001; Shane 1995; Rodriguez-Pose 1999).

One can distinguish four main types of entrepreneurial culture – *all-inclusive*, *stable and balanced*, *rational*, and *width-wise* – each of which highlights different characteristics that produce different processes in the business and in the entrepreneurs' daily lifestyle

- *All-inclusive entrepreneurial culture*. An all-inclusive entrepreneurial culture is a way of life: the individual's entrepreneurial characteristics are adapted and applied to all spheres of life. In this context, entrepreneurship is an ongoing adventure or exploitation, and the individual utilizes such major personal characteristics as creativity, innovation, risk-taking, autonomy and proactivity in making decisions and in carrying them out, not only in business-related matters but also in personal and family-related issues, such as choice of residence, children's schools, use of leisure time, etc.
- *Stable and balanced entrepreneurial culture*. Stable and balanced entrepreneurial culture addresses the individual entrepreneurs' self-awareness of the areas in which they are qualified or not qualified, to use their entrepreneurial characteristics for their venture; it is thus called the *anatomy of an entrepreneur*. In those areas in which entrepreneurs are aware of their limitations, and perceive themselves as being non- or underqualified, or simply not suited (e.g., impatience with administrative tasks; non-conformity), they hire other people to carry out the tasks for which they are unfit. The consequential result of hiring persons that possess the complementary personal qualifications is a balanced and stable culture. When entrepreneurs are unaware of their weaknesses, and how these negatively affect their business's functioning, an unsteady, unpredictable culture may grow.
- *Rational entrepreneurship*. Building opportunities from ideas typifies entrepreneurship practices that evolve into a rational entrepreneurial culture; such a culture encourages careful assessments of each innovative idea, sometimes with the assistance of professionals and experts, in order to estimate its application to the market. As assessments of the feasibility of the ideas are obtained, the rational-entrepreneurial culture encourages the people involved in the business of creating opportunities to implement their innovative ideas through exploitation. The 'spark' for many entrepreneurs, however, is seeing an opportunity that does not yet exist. By laying the foundation for the opportunity's feasibility, a rational-entrepreneurial culture may advance the business to the achievement of its goals (Boyd and Vozikis 1994).
- *Width-wise entrepreneurial culture*. A width-wise entrepreneurial culture is typified by the entrepreneur's broader vision, and by 'thinking big'; the business or the entrepreneurial actions are not limited to a single place or product. In order to identify potential opportunities, the entrepreneurs must be engaged in an ongoing process of learning about the local

31

and global markets, tastes and new developments; they have to use multiple and varied means to acquire this information, such as the internet, attending social and/or professional conferences, acquiring relevant and useful networks, and more. Such entrepreneurs may seem constantly agitated and restless in their ongoing search for relevant information and knowledge. For most of the entrepreneurs who live in such an entrepreneurial culture, 'climbing the mountain of success' may appear to be only a stepping stone to reaching higher summits (Stewart and Roth 2001).

The business's entrepreneurial culture must be led, nurtured, constantly monitored and adjusted. Much like preparing a culinary dish, establishing an entrepreneurial culture requires a combination of the right ingredients and the right pace, to ensure that it develops and manifests itself in the business as expected and supports the business and entrepreneur's goals. Identifying the entrepreneurial culture that is best suited to one's intentions is thus crucial for the business's operation.

PROCESSES THAT STRUCTURE THE ENTREPRENEURIAL CULTURE

In a survey of seventy leading entrepreneurs from forty-eight countries around the world conducted specifically for this book, the respondents were asked to rank the most important factors in the process that structures their entrepreneurial culture. As seen in Figure 2.2, *identification of opportunities*, *differentiation*, *creative teams*, *stimulating partners and role models* were considered the most important factors for a vivid, entrepreneurial culture.

Researchers have begun to stress that the *identification of opportunities* can lead to a competitive advantage; the individual entrepreneur's ability to recognize opportunities is thus a highly beneficial aptitude. Most opportunities do not appear 'out of the blue', but result from the entrepreneur's

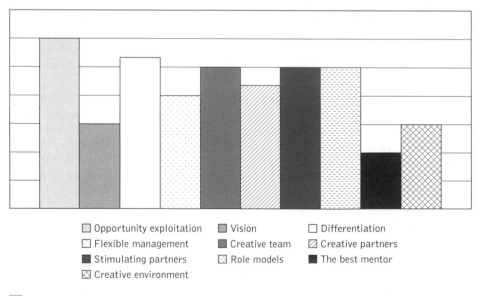

□ Opportunity exploitation ▨ Vision □ Differentiation
□ Flexible management ■ Creative team ▨ Creative partners
■ Stimulating partners ▦ Role models ■ The best mentor
▨ Creative environment

Figure 2.2 *Ranking of the most important factors in an entrepreneurial culture*

alertness to possibilities and knowledge of how to exploit them, and from fine-tuning the mechanisms needed to identify potential opportunities at an early stage. The types of exploitable opportunities and the mechanisms available to look for them delineate the character of the entrepreneurial culture; for example, exploiting financial opportunities will generally develop into a finance-oriented entrepreneurial culture. The exploitation of opportunities to introduce new products or develop new and different products and services will be discussed in the section dealing with the marketing-related aspects of the entrepreneurial culture, etc.

Visions also play a major role in shaping the structure and character of the entrepreneurial culture; however, since visions are usually reflections of dreams, hopes or desires, they are often quite undefined, and do not necessarily match the presently accessible or potentially available resources. The vision of a venture should be clearly defined by developing a *mission statement*; the purpose of such a document is to put the spotlight on how the business should be established and run in order to realize a profit or a goal. Mission statements set practical goals and these underlie the *business plan* and the *practical action plans*. The business culture of the firm is derived from the vision while the behavior, daily conduct and norms derive from the action plans, as described in Figure 2.3.

SUMMARY

Each entrepreneurial culture evolves from the influence of several main sources: the sociocultural environment, the stage of development of the local economy and the personal traits of the majority of its entrepreneurs. Each type of entrepreneurial culture reflects one of the many possible combinations of its sources. An entrepreneurial culture in which the business economy is open and managed by people who are overall more creative and risk-taking would be considered a mature and developed one, while one operating under similar economic and resource conditions, but managed by people who are overall less creative and less risk-taking might be considered more 'planned' and less creative. Most important, the entrepreneurial culture is critical to the development and evolution of the businesses operating within it, and is reflected throughout the entrepreneurial process. The more dominant the entrepreneurial culture, the more transparent its influence, both within and outside the businesses, and in most of the businesses' processes and practices.

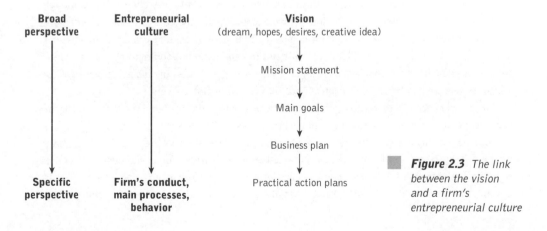

Figure 2.3 *The link between the vision and a firm's entrepreneurial culture*

CASE STUDY 2.1   Leonidas, Israel

Shlomi and Osnat Zingler, Israeli franchisors of Leonidas Belgian Chocolates, opened their *chocolaterie* in Israel in 2005. They hoped to break into the Israeli market with a very up-market, fine-quality product – high-priced artisan chocolates, produced in accordance with the demanding quality standards of the Leonidas head company in Belgium. To penetrate the market with such a luxury product, at a time when the Israeli economy was still coming out of a minor economic recession, was a very ambitious goal, and the potential clients' anticipation of 'something new' in the realm of chocolates was still unclear. A survey made prior to launching Leonidas, Israel produced mixed results regarding the maturity level of Israelis vis-à-vis their lifestyle as a whole and specifically with regard to fine chocolates. Some respondents stated that they would be willing to pay for high-quality chocolates, while others were unsure or were unfamiliar with Leonidas's reputation; and some were unwilling to pay 'high prices' for an unnecessary product such as fine chocolate. However, a small but nevertheless sufficiently large proportion of the respondents were keen on being able to further satisfy their desire for luxury items, and quality chocolate was viewed as a desirable luxury item.

The Zinglers followed all of the predetermined steps of their very structured business plan, but they remained concerned with how to ascertain their Israeli clients' tastes, and especially with how to differentiate themselves from the other artisan *chocolateries* that had begun to spring up in well-to-do Israeli cities. Follow-up surveys and in-depth individual interviews of the potential clientele indicated that there was an incipient demand for products that are innovative rather than 'more of the same'; this clientele wanted things that were pleasurable, and that emphasized their high lifestyle. At this point, the Zinglers's creative thinking led them to change their mission statement from 'to sell high-quality chocolates' to 'to sell fine experiences', thus transforming their merchandise from 'a product' to 'sensual anticipation'. They believed that this would differentiate them from other *chocolateries*.

The Zinglers decided to establish their *chocolaterie* in a prosperous suburb of Tel Aviv, and to furnish it, with attractive elegance, around themes of sensual experiences. This was very risky, as the rental cost in a high-market location, as well as the cost of the planned decor, was very high. The Zinglers were also unsure as to whether their venture would succeed at all, and if so, how successful it might be. Osnat – who at the age of twelve had disobeyed her parents and secretly sold her own handicrafts – decided at this point that they should take a chance '. . . although Leonidas seemed too big for us: a hundred-year-old tradition of chocolate production, with more than ninety types of chocolates and a large number of other complementary products'. In addition, according to Osnat's husband Shlomi, 'it's difficult to penetrate the food market in Israel since a considerable part of the population is religiously observant and eats only foods that have kosher approval, and we had to take this central issue into consideration as well'.

The Zinglers decided that differentiating themselves by the quality of their products and decor was not enough. They decided to treat their clients as guests: 'We love to host friends and relatives in our home, so this was very natural for us,' says Osnat. 'In Belgium, where we spent three years working in an Israeli company, we always talked about the professional and personal service suppliers provided. We felt that we had to adopt this way of doing things, to bring it here,' reveals Shlomi. 'Our main guideline,' adds Osnat, 'is to always treat our clients as very welcome guests.'

The unique, personalized service the couple provides includes tastes of entire pieces of the different flavored chocolates. Shlomi: 'As a client, I could never stand being offered a small piece of cake or cheese cut off from the whole piece, so I decided that this would not happen in our business,' and Osnat adds that 'we offer our guests a whole chocolate bon-bon.'

The Zinglers also chose unique furnishings and decor for their shop – an elegant sofa and coffee table where each guest can sit for a while, rest, and taste chocolates. They also learn and remember the names of their return clients; not only do they call them by name but they also offer them special deals, involving products that are tailor-made to their needs. They are also attentive to the needs of new clients, as exemplified by an incident that occurred only three months after they opened their shop. At closing time on a very busy pre-holiday evening, a young man came in to buy, at his mother's request, 'a really nice box of chocolates for her important dinner hosts', and cost was no object. He was willing for them to improvise a nice package of whatever chocolates were left, but the Zinglers were neither willing to lower their standards nor fail a customer. With only two or three different types of chocolates still unsold, they took the time to put together an elegant basket with a bottle of fine wine, two elegant wine glasses, a couple of flasks of artisan syrups, and some of the remaining chocolates. Their wide-ranging analysis of the situation and their creative solution – to create and sell an elegant basket rather than a box of chocolates – bolstered their rising reputation.

Moreover, the Zinglers treat their workers as partners: they manage the enterprise, but their workers have a great deal of autonomy, never being asked for details on what they did or to report their work hours: 'We trust them . . . and they return the favor,' says Osnat. All of the workers are very carefully selected and trained. 'Our workers are our most precious asset and our most important "display",' they say. The Zinglers believe that their workers represent their business and its values, and they therefore guide their staff to adopt their own very high standards in terms of attire, service, generosity and hospitality.

Their broad perspective and creativity guaranteed their reputation. The results of the first months showed a very steep growth in revenues; after six months, the couple opened a second Leonidas *chocolaterie* in Jerusalem and then a third in Tel Aviv, and they mentored new franchisers to manage each one.

QUESTIONS FOR DISCUSSION

1   Which of the processes that 'structure entrepreneurial culture' do you think the Zinglers addressed the most? What do you think were the reasons for their focus on these different aspects?
2   What were the main risks that the Zinglers faced?
3   What can you learn about the Zinglers's entrepreneurial spirit?
4   Discuss the relationship between 'entrepreneurial spirit' and 'entrepreneurial culture'.

NOTE

1   Hofstede (2001) measured an aspect of entrepreneurial culture – individualism versus collectivism – in different countries and showed that entrepreneurship declines when collectivism is emphasized. Shane (1992) related cultural norms to levels of innovation and economic development.

REFERENCES

Ács, Z.J. and Audretsch, D.B. (2003) *Handbook of Entrepreneurship Research: An Interdisciplinary Survey and Introduction*, New York: Springer.

Boyd, N.G. and Vozikis, G.S. (1994) 'The influence of self-efficacy on the development of entrepreneurial intentions and actions', *Entrepreneurship Theory and Practice*, 18: 63–78.

Hofstede, G. (1980a) 'Culture and organizations', *International Studies of Management and Organization*, 10: 15–41.

Hofstede, G. (1980b) *Culture's Consequences: International Differences in Work Related Values.* Beverly Hills, CA: Sage Publications.

Hofstede, G. (1980c) 'Motivation, leadership, and organization: do American theories apply abroad?', *Organizational Dynamics*, 9: 42–63.

Hofstede, G. (1983a) 'National cultures in four dimensions: a research-based theory of cultural differences among nations', *International Studies of Management and Organization*, 13: 46–75.

Hofstede, G. (1983b) 'The cultural relativity of organizational practices and theories', *Journal of International Business Studies*, 14: 75–90.

Hofstede, G. (1984) 'The cultural relativity of the quality of life concept', *Academy of Management Review*, 9: 389–99.

Hofstede, G. (2001) *Culture Consequences: Comparing Values, Behaviors, Institutions and Organizations Across Nations*, Thousand Oaks, CA: Sage Publications.

Kirzner, I.M. (1997) 'Entrepreneurial discovery and the competitive market process: an Austrian approach', *Journal of Economic Literature*, 35: 60–85.

Leibenstein, H. (1968) 'Entrepreneurship and development', *American Economic Review*, 58: 72–83.

Rodriguez-Pose, A. (1999) 'Innovation prone and innovation averse societies: economic performance in Europe', *Growth and Change*, 30: 75–105.

Shane, S.A. (1992) 'Why do some societies invent more than others?', *Journal of Business Venturing*, 7: 29–46.

Shane, S.A. (1995) 'Is the independent entrepreneurial firm a valuable organizational form?', *Academy of Management Journal*: 110–14.

Stewart, W.H. and Roth, P.L. (2001) 'Risk propensity differences between entrepreneurs and managers: a meta-analysis review', *Journal of Applied Psychology*, 86: 145–53.

Chapter 3

'Entreprening'

OBJECTIVES

After studying this chapter you will be able to:

■ Explain the nature and roots of the term 'entrepreneurship' and how it is related to the characteristic entrepreneurial path.

■ Uncover the different backgrounds that foster entrepreneurship among individuals, consequently engaging factors that will facilitate the development of such backgrounds in the business to stimulate entrepreneurial spirit and conduct among teams and employees.

■ Recognize that individuals differ in finding entrepreneurship as the most desirable career path, subsequently facilitating the way to entrepreneurship for those who are attracted to it as well as introducing entrepreneurship to those who are less attracted to it, to enable them to make more conversant choices along their future career path.

■ Understand the different drivers toward entrepreneurship.

■ Identify the main characteristics of today's entrepreneurs (e.g., human capital-related factors, vision, motivation, and psychological traits).

■ Discuss factors related to individuals' readiness to enter into entrepreneurship.

■ Articulate the multifaceted relationships between entrepreneurial businesses and their ecosystems, and be able to take knowledgeable decisions on the relevant niche in which to set up a business.

WHAT DOES IT TAKE TO BE AN ENTREPRENEUR?

Before discussing what it takes to be an entrepreneur, the term *entrepreneur* itself has to be defined, and the various activities and actions involved in *entrepreneurship* examined and understood. To date, no firm agreement on either of these has been reached, and the numerous proposed definitions and suggestions are usually sketchy and inconsistent. Many researchers, as well as many organizations, have highlighted the need for a collaborative international approach to entrepreneurship and have voiced strong support for the development of a core set of measures, within an agreed-upon framework, to identify the attributes and activities of the entrepreneur. In the belief that such a model can serve to promote entrepreneurship the world over, efforts have been made to build models and establish indicators that would benefit professionals in the area of entrepreneurship (e.g., counselors, mentors), as well as help academic researchers identify those measures. In this section, we attempt to 'crack the entrepreneur code' by delineating the attributes of today's entrepreneur and the main activities that he or she must be able to manage successfully.

Some researchers define entrepreneurs as creative and motivated individuals who take a risk and establish a business, the risk being that of selling at uncertain prices after buying at certain ones (Brockhaus 1980; Carland et al. 1984; Palich and Bagby 1995; Chell 2008); others suggest that entrepreneurs are those who are willing to take risks, and are able, via networking ability and relationship-building skills, to bring different parts of the market together (Dubini and Aldrich 1991; Ostgaard and Birley 1996; Greve and Salaff 2003; Jack, Dodd and Anderson 2008). Entrepreneurs have been defined in myriad other ways, the predominant ones being: inventors of ideas that they evolve to creation; people able to maintain and ensure the growth of an enterprise; developers of new technologies or products that change the field in which they are working; creators and exploiters of new opportunities, and people who change the way in which we think and function in a given area of social activity (Sandberg and Hofer 1987; Bygrave and Hofer 1991; Sarri and Trihopoulou 2005; Taormina and Kin-Mei Lao 2007).

The 'Bill Gates syndrome',[1] typifying 'ordinary' children who become powerful and influential entrepreneurs, is a recognized and acknowledged example, but it is the exception – albeit a notable one – rather than the rule. In many ways, the original failure to recognize Bill Gates' abilities, as proven by the later outburst of his creative abilities and resultant success story, should actually be considered a failure of the educational system.

The educational system, and bodies such as labor- and market-related ministries, industrial ministries and associations and institutions of higher learning, among others, should develop measures to identify potential entrepreneurs and initiate programs to stimulate and encourage innovation, creativity, and other qualities that are necessary for entrepreneurial success. This should also be done among young people, even pupils in elementary and high schools, since identifying and developing the traits, abilities and other resources that are vital for entrepreneurship can facilitate their future careers as successful entrepreneurs.

IS THERE A BACKGROUND THAT PROMPTS ENTREPRENEURSHIP?

Two random examples of successful and renowned entrepreneurs depict very different background scenarios: Oprah Winfrey and Conan O'Brien, the host of NBC's *Tonight Show*, both recognized television personalities in the United States. Oprah Winfrey's life story[2] tells of a traumatic childhood and a young woman whose rebellious spirit enabled her to break through and overcome social and racial barriers. Determined to excel, she rose to become a prominent and innovative television talk-show host, and an influential multipreneur who owns a film company, a widely read monthly magazine and a cable network, in addition to establishing several philanthropic organizations. She has been quoted as saying that: 'with every experience, you alone are painting your own canvas, thought by thought, choice by choice',[3] stressing that despite her background, her attitude toward life experiences is that they can be translated into choices that craft opportunities. Conan O'Brien was born and raised in an Irish Catholic family in a suburb of Boston, Massachusetts, to a mother who was an attorney, and a father who was a physician and professor of medicine. He graduated from Brookline High School, as valedictorian, and entered Harvard University, where he was a writer for the *Harvard Lampoon* humor magazine. In 2001, he formed his own television production company, Conaco, which has shared in the production credits for *Late Night*. Emerging from vastly different backgrounds, and active in entirely different realms, both Oprah Winfrey and Conan O'Brien are undoubtedly what we term *entrepreneurs*. It thus appears that there is no single 'right' or 'propitious' background or family history that prompts or leads to entrepreneurship.

Alfred Marshall, in his foundational treatise *The Principles of Economics* (1890), listed four factors of production: land, labor, capital, and organization. He further asserted that entrepreneurship is the driving element behind organization, and that entrepreneurs must have a thorough under-standing of the industries connected with their enterprise, be natural leaders, have the ability to foresee changes in supply and demand, and be willing to act on risky forecasts, even in the absence of all the relevant information. These are no longer the only universally accepted characteristics that typify entrepreneurs. A combination of in-born psychological traits, cultural, family and educational backgrounds, and social values are considered to underlie the nature and attributes of the quintessential entrepreneur.

A number of studies have revealed that role models, as well as positive attitudes toward entrepreneurship expressed by family members, especially parents, and by teachers and peers, are of prime importance in stimulating behavior that can lead to entrepreneurial activities. Parents and a home environment that support and encourage independence, achievement, and respon-sibility on a daily basis appear to be highly important factors in prompting entrepreneurship, especially among women. It appears that children whose parents' educational viewpoint directed them toward achievement, autonomy and responsibility found satisfying careers and lifestyles in entrepreneurial ventures – but so, too, did children who were not supported, or were even severely neglected by their parents, but whom life itself forced to become responsible, autonomous, and achievers. Oprah Winfrey and Conan O'Brien exemplify these radically different, even antithetical, explanations.

Recent research in entrepreneurship has also shown that the cultural environment is a dominant factor in a person's motivation to start a business. Cultures such as those of the United States and, more recently, Canada, which place a high value on creativity, innovation and autonomy, or on 'making money', will generate more business formations than those that do not. In his inspirational book *The Protestant Ethic and the Spirit of Capitalism* (1905), Max Weber, the German economist and sociologist, wrote that the Protestant ethic influenced people to engage in work in the secular world, developing their own enterprises and engaging in trade and in the accumulation of wealth for investment. This ethic led to the development of capitalism and, in the largely Protestant United States, to immense economic development.

Some studies (Stephenson 1958; McClelland 1961; Furlong, Biggart and Cartmel 1996; Drennan, Kennedy and Renfrow 2005) have addressed the effects of social, demographic and class differences on children's mental and psychological attitudes and on their life choices. These studies showed that children's first impressions of the labor market, and their later occupations or professions, as well as their orientation toward work, are based on the general nature and significance of the work world of the adults around them. This ultimately affects both their capabilities and their ambition to exploit opportunities and become entrepreneurs.

Other findings of these studies, however, are mixed: some children from dysfunctional families were found to have little or no curiosity in their environment and to lack confidence in their ability to learn and to deal with the difficulties that life presents; others with the same or similar backgrounds were found to be eager to explore their surroundings, and were both motivated and prepared to devote their energies and resources to developing their capabilities, and to using them to get ahead in life. It is the latter group that may choose entrepreneurship as a promising path to success (McClelland et al. 1953; Caird 1963; McClelland 1965; Durand and Shea 1974;

Litvak and Maule 1976; Begley and Boyd 1987; Lee and Tsang 2001; Chowdhury 2005; Drennan, Kennedy and Renfrow 2005).

MAIN CHARACTERISTICS OF TODAY'S ENTREPRENEURSHIP AND ENTREPRENEURS

The multifaceted aspects of entrepreneurship and entrepreneurs are summarized in Table 3.1, which lists some of the major findings on human capital (HC) and the ecological and psychological aspects of entrepreneurship, along with several such entrepreneurial-related topics as networking, team work, career path and more. These characteristics have been identified in a large number of studies to date, but since the phenomenon of entrepreneurship is growing rapidly and is appearing in more and widely dissimilar countries all over the world, entrepreneurs, too, are becoming increasingly dissimilar.

Today's entrepreneurs may be highly educated, uneducated, or even illiterate; they may be trained professionals or lacking any trade or occupation; they may be very young (adolescents have established their own enterprises) or old enough to be out of the workforce; they may have had formal preparation for entrepreneurship or have learned about it along the way; finally, more and more women have entered the field of entrepreneurship (WE) as the constraints of work and home have become less limiting for women in most countries.

Theoretically, entrepreneurship can provide the best fit between a person and a profession or career, as the enterprise and how it is managed are determined by the entrepreneur's own predilections and decisions, rather than by those made by others, while within the corporate system employees have to adapt themselves to the dictates of employers or prestructured jobs (Gupta, MacMillan and Surie 2004; Mayo 2005).

Vision and motivation

Visions are all around us, in everything we see and think about. They can be things that we would like to see exist or happen, or things we would like to improve; they may be things that we think would help us handle our lives more effectively and pleasantly. A vision can also be a bright and exceptional idea that springs forth unexpectedly and with no apparent connection to ongoing affairs. In the context of entrepreneurship, however, vision means seeing something that others do not, and implementing it before they do. This kind of vision is an underlying requisite of venture creation and the motivating factor for the establishment of an independent and self-run enterprise.

Visions that emerge from very personal needs or experiences can grow and develop into entrepreneurial enterprises, as exemplified by the successful chain of Starbucks coffee shops. Howard Schultz, the former CEO of Starbucks, was drinking a cup of coffee in an Italian coffee bar during one of his trips to Europe. He loved the taste, the service and the atmosphere, and realized that he did not mind paying a little extra for them. This experience stimulated him to create the same atmosphere and presence in the United States. Schultz's vision led to a chain of Starbucks throughout North America, and in several countries in Europe and Asia, among other places (Hinterhuber and Popp 1992; Olsen 1994).

The normative process of decision-making in selecting a job, staying in or quitting an active job, or entering entrepreneurship, moves through three main circles (illustrated in Figure 3.1). The first, innermost circle in a person's motivation to select a specific job or profession is basically concerned with his or her personal desires and aspirations, and the answer to the existential question 'What do I want to do for a living?' or, perhaps, 'What do I want from life?' The primary

Table 3.1 The main characteristics of today's entrepreneurs

Human capital	Ecology	Psychological aspects	Entrepreneurship and SME
Gender	*Local, embedded*	*Motivations*	*Features*
■ Men launch businesses more than women do ■ Men's businesses are more successful in terms of survival time and revenues than those of women ■ More women are launching and managing their own businesses today than in the past ■ More women consider entrepreneurship a career path today than in the past ■ More women are attracted to entrepreneurship today because the home–work conflict is more manageable	■ There are more transformations from cluster entrepreneurships to global, multinational and borderless ones ■ Specific groups are more locally embedded: ethnic groups, low-tech sectors, local-oriented businesses, women more than men	■ Diverse motivations to enter entrepreneurship: *personal*, such as, autonomy, fulfillment of personal needs; *economic*, such as the need for rapid growth and financial benefits; *political*, to establish the 'right' networking, resources and power	■ Very diverse configurations (e.g., partnerships, multipreneurships, intrapreneurships, franchises) ■ Leading entrepreneurs have or develop different roles; involvement in one feature (i.e., creator of ideas, investor, launcher of start-ups, manager of the firm), does not predict engagement in others
Human capital (HC)	*Competition for scarce resources*	*Traits*	*Networking*
■ Today's entrepreneurs' HC is more varied than in the past ■ Wide-ranging HC is not necessarily related to entrepreneurial and/or professional activities: physicians may launch a computer-based venture, and retired teachers may launch websites for adult recreation possibilities ■ Most entrepreneurs lack specialization in entrepreneurship and management	■ Power plays a crucial role in securing scarce resources ■ Entrepreneurs utilize networking, political connections and innovation in order to compete against both entrepreneurial and corporate businesses in securing scarce resources	Entrepreneurs possess diverse psychological traits: ■ Ambition ■ Nonconformism ■ Difficulty adjusting to a corporate system ■ Adventure-seeking ■ Risk-taking ■ Creativity ■ Restlessness	■ Most successful entrepreneurs are able to communicate their ideas and 'sell' them to their relatives, friends and family on an ongoing basis, thus establishing networks

Table 3.1 Continued

Human capital	Ecology	Psychological aspects	Entrepreneurshaip and SME
Personal characteristics	*Spatial heterogeneity*	*Core traits required*	*Team work*
■ Age – younger individuals are more likely to start a business ■ Individuals in mid-career and retired people are turning to entrepreneurship more than in the past. The main explanations for this refer to longer life spans, better health care, past experience in the labor market, and the desire to fill free time with meaningful activities ■ Women at a child care stage of life are more involved in entrepreneurial activities than in the past	■ Less rigidity in organizational structures ■ Heterogeneity and adaptive organizational forms in different environments (i.e., working from home, diffuse hierarchy in entrepreneurial businesses, partnerships, weakened bureaucracy, among others)	■ Innovation, creativity and proactiveness are core traits throughout the entrepreneurial venture ■ Communication, emotional intelligence and risk-taking are prime traits needed to sustain a competitive advantage ■ Each entrepreneurial stage requires different individual traits: *launching stage* – creativity and risk-taking; *operation and maintenance stage* – managerial competence ■ Leadership, persistence and managerial attributes are valuable in crisis phases	■ Team hierarchy and traditional chain-of-command rules are less common today than in the past ■ Teams are based on expertise. Relations in teams that are professional, interest-driven, informal and non-obligatory are more likely to lead to win–win situations, which are more likely to lead to a successful venture
Ethnic groups and minorities			*Career path*
■ Ethnic groups and minorities are under-represented in most entrepreneurial activities ■ Female entrepreneurship in these groups is significantly under-represented ■ In immigration countries (e.g., the US and Canada), ethnic entrepreneurship is addressed more than in non-immigration countries (e.g., most European and Asian countries)			■ Potential entrepreneurs should attend preparatory programs ■ Active entrepreneurs should participate in training programs ■ Mid-career employees tend to go back to specific training programs prior to switching careers to entrepreneurship ■ Entrepreneurs find that their careers are ongoing learning experiences

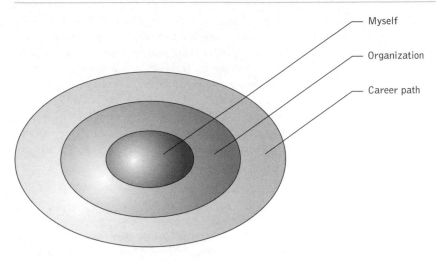

Myself

Organization

Career path

Figure 3.1 *The process of decision-making in selecting a job*

focus is therefore on *myself*,[4] which encompasses other questions such as: What is best for me? What interests me? Where and how can I utilize my knowledge and skills? How can I grow and develop in the course of my working life? Some individuals find their way to a job that provides them with a sufficient degree of satisfaction, while others must compromise and, in order to make a living, work in whatever job the market offers, with a lack of interest and enthusiasm.

The middle circle refers to one's identification with the *organization* that he or she is actually working in. An individual may be satisfied with his job per se, but not with the values, culture, rules or atmosphere of the workplace. This will lead to a feeling of detachment, or to a lack of commitment and identification with the organization, and although individuals in such a situation may continue to work in their organizations, their lack of identity will lead some of them to search for employment elsewhere.

The outermost circle represents the individual's *career path*. Within this circle are past and present jobs, as well as envisioned future jobs and other possibilities. Commitment, contentment and enthusiasm with past and present jobs or organizations, or the lack of any or all of these, are likely to affect or even determine perceptions of a future career path. Individuals who are satisfied with their present or past jobs and organizations may nevertheless have doubts about their potential for success in other places of work or in an independent enterprise.

Movement from one circle to another is not always in what the individual considers a desired or forward direction. For example, a professor who is highly competent in and satisfied with his or her chosen academic field may be called upon to fill an even higher level position in administration, as a dean or as head of a university department. Since such administrative positions are very demanding, full-time posts, very little time is left for academic research. There is also an additional, two-sided dilemma: neglecting or abandoning research for three or four years is likely to endanger progress in one's academic career path, but refusing such administrative jobs can often mean renouncing prestigious and well-networked appointments.

For many individuals in the workforce, entrepreneurship has proven to be an excellent choice, since it can provide a satisfactory or even excellent livelihood, as well as fulfillment of the individual's desires and aspirations (the innermost circle). In terms of many individuals' need for *organization* (the middle circle), entrepreneurship is likely to fulfill the need for commitment and identification with their own creation, and to do so in an organization that is planned, established and developed by the entrepreneur, according to his or her own vision and desires, thereby promoting the entrepreneur's *career path* (the outermost circle), in a way that answers the needs of the *id* (a return to the innermost circle). Many entrepreneurs are more comfortable in a protean career (Hall 1976, 2002); that is, a career process in which the person, not the organization, manages his or her career; as such, the protean person's own personal career choices, desires, and their implementation are unified, controlled and adjusted by that person, promoting his or her self-fulfillment. As protean core values are freedom and growth, mobility between jobs is high, success criteria are subjective, and professional and job preferences fluctuate. Entrepreneurship is the best format for such a career type. Thus, for many individuals, entrepreneurship is highly likely to satisfy the needs found in all three circles.

Psychological traits

Psychological theories focusing on the personal traits, motives and incentives of entrepreneurs stress their need for achievement, a propensity for risk-taking, and an 'internal locus of control', all of which are considered major characteristics of the entrepreneurial personality. The strong need for achievement, in terms of accomplishing difficult tasks, organizing ideas, overcoming obstacles and/or attaining a high standard of work, is considered a significant psychological variable associated with new venture creation; independence and a strong internal locus of control, which are both associated with self-awareness, self-development and ongoing learning, as well as with self-regard and sometimes competitiveness, are also significant factors (McClelland 1961; Pandey and Tewary 1979; Sexton and Smilor 1985; Shaver and Scott 1991; Kaufmann, Welsh and Bushmarin 1995; Mueller and Thomas 2001).

Entrepreneurs have been found to be creative and enthusiastic about the fruits of their creativity, and to have a zeal for the challenge of inventing new products and exploiting new ways of marketing. They are restless, and even the most successful ones are never fully satisfied with their accomplishments: they tend to continually look for additional and different paths to achieve their goals and realize their vision. Sustaining goal-directed action and utilizing coping strategies when faced with obstacles are also traits identified with entrepreneurs, as is tenacity, which has been consistently identified as a typical trait of both inventors and entrepreneurs.

Researchers in cognitive theories that address entrepreneurs' perceptions of the startup process assert that in order to keep their long-term goals alive in the face of surprises, shortages and barriers, entrepreneurs develop intense mental images of desirable futures. These researchers also found that to cope with the uncertainties and urgencies they face, entrepreneurs draw upon tacit knowledge, similar to intuition, through cognitive processes based on compressed experience, rather than on strategic thinking. The combination of these images and tactics comprises the overall scheme of the venture that the entrepreneurs want to create. All of these are important in the entrepreneur's exploratory and experimental setting, when information is scarce and outcome probabilities unclear, and in which rational decision-making processes strain limited resources and provide little gain (Brockhaus 1980; Sexton and Bowman 1986; Low and MacMillan 1988; Chen, Greene and Crick 1998; Ireland and Miller 2004).

The main resource: human capital (HC)

The combination of higher education, work experience and expertise has a strong impact on entrepreneurship. Explanations for this derive from the laws of supply and demand. In the job market, education, experience and specific expertise are exchangeable assets that enable job applicants to construct their credentials to suit the type of employment offered; job seekers with fewer exchangeable HC assets need to compromise, and accept lower paid positions, or hard or boring jobs. Employers, even those able and willing to pay fairly for their workers' educational and professional attainments, rarely need all of their employees' specific knowledge or know-how for performing most of the tasks in their companies. The well-known description 'over-qualified' illustrates the disproportion between job availability and HC availability: since employers neither want nor can afford to pay the costs attached to highly qualified (i.e., over-qualified) workers, over-qualified individuals often seek a more remunerative and satisfying solution, which can be found in entrepreneurship (Robinson and Sexton 1994; Edwards and Muir 2005).

Ecology characteristics

Ecological theories have addressed the multifaceted relationships between new businesses and their environments. These studies are based on the concept known as the Competitive Exclusion Principle (Hannan and Carroll 1992; Aldrich and Wiedenmayer 1993), which asserts that two similar businesses cannot occupy the same niche at the same time in the same ecosystem. In order to succeed, new entrepreneurial businesses must have or construct unique products or services, or fashion or devise attractive conditions or characteristics that suit their particular environment. The multifaceted relationship between environment and business is the prime concern in ecological studies. Ecological models focus on how organizations change over time, especially through the demographic processes of selective replacement – organizations' founding, growth and mortality. The major theories of organizational ecology dealing with the founding of new businesses include, among other topics: the rate of new venture launches or launch attempts; competition across regions; rates of founding across geographical locales; the contribution of initial resource endowments; allocation of power; risk-taking under conditions of uncertainty, and information asymmetry.

The ecological conditions upon which entrepreneurial viability is dependent are difficult to define and measure, and the long-term or continued success of such ventures, both newly launched and 'up and running', is therefore highly unpredictable. Ecological models are beginning to provide clearer explanations for these relationships (Aldrich, Zimmer and McEvoy 1989; Reynolds 1991; Ács and Audretsch 2005).

SUMMARY

Today, anyone can be an entrepreneur, be they young or old, male or female, with formal preparation for entrepreneurship or thrilled to explore this path with no previous knowledge, with concrete or amorphous visions. All have a common drive – they are keen to develop themselves into their own, extant venture. Yet entrepreneurship is quite a difficult matter: it confronts individuals with various vague, risky and uncertain business situations. Although entrepreneurship is encouraged by many national agencies and governments in many countries, and is culturally incorporated into many communities, some individuals will be more attracted to entreprenurship than others, as this demanding, tough yet challenging and stimulating career path is more appealing to individuals possessing the combination of specific human capital determinants, psychological traits and family encouragement, along with positive values toward entrepreneurial spirit (e.g., independence, risk-taking, onoing learning, learning through doing).

Some people find entrepreneurship a satisfactory, self-fulfilling career path as it provides them with their desired livelihood, matches their aspirations and fits their independent, free-spirited psychological characteristics; others are attracted to entrepreneurship as it fulfills their need for commitment and identification with their own creation, their own venture; yet others find it the best path for a protean career. Entrepreneurship fulfills different needs in different people as a preferred job and way of life.

CASE STUDY 3.1   Jemex, Croatia

After twenty years as a consultant in a large company, Luka Brstilo was bored with his job. 'I get bored easily,' he confesses. Brstilo was employed as a consultant in information technology (IT) management and marketing-related matters. He was earning well, but always felt that something was missing in his life. At work, Brstilo was considered 'rebellious', as he was frequently involved in disputes and disagreements with his boss and colleagues. They wouldn't fire him, however, due to his creative thinking and his commitment to the company's projects and clients: every project was carried out quickly and completely, and there was widespread satisfaction with his devotion and professionalism. In fact, after one particular disagreement, Brstilo was actually fired, but clients' threats to leave the company if he wasn't there resulted in his boss's rehiring him the very next day. Brstilo's creative solutions often entailed risks, and the company he worked for could not afford to take them. Such refusals frustrated him. He felt that he was going downhill. One evening, on the way to soccer practice with his son, a neighbor told him that he looked 'gray'. Although Brstilo wasn't sure he understood exactly what this meant, he did feel old and run-down and bored. Brstilo quit his job the very next morning. Within a month, he launched two businesses – simultaneously. 'My wife was very worried about my decision to quit. She has a job, but we have two children, and there was no guarantee that things would work out for us. So I decided to have two businesses: one of them is solidly based, that is, it specializes in what I do best – marketing and management consulting – and I'm the only "player" there. My clients are only large companies, and I work for them when I really need money. The other one, Jemex, is a company that provides internet services. The internet activity was launched early last year, and I have been running it full time since September. I manage this second business, but my income is mainly from the first one.' Jemex is still in its infancy, and it faces several constraints, but Brstilo is very devoted to his entrepreneurial activity: he works longer hours and his work often spills over into his personal and family life, but Brstilo is happy: 'Croatia is an economically emerging country, but it has some old legal and economic structures, with so many rules that it is sometimes difficult to distinguish between them. The country suffers from very long decision-making processes and a lot of bureaucracy. Many people that I have spoken with avoid entrepreneurship for just those reasons,' he says. Brstilo is a restless doer with irrepressible creative energies, and he decided to turn these attributes to his advantage. He saw that the government's procedures were slow and burdensome, which made it difficult for new businesses to become established, including those related to the internet. He saw an opportunity there, and launched a company. He also began to look for other mergers, partnerships or opportunities that would make it possible to circumvent the government's cumbersome bureaucracy and provide services that were becoming more in demand. 'Suddenly, it occurred to me that in some parts of Croatia's main cities, especially in the south where I live, there is a lot of low-cost housing; and the residents there can't afford to be connected to the internet. I realized that in the virtual labor market we live in, the unemployed, who constitute a relatively large part of the population in these areas, lack the major means for entering the labor force today: access to the internet. In the housing projects there are higher proportions of unemployed, old people, and families with many children. I thought to myself, "There are thousands living in low-cost housing in Croatia, so there should be a huge potential there." I decided to offer these inhabitants wireless DSL [digital subscriber line]. I knew this would be in the government's interest as well. Along with two partners in this project, I structured a specific strategy and we constructed our niche,' says Brstilo. 'The growth of my company relies on four things: the partners; its positioning; its clear strategy and attainable goals, and funding. I am constantly searching for money . . . this is what I do every day.' Brstilo is a great believer in networking and direct communication: he considers networking the key to success, and suggests that a small, entrepreneurial company can develop its activities thanks to strong relationships with major players (e.g., large companies and government firms). Luka Brstilo says that he is not a workaholic: 'I hope to have such success that I will be able to give up working.' But until such success is reached, he does not rest; he seeks more and more opportunities to exploit.

QUESTIONS FOR DISCUSSION

1   What are Luka Brstilo's main entrepreneurial strengths – psychologically, and in terms of human capital and motivation?
2   How did Brstilo's entrepreneurial psychological traits affect his behavior and his life when he was an employee in a large company?
3   Analyze the beneficial effects of Brstilo's entrepreneurial traits on his business, well-being, motivation and drive, and personal life.
4   Analyze the potential disadvantages of Brstilo's entrepreneurial traits for his business, his well-being, his motivation and drive, and his personal life.
5   Identify Brstilo's motivations to launch his businesses.
6   Is Brstilo typical of today's entrepreneur? Specify.
7   How would you advise Brstilo to proceed with his businesses? Explain.

NOTES

1   World Changers: Bill Gates, www.wc.pdx.edu/billgates/billy.html; Microsoft, Bill Gates's home page, www.microsoft.com/billgates/default.aspx.
2   Oprah Winfrey's biography, at Oprah Winfrey's official site, www.oprah.com.
3   Experience Quotes, www.wow4u.com/experiencequotes/index.html.
4   Adapted from Sigmund Freud's theory of the *id*, the part of the personality that contains our primitive impulses, such as anger and hunger, and is based on the pleasure principle.

WEBSITES FOR ENTREPRENEURIAL COUNSULTING

ACE, Action Community for Entrepreneurship, http://www.ace.org.sg/Site/index.aspx.
Disney Entrepreneur Center, www.disneyec.com/.
DIY.BizPlan.com, www.diybizplan.com/HELP!_Free_Consulting_for_Entrepreneurs.
ECWT, European Centre for Women and Technology, www.womenandtechnology.eu/digitalcity/news/
    w_all.jsp?dom=AAABECDQ&prt=AAABDUAV&fmn=AAABDVVL&men=AAABDVWA&ktg=AAA
    AIGTK.
FKCCI, Federation of Karnataka Chambers of Commerce and Industry, India, www.fkcci.org/services.php.
Networked Intelligence for Development, www.networkedintelligence.com.
SBA programs, www.world-entrepreneurship-forum.com/.
SCORE, Counselors to America's Small Business, www.score.org/index.html.
SMEtoolkit, http://us.smetoolkit.org/us/en/.
SPRING, Singapore, www.spring.gov.sg/Content/HomePage.aspx.

REFERENCES

Ács, Z.J. and Audretsch, D.B. (2005) *Foundations and Trends in Entrepreneurship*, Boston: Now
    Publications.
Aldrich, H.E. and Wiedenmayer, G. (1993) 'From traits to rates: an ecological perspective on
    organizational foundings', in J. Katz and T. Lumpkin, *Advances in Entrepreneurship, Firm
    Emergence, and Growth*, Greenwich, CT: JAI Press, 145–95.
Aldrich, H.E., Zimmer, C. and McEvoy, D. (1989) 'Continuities in the study of ecological succession:
    Asian businesses in three English cities', *Social Forces*, 67: 920–45.
Begley, T.M. and Boyd, D.P. (1987) 'Psychological characteristics associated with performance in
    entrepreneurial firms and smaller businesses', *Journal of Business Venturing*, 2: 79–93.
Brockhaus, R.H. (1980) 'Risk taking propensity of entrepreneurs', *Academy of Management Journal*,
    23: 509–20.
Bygrave, W.D. and Hofer, C.W. (1991) 'Theorizing about entrepreneurship', *Entrepreneurship Theory
    and Practice*, 16: 13–23.
Caird, S.P. (1963) 'What do psychological tests suggest about entrepreneurs?', *Journal of Managerial
    Psychology*, 8: 11–20.
Carland, J.W., Hoy, F., Boulton, W.R. and Carland, J.A. (1984) 'Differentiating entrepreneurs from
    small business owners: a conceptualization', *Academy of Management* Review, 9: 354–9.
Chell, E. (2008) *The Entrepreneurial Personality: A Social Construction*, London: Routledge.
Chen, C.C., Greene, P.G. and Crick, A. (1998) 'Does entrepreneurial self-efficacy distinguish
    entrepreneurs from managers?', *Journal of Business Venturing*, 13: 295–316.
Chowdhury, S. (2005) 'Demographic diversity for building an effective entrepreneurial team: is it
    important?', *Journal of Business Venturing*, 20: 727–46.
Drennan, J., Kennedy, J. and Renfrow, P. (2005) 'Impact of childhood experiences on the development
    of entrepreneurial intentions', *International Journal of Entrepreneurship and Innovation*, 6: 231–8.
Dubini, P. and Aldrich, H. (1991) 'Personal and extended networks are central to the entrepreneurial
    process', *Journal of Business Venturing*, 6: 305–13.
Durand, D. and Shea, D. (1974) 'Entrepreneurial activity as a function of achievement motivation and
    reinforcement control', *Journal of Psychology*, 88: 57–63.
Edwards, L. and Muir, E.J. (2005) 'Promoting entrepreneurship at the University of Glamorgan through
    formal and informal learning', *Journal of Small Business and Enterprise Development*, 12: 613–26.

Furlong, A., Biggart, A. and Cartmel, F. (1996) 'Neighbourhoods, opportunity structures and occupational aspirations', *Sociology: The Journal of the British Sociological Association*, 30: 551–65.

Greve, A. and Salaff, J.W. (2003) 'Social networks and entrepreneurship', *Entrepreneurship Theory and Practice*, 28: 1–22.

Gupta, V., MacMillan, I.C. and Surie, G. (2004) 'Entrepreneurial leadership: developing and measuring a cross-cultural construct', *Journal of Business Venturing*, 19: 241–60.

Hall, D.T. (1976) *Careers in Organizations*, Glenview, IL: Scott, Foresman.

Hall, D.T. (2002) *Careers in and out of Organizations*, Thousand Oaks, CA: Sage Publications.

Hannan, M.T. and Carroll, G.R. (1992) *Dynamics of Organizational Populations: Density, Legitimation, and Competition*. New York: Oxford University Press.

Hinterhuber, H.H. and Popp, W. (1992) 'Are you a strategist or just a manager?', *Harvard Business Review*, 70: 105–14.

Ireland, R.D. and Miller, C.C. (2004) 'Decision-making and firm success', *Academy of Management Executive*, 18: 8–12.

Jack, S., Dodd, S.D. and Anderson, A.R. (2008) 'Change and the development of entrepreneurial networks over time: a processual perspective', *Entrepreneurship and Regional Development*, 20: 125–59.

Kaufmann, P.J., Welsh, D.H. and Bushmarin, N.V. (1995) 'Locus of control and entrepreneurship in the Russian Republic', *Entrepreneurship Theory and Practice*, 20: 43–58.

Lee, D.Y. and Tsang, E.W. (2001) 'The effects of entrepreneurial personality, background and network activities on venture growth', *Journal of Management Studies*, 38: 583–602.

Litvak, I.A. and Maule, C.J. (1976) 'Comparative technical entrepreneurship – some perspectives', *Journal of International Business Studies*, 7: 31–8.

Low, M.B. and MacMillan, I.C. (1988) 'Entrepreneurship: past research and future challenges', *Journal of Management*, 14: 139–62.

Marshall, A. (1890) *The Principles of Economics*, London: Macmillan and Co., Ltd.

Mayo, A.J. (2005) 'Zeitgeist leadership', *Harvard Business Review*, 83: 45–60.

McClelland, D.N. (1961) *The Achieving Society*, Princeton, NJ: Van Nostrand.

McClelland, D.N. (1965) 'Achievement and entrepreneurship: a longitudinal study', *Journal of Personality and Social Psychology*, 1: 389–92.

McClelland, D.N., Atkinson, J.W., Clark, R.A. and Lowell, E.L. (1953) *The Achievement Motive*, New York: The Free Press.

Mueller, S.L. and Thomas, A.S. (2001) 'Culture and entrepreneurial potential: a nine country study of locus of control and innovativeness', *Journal of Business Venturing*, 16: 51–75.

Olsen, D. (1994) *Starbucks Passion for Coffee*, Menlo Park, CA: Sunset Publishing.

Ostgaard, T.A. and Birley, S. (1996) 'New venture growth and personal networks', *Journal of Business Research*, 36: 37–50.

Palich, L.E. and Bagby, D.R. (1995) 'Using cognitive theory to explain entrepreneurial risk-taking: challenging conventional wisdom', *Journal of Business Venturing*, 10: 425–38.

Pandey, J. and Tewary, N.B. (1979) 'Locus of control and achievement values of entrepreneurs', *Journal of Occupational Psychology*, 52: 107–11.

Reynolds, P.D. (1991) 'Sociology and entrepreneurship: concepts and contributions', *Entrepreneurship Theory and Practice*, 16: 47–71.

Robinson, P.B. and Sexton, E.A. (1994) 'The effect of education and experience on self-employment success', *Journal of Business Venturing*, 9: 141–57.

Sandberg, W.R. and Hofer, C.W. (1987) 'Improving new venture performance: the role of strategy, industry structure, and the entrepreneur', *Journal of Business Venturing*, 2: 5–29.

Sarri, K. and Trihopoulou, A. (2005) 'Female entrepreneurs' personal characteristics and motivation: a review of the Greek situation', *Women in Management Review*, 20: 24–36.

Sexton, D.L. and Bowman, N. (1986) 'Will the real entrepreneur please step forward?', *Baylor Business Review*, 4: 10–14.

Sexton, D.L. and Smilor, R.W. (1985) *The Art and Science of Entrepreneurship*, Cambridge, MA: Ballinger, 25–48.

Shaver, K.G. and Scott, L.R. (1991) 'Person, process, choice: the psychology of new venture creation', *Entrepreneurship Theory and Practice*, 16: 23–45.

Stephenson, R.M. (1958) 'Stratification, education, and occupational orientation: a parallel study and review', *British Journal of Sociology*, 9: 42–52.

Taormina, R.J. and Kin-Mei Lao, S. (2007) 'Measuring Chinese entrepreneurial motivation: personality and environmental influences', *International Journal of Entrepreneurial Behaviour and Research*, 13: 200–21.

Weber, M. (1905) *The Protestant Ethic and the Spirit of Capitalism*, New York: Charles Scribner's Sons.

Part II

The process-oriented perspective in entrepreneurship

Chapter 4

Creativity in entrepreneurship

OBJECTIVES

After studying this chapter you will be able to:

- Discuss the meaning of creativity through its different definitions, and by introducing the paradoxes, challenges, gaps and asynchronies it raises in the entrepreneurial realm.
- Delineate the role and relevance of creativity in entrepreneurship and specifically in the process of venture creation.
- Identify the key factors of creativity in the course of the entrepreneurial life cycle.
- Recognize the relationships of creativity with: the environment, the business's idea and vision, the business's structure and organization, the team and employees.
- Distinguish between the different factors that stimulate the development of a creative idea.
- Understand how creativity functions in the entrepreneurial realm and be able to apply it in entrepreneurial businesses, projects or other undertakings.
- Discuss the role of creativity as a foremost competitive advantage for the entrepreneurial business.
- Discover more about the different practices, means and tools to both enhance and use creativity along the business's life cycle.
- Learn ways to foster creativity in the business (e.g., business atmosphere, business plan, strategy and staff).
- Operate a new and practical model of creativity in order to enhance creativity in a new business.

In ancient Greece and during the Italian Renaissance, creativity flourished. These and similar epochs in history reflect the notion that when a society enjoys economic prosperity, along with the psychological and sociological conditions embedded in the culture at such times, creativity emerges. Creativity is stimulated by 'the proportion of social resources which is allocated to non-instrumental pursuits' (Kavolis 1964: 334). At the same time, creativity can emerge in individuals who are experiencing poverty, distress and either unemployment or poor environmental conditions: creative ideas at such times may be translated into tangible, sellable products or businesses, and creativity becomes the escape-hatch for dire circumstances. Nevertheless, creativity is not only an outcome of economic or cultural circumstances: it is a phenomenon that embodies the individual as well as the larger sociocultural representations.

DEFINING CREATIVITY

Creativity, for the purposes of entrepreneurialism, is the envisioning of new combinations of resources and market realities, often through the questioning of conventional wisdom, the discovery of new knowledge with respect to market needs, technology, or the availability of vital resources, and/or finding new applications for pre-existing knowledge. Edward de Bono, a leading authority on thinking processes who is widely regarded as the father of lateral thinking and whose ideas have influenced research into creativity, emphasizes the individual's ability to change concepts and perceptions through thinking skills, such as lateral thinking and creative thinking, and introduces three leading concepts that represent creativity: creation, synthesis (i.e., combining separate elements into a connected system), and modification (i.e., adapting or changing resources, structures, processes or ideas, among others, to develop a new concept).

Creativity has been defined in many ways. Webster's Dictionary defines it as the ability or power to create, to invest with a new form, to produce through imaginative skills, to make or bring into existence something new. H.H. Fox, an influential researcher in the field, defines creativity as any thinking process in which original patterns are formed and expressed. E. Paul Torrance, an educator and creativity researcher, focuses on the fluency of ideas, flexibility and originality of thinking, and sometimes elaboration. Other definitions include the ability to make new combinations of social worth, imagining familiar things in a new light, digging below the surface to find previously undetected patterns, finding connections among unrelated phenomena, and the ability to use different modes of thought to generate new and dynamic ideas and solutions (Carnevale, Gainer and Meltzer 1990; de Bono 1996; Kruger 2004; Von Oech 2008).

The many definitions of creativity make an assessment of its different forms a challenging task. Are atypical, inventive ideas for solving ordinary, everyday, practical problems comparable to artistic or intellectual oeuvres, revolutionary scientific discoveries, or the creation of products for which market demand has not yet developed? Apparently not. Thus an exclusive definition of creativity needs to be constructed for the entrepreneurial context that will decipher the main elements configuring entrepreneurial creativity and differentiate them from general creativity (Amabile 2000; Abraham and Knight 2001; De Weerd-Nederhof and Fisscher 2003; Amabile and Mueller 2008; Fischer and Amabile 2009).

One such attempt addresses creativity in the entrepreneurial realm according to its practical outcome: *innovation*, *regularity*, and *recognition and acceptance*. It is not only these elements, but the interaffective relations among them that coalesce into *entrepreneurial creativity*.

CREATIVITY IN THE ENTREPRENEURIAL REALM

Founding a new business, developing products and services, or exploiting new organizational or business processes requires creativity, as a certain degree of thinking 'outside the box' is needed to transform the business, products or services into ones that are not simply 'more of the same' but at the same time remain appealing and attractive to potential clients. Creativity as an attribute is based on the prevailing social, cultural, economic and political climates, as these determine the direction that creativity will take. Creative ideas in the framework of the 2008 global financial

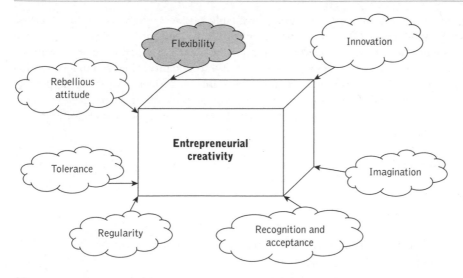

Figure 4.1 *The elements of entrepreneurial creativity*

crisis,[1] for instance, are quite different from those created in affluent times, when most countries are experiencing wealth and prosperity. However, creativity is also attributed to the individual: by his or her ideas, the 'process of bringing something new into being', passion, commitment, and most of all, by revealing that which is hidden from 'ordinary' people's view and pointing to something that will be new, creativity emerges (Engle, Mah and Sadri 1997; Hao and Scott 2006).

Creativity is a multifaceted concept that is manifested differently in different domains: it acquires different meanings for different organizations. This pluralism in perspective and definition makes creativity difficult to define in entrepreneurial research and to assess in entrepreneurial practice. Nevertheless, there is some consensus among researchers in entrepreneurship as to two defining characteristics of creativity: originality and usefulness. In this sense, being creative is not enough to become an entrepreneur: entrepreneurial creativity surfaces when it has an impact on individuals, businesses, cultures or other systems. In its largest sense, creativity is the ability to produce something that is novel, i.e. original, unexpected, and appropriate (useful, adaptable to task constraints) (Amabile 1988, 1998, 2000; Plucker and Runco 1998; Mayer 1999; Rickards and De Cock 1999; Runco 1999; Sternberg and Lubart 1999).

In the entrepreneurial realm, creativity can be defined as an idea or product that is original, valued, and implemented, as well as the ability to respond adaptively to the need for new approaches and new products. It is in essence the ability to bring something new into existence purposefully, though this does not necessarily have to be an innovative product that has never existed. Moreover, creative ideas must somehow influence the way business is done and implemented, in terms of developing a product or service, creating a new way to approach a process, or penetrating a new market that has never used a specific product. In essence, creativity is considered by many entrepreneurial researchers and practitioners as the mental part of the entrepreneurial process (Amabile 1998; Csikszentmihalyi and Wolfe 2000).

Research on entrepreneurial creativity has revealed that such an impact does not emerge exclusively from the creation of 'something new' or of 'something that did not exist before': entrepreneurs need to implement their creative ideas. Entrepreneurial creativity is about coming up with ideas that are 'outside the box' at the outset, be they novel or already existing, and most important, turning them into value-creating, profitable business activities. Unlike creative individuals who think beyond the standard paradigms, creative entrepreneurs have to go a step further and execute their creative idea by committing to the pursuit of the opportunity, organizing the necessary arrangements, processes and resources to do so, and managing the implementation of a strategy that will transform their creative ideas into a business. Most researchers in entrepreneurship consider the active implementation of a creative idea to be the primary difference between creative individuals and entrepreneurs (Witt 1998). As such, the formula for creativity in entrepreneurship is:

$$\textbf{Entrepreneurial creativity} = \text{Individual's creativity F (sociocultural environments)} \times \text{entrepreneurial action}$$

Entrepreneurial creativity includes:

- Creation of something that is not usually seen in the context of the business
- Expansion of opportunities for a creation
- Synthesis of separate elements into a different product, idea, or service
- Modification of an already known creation in order to develop a different concept
- Imitation combined with adaptation of an already known creation in order to adjust it to a specific need or demand.

Entrepreneurial 'creativity' conceals some inherent paradoxes for the typical entrepreneur. The first has to do with planning and structuring the entrepreneurial process: in contrast to being 'just' creative and emitting streams of ideas, entrepreneurial creativity engages individuals into an at least partially planned and structured activity, in executing their ideas into products, services, projects or processes. The second paradox has to do with knowledge: creativity in entrepreneurship means discovering new knowledge or finding new applications for pre-existing knowledge – for the latter, entrepreneurs need to know what already exists. Knowledge itself, however, can inhibit creativity, as it may bias, influence or limit it. Interestingly, in ancient Greece, although the concept of creativity referred to freedom of action, it was actually coerced into following laws and rules: *techne* (the Greek word for art) meant 'the making of things, according to rules'. Finally, there is a certain flexibility in today's definition of creativity in the entrepreneurial realm, seemingly distinct from the ultimate definition of creativity, in that entrepreneurial creativity embodies imitation, modification and invention, rather than the exclusive creation of new ideas. Examples of modifying existing solutions, rather than inventing new ones, for different problems or for the changing times include the modification of cloth diapers to disposable ones, as more mothers went to work and had less time to wash the cloth ones; producing microwavable food in kid-size portions as more children returning from school had to cook their own meals. Entrepreneurial creativity, far from referring solely to discovery or invention, takes on a larger definition which apparently does not require pure 'creativity' for the implementation of ideas.

CREATIVITY AND ENVIRONMENT

One prominent and inherent element of creativity that is recognized by all researchers in the field is that it functions through a combination of both person and context (Woodman, Sawyer and Griffin 1993; Kristof 1996; Oldham and Cummings 1996; Zhou and George 2001). Multifaceted sociocultural, business and organizational environments have two opposing impacts on entrepreneurial creativity. They may foster creativity, but they can also obscure it among entrepreneurs and their employees or teams. One principal factor that is both tangible and intangible, prevalent and most important in stimulating creativity in different environments is 'support', which is reflected in financial resources, technology, managerial support, etc. Support that is hidden or unspoken can influence creative ideas because entrepreneurs and/or their employees may consider the environment intolerant of these ideas or devoid of supportive resources to implement them. On the other hand, some ideas that may initially be seen as imaginative, unrealistic or unfeasible may come to light when individuals perceive the environment as supportive and potentially helpful in their realization. A supportive environment should therefore be integral to the organizational strategy of entrepreneurial businesses.

As such, organizational creativity can be seen as a phenomenon that is structurally embedded in the organization rather than as some innate quality of a few extraordinary individuals. In effect, organizational creativity in entrepreneurial businesses is much more than a collection of creative individuals. It is the creation of an environment – the management and teams, organizational structures, business strategies, etc. – that stimulates creativity, i.e., motivates and encourages the use of creativity at work. Above all, this supportive environment must treat creative ideas as valuable seeds that have to be carefully cultivated in the business, incubated and improved on an ongoing basis in order to use them in the short or long term to accomplish the business's goals.

One example that illustrates this is the story of fourteen-year-old Daniell Sørensen, awarded first prize in a competition for young entrepreneurs in Denmark, who developed a device which flashes a red light (like the red light on a police car) when noise in the classroom exceeds 100 decibels: as a consequence, the teacher does not have to comment on the noise in class and the class takes responsibility for its own conduct. This device and the process of its development were highly evaluated in the competition, but Daniell said that his creative idea of such a device had been incubating in his mind for five years. When it was first conceived, he asked his former science teachers to assist him with the development of the device, but they told him that he was just 'imagining unrealistic visions'. Daniell therefore dropped his idea, until a few months before the competition. His current school is oriented toward innovation and creativity and is built around the concept of creating a supportive environment for young students in order to stimulate their creative ideas. 'I found myself locked away by choice in the R&D hall of our school, mainly with my brother, also a student in the school, developing my ideas. Our teachers were helpful and the person in charge of the R&D projects was cooperative and very supportive. They all engaged the science class to assist me with the development of my idea and raised money to assist me in implementing it properly.'

Moreover, collaborative work, teamwork, the sharing of knowledge, the promotion of dialogues that involve multiple domains of scientific/professional knowledge to produce value for the organization's mission, and the marketing and transfer of learning, are all activities via which new ideas and new ways of solving problems can emerge through a collaborative effort. Meaningful entrepreneurial creativity will emerge when the business develops formal and instituted procedures and tools, and provides resources to encourage meaningful creativity in the organization (Bharadwaj and Menon 2000; Styhre and Sundgren 2005).

TYPES OF CREATIVE IDEAS

In the context of entrepreneurship, the creation of an original idea is usually the first stage, occurring during a deep and often prolonged incubation in the individual's mind, long before it takes on a concrete form. To enhance entrepreneurial profitability, a creative idea should involve one or more of the following:

- It is an innovative product and/or service.
- It is an improvement on the existing product and/or service.
- There is a market for it, and new commercial possibilities (gaps).
- There is a new unexploited market for it.
- There are new, more efficient or effective fabrication processes for it.
- It involves innovation in the structure and culture of an existing business.
- It involves innovation in R&D.
- It exploits new, and less costly or more worthwhile, raw resources.
- There are new resources for its distribution.
- New forms of relationships with governmental agencies, community associations, etc. will evolve from it.

THE 'IDEA'

The hazardous road from ideas that pop up to the actual startup and operation of a venture is complex and may be frustrating if the entrepreneur is unaware of the critical points he or she must consider and the obstacles that will inevitably be encountered. Focusing on the first stages of the venture creation, this section illustrates the entrepreneurial trail from the pre-launch stage to the establishment of a profitable and sustainable business.

Enthused by their inventions and ideas, novice entrepreneurs are likely to underestimate the practical processes; they may lack sufficient knowledge of the basic facts and issues associated with venture creation – the nitty-gritty of the business world – and thus endanger the potential growth of their planned ventures. The implementation of an idea is far different from the preceding stage of creative and inventive flowering of novel ideas. Implementation necessitates a thorough understanding of the industry and the sector where similar products and/or services are active, recognition of an opportunity, assessing the market's needs for the new products or services, clients' demands, and the market's saturation point (Alvarez and Busenitz 2001; Delmar and Shane 2004).

Creativity is essential for the generation of novel ideas. Creative ways of thinking, interpreting and problem-solving, and using one's imagination, intuition and feelings on a day-to-day basis at work, are among the creative means of stimulating ideas (Okpara 2000; Buijs, Smulders and van der Meer 2009; Goffin and Visscher 2009; Glaveanu 2010).

To stimulate the use of creativity, to accelerate the pace and quality of emerging ideas, entrepreneurs must train themselves to go beyond the traditional interpretation of a problem and then turn their novel interpretation into an opportunity. They need to employ creativity to see their surrounding circumstances in a new light, which will provide them with a competitive advantage. For example, a buffet-restaurant owner was losing money because of the large amounts of food being thrown away on a daily basis. He decided to collaborate with nearby farmers by selling them the leftover food for their cattle, while his competitors were using financial means to minimize their waste-related losses. By being creative, the buffet-restaurant owner profited from his collaboration with the farmers and gained a competitive advantage. Creative ideas can target many aspects of a business (e.g., improving productivity and efficiency, achieving speed, enhancing comfort and convenience or positively influencing returns); creative thinking can produce various alternatives leading to the evolution of new ideas.

Competing on well-known playing fields and in familiar environments is difficult for entrepreneurs: competitors, especially the more established ones, usually have the advantage due to prior experience, larger and more efficient networks and an established business reputation. However, entrepreneurs may alter the well-known playing field by being creative, thus transforming the familiar into an unfamiliar, ambiguous environment where they, the entrepreneurs, set the rules, because they are the ones who produced the environment-altering ideas: on this now unfamiliar playing field, the creative entrepreneurs gain a competitive advantage over well-established companies. Entrepreneurs have smaller businesses, which means that they are more flexible and can adjust those businesses more easily to new environments: they can therefore alter the playing field more frequently. Creative ways of changing the field via the initiation of ideas that are unexpected and unknown provide a critical competitive advantage for entrepreneurs.

CREATIVITY IN THE CONTEXT OF ENTREPRENEURIAL PROJECTS

The word 'entrepreneurship' was adopted into the English language from the French *entreprendre*,[2] meaning to undertake, launch or found something. Entrepreneurship, however, is a term that covers a much broader range of actions. 'Launching' or 'founding' is only the first stage in the creation of a venture, while entrepreneurship includes its successful – and profitable – continued existence. To launch and successfully run a venture requires certain critical resources, skills and abilities, one of which is creativity – which in many entrepreneurial situations may appear in the form of innovation, inventive thinking, novel ideas, visions and dreams, or even curiosity, among others. Creativity is, in its totality, an expression of the unique ability to meld together into a working relationship both the tangible and the intangible resources required throughout the existence of a business.

How creativity functions

A useful example of how creativity functions can be found in music, literature, the arts and cinema, where it is clearly seen as a cyclical process: new artists borrow from the works of their predecessors and create new ones to be valued or appreciated in their own time and in the future. In the ensuing years, rising artists may look back upon and be inspired by these latter works and create newer and even more innovative ones.

However, there is often a unique harbinger. For example, with regard to modern popular music, The Beatles may be viewed as the forerunners. Pioneering advanced, multilayered arrangements in rock and pop, they played a key role in the development of some of the musical styles of the 1960s. Their musical innovations propelled the rock-and-roll of the 1950s in a completely new direction, which many different artists of the 1960s transformed into wholesome bebop, or into less than wholesome psychedelic music. But The Beatles were almost instantaneously listenable, enjoyable and musically esthetic, and – most of all – their music and their social messages were timely: they spoke to the spirit of the times, and they perfectly suited the state of mind and tastes of their British fan base, and then of their American one (Brazeal and Herbert 1999; McIntyre 2006).

Much of the entrepreneurial literature suggests that entrepreneurs are more creative than others, and that they tend to think and sometimes act in non-conventional ways, to challenge existing assumptions and to be flexible and adaptable in problem-solving, decision-making and planning. All of these attributes are integral to creativity and the creative process. Creativity emerges in the entrepreneurial business realm mainly as a result of the interaction between the individual and the environment,[3] but certain environmental conditions are needed in order to encourage and stimulate creativity. Creative individuals are usually prepared to engage in challenging activities, and they are able to learn from their experiences; they will take the risk of failure, but only when they feel that there is sufficient scope for freedom of action. Creativity is fostered in environments in which ideas, feedback and evaluation are constantly exchanged, and where the creators can draw on diverse sources of information and expertise. Creative ability and the motivation to create are reinforced by the positive effects of having made an impact – of having achieved concrete outcomes and of changing the way things are done (Kirton 1976; Solomon and Winslow 1988; Whiting 1988; Timmons 1989; Livingstone, Nelson and Barr 1997; Utsch and Rauch 2000).

Figure 4.2 illustrates creative entrepreneurial activities, tools and means that can be applied at the different stages of the business's life cycle. Creativity can be introduced as *input* (i.e., recruiting different, unique or creative people, or building a non-bureaucratic business); as a *process*, (e.g., gathering different and unconventional ideas from team members and discussing them, or managing creative-marketing processes); or as *output*, such as merging existing products with other products' parts/functions to develop added value, or supplying creative services. Creative activities and tools can be tangible, addressing the product or the team, or intangible, focusing on a state of mind, attitudes or experimentation.

Creativity can be employed in the business in different forms and stages, and at the entrepreneur's pace, discretion and convenience, as shown in Figure 4.2.

Fostering creativity

Entrepreneurs and their teams become more creative when they are motivated and enthused about their work, when they have passion and an interest in what they are doing and when they feel satisfaction with the challenge posed by the situation, their ideas and their achievements. Although some people probably possess more creative skills than others, a creative atmosphere that is developed and introduced into the business may intensify the creativity there. However, the first step to developing a creativity-stimulating atmosphere is knowledge. Any type of creative work must start with research into what already exists; then stimulating and creative atmosphere can be crafted (Amabile 2000; Rickards and Moger 2006; Chen 2007; Fangqi and Tudor 2007; Sandberg 2007; Wang and Casimir 2007; Fischer and Amabile 2009; Manimala 2009; Moneta et al. 2009).

For a creative atmosphere:

- Creativity is enhanced when people have some but not too much freedom.
- Allow for trial and error and discuss these experiences with the staff in order to learn from them; experiences stimulate creative ideas by freeing the mind.
- Reflect on new linkages, possible new combinations, original solutions that are being contemplated by the people in the business.
- Suspend or minimize judgment on originality or creativity exhibited by your staff.
- Include creative, open-minded people in your business: they are inclined to be more adaptable, and more prepared to consider a range of alternative approaches and to challenge the status quo.
- Provide your staff with opportunities to search for outstanding ideas or solutions, encourage breakthroughs in different segments of your business, allocate time for creative work; appraise and reward people that produce such breakthroughs.
- Include creative thinking games and assignments at your staff meetings.

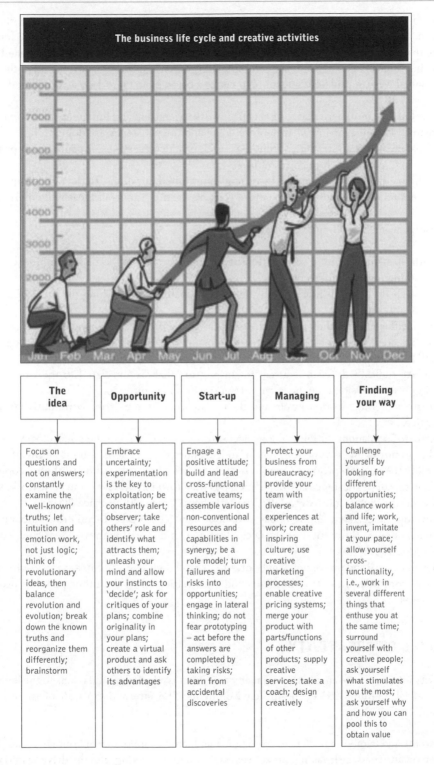

The business life cycle and creative activities

The idea	Opportunity	Start-up	Managing	Finding your way
Focus on questions and not on answers; constantly examine the 'well-known' truths; let intuition and emotion work, not just logic; think of revolutionary ideas, then balance revolution and evolution; break down the known truths and reorganize them differently; brainstorm	Embrace uncertainty; experimentation is the key to exploitation; be constantly alert; observer; take others' role and identify what attracts them; unleash your mind and allow your instincts to 'decide'; ask for critiques of your plans; combine originality in your plans; create a virtual product and ask others to identify its advantages	Engage a positive attitude; build and lead cross-functional creative teams; assemble various non-conventional resources and capabilities in synergy; be a role model; turn failures and risks into opportunities; engage in lateral thinking; do not fear prototyping – act before the answers are completed by taking risks; learn from accidental discoveries	Protect your business from bureaucracy; provide your team with diverse experiences at work; create inspiring culture; use creative marketing processes; enable creative pricing systems; merge your product with parts/functions of other products; supply creative services; take a coach; design creatively	Challenge yourself by looking for different opportunities; balance work and life; work, invent, imitate at your pace; allow yourself cross-functionality, i.e., work in several different things that enthuse you at the same time; surround yourself with creative people; ask yourself what stimulates you the most; ask yourself why and how you can pool this to obtain value

Figure 4.2 *Improving and using creativity along the business life cycle*

- Design the workplace in a creativity-oriented way, where people will have the chance to think, feel, brainstorm and create while being stimulated and inspired. Some high-tech companies have designed special halls with games and sports facilities for the staff to use during their breaks, with the aim of stimulating invention and creativity; some others have designed weekly, paid hours devoted to taking a break from their daily activities and to think and invent.
- Develop an atmosphere that supports teamwork, friendship and fun: people tend to be more creative when they enjoy what they are doing and the place they are doing it in.
- Enable creativity in: strategy, technology used, products/services, organizational processes, financing, marketing, human resources.
- Challenge the staff and yourself by raising complicated questions. Reduce the proportion of answers relative to questions: the more you ask, the more spin-off ideas will emerge.

For creative teams, encourage your staff to:

- Synthesize ideas from several different existing projects/tasks and combine them into something new and different.
- Research the existing market and then intentionally do something original, unusual and completely different.
- Imagine the future of their project/task or design, and then create something that goes beyond the expected, via step-by-step additions or changes/reductions in the original project's aim until it no longer resembles the original starting point.
- Look to radically different sources for inspiration that are unrelated to the work they are doing – such outside influences can often provide a new direction.
- Create something from scratch, and then compare it with existing competitive products/services.
- Perform simulations – look at the project/product/service from the point of view of people who do not know its function, use or added value (e.g., a client, a user, an investor); then modify the project/product/service so that it will be more appealing to these people.
- Enjoy sensory experiences through 'methods' that foster creativity – music at work, sounds, new design, lights, mini-waterfalls, among others (Coyne 2009; Price 2009).
- Develop uncertain, ambiguous situations and embrace turbulent, uncontrollable environments, different experiences, learning and creating new ideas and solutions (Gryskiewicz 2009).
- Develop social and professional networks to expand their exposure to a variety of people and learn from their insights, comments and even criticisms of the other people's products/services.

A MODEL OF CREATIVITY

Creativity is known to be an innate personality trait but it is affected by and reacts to the individual's family, social, cultural and economic environments. The interaction of all of these leads to 'creation':

- Parents and family: experiences from home and family support or encourage creativity.
- Personality traits: risk-taking, proactiveness, innovative thinking, and the drive to initiate turn creativity into action.

- Specific area and network: the sociocultural environment informs creativity and the network is a complementary social component that may stimulate creativity.
- Readiness to create: autonomy and self-direction to visualize, invent, dream.
- Incubation: an idea germinates and develops through a non-linear path; it grows, fades, mutates, etc., as per the individual's imaginative or innovative capabilities.
- Niche: the location, process, or market segment where the idea is turned into a useful or desirable end-product.
- People assisting or impeding: the people around the creator, who may be needed for assistance or support, may assist in the development of an idea or of its cultivation into the creation, but there may also be people that impede the process.
- Creative process: the course through which the idea becomes a concrete end-product.
- Awareness of what is acceptable: the proactive feedback process; asking people's opinions, looking around and deciphering the trends.
- The creation: the end-result or end-product of the original idea.

The flow chart in Figure 4.3 shows the creative individual's path to his or her creation. It begins in the family, which may constitute the underlying basis of creativity. Individuals may inherit or be born with 'creative genes', or grow up in a supportive framework, each of which can stimulate the naturally creative person to choose a field of endeavor in which he or she can fulfill their need to create. In the case of entrepreneurship, the individual may be stimulated by the experience of growing up in a family that owns or runs a business.

A creative idea arises, or perhaps springs up as a vision or phantasmagoria, and evolves during its incubation period in the individual's subconscious or semi-conscious – or even fully conscious – mind. It is during this stage that connections are made between the existing elements and imaginary ideas, some even seemingly contradictory, unsuitable or unrealistic. The incubation phase has both mental and emotional aspects: it is not enough to have or to acquire the ability to make mental connections between the real and the imagined ideas or situations; there has to be an emotional driving force that fosters creativity. For example, given equal shares of 'creative genes', complacent individuals are apt to be less creative or innovative than restless ones. It is the restless, mentally energetic ones that are more likely to turn their images, fantasies and visions into original or innovative ideas. This creative process can be modified by supportive goal-oriented people who help the creator in the implementation of the ideas, or it can be intentionally or unintentionally blocked by their non-supportive, or even harmful counterparts (Fiol 1995).

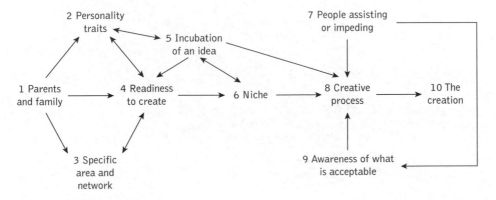

Figure 4.3 *A model of creativity*

GAPS AND ASYNCHRONICITIES

Original or innovative ideas originate in thoughts about 'gaps' or 'asynchronies', which some researchers in entrepreneurship have defined as the absence of sufficient, suitable, or convenient products or services. Such gaps and asynchronies constitute the niches for useful products, services or knowledge that can solve or relieve existing problems. For example, an Israeli small-medium enterprise (SME) developed an ultrasonic toothbrush for pet dogs and cats. The need for such an item was exploited by this SME after they learned that pet owners had begun to recognize that good dental and oral hygiene would protect their pets from medical and health problems caused by oral bacteria, and that the overall health benefits to their pets were worth the cost of buying and the effort of using the toothbrush. A very different project emanated from an original idea for a diabetes program at the University of Michigan. In an innovative pilot program aimed at encouraging the use of medicines that can help prevent the debilitating long-term effects of the disease, employees and their dependants with any early form of diabetes were able to receive some of their medications for free. In this case too, by identifying a gap – an unexplored area in the treatment of diabetic diseases – a niche was found and an original and practical project was created

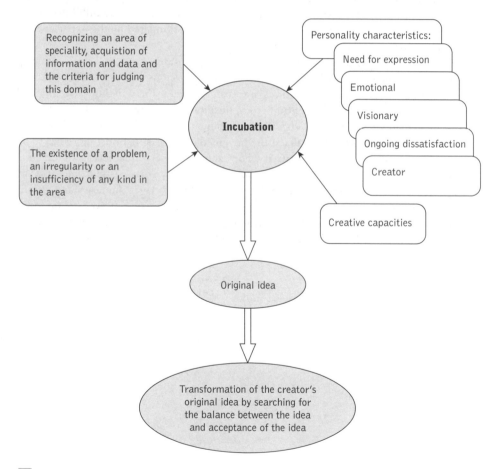

Figure 4.4 *Creation of an original idea*

and implemented. Both assistance from others and proactive feedback processes are needed to put an original, innovative idea into practice.

CREATIVITY IN THE CONTEXT OF THE BUSINESS PLAN

There has been considerable criticism regarding the efficacy of using business plans. Some researchers and practitioners maintain that following a business plan may reduce the positive results of intuition and creativity – two basic characteristics of successful entrepreneurship. The main weakness of the strictly adhered-to business plan is that decisions are made before opportunities to explore or discuss different options have arisen, and the entrepreneur thus automatically forfeits possibilities for improving on ideas and possibly incorporating them into better solutions. Other researchers and practitioners maintain that creativity should be put into effect throughout the different stages of establishing and running a business, rather than be relegated to the idea-creation stage alone. Taking these arguments into consideration, and acknowledging the importance of acquiring information about the market and the potential clients prior to launching a venture, this section is about the important role of creativity in the process of formulating the business plan.

The business plan is usually based on information gathered regarding the launching, financing and marketing processes of a business venture. It addresses topics such as balance sheets and results *pro forma*, forecasting needs and liquidity, assessing the target market and market size, forecasting the market's segments, forecasting the business's growth, and so on. A combination of two main types of creativity should be incorporated into business plans in order to benefit from the entrepreneur's common sense and intuition in the creation and management of the venture: enlarging the scope of the issues that are usually included in the business plan, and integrating different types of information that could improve the business plan's effectiveness (Delmar and Shane 2003; Wen and Chen 2007).

- *Enlarging the scope.* This includes gathering information on a broad range of activities in the proposed field of activity. For example, the attitudes and expectations of other entrepreneurs toward their businesses or toward the market: Are they planning to enlarge the range of their products? To diversify it? Are they satisfied with their business's activity? And if so, in what respect? Are they planning to launch a different business in the future? Or change the direction of the present one? And if so, why? A different kind of soft data can be collected by asking for people's feedback on the proposed business, including both positive and negative criticisms of the plan and suggestions for modifications or additions.
- *Integrating different types of information.* The creativity in this process is manifested in turning hard data into soft data, and in giving it a 'human touch', usually by being attentive to people's common sense and experience. Using various creative techniques, for example, may be very useful for brainstorming business plans in order to break the mold of group thinking and open the door to creative thinking. One of these is the 'devil's advocate' technique. This involves a gathering of six to twelve people, preferably from different disciplines, to discuss an entrepreneur's business plan. One of the participants is chosen to be the devil's advocate. As the entrepreneur begins to present his or her plan for the business, the devil's advocate quashes it, piece by piece, with negative criticism; this stimulates the others in the group to voice their own suggestions, thus eliciting new ways of looking at the business plan.

Another technique for gathering information relevant to the business plan is by conducting simulations and gaming exercises. These have long been recognized as effective means for salesmen and managers to hone their techniques, but by enabling them to scrutinize their business-planning strategies, they are also useful for entrepreneurs: by experiencing their clients' (simulated) experiences and analyzing the relative success or failure of the different outcomes derived from those simulations or games, entrepreneurs gain more information and may be able to make some forecasts regarding their planned businesses that would not otherwise emerge.

Creativity may serve the business plan by expanding the breadth of the planned topics, or by introducing different and unconventional ones; in doing so, valuable advantages in information over the competitors may be gained.

DIFFERENTIATION OF THE BUSINESS

Differentiation of the business can ensure its competitive advantage. The entrepreneur can establish the uniqueness of the product and/or service being offered by emphasizing its quality, its innovative design, or the special niche it occupies. Lateral thinking, an attribute of creative people, intuition and an open mind stimulate original ideas – ideas that can differentiate a business from similar ones in the same area. Ideas that are put into effect earlier than those of the rival business become a competitive advantage. Differentiation requires (Thompson and Poon 2004; Clarkin and Rosa 2005):

- Familiarity with the domain and the industry of active and potential competitors, the market's saturation point, and product feasibility in specific markets.
- Developing the ability to observe and assess how other businesses differentiate themselves.
- Gathering relevant, up-to-date information by improving questioning techniques.
- Developing one's ability to objectively evaluate one's own ideas.
- Broadening communication through brainstorming and exchanging ideas, and finding the links between different ideas.

SUMMARY

Creativity is a major component in the complex process of venture creation, and it should be practiced by entrepreneurs and potential entrepreneurs in order to maintain mental flexibility and prove themselves capable of coping with, and utilizing, different ideas. Creativity can and should be implemented throughout the entrepreneurial process, including creation of the business plan and the differentiation processes. Creativity embedded within these seemingly non-creative processes confers a competitive advantage to the entrepreneurial business. To foster such ongoing creativity, the entrepreneurial business should establish environments that will stimulate creativity among its staff. In order to maintain their creativity, entrepreneurs should be accepting and tap into that side of themselves that is the dreamer or the visionary, and not be judgmental or self-judgmental about creative ideas. This means accepting the need to think freely and boundlessly, to try out new possibilities, and to play with new ideas.

To fuel their creative drive, entrepreneurs should establish rituals or a discipline that incorporates time for creative thinking: these may include teamwork, allocating weekly 'time out' for activities that stimulate creativity – analyzing brainteasers, figuring out complicated dilemmas, or even solving high-quality riddles and puzzles.

CASE STUDY 4.1   Photoart, the Netherlands

During her school years, Emily Porter was considered a shy and quiet girl. She avoided the companionship of her classmates and spent much of her time exploring the 'artistic and visual aspects' of her environment. She was so enthusiastic about 'how things are seen by the eyes' that nothing else interested her. She sometimes secretly formed a pseudo-camera with her fingers and peered through 'the eye of the camera' at things around her. She loved pretending to take photos from different angles; it inspired and fulfilled her. Although she was an excellent student, her teachers were very concerned about her, as was her mother. Her father, however, a choreographer and stage manager of the community's dance group, who carried with him a lifelong feeling of missed opportunities, supported his daughter's feelings and interests, and encouraged her to follow them. 'My family could not afford to buy me a camera [when I was young],' says Porter, 'but when I grew up and had to decide on my future career, I knew what I wanted to do. But I also knew that I must get paid for it, and I hoped to earn lots of money. One part of me was afraid to "miss my life" as my father felt he had, and the other part was determined to earn money.' When she was nineteen years old, Porter's family managed to help her buy a very expensive camera with a large-format camera lens. She began taking still pictures, which she sold on the sidewalks of a tourist village in the Netherlands on the weekends. The money she earned enabled her to buy a second, more sophisticated camera, and she was able to devise a unique technique by which 'stills were seen as if in motion, and everything seemed to be dynamic'. People liked her unique pictures and most of her photographs were sold each week. Then Porter purchased some wooden frames for her pictures, which she colored and decorated, and she started to sell them as well. About a year later, an American woman visiting the Netherlands saw her art and offered Porter a job as the photographer of the association she was managing in New York City. Porter accepted the offer and moved to New York. She began to attend classes in photography at New York University, and developed more varied techniques in black-and-white photography; she combined these with computer graphics and developed an expertise in this area. Determined 'to earn money for her dreams', Emily asked the American woman's permission to exhibit her work at one of the association's reunions. Her photographs, in their decorated frames, were a great success; most were sold that night and she got many offers for more projects. Porter was very encouraged. She registered for academic studies at New York University, but unexpectedly had to go back to the Netherlands when her father became very ill. On her flight home, Porter met Paul, an artist, who later became her husband. They returned to New York two years later, but the association she was working for had hired another photographer and the university would not accredit her previous studies after two years. She had to start all over again. She designed a very attractive website for the products and services she was offering and orders for projects began to arrive. She kept updating her equipment and developed high-quality photographs. She was keen and capable, and invented techniques that combined photography and computer graphics, which she then used to produce eye-catching photos on a broad assortment of items, such as cups, calendars and pillows. Porter loved her work and spent hours doing it. Although they had no money and Paul was not working at the time, they decided to take out a bank loan and open a store in New York. This was risky, but after less than a year they were able to repay the loan. Paul Porter, however, was unable to find a proper job in New York and they decided to return to the Netherlands. Emily Porter is now thirty-six years old, and she and Paul are the parents of nine-year-old twins. They live in the Utrecht area, in the Netherlands, having moved there after ten years in New York. Five years ago, Porter launched a unique photography business in Utrecht, and now owns a chain of franchised photography stores all over the Netherlands.

QUESTIONS FOR DISCUSSION

1   What was the role of creativity in Emily Porter's entrepreneurial life?
2   How did creativity affect Emily Porter's childhood? Do you think that creative people need support – such as the support Emily Porter received from her father – to implement their dreams?
3   How does creativity enhance a firm's success?
4   What are the main pitfalls of creativity in a person's work life?
5   Give a brief profile of a creative person who you know. Where and how is his or her creativity manifested?

NOTES

1   Around the world, stock markets have fallen, large financial institutions have collapsed or been bought out, and governments in even the wealthiest nations have had to come up with rescue packages to bail out their financial systems. *Financial Times*, 17 December 2008, www.ft.com/indepth/global-financial-crisis.
2   Its roots come from the German, to be discussed in Chapter 5.
3   The model of Person–Environment (P-E) Fit, developed in the early 1970s by researchers at the University of Michigan, states that a discrepancy between the motives of the person and the supplies of the environment (job) may induce job stress and strain (Caplan et al. 1975; Van Harrison 1978; Baker 1985). This model is related to creativity in different environments (Livingstone, Nelson and Barr 1997).

REFERENCES

Abraham, J.L. and Knight, D.J. (2001) 'Strategic innovation: leveraging creative action for more profitable growth', *Strategy and Leadership*, 29: 21–7.

Alvarez, S. and Busenitz, L. (2001) 'The entrepreneurship of resource based theory', *Journal of Management*, 27: 755–75.

Amabile, T.M. (1988) 'A model of creativity and innovation in organizations', in B.M. Staw and L.L. Cummings (eds) *Research in Organisational Behavior*, vol. 10, Greenwich, CT: JAI Press.

Amabile, T.M. (1998) 'How to kill creativity', *Harvard Business Review*, 76: 76–87.

Amabile, T.M. (2000) 'Stimulate creativity by fueling passion', in E.A. Locke (ed.) *Basic Principles of Organizational Behavior: A Handbook*, Oxford: Blackwell.

Amabile, T.M. and Mueller, J. (2008) 'Assessing creativity and its antecedents: an exploration of the componential theory of creativity', in J. Zhou and C.E. Shalley (eds) *Handbook of Organizational Creativity*, Hillsdale, NJ: Lawrence Erlbaum Associates.

Baker, D.B. (1985) 'The study of stress at work', *Annual Review of Public Health*, 6: 367–81.

Bharadwaj, S. and Menon, A. (2000) 'Making innovation happen in organizations: individual creativity mechanisms, organizational creativity mechanisms or both?', *Journal of Product Innovation Management*, 17: 424–34.

Brazeal, D.V. and Herbert, T.T. (1999) 'The genesis of entrepreneurship', *Entrepreneurship: Theory and Practice*, 23: 29–45.

Buijs, J., Smulders, F. and van der Meer, H. (2009) 'Towards a more realistic creative problem solving approach', *Creativity and Innovation Management*, 18: 286–98.

Caplan, R.D., Cobb, S., French, J.R.P., Harrison, R.V. and Pinneau, S.R. (1975) *Job Demands and Worker Health*, Cincinatti, OH: National Institute for Occupational Safety and Health (HEW Publication No. NIOSH, 75-160).

Carnevale, A.P., Gainer, L.J. and Meltzer, A.S. (1990) *Workplace Basics*, San Francisco, CA: Jossey-Bass Inc.

Chen, M.H. (2007) 'Entrepreneurial leadership and new ventures: creativity in entrepreneurial teams', *Creativity and Innovation Management*, 16: 239–49.

Clarkin, J.E. and Rosa, P.J. (2005) 'Entrepreneurial teams within franchise firms', *International Small Business Journal*, 23: 303–34.

Coyne, R. (2009) 'Creativity and sound: the agony of the senses', in T. Rickards, M.A. Runco and S. Moger (eds) *Routledge Companion to Creativity*, London: Routledge, 25–37.

Csikszentmihalyi, M. and Wolfe, R.N. (2000) 'New conceptions and research approaches to creativity: implications of a systems perspective for creativity in education', in K. Heller, F. Monks, R. Subotnik and R. Sternberg (eds) *International Handbook of Giftedness and Talent*, 2nd edn, Oxford: Pergamon Press.

de Bono, E. (1996) *Serious Creativity Using the Power of Lateral Thinking to Create New Ideas*, London: HarperCollins.

Delmar, F. and Shane, S. (2003) 'Does business planning facilitate the development of new ventures?', *Strategic Management Journal*, 24: 1165–85.

Delmar, F. and Shane, S. (2004) 'Legitimating first: organizing activities and the survival of new ventures', *Journal of Business Venturing*, 19: 385–410.

De Weerd-Nederhof, P.C. and Fisscher, O. (2003) 'Editorial', *Creativity and Innovation Management*, 12: 63–4.

Engle, D.E., Mah, J.J. and Sadri, G. (1997) 'An empirical comparison of entrepreneurs and employees: implications for innovation', *Creativity Research Journal*, 10: 45–9.

Fangqi, X. and Tudor, R. (2007) 'Creative management: a predicted development from research into creativity and management', *Creativity and Innovation Management*, 16: 216–28.

Fiol, C.M. (1995) 'Thought worlds colliding: the role of contradiction in corporate innovation processes', *Entrepreneurship Theory and Practice*, 19: 71–90.

Fischer, C.M. and Amabile, T. (2009) 'Creativity, improvisation and organizations', in T. Rickards, M.A. Runco and S. Moger (eds) *The Routledge Companion to Creativity*, London: Routledge, 13–25.

Glaveanu, V.P. (2010) 'Paradigms in the study of creativity: introducing the perspective of cultural psychology', *New Ideas in Psychology*, 28: 79–93.

Goffin, K. and Visscher, K. (2009) 'Editorial', *Creativity and Innovation Management*, 18: 143–6.

Gryskiewicz, S.S. (2009) 'Leading for renewal: the value of positive turbulence', in T. Rickards, M.A. Runco and S. Moger (eds) *The Routledge Companion to Creativity*, London: Routledge, 99–109.

Hao, Z. and Scott, E.S. (2006) 'The big five personality dimensions and entrepreneurial status: a meta-analytical review', *Journal of Applied Psychology*, 91: 259–71.

Kavolis, V. (1964) 'Economic correlates of artistic creativity', *American Journal of Sociology*, 70: 332–41.

Kirton, M.J. (1976) 'Adaptors and innovators: a description and measure', *Journal of Applied Psychology*, 61: 622–9.

Kristof, A.L. (1996) 'Person–organisation fit: an integrative review of its conceptualizations, measurement, and implications', *Personnel Psychology*, 49: 1–49.

Kruger, M.E. (2004) 'Creativity in the entrepreneurship domain', unpublished thesis, University of Pretoria.

Livingstone, L.P., Nelson, D.L. and Barr, S.H. (1997) 'Person–environment fit and creativity: an examination of supply–value and demand–ability versions of fit', *Journal of Management*, 23: 119–46.

Manimala, M. (2009) 'Creativity and entrepreneurship', in T. Rickards, M.A. Runco and S. Moger (eds) *The Routledge Companion to Creativity*, London: Routledge, 119–32.

Mayer, R.E. (1999) 'Fifty years of creativity research', in R.J. Sternberg (ed.) *Handbook of Creativity*, Cambridge: Cambridge University Press, 449-60.

McIntyre, P. (2006) 'Paul McCartney and the creation of "Yesterday": the systems model in operation', *Popular Music*, 25: 201–19.

Moneta, G.B., Amabile, T.M., Schatzel, E. and Kramer, S.J. (2009) 'Multi-rater assessment of individual creative contributions to team projects in organizations', *European Journal of Work and Organizational Psychology*, May.

Okpara, F.O. (2000) *Entrepreneurship: Text and Cases*, Enugu: Precision Printers and Publishers.

Oldham, G.R. and Cummings, A. (1996) 'Employee creativity: personal and contextual factors', *Academy of Management Journal*, 39: 607–34.

Plucker, J.A. and Runco, M.A. (1998) 'The death of creativity measurement has been greatly exaggerated: current issues, recent advances, and future directions in creativity assessment', *Roeper Review*, 21: 9–36.

Price, I. (2009) 'Space to adapt: workplaces, creative behaviour and organizational memetics', in T. Rickards, M.A. Runco and S. Moger (eds) *The Routledge Companion to Creativity*, London: Routledge, 46–59.

Rickards, T. and De Cock, C. (1999) 'Sociological paradigms and organizational creativity', in R.E. Purser and A. Montuori (eds) *Social Creativity*, vol. 2, Cresskill, NJ: Hampton Press, 235–56.

Rickards, T. and Moger, S. (2006) 'Creative leaders: a decade of contributions from Creativity and Innovation Management Journal', *Creativity and Innovation Management*, 15: 4–18.

Runco, M.A. (1999) 'Time', in M.A. Runco and S.R. Pritzer (eds) *Encyclopaedia of Creativity*, London: Academic Press, 658–63.

Sandberg, B. (2007) 'Enthusiasm in the development of radical innovations', *Creativity and Innovation Management*, 16: 265–73.

Solomon, G. and Winslow, E. (1988) 'Toward a descriptive profile of the entrepreneur', *Journal of Creative Behavior*, 22: 162–71.

Sternberg, R.J. and Lubart, T.I. (1999) 'Concept of creativity: prospects and paradigms', in R.J. Sternberg (ed.) *Handbook of Creativity*, Cambridge: Cambridge University Press, 3–15.

Styhre, A. and Sundgren, M. (2005) *Managing Creativity in Organizations: Critique and Practices*, New York: Palgrave Macmillan.

Thompson, E.R. and Poon, J.P.H. (2004) 'Convergence or differentiation? American and Japanese transnational corporations in the Asia Pacific', *Geoforum*, 35: 111–25.

Timmons, J.A. (1989) *The Entrepreneurial Mind*, Andover, MA: Brick House Publishing.

Utsch, A. and Rauch, A. (2000) 'Innovativeness and initiative as mediators between achievement orientation and venture performance', *European Journal of Work and Organizational Psychology*, 9: 45–62.

Van Harrison, R. (1978) 'Person–environment fit and job stress', in C.L. Cooper and R. Payne (eds) *Stress at Work*, Chichester: Wiley, 175–208.

Von Oech, R. (2008) *A Whack on the Side of the Head: How You Can Be More Creative*, New York: Warner Books.

Wang, K.Y. and Casimir, G. (2007) 'How attitudes of leaders may enhance organizational creativity: evidence from a Chinese study', *Creativity and Innovation Management*, 16: 229–38.

Wen, Y.Y. and Chen, D.F. (2007) 'Teaching cultural literacy to students in TVES, Taiwan: an integrated-skills approach', In *Proceeding of the 2007 International Conference and Workshop on International Education: The Prospect of International Education in the Twenty-first Century*, CD-ROM, Taoyuan, Taiwan: Ming-chuan, 30–46.

Whiting, B.G. (1988) 'Creativity and entrepreneurship: How do they relate?', *Journal of Creative Behavior*, 22: 178–83.

Witt, U. (1998) 'Imagination and leadership – the neglected dimension of an evolutionary theory of the firm', *Journal of Economic Behavior and Organization*, 35: 161–77.

Woodman, R.W., Sawyer, J.E. and Griffin, R.W. (1993) 'Toward a theory of organizational creativity', *Academy of Management Review*, 18: 293–321.

Zhou, J. and George, J.M. (2001) 'When job dissatisfaction leads to creativity: encouraging the expression of voice', *Academy of Management Journal*, 44: 682–96.

Chapter 5

Innovation

OBJECTIVES

After studying this chapter you will be able to:

- Recognize the main features of innovation, and distinguish between innovation, creativity and adaptation.
- Understand the role of innovation in the context of the entrepreneurial realm.
- Recognize the design of innovation in the entrepreneurial business in order to implement it in an existing/potential business.
- Link the concept of innovation to robust theories in entrepreneurship and strategy, such as the dynamic capabilities (DC) perspective; consider the ongoing changes that are occurring around the business; understand that innovation can be implemented to facilitate the business's accomplishment of its goals; further investigate innovation within the framework of the DC perspective.
- Identify the key features of innovation and ways of enhancing it in the business.
- Acknowledge how innovation can be implemented in the different business processes, structures and activities.
- Apply innovative thinking toward complementing the business's goals.

THE DESIGN OF INNOVATION IN THE ENTREPRENEURIAL CONTEXT

Innovation has been studied in a variety of contexts (e.g., in relation to technology, commerce, social systems, economic development, policy construction). There are naturally, therefore, a wide range of approaches to conceptualizing innovation in the scholarly literature. Following Schumpeter, Drucker, Amabile and other influential theoreticians in the realm of innovation, one widely accepted definition of innovation is that it is the successful implementation of creative ideas within an organization. Some other definitions consider innovation as the sum of invention and the commercialization of that invention, through turning an idea, mainly a creative one, into a feasible, profitable opportunity; a different definition shared by many researchers in this field is that at the core, all innovation begins with creative ideas.

Joseph Schumpeter considers entrepreneurs as innovative individuals: 'the function of entrepreneurs is to reform or revolutionize the pattern of production by exploiting an invention, or more generally, an untried technological possibility for producing a new commodity or producing an old one in a new way by opening up a new way of supply of materials or a new outlet of products by reorganizing an industry and so on' (1942: 82–3). Peter Drucker (1993, 1998, 1999) – one of the most influential management consultants – building upon Schumpeter's premise of entrepreneurship considers the very foundation of entrepreneurship in the practice of systematic innovation, which he defines as the effort to create purposeful, focused change in a venture's economic potential; the essence of entrepreneurship according to Drucker is in creating new or different things rather than improving the already existing things. As such, according to Drucker, the intensive quest for innovation pushed many businesses to operate in dynamic, risky environments and to engage in an innovation-oriented business culture. Researchers in entrepreneurship and innovation stress that the dynamic, shaky environment entails high and unexpected risks and that innovation is an inherent entrepreneurial means to construct, reconstruct and then establish the business's competitive advantage. The entrepreneur's action is therefore twofold: they manage the existing business processes but also apply their innovative ideas within the setting of these existing processes; subsequently, the existing processes change and take on different forms during the course of the business, based on the entrepreneur's response, which involves mainly applying innovative coping strategies to the changing environment's demands (DiMaggio 1992; McGuire, Granovetter and Schwartz 1993; Brown and Eisenhardt 1997; Drucker 1999).

In *Innovation and Entrepreneurship* (1985a), Drucker presents seven sources of innovative opportunity that should be explored by entrepreneurs when starting an entrepreneurial business. Potential opportunities may emerge from the following situations:

- An unexpected success or failure could be a potential opportunity
- Discrepancy between reality and how it is interpreted by others can create an innovative opportunity
- Innovation based on the 'missing link' between the need and what is done to respond to that need
- Changes and shifts in industry or market structure are opportunities for an innovative product, service or business approach
- Changes in the population's size, age structure, composition, employment, level of education and income can create innovative opportunities
- Changes in perception, general assumptions, attitudes and beliefs are unique opportunities for innovations
- Advances in knowledge can create new products and new markets.

The best practices that can assist entrepreneurs in creating an advantage out of a new innovation are:

- Analyzing opportunity for identification of the potential customers' interest in using the innovation.
- Modifying the innovation so that it will be simple and clearly focused on a specific need.
- The 'elevator effect' – innovations should be determined as if they needed to be introduced to an investor while going up in an elevator: very short, simple and clear.
- Innovations targeted and appealing to a small and focused market require limited amounts of money from the founder; as the market and demand grow, the business will be able to use its

resources, networks and expertise to fine-tune its processes and stay ahead of the emerging competition.

■ Innovators aim at market leadership, i.e. dominating a niche, being the leading business for a product/service/process, etc.

INNOVATORS AND ENTREPRENEURS

Innovators are the pioneers in developing new 'entities'. Studies describe them as more open to new ideas, concepts, and ways of thinking, more imaginative, more reflective, more free-spirited and more non-traditional than the everyday person. Not all innovators are entrepreneurs, and not all entrepreneurs are innovators; however, the more innovative the business, the better its odds of succeeding.

Innovators develop new technologies 'out of thin air', like Thomas Edison, one of those who developed the light bulb, Edwin Belin, who held the patent in 1922 for the transmission of photographs by wire as well as fiber optics and radar, and demonstrated a mechanical scanning device that was an early precursor to today's television set, or Steve Jobs, the CEO and entrepreneur who built up Apple and was reported to be 'as famous as a 1970s rock star' in the newspapers at the time; new concepts, like Gabrielle 'Coco' Chanel (1883–1971), who is the most influential and innovative fashion designer to date, or Miles Davis, who legitimized a new genre, 'fusion jazz', when the jazz model was a radical innovation; new marketing and selling concepts, like Philip Kotler and Gerald Zaltman, who 'sold' ideas, attitudes and behaviors through the innovative 'social marketing' (Kotler and Roberto 1989); new adventures, like Neil Armstrong, Buzz Aldrin and Michael Collins, the pioneering crew that put two astronauts on the moon.

The literature in innovation and creativity distinguishes innovators from adaptors (e.g. Isaksen and Kaufmann 1990; Nias 1998). However, innovators may also find innovative ways to improve applications of either new or existing technologies or processes; they may apply existing technologies and/or processes in new ways, or amend existing technologies via innovative business models.

The Schumpeterian conceptualization of entrepreneurship focuses on the innovator, i.e., the one who disturbs the even flow of production by breaking away from routine activity and by creating new ways of doing things and new things to do. Schumpeter (1912, 1934) argued that innovation and technological change in the market spring from the wild spirit of entrepreneurs. Schumpeter, who was a very influential scholar in the field of entrepreneurship, promoted the use of the term, which is based on the translation of the German word *Unternehmergeist*, meaning entrepreneurial spirit. In his many publications, he emphasized the imperative role of innovation, which he considered a major component of each and every stage of venture creation. Identifying innovation as an inseparable element in the whole process of entrepreneurship was Schumpeter's main contribution to the theoretical foundation of this field (McCraw 2007). Peter Drucker (1985a, 1985b) also considered innovation to be the backbone of entrepreneurship, and claimed that entrepreneurial businesses become successful only by being innovative. He further suggested that entrepreneurs, who are by nature innovative, are uniquely inspired individuals who are able to grasp possibilities from the mundane and turn them into a different reality.

The research in innovation and entrepreneurship revealed five key elements that have been used to characterize and illustrate the entrepreneurial spirit; and innovation is considered as having a predominant role, especially in the basics of entrepreneurial businesses; along with the other four dimensions (i.e., autonomy, risk-taking, proactiveness and competitive aggressiveness), innovation is treated as the foremost element elevating the performance of entrepreneurial businesses and contributing to their success and profitability. Other types of businesses, less innovative in 'spirit' (e.g., imitative or acquisitive types of businesses) have been found to be less successful in the entrepreneurial realm (Miller 1987; Covin and Covin 1990; Covin and Selvin 1991; Kariv 2010).

However, innovation does not emerge only as a positive outcome for the business: many entrepreneurial businesses that are in a stage of scarce resources yet are striving for innovation and invention have to cope with the difficult trade-off between exploitation of existing technologies, capabilities and markets with the exploration of innovative technologies or capabilities. Christensen (2000) identified this as the 'innovator's dilemma', but the potential damage innovators can 'cause' is mainly to the businesses that engage such innovations. For example, by engaging new technologies, entrepreneurial businesses can end up losing customers who are not yet ready for such innovation; using different marketing innovations may result in the loss of current customers for newcomers. Entrepreneurial businesses, however, cannot renounce innovators in their businesses since they are the ones who can produce the added-value, sustainable advantage for the business. The question lies in whether to invest in potential capabilities that may support long-run sustainability or harvest short-term benefits from current capabilities, as well as in how to trade-off the costs of exploration (investments in survival) with the benefits of exploitation (maximizing returns to investors).

Such a dilemma may be dealt with in several ways: first, the 'mindset' of entrepreneurial businesses is typically highly tolerant of ambiguity and high risk-takers. As such, entrepreneurial businesses will take risks; in addition, businesses should be attentive to the 'hints' of up and coming trends from their environments, which can then be developed into an innovative product, service, technology, etc. Finally, entrepreneurial businesses explicitly eschew prediction and choose instead to create the future; they then 'sell' new concepts, ideas and mindsets, rather than a product/service, through today's emerging and expanding networks and the imaginative leveraging of unexpected contingencies into unforeseen opportunities.

THE DYNAMIC CAPABILITIES PERSPECTIVE AND INNOVATION

Taking the 'dynamic capabilities' (DC) perspective (Teece et al. 1997; Warren 2002), it is particularly important to apply innovation in a business as it helps the business adjust its capability in the existing resource mix, thereby creating a competitive advantage which might otherwise quickly erode. While the DC perspective regards innovation as critical to a business's sustainability, it is also the subject of particular challenges in most entrepreneurial businesses: as they are difficult to plan, the nature of innovative activities in most businesses is episodic; improvisation plays an important role in many businesses, and innovation is unpredictable. Thus innovation in the entrepreneurial context is a challenge that needs to be dealt with, planned and incorporated into the business strategy. Finding the balance in innovation which will create and maintain a competitive advantage without facing too many risks and thus endangering it (e.g., by planning the innovation process in terms of 'when, where and how' to apply it) is the ultimate challenge for an entrepreneurial business.

One interesting example of the power of innovation as an asset for a sustainable, beneficial entrepreneurial business is that of the Israeli company Mirabilis.[1] Founded in 1996, Mirabilis pioneered the internet-wide instant messaging phenomenon ICQ (read: 'I seek you'), making it one of the most successful and popular internet products of all time. With currently close to 400 million downloads, this community of subscribers constituted an extraordinary capital. Mirabilis was acquired by AOL in 1998 for a total of US$400 million. Its impressive success provided a model for 'startuppers' and helped open the floodgates for numerous Israeli entrepreneurs as well as inspired hi-tech entrepreneurs worldwide. Dr Yossi Vardi,[2] the founding investor of Mirabilis, is one of Israel's early high-tech entrepreneurs – and undoubtedly the leading and most well known of them. He has founded and nurtured over sixty high-tech companies in over forty years in diverse areas of software, energy, internet, mobile communications, electro-optics, clean water and others; but he is certainly most recognized for ICQ and the sale of Mirabilis to AOL. The four young and avid computer users, Arik Vardi, Sefi Visiger, Yair Goldfinger and Amnon Amir, who established Mirabilis wanted to introduce a new way of communicating over the internet; the innovation of ICQ, according to Vardi, was that 'it was just something brilliant',[3] as it did not define a 'need' but eventually created one that was still unknown and merely existed, and most of all, derived by the founders' own experiences of 'what was missing' – users surfed the internet without communicating with each other. Goldfinger perfected the client, Vardi wrote the server, and Visiger designed ICQ's whimsical interface: it was he who conceived the ICQ icon,[4] the unique 'flower power'. Mirabilis managed to sell both the founders' innovative idea of people instantly communicating over the internet, and their innovative product. But their innovation emerged in several phases, from the idea to the exploitation of the opportunity, the application of the product, implementation and sustainability of the product, despite the many competitors who have surfaced over the years (Saperstein and Rouach 2002; Guangya, Ni and Ren 2006).

HOW TO STIMULATE INNOVATION

Scholars in the field of entrepreneurship stress that maintaining intellectual curiosity, exploring novel ideas and having or developing an openness to new experiences are the factors that have the greatest effect on enhancing innovation; others propose that a proactive search for new experiences and being open-minded fuel innovativeness in business, and can lead to gaining a sustainable competitive advantage; still others propose that innovative ideas and methods, and problem-solving strategies, are or should be used on a daily basis. Innovative ideas reveal where there is a dissonance between reality and the vision or even the perception of reality at the outset. Peter Drucker asserts that when people are satisfied and complacent, their drive to invent something new dissipates. Therefore, entrepreneurs should purposely confront their staff with complex problems and/or dilemmas in the business, thereby creating situations in the business that will activate the staff to invent solutions in order to confront these problems and dilemmas. Satisfied, fulfilled staff are more resistant to new solutions.

Other practices for stimulating innovation in entrepreneurial businesses include training the staff to create innovative ideas and solutions in uncertain, challenging situations through training courses, engaging mentors and experts in entrepreneurship and innovation, and benefitting from existing inventors, creators or innovators, inside or outside the business, for a planned process of transfer of learning, i.e., sharing their insights on innovation and innovative ideas with the staff and providing them with a model on how to use innovation in their ongoing processes (Venkatraman and Price 1990; Bull, Thomas and Willard 1995; Valente 1995; Klein and Sorra 1996; Gibbons 2004).

INNOVATION AND BUSINESS SUCCESS

The result of an innovative idea has to be examined for characteristics that will enable it to be evaluated for its likely success. Following Filion (2001, 2003), Filion, Luc and Fortin (2003) and

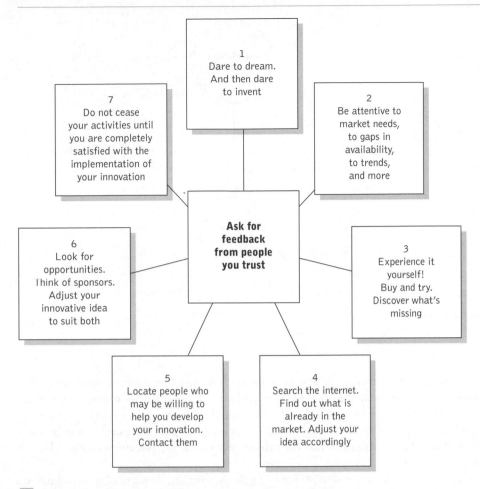

Figure 5.1 *Practical steps for practicing innovative thinking*

Filion and Fayolle (2006), business success will appear when innovation is correlated with the following factors: relative advantage, compatibility, simplicity, trialability, and observability. There is a certain amount of interplay among these characteristics and between each of them and the environment.

- *Relative advantage* is the degree to which an innovative idea is perceived as being better than the idea it supersedes, thus giving the business an advantage over businesses offering the old product or performing the same tasks in the old way. For example, upgrading the mechanical gas pumps in gas stations to computerized ones speeds up the process and facilitates payment and bookkeeping processes.
- *Compatibility* is the degree to which an innovation is perceived as consistent with the existing values, past experiences, and needs of the potential adopters. For example, some medical clinics initiated more realistic procedures for setting doctors' appointments following complaints from patients that they were not being received as scheduled and had long waits before being seen by their doctor. Entrepreneurial businesses should seek to determine their customers' needs, and then find the innovative solution to fulfill those needs.

Figure 5.2 *Innovative idea and potential success*

- *Simplicity* refers to the relative ease in understanding and using an innovation. Innovations that are easy to understand will be adopted more rapidly than those that require the development of new understanding, know-how and skills. For example, for some sectors of the population, e-commerce is too complicated to use and they continue to make their purchases only in the traditional way. In order to penetrate the market and gain broad use, an innovative idea has to be user-friendly.
- *Trialability* refers to the possibility of first using the innovation, or parts of it, on a limited, experimental or trial basis. Innovations that can be divided into their component parts, with each part being tried separately, are generally adopted more rapidly than innovations that are not divisible.
- *Observability* is the degree to which the end results of an innovation are visible to others. Many innovative products or procedures whose advantages are not immediately visible may not be treated as innovative.
- *Implementation* of one's innovation is the final step in a process involving a number of actions, some or all of which may be happening concurrently.

UNEXPECTED BUSINESS RESULTS

The positive and negative results of attempts to introduce an innovative idea, product or service to the market should be analyzed in order to improve the quality or effectiveness of the end-product. Whether the business results are surprisingly successful or unexpected failures, they should be studied in depth to determine the real causes for the results. There is a universal tendency to happily accept successful results but to focus attention only on the failures; in doing so, entrepreneurs can fail to learn what contributed to the successful results which can be applied elsewhere in order to ensure further successes. Feedback and lesson learning, as well as brain-storming, have been found to lead to positive results in both the short and long terms.

Entrepreneurs constantly challenge themselves to realize their visions and turn them into successful realities. When faced with disappointing results, they usually look for other opportunities and other ways of implementing their vision. The adage 'When a door closes, a window opens' illustrates the motivating role of innovation in the entrepreneurial realm.

THE EFFECTS OF MARKET DEMAND

Clients always want more and better! Changing tastes and demands generate creative and innovative ideas. The growing demand for environmentally friendly products, for example, has led to the development of innovative products and manufacturing procedures. Thus the demand for cheaper, better, safer, and environmentally friendly air travel has mushroomed into a massive challenge for the world's aeronautics industry: innovative engineering to improve mechanical efficiency and performance, reduce fuel consumption, lessen noise and air pollution, and improve passenger comfort is continually being created. Attitudes against the unnecessary suffering of animals during the testing of cosmetics and household products have led to creative and innovative testing techniques to ensure the safety of these products without causing the suffering in laboratory animals.

OPPORTUNITY EXPLOITATION IN THE CONTEXT OF INNOVATION

Opportunity exploitation is one of the first stages in the entrepreneurial process (discussed later on in this book), typically following the stage in which entrepreneurs develop ideas for unique products and/or services. The unique application of innovation in the entrepreneurship domain therefore lies in the opportunity exploitation stage and it involves both the process and outcome. The process refers to innovation introduced into the exploitation process, i.e., entrepreneurs engage innovative ways to penetrate the market or locate opportunities, while the outcome refers to an innovative product or service introduced to the market at that stage.

Based on the Kirznerian concept of 'entrepreneur-producer', in process terms, the entrepreneur sees an opportunity for profit where it is still invisible for the market. At this point the entrepreneur is a type of catalyst that identifies the opportunity in the market; an innovative process of exploitation is very advantageous for the entrepreneur by being the first to uncover it. In addition, innovative opportunity exploitation 'interrupts' the balanced equilibrium of the market by intriguing the market through an innovative process, with opportunities that were unknown as a result of market ignorance at a specific time and place. Being the first to exploit an opportunity and being in the 'right time and place' means profiting from disclosing the innovation level for the whole market; moreover, being quicker and more innovative relative to the others' knowledge means generating a competitive advantage which is critical for the process of opportunity exploitation.

Carefully and thoroughly managing the processes involved in the disclosure of an opportunity is associated with fueling the opportunity with a meaningful content (e.g., innovative products or services), which will provide the entrepreneur with a valuable competitive advantage; this represents the significance of innovation in the outcome. This provides an exceptional momentum for entrepreneurs; therefore incorporating innovation at this point is critical. Imitators will then appear in the market and attempt to compete with the original entrepreneur (with reduced prices, more attractive conditions, more personal service, etc.), and will expose the outcome in danger. The more innovation has been used, the more rare and less imitable the outcome will be, and a more sustainable competitive advantage is then guaranteed (Kirzner 1997; Shane 2001; Eckhardt and Shane 2006).

Exploiting changes in industry structure

Constant changes in structure encourage the turnover of manpower across organizations and therefore the exchange of ideas between different organizational cultures and different countries; these, in turn, motivate more innovation and creative thinking. Innovation both derives from and cultivates team-thinking, spin-off activities, and 'intra-preneurship'. There are also cross-effects of processes occurring both within and between firms, and these can have positive effects on innovation (Gauvin and Sinha 1993; Kessler and Chakrabarti 1996).

Changes in the demography of the workforce

The entry into the labor market of women, ethnic minorities, very young people, and retirees has enlarged the spectrum of human abilities and contributed to market viability. The market benefits from the unique characteristics and strengths of these new groups, as well as from their differences. Their entry into the market has also necessitated changes in both the organization of the workplace (e.g., on-site cafeterias, work-out rooms, nursing rooms) and work schedules (e.g., flexible hours). The employment of members of minority groups has led to changes in welfare rules, and employment of the physically and/or mentally challenged has necessitated the provision of services and facilities to enable their participation in the labor market. All of these require ongoing innovative and creative thinking for planning, designing and implementing methods and practices that will match the different and constantly changing needs as they arise (Gustavsen, Finne and Oscarsson 2001).

DIFFERENTIATING CREATIVITY AND INNOVATION IN THE ENTREPRENEURIAL CONTEXT

Creativity and innovation often tend to overlap in much of the research in entrepreneurship and complex, though nourishing and dynamic realtionships exist between them; in certain situations creativity can be considered an element of innovation, as innovation is the successful implementation of creative ideas, the phase in which creative ideas are adapted and turn into the process that develops an idea into a feasible, attainable and money-generating business; in other situations creativity is treated as 'only accessible to people with certain qualities' (Schumpeter 1934: 228), and perceived as either an inborn or developed qualification to produce novel ideas by an individual or small group of individuals working together; it still does not guarantee the production of useful and practical ideas that may be developed into valuable, successful products. Researchers in entrepreneurship tend to make the distinction between innovation and creativity by treating creativity as the generation of ideas for new, improved ways of doing things and innovation as their implementation in practice (Amabile 1988; West and Farr 1990; Scott and Bruce 1994; Brazeal and Herbert 1999; West and Rickards 1999).

Figure 5.3 illustrates the complex yet nourishing interrelations of creativity, innovation, and their shared areas, along with their effects on the implementation process; implementation is

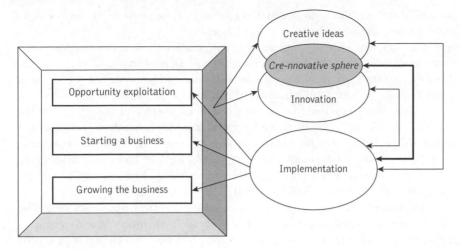

Figure 5.3 *The relationships between creativity, innovation and implementation in the entrepreneurial activity*

directly affected by innovation and indirectly affected by creativity, i.e., the shared parts of creative ideas join with innovation, while the implementation process affects creativity.

Creative products or ideas do not come 'out of the blue'. Most already existed, but by being viewed through the lens of innovation, they were put to different uses and/or directed to different users. Innovative products can bear the special imprint of creative individuals as well as modifications generated by their professional or life experiences.

Innovation is seen as adding to creative ideas via recognition of their usefulness and acceptance of their value. Recognition and acceptance are warranted as it typically takes considerable time and effort before the public accepts a new product or service. Cellular and wireless telephones, which are omnipresent today and being used at an unprecedented rate worldwide, represent a creative idea that has been penetrating the market for over thirty years; it is only by becoming an innovative idea, not just a creative one, that cell phones began to enjoy more frequent use, and this change occurred when the meaning or value of these telephones became recognized, understood and accepted (Puro 2002; Schejter and Cohen 2002). Recognition and acceptance are also dependent on how alert the creator is to the demands of the time and culture, and how well he or she assesses the potential market. It is even more important that the creator sense the potential clients' tastes and openness, enabling modification of the creative idea into a marketable product. If this is not done, the creative idea is likely to be perceived as senseless and useless; innovation is thus the generation of creative ideas into a new, unrevealed product or service that is considered useful or valuable by the potential customers (Stevenson and Gumpert 1985; Dimov 2007; Kor, Mahoney and Michael 2007).

SUMMARY

Researchers and practitioners in the field of entrepreneurship have called for a new debate on innovation in the context of entrepreneurship, and have positioned it at the forefront of entrepreneurial activity – before opportunity exploitation or creativity, as this is the essence of the entrepreneurial activity. This notion, which is related to Schumpeter's writings, will be scrutinized in the coming years in both theory and practice.

Innovation is the backbone of entrepreneurship, and studies show that entrepreneurial businesses become more successful by being innovative in their ideas, products/services, processes, technologies, and management practices, among others. Innovation, however, is not an isolated phenomenon that is simply a matter of funding top-down innovative programs and rolled-out solutions: it arises from social, economic and cultural contexts, which typically operate at the regional and organizational levels. Innovations may be perceived as likely to achieve envisioned or planned organizational goals and be highly valued and desired in one market but undesirable in another; they may be perceived as too creative, puzzling or non-feasible. Innovation requires the attentiveness of the entrepreneurs to such tastes, in order to turn undesired, innovative products into not only new but also valuable and useful practical products or services.

In addition, entrepreneurs wishing to introduce innovation into their businesses should be aware of its different representations, and they should incorporate it into processes and techniques aimed at stimulating innovation from creative ideas; such processes or techniques should be inherent parts of the business process (e.g., opportunity exploitation, product development, and locating the niche, product or service). A planned, strategic combination of creativity and innovation in entrepreneurial businesses will produce a competitive and sustainable advantage in the market.

WEBSITES

Bis, UK, www.bis.gov.uk/bis-announcement.
expertsOn, www.expertson.com/Innovation/innovation.html.
GrandLyon, http://business.grandlyon.com/Innovation.3+M52087573ab0.0.html.
InnovationCanada.ca, http://innovationcanada.ca/.
InnovationTools, www.innovationtools.com/.
Innovation websites, United States, www.chsbs.cmich.edu/leader_model/Development/media/websites/innovation_websites.htm.
Israel Innovation 2.0, www.israelinnovation20.com/category/israeli-websites/.
WBC-inco.net, Balkan countries, www.wbc-inco.net/object/news/list.

CASE STUDY 5.1   Speak-ing-4-u, Australia

Some scholars of entrepreneurship assert that creativity and innovation are more complex in affluent economies, since there is nothing that has not been created or invented in such societies. Lachlan Lucht, from Australia, is living proof that creativity and innovation are still pertinent in affluent economies, and that they not only contribute to one's business, but are also a way of life.

Australia has a very healthy economy and a stable government. By nature Australians are very relaxed and easy-going, and it is often said that they can take things *too* easily. However, along with its prosperity, Australia is relatively isolated from 'the rest of the world' and, according to Lachlan, 'sometimes people tend to ignore many of the world's problems . . . Being isolated is an advantage for [Australia's] internal businesses, but it is a major constraint for international businesses, even though the entry of the internet has facilitated a lot in this matter. People tend to become very reactive to international entrepreneurial activities and prefer to concentrate on the national terrain.' Lachlan, however, was determined to develop an international career and turned the constraints of Australia's location into a driving force to build an international entrepreneurial business.

Lachlan started his career as a self-employed business consultant and speaker, providing services to Australian companies. He was successful, but wanted to penetrate the 'global market'. He knew that he had to find a unique niche to make this happen, since there were many consultants in his field in almost every developed country and the need for his expertise was very limited. In the course of his search for international opportunities, Lachlan met a Russian manufacturer, Boris, who spoke to him about his lack of marketing know-how. Although Lachlan was not a consultant in marketing-related areas, he offered the Russian manufacturer his advisory services, for which he asked a very low price.

The project was not cost-effective for Lachlan, but it was greatly appreciated by Boris and his team: 'The price I charged Boris didn't cover the hours I spent studying the subject, or the hours I spent with him or his staff. But it was a turning point for me, and it was worthwhile,' says Lachlan. Not only did the work with the Russian manufacturer provide Lachlan with experience with another country, it created opportunities to establish direct contacts with other Russian manufacturers. At this stage, Lachlan visited Russia frequently, coming and going at his own expense. Many independent businessmen would probably have turned down such a business deal, or soon abandoned it, but Lachlan believed that it could be the opportunity he was looking for to build meaningful networks outside Australia. Two years of work in collaboration with Boris resulted in an invitation from a Russian food manufacturer to give a speech on communication skills to 200 Russian food manufacturers. This was a stroke of luck, as well as a great surprise for Lachlan, as such things were so uncommon at that time in Russia, before the political and economic changes of the 1990s.

'I had the feeling I was doing the right thing. I knew that I had what it takes, that I know how to convince people to use my services, and how to approach them at the right time and place. It took me time to study the Russian culture and market – a long time – but I began to understand what they lack, and what I could do there. Money, for example, was not the main factor in these manufacturers' decisions about whether to use my services and, surprisingly, neither was the language barrier. I already spoke some Russian and they spoke some English . . . I had to "decipher" their suspicions, and discover what stopped them from hiring me. I decided to put everything on the table: I invited five of my Russian manufacturer friends to a restaurant and initiated a brainstorming session on counseling in Russia. I figured out that they needed to have a very precise idea of what they could get from counseling, and that they were also concerned that there might be chaos, with workers speaking out against their bosses and companies in the counseling sessions. This valuable information allowed me to structure my marketing methods in Russia differently. I also realized that I should have two different marketing strategies: an Australian-oriented one, and a Russian-oriented one,' says Lachlan.

Lachlan's next presentations were a great success, apparently because he presented and explained techniques for coping with stress, and also gave practical tips. From that moment on, invitations for his speeches and presentations started to stream in, and Lachlan realized that he had found the niche he had been seeking: 'speaker' and 'presenter', rather than 'advisor' and 'counselor'. His charisma and appealing personality, and his ability to communicate, attracted an increasingly large number of listeners and led to a widespread reputation.

Lachlan launched his first business, Speak-ing-4-u, in Australia, in 1980, before the widespread use of the internet for marketing. Since both Australia and Russia were relatively isolated, from each other and from the rest of the world, Lachlan knew he had a long way to go in order to develop the international career he had been dreaming of for so many years. On his flights to Russia he sometimes arranged to travel through various other countries, which he thought might present opportunities to meet different business people. On one occasion, in an airport in the Netherlands, Lachlan quite fortuitously met a man who worked for the government in The Hague. Their meeting resulted in a fruitful collaboration, as the man was interested in Lachlan's expertise for his department. Lachlan's speaking career continued to expand and developed into a business. Over the course of twenty years, he has helped more than 5,000 people improve their marketing and personal business-related skills. Lachlan then founded a transnational speakers' association headquartered in Canberra, and initiated the foundation of a different business, organizing conferences for leading companies around the world. At present, he is founding an association of small- and medium-sized manufacturers for the purpose of enhancing their personal skills in order to facilitate international networking for commercial purposes.

QUESTIONS FOR DISCUSSION

1 In what sense is Lachlan Lucht *creative*?

2 In what sense is he *innovative*?

3 How did he establish the competitive advantage for his businesses? Is this the usual way?

4 What did he gain and what did he lose along his entrepreneurial way?

5 Would you consider Lachlan Lucht's successes the result of planning or of good luck? Explain.

CASE STUDY 5.2   Wastemania, Hamburg

Jeffrey Kershner, from Hamburg, Germany, is a twenty-seven-year-old 'genius' who has won first prizes in many national and international competitions for young inventors, young entrepreneurs and for 'most innovative product/development'. He invented a new software line aimed at decreasing the energy consumption of desktop computers. He is now in a very advanced stage of negotiation with investors on funding his invention: he really hopes it 'will work this time'. Throughout his working life, which began at the age of sixteen, Kershner has invented fifteen new technologies for different goals and has launched two very active, though not yet profitable, businesses in Germany and Singapore.

Kershner's road to the high-tech business arena was unusual and fraught with many difficulties. As a child he lived with his father in a working-class district in the north of Germany, his mother having died during his very early childhood. Kershner was raised in the atmosphere of her work as an artist, which consisted of decorating their and their friends' and neighbors' houses. Kershner's father was away at work all day long and Kershner spent most of his time after school alone in the house. He liked it, as he could then let his imagination flow; his father was a practical, goal-oriented person, and Kershner was always asked to keep busy, 'to do something rather than dreaming all day long' when his father was at home.

He knew from the neighbors that his late mother had been a sensitive person, imaginative and very creative; he felt that they were alike in this respect. At school, Kershner was frequently mocked for his emotionality and sensitivity: they called him names and he had very few friends. Being thus isolated, he turned to books, the internet and especially the physics course he took after school at the neighborhood educational center. He was very active at this center and won all of the prizes for his inventions.

One day, as he was walking back from school, Kershner stopped at a red light, and a woman with her baby in a carriage was standing next to him waiting for the red light to change, when an old car sped by spewing exhaust directly into the baby's face: the baby began to cough heavily. Kershner felt sorry for the baby and decided to invent 'something' to reduce automobile pollution. He discussed this with the physics teacher at that afternoon's class, but they agreed that the lab resources at the center were inadequate for such an invention. Kershner was very disappointed, as he had already visualized how he would invent such a technology. To encourage him, Kershner's teacher told him about her own experience as a promising young researcher when she invented the first electronic calendar to be connected to personal computers (PCs); she was highly respected and planned to patent the invention, then produce and sell it. But at that time she was tackling severe family difficulties which ended in her divorce. As a single mother of two young children, she abandoned her dreams to patent the electronic calendar and became a physics teacher in an afterschool program instead, but she told him that she still hoped to achieve her dream some day.

Kershner was so inspired by his teacher's story that he decided to work on the development of the PC-connected electronic calendar. After eight months, Kershner developed a prototype and was very encouraged by the product's development. He decided to search for investors to fund his R&D, searched the internet and set up meetings. However, he was naïve and worked alone, and did not consult more experienced entrepreneurs, and he therefore chose the wrong person to invest in his product. This very unfortunate experience ruined Jeffrey's idea and his eight months of work; he was then sued by the investor. His father was so furious and disappointed that he threw Kershner out of the house.

At the age of seventeen, Kershner had to make his own living and find places to spend the night at family, friends and neighbors. He found a night job at a twenty-four-hour fast-food restaurant, then was hired as an assistant programmer for a very low salary in a local company. In addition, he assisted in the afterschool physics class to earn a little more money. He also advertised himself on the school's bulletin board as a private tutor for younger students in mathematics and physics. He got some students and eventually found himself working three different jobs during the week while studying in his last year of high school. He had a lawsuit against him, the German welfare system was looking for him and he faced many difficulties with his father; nevertheless, Kershner completed his high-school studies with 'remarkably excellent' grades and got a grant for college studies.

As a sensitive person, he was very attentive to people's needs and was intrigued by how to produce the 'missing link' between their needs and reality. One day, he took the bus to Hamburg to look for an apartment to rent near the university that he was going to study at the following year when he saw a handicapped person struggling to get on the bus. Kershner then spent six months inventing a technological device for wheelchairs that would facilitate bus accessibility for the handicapped; this technology already existed but Kershner's invention promoted it and was resource-conserving. A professor at his university partnered with him in this invention and they then sold it to a large company for a lower price than it could get elsewhere. At the same time, while sitting in a bar with some friends from the university, one of his friends, who was drunk, could not find his wallet. Kershner spent one year developing a kind of nanotechnological GPS device which could be used to locate valuables. He sold this invention to a well-known company and, for the first time in many years, finally felt financially solvent.

He bought a nice house in the Hamburg area and anticipated better days. This did not last for long, however, as he lost in court and had to pay a lot of money to the investor whom he had connected with when he was a young inventor. Then Kershner's father, learning of his son's success, sued him for reimbursement of the money it had cost to support Kershner when he was living at home; in a court compromise, Kershner paid his father the money, and he was once again broke. Kershner was very successful in school and received grants for his studies; he was then recommended to a very prestigious university in Germany for his Master's degree. The more knowledge he gained the more innovations he invented, most of them in order to satisfy his curiosity, since he felt that analyzing opportunities or identifying potential customers was a waste of time. 'Everybody knows what he or she needs; they will find the inventor. An inventor is not a marketing person and he or she should not be looking for clients,' he once told his partners.

His technologies were poorly advertised or published in the newspapers; they were only reported in academic journals. Only those inventions that Kershner developed with partners produced money, as the partners sold the idea, the prototype or the technology itself. While Kershner was very proactive professionally, he was reluctant in business terms; he did not expose his inventions at the forefront: it was only when his colleagues, the researchers, 'found out' about his inventions that they urged him to publish them or to put them on the market. The nanotechnological GPS, for example, could have been much more profitable if Kershner had been willing to modify it according to the demands of a very wealthy client. Kershner, however, thought this modification would diminish the device's sophisticated technology and withdrew from the deal.

The two businesses that he launched were not his idea, but his colleagues', who became his partners in these endeavors. In his own mind, Kershner was still the 'young child that let his imagination flow' rather than a businessman or entrepreneur. The coughing baby's face stayed in Kershner's mind for many years, and in the past fifteen months he has engaged a team of four bright researchers to invent a device that will reduce automobile pollution. He is very enthusiastic to launch a third business in Germany to deal with this emerging problem.

QUESTIONS FOR DISCUSSION

1   Trace the sources of innovation throughout Jeffrey Kershner's life.
2   What were the relationships between Jeffrey Kershner's innovation and production aspects? Explain.
3   What was the role of Jeffrey Kershner's childhood experiences and parents' traits in his career path?

4   What were Jeffrey Kershner's competitive advantages and how did he reveal them?

5   What were Jeffrey Kershner's main advantages in his innovations and inventions? What were his main disadvantages?

6   Do you think Jeffrey Kershner is the type of potential entrepreneur who may run a successful, sustainable business? Under what circumstances could such a business be applicable? Explain your answer.

7   In what sense was Jeffrey Kershner a leader?

8   What are the main differences in terms of innovation between Lucht of Speak-ing-4-u in Australia and Kershner in Germany?

NOTES

1   The following description of Mirabilis was read and personally approved by Dr Yossi Vardi, December 2008.

2   Yossi Vardi, from Wikipedia, the free encyclopedia, 2006, http://en.wikipedia.org/wiki/Yossi_Vardi.

3   Stacy Perman, 'A conversation with Yossi Vardi', *Business Week*, 2 January 2008.

4   A daisy that morphs to designate whether one is available to chat online, busy or even invisible to certain individuals.

REFERENCES

Amabile, T.M. (1988) 'A model of creativity and innovation in organizations', in B.M. Staw and L.L. Cummings (eds) *Research in Organisational Behavior*, vol. 10, Greenwich, CT: JAI Press.

Brazeal, D.V. and Herbert, T.T. (1999) 'The genesis of entrepreneurship', *Entrepreneurship:Theory and Practice*, 23: 29–45.

Brown, S.L. and Eisenhardt, K.M. (1997) 'The art of continuous change: linking complexity theory and time-paced evolution in relentlessly shifting organizations', *Administrative Science Quarterly*, 42: 1–34.

Bull, I., Thomas, H. and Willard, G. (1995) *Entrepreneurship – Perspectives on Theory Building*, Oxford: Pergamon.

Christensen, C.M. (2000) *The Innovator's Dilemma*, Boston, MA: Harvard Business School Press.

Covin, J.G. and Covin, T.J. (1990) 'Competitive aggressiveness, environmental context, and small firm performance', *Entrepreneurship Theory and Practice*, 14: 35–51.

Covin, J.G. and Selvin, D.P. (1991) 'A conceptual model of entrepreneurship as firm behavior', *Entrepreneurship Theory and Practice*, 16: 7–25.

DiMaggio, P. (1992) 'Cultural boundaries and structural change', in M. Lamont and M. Fournier (eds) *Cultivating Differences*, Chicago: University of Chicago Press: 21–57.

Dimov, D. (2007) 'Beyond the single person, single insight attribution in understanding entrepreneurial opportunities', *Entrepreneurship Theory and Practice*, 31: 713–31.

Drucker, P.F. (1985a) *Innovation and Entrepreneurship: Practice and Principles*, New York: Harper & Row, Inc.

Drucker, P.F. (1985b) 'The discipline of innovation', *Harvard Business Review*, 63: 67–73.

Drucker, P.F. (1993) *Managing for the Future*, New York: Penguin Books.

Drucker, P.F. (1998) *Peter Drucker on the Profession of Management*, Boston: Harvard Business School Press.

Drucker, P.F. (1999) *Management Challenges for the 21st Century*, New York: HarperCollins.

Eckhardt, J. and Shane, S. (2006) 'Innovation and small business performance: examining the relationship between technological innovation and the within-industry distributions of fast growth firms', *Report for the Small Business Administration*.

Filion, L.J. (2001) *Réaliser son projet d'entreprise*, Montreal: Editions Transcontinental.

Filion, L.J. (2003) *Savoir entreprendre*, Montreal: Presses de l'Université de Montreal.

Filion, L.J. and Fayolle, A. (2006) *Devenir entrepreneur: des enjeux aux outils*, Paris: Pearson Education France.

Filion, L.J., Luc, D. and Fortin, P.A. (2003) *L'essaimage d'entreprises. Vers de nouvelles pratiques entrepreneuriales*, Montreal: Editions Transcontinental.

Gauvin, S. and Sinha, R.K. (1993) 'Innovativeness in industrial organizations: a two-stage model of adoption', *International Journal of Research in Marketing*, 10: 165–83.

Gibbons, R. (2004) 'Globalisation, innovation and socially robust knowledge', in R. King (ed.) *The University in the Global Age*, Basingstoke: Palgrave Macmillan.

Guangya, X., Ni, J. and Ren, L. (2006) 'Imitation innovation in China: a case study of the software industry', *Technology Management for the Global Future*, 2: 988–91.

Gustavsen, B., Finne, H. and Oscarsson, B. (2001) *Creating Connectedness: The Role of Social Research Innovation Policy*, Amsterdam/Philadelphia: John Benjamin's Publishing Company.

Isaksen, S.G. and Kaufmann, G. (1990) 'Adaptors and innovators: different perceptions of the psychological climate for creativity', *Studia Psychologica*, 32: 129–41.

Kariv, D. (2010) 'The role of management strategies in business performance: men and women entrepreneurs managing creativity and innovation', *International Journal of Entrepreneurship and Small Business*, 9: 243–64.

Kessler, E.H. and Chakrabarti, A.K. (1996) 'Innovation speed: a conceptual model of context, antecedents, and outcomes', Academy of Management, *Academy of Management Review*, 21: 1143–91.

Kirzner, I. (1997) 'Entrepreneurial discovery and the competitive market process: an Austrian approach', *Journal of Economic Literature*, 35: 60–85.

Klein, K.J. and Sorra, J.S. (1996) 'The challenge of innovation implementation', *Academy of Management Review*, 21: 1055–80.

Kor, Y.Y., Mahoney, J.T. and Michael, S.C. (2007) 'Resources, capabilities and entrepreneurial perceptions', *Journal of Management Studies*, 44: 1185–210.

Kotler, P. and Roberto, E. (1989) *Social Marketing: Strategies for Changing Public Behavior*, The Free Press (Latest title in Philip Kotler and Nancy Lee, Social Marketing: Influencing Behaviors for Good, Sage, 2008).

McCraw, T.K. (2007) *Prophet of Innovation: Joseph Schumpeter and Creative Destruction*, London and Cambridge: Belknap Press of Harvard University Press.

McGuire, P., Granovetter, M. and Schwartz, M. (1993) 'Thomas Edison and the social construction of the early electricity industry in America', in R. Swedberg (ed.) *Explorations in Economic Sociology*, New York: Russell Sage Foundation, 213–46.

Miller, D. (1987) 'Strategy making and structure: analysis and implication for performance', *Academy of Management Journal*, 30: 7–32.

Nias, D. (1998) 'Adaptors and innovators: styles of creativity and problem solving', *Journal of Occupational and Organizational Psychology*, 71: 366–8.

Puro, J. (2002) 'Finland: a mobile culture', in J. Katz and M.A. Aakhus (eds) *Perpetual Contact, Mobile Communication, Private Talk, Public Performance*, Cambridge, UK, and New York: Cambridge University Press, 19–29.

Saperstein, J. and Rouach, D. (2002) *Creating Regional Wealth in the Innovation Economy: Models, Perspectives, and Best Practices*, Upper Saddle River, NJ: FT Press.

Schejter, A. and Cohen, A.A. (2002) 'Israel: chutzpah and chatter in the Holy Land', in J. Katz and M.A. Aakhus (eds) *Perpetual Contact, Mobile Communication, Private Talk, Public Performance*, Cambridge, UK, and New York: Cambridge University Press, 63–9.

Schumpeter, J.A. (1912) *Theorie der wirtschaftlichen Entwicklung*, Leipzig: Duncker & Humbolt.

Schumpeter, J.A. (1934) *The Theory of Economic Development,* Cambridge, MA: Harvard University Press (first published in German in 1911).

Schumpeter, J.A. (1942) *Capitalism, Socialism and Democracy,* New York: Harper & Row.

Scott, S. and Bruce, R. (1994) 'The influence of leadership, individual attributes, and climate on innovative behavior: a model of individual innovation in the workplace', *Academy of Management Journal,* 37: 580–607.

Shane, S. (2001) 'Technology opportunity and firm formation', *Management Science,* 47: 205–20.

Stevenson, H.H. and Gumpert, D.E. (1985) 'The heart of entrepreneurship', *Harvard Business Review,* 85: 85–94.

Teece, D.J., Pisano, G. and Shuen, A. (1997) 'Dynamic capabilities and strategic management', *Strategic Management Journal,* 18: 509–33.

Valente, T.W. (1995) *Network Models of the Diffusion of Innovations,* Cresskill, NJ: Hampton Press.

Venkatraman, M.P. and Price, L.L. (1990) 'Differentiating between cognitive and sensory innovativeness: concepts, measurement and implications', *Journal of Business Research,* 20: 293–315.

Warren, L. (2002) 'Towards critical practice in a teaching company scheme', *OR Insight,* 15: 11–19.

West, M.A. and Farr, J.L. (1990) 'Innovation at work', in M.A. West and J.L. Farr (eds) *Innovation and Creativity at Work: Psychological and Organizational Strategies,* Chichester: Wiley, 3–13.

West, M.A. and Rickards, T. (1999) 'Innovation', in M.A. Runco, and S.R. Pritzker (eds) *Encyclopedia of Creativity,* New York: Academic Press.

Chapter 6

Opportunity exploitation

OBJECTIVES

After studying this chapter you will be able to:

■ Discuss the availability of entrepreneurial opportunities and give examples of successful businesses started by entrepreneurs who considered the different aspects of the opportunity-exploitation processes.

■ Recognize the key features of the process of opportunity exploitation and distinguish between opportunity identification, exploitation and creation.

■ Comprehend the significance of the process of opportunity evaluation for business success.

■ Discover main practical ways of identifying opportunities in the environment.

■ Recognize the role of incubators in opportunity creation and exploitation, as a facility enabling the cultivation of opportunities.

■ Develop appropriate strategies for the promotion of active opportunity-exploitation processes.

OPPORTUNITY IDENTIFICATION

For a business venture to survive, and to succeed, it is not enough that the entrepreneur be 'in the right place at the right time'. Entrepreneurs also have to develop the ability to stay on top of the trends, largely by adapting to them and making adjustments in the plans on which the business was originally founded. To do so requires continual opportunity identification, through ongoing learning about the general market trends and the core business, and by locating and evaluating the key adaptive features.

Based on Schumpeter (1934) and Kirzner (1973), an opportunity means meeting (or creating) a market need or interest and turning it into superior value through a variety of resource and ability combinations. Many opportunities already exist 'out there', and the entrepreneur is the 'agent' who is able to discern them, as 'entrepreneurship is about the processes of discovery and exploitation of opportunities to create the future goods and services' (Davidson 2009: 125). Simply coming across valuable information is not enough for entrepreneurship: the difference between those who identify an opportunity and those who do not lies mainly in the ability to make a connection between specific knowledge or information and a commercial opportunity; such a connection, however, requires a set of skills and insights that some individuals possess more than others. According to Shane and Venkataraman (2000), opportunities are those situations in which raw materials, products or methods can be sold to produce more revenue than their cost of production. But such 'situations' do not reveal themselves to all of us: some individuals can more easily observe imperfect phenomena and be triggered to introduce solutions to remedy them. Entrepreneurs who transform their new ideas or solutions into market and commercial potential have performed a successful opportunity-recognition process.

The next step in opportunity recognition consists of exploiting or creating opportunities, evaluating the nature of the opportunity and moving ahead with the entrepreneurial process. Frequent errors occur in the recognition phase, especially in differentiating between actual and perceived opportunity: a wrong perception of the opportunity at this stage may intensify a waste of resources that are typically scarce at the startup stage (Kirzner 1997). Entrepreneurs should accumulate relevant information on market needs, demands, complexities and hurdles from their own or their colleagues' experimentation, be alert to trends, test further developments and technologies, and conduct market research, to be able to establish an idea that can break the existing means–ends framework and provide, via this idea, 'added value' to the market; in this way, they will accomplish the opportunity-recognition process.

Two broad perspectives relating to opportunity identification in the context of search behavior exist: the first presumes a rational search process and is based on the assumption that entrepreneurs know better than non-entrepreneurs where an innovation can be found and can more accurately evaluate the cost and benefits of acquiring new information on this innovation. The second perspective suggests that entrepreneurs possess a constant alertness to circumstances and situations and are in an ongoing process of discovery, which involves a distinctive set of perceptual and cognitive processing skills that direct the opportunity identification.

In both cases, the practical manifestation of opportunity identification may appear in two different behaviors: opportunity exploitation and opportunity creation. Both refer to building an efficient, full-scale operation that will transform the innovative idea into a profitable business, by testing the concept and product, completing the prototype, completing the initial plant tests, market testing, etc. The difference between these two manifestations is that exploiting opportunities focuses on using existing resources or combining them to gain economic returns from the potential entrepreneurial opportunity, while creating an opportunity means to form new, innovative possibilities to be used for the new idea. The outcome of either of these processes will be selection of the final act in the opportunity-recognition phase, when the entrepreneur decides on whether to proceed with or exit the entrepreneurial process, given the accumulated information and depending on the type and cost of the resources required to exploit the opportunity (Kirzner 1973, 1997; Venkataraman 1997; Shane 2000; Ucbasaran et al. 2003).

A different branch of research addresses 'accidental' discovery which, in contrast to a proactive, intended search, stems from a 'passive search' for opportunities to be subsequently developed. Some studies have found that many entrepreneurial businesses favor non-systematic approaches to searching for opportunities, and prefer to 'accidentally' discover business concepts which have not been subjected to formal screening.

This phase includes three main elements: *perception*, sensing or perceiving market needs and/or under-employed resources; *discovery*, recognizing or discovering the 'fit' between these market needs and the resources; and *creation*, turning the newly discovered 'fit' into a business concept. Different kinds of opportunities exist everywhere and can be recognized by most people, but some

91

individuals are able to identify useful opportunities that few others see, and they do so with greater ease.

OPPORTUNITY EXPLOITATION

Opportunity exploitation is considered to be a very critical step in the entrepreneurial process; nevertheless, only minimal attention has been paid to how opportunities are exploited once they are identified. We will build on three theoretical and practical frameworks to explain the process of opportunity exploitation; the first is economy-oriented, stressing that entrepreneurial opportunities exist as a result of the distribution of information about material resources in society. Accurate, relevant and 'right time and place' information are critical for the exploitation phase. Some experienced entrepreneurs may simply have had a fortuitous prior business-ownership experience and may subsequently have little idea about identifying additional profitable projects. Over time, however, entrepreneurs are likely to acquire information and contacts that provide them with a flow of information related to opportunities. The ability of entrepreneurs to learn from previous business ownership experiences can influence the quantity and quality of subsequently collected information (Cooper, Folta and Woo 1995; Gaglio 1997, 2004; Crossan, Lane and White 1999; Gaglio and Katz 2001; Gartner, Carter and Hills 2003; Cope 2005; Corbett 2005, 2006).

As such, the entrepreneur's role is twofold; he or she should be alert and proactive in both accumulating and evaluating information, but also foster this information further on, so that the new product/service will be perceived as valuable for the market. Information is a raw substance that needs to be interpreted for the customers. From this perspective, opportunity exploitation is the outcome of a successful rational search process, manifested as superior information-processing ability, search techniques or scanning behavior (Shaver and Scott 1991; Fiet 1996; Caplan 1999).

The second orientation addresses culture and environment, and argues that entrepreneurial opportunities exist as a result of environmental ambiguity and the cultural resources available to interpret and define those opportunities. An intensified demand for vaccines against the swine flu in 2009, whose appearance in 1976 was believed to be a reincarnation of the infection that killed tens of millions of people in 1918 and 1919, is an example of environmental influences on opportunity exploitation; as such, pharmaceutical companies undertook crash programs to make enough of the vaccine for the start of the flu season in October 2009; the insurance industry reacted to this situation, and many other business people and entrepreneurs were prepared to get involved. This path addresses opportunity exploitation by entrepreneurs locating the 'right' place, where environmental occurrences and/or culture support their new ideas to remedy the situation. A third orientation stresses the role of networking in defining entrepreneurial opportunities. Networking and meaningful networks are an opportunity corridor for the entrepreneur (i.e., the 'corridor principal'), as they develop broad social and professional networks which can promote opportunity detection (Ronstadt 1988; McGrath 1999).

In practice, many entrepreneurs refer to each one of these suggested orientations to exploit their possibilities in proceeding with their innovative product/service. Yet differences still appear, as two main factors influencing the potential of the new product/service: the nature of the opportunity (e.g., available, in daily use, cheap/expensive) and the nature of the entrepreneur (e.g., risk-taker, managing vague situations, having prior experience in such phases) (Kirzner 1973; Christiensen, Madsen and Peterson 1994; Shane and Venkataraman 2000; Shane 2003).

The following two simple examples demonstrate the role of resource availability in the opportunity-exploitation phase. Debbi Fields,[1] a twenty-year-old housewife in Palo Alto,

California with no prior business experience, used a recipe for chocolate-chip cookies to build a business – 'Mrs. Fields' Cookies' – and became the most successful cookie company owner. Cookies were neither an innovative product in her region nor a product in short supply, and therefore penetrating the market with this product was quite difficult. On the first day there was such poor attendance in her new shop that she went outside and distributed her cookies for free on the street. Her entrepreneurial way was not easy at first. Yet, the resources she needed to exploit this opportunity (cookie ingredients, baking equipment) were available and cheap, and this allowed her to proceed with this opportunity-exploitation phase. Fields' business success stemmed from her effective recognition and exploitation of an opportunity. In contrast, John Cagadas,[2] a young inventor from the Philippines, developed and produced a gene chip that he believed was able to detect the causes of autoimmune illness. He tried to attract investors and clients for his product for over two years, with no success. According to Cagadas, professionals kept praising this important invention, yet were unwilling to engage in it. Cagadas abandoned the entrepreneurial process as the resources required for exploiting and proceeding with his invention were unavailable and such devices were not yet in common use. His perception of the opportunity was unrealistic and caused definitive financial damage to his business.

The entrepreneurial process requires the opportunity-exploitation phase to minimize the sort of damage John Cagadas incurred. According to Kirzner (1973), perceptive entrepreneurs identify situations that are unsolved or imperfect and decide to develop a product or service to solve or improve them, while perceiving the existing resources that can be redeployed and used to create more promising outcomes. Their enthusiasm to start a business around their product/service therefore emerges when resources are identified and the entrepreneurs move from creating visionary, 'pie in the sky' ideas to fleshing out those ideas and turning them into products that are feasible and marketable. This is the process of exploitation. The process itself has a unique effect on the entrepreneur, eventually as much of an effect as its outcomes have on the entrepreneur and on the business. Studies show that while engaged in the exploitation phase, entrepreneurs are highly motivated and fueled with enthusiasm, they are optimistic and keen to proceed with their innovations. This enthusiastic spirit is associated with the multiple activities involved in this dynamic phase, e.g., accumulating the critical resources necessary to exploit the opportunity, refinement, decision-making, organizing institutional arrangements to exploit the opportunity, testing technologies, models and new information, assimilating the new information and applying it for commercial ends, negotiating with venture capitalists and suppliers, learning to accumulate experience and new capabilities over time, and improving the content of the entrepreneur's knowledge stock so that it will not be built only upon prior knowledge.

Many studies point to two major modes of exploitation – the creation of new firms and the sale of opportunities to existing firms. The chosen model of exploitation lies in the entrepreneur's perceptions of the probability for success. Normally, buyers will not engage in opportunistic behavior by exploiting the entrepreneur's knowledge base for their own advantage, as in the example of John Cagadas; in such cases, sale of opportunities to an existing firm is the better choice. However, once the knowledge is revealed to potential buyers and the entrepreneurs create new ventures, the likelihood for business success is higher than by choosing the 'selling' mode.

Entrepreneurs differ in the way they think about new capabilities and their potential applications. Some are more sensitive to, or more curious about, potential clients' needs, more aware of the market's gaps, and more easily perceive possibilities for new solutions to fill these needs or gaps. Entrepreneurs with this kind of perceptiveness can often identify possibilities simply by observing daily and routine situations; for example, a colleague's complaint about unfriendly computer software or a newspaper report of an increase in car accidents in the vicinity may stimulate them to think about producing new, innovative solutions to the problems. Such inventive processes require exploitation of the innovative solutions, as enthusiasm over the invention or creation is sometimes blinding. There are creative and innovative individuals who are very perceptive and able to recognize unexploited resources, e.g., underutilized technology, non-functional businesses or underperforming financial assets. The very presence of these unexploited resources often has a dynamic impact on these individuals, and they attempt to find worthwhile uses for them – to define what can create value for them in terms of market acceptance and commercial viability. However, merely exploiting opportunities will not necessarily develop into a profitable business venture, and entrepreneurs must create value for their ideas and potential opportunities: simply readjusting current matches of resources and needs is insufficient, and entrepreneurs must recombine the resources in order to create value superior to that which is currently available. However, exploitation of unexploited resources and market acceptance and viability will not result in a profitable business venture unless the value of the new product or service is noticeably superior to that which is currently available (Schumpeter 1934; Ardichvili, Cardozo and Ray, 2003; Shepherd and DeTienne 2005; DeTienne and Chandler 2007; Kor, Mahoney and Michael 2007).

OPPORTUNITY CREATION

Severe doubts have been raised as to the existing technology for the development of hybrid vehicles to preserve the environment, and as to the costs of many rare materials used in the manufacture of such hybrid vehicles; yet their sales have increased around the world. Today, we cannot imagine ourselves without a television, yet at its inception there was broad public antagonism toward the television, or to 'seeing by electricity' as it was referred to in 1880, as professionals were concerned that it would sabotage human interactions; yet most houses today have more than one television set. These two examples illustrate the need to create opportunities when they are unavailable or not in use. Scientific breakthroughs, innovative thinking, or creative solutions to add comfort to our daily lives may be overlooked because opportunities do not exist or are unavailable. A lack of available resources, knowledge, technology or even unresponsive market attitudes toward an innovation may result in abandoning the potentially brightest inventions.

In such situations, some entrepreneurs create opportunities from scratch; others use a cross-breeding process of different resources, while yet others merge existing resources, or use existing or merged resources for completely new purposes. Some new opportunities for entrepreneurial activity emerge as byproducts of a R&D process or of market attitudes. The common ground is the creation of new opportunities for an invention rather than abandoning an invention because of a lack of extant possibilities to exploit it. Shane defines an entrepreneurial opportunity as 'a situation in which a person can create a new means–ends framework for recombining resources that the entrepreneur believes will yield a profit' (2003: 18), while Shane and Venkataraman (2000) argue that opportunities are not known to all parties at the same time, and that some individuals are more sensitive than others and can either exploit or create in their minds particular opportunities that others still do not observe. A stream of researchers in the field of opportunity recognition argue that while elements of opportunities may be objective and recognized, opportunities are made and formed, and exist in the mind of the entrepreneur as creative constructions, rather than being discovered or identified; creation of opportunities is thus an outcome of the sense-making activities of individuals (Hench and Sandberg 2000; McGrath and MacMillan 2000; Ardichvili, Cardozo and Ray 2003; Gartner, Carter and Hills 2003). Some people habitually activate their mental schema to process information and notice it in the midst of an otherwise overwhelming amount of stimuli (Gaglio 1997). This may explain why the pursuit of one set of ideas and opportunities invariably leads entrepreneurs to additional innovative and previously unrecognized ones (Ronstadt 1988). McGrath (1999) has argued that entrepreneurs have access to numerous shadow options (i.e., opportunities that have not been recognized). Over time, valuable information regarding the real option can be made available or suitable venture opportunities may emerge. Although McGrath (1999) focused on the ability to learn from entrepreneurial failure, shadow options may also arise with more successful entrepreneurs.

Cognitive and behavioral differences between individuals explain why certain individuals visualize and create opportunities more easily than others: the ability to make the connection between different pieces of knowledge and information, even those that are unrelated, requires a set of skills and aptitudes, e.g., being 'alert' to opportunities, being flexible, thinking outside the box, having the ability to optimize existing opportunities, even if they are only in their minds, risk propensity, achievement motivation, and preference for innovation rather than imitation or copying the competition in order to 'make more of the same'. Search behavior can be bounded by the individual's knowledge, motivation, creativity, dynamism and vigor, as well as by his or her ability to gather an appropriate amount of information and produce meaningful bits of information (Kirzner 1973; Woo, Folta and Cooper 1992; Cooper, Folta and Woo 1995; Venkataraman 1997; Stewart et al. 1998).

OPPORTUNITY EVALUATION

Entrepreneurship entails taking risks. Giving up an established or solidly based career and entering into an uncertain venture, and above all, facing the danger of misjudging opportunities and investing one's internal resources, and possibly one's financial resources as well, by plunging into a new undertaking, is an unpredictable and precarious step. The risks might be very harmful for the entrepreneur, the venture itself, and the people who depend on the entrepreneur's income. In light of such risks, evaluating the available opportunities correctly is critical. It is possible to do this by setting up a reliable mechanism that can predict the feasibility of the business's success and the likelihood of its achieving the planned goals, and of alerting the entrepreneur to the risks involved.

Opportunities change. They have to be reassessed as they evolve and develop. The entrepreneur must also address the question of whether the combination of resources available for investment in the proposed venture can, in fact, turn it into an economic success. Some entrepreneurs, investors and scientists who develop products and procedures are so eager to turn their developed products into businesses that they fail to examine the product's marketability objectively.

Several evaluation procedures have been devised for entrepreneurs making decisions about whether to commit resources for further development, investment or acquisition. 'Due-diligence tests' (e.g., Bing 1996; Manigart et al. 1997; Brockner, Higgins and Low 2004) and the 'stage-gate procedure' (Cooper and Edgett 2005) are two popular evaluation procedures; the 'knowledge corridor' is a criterion-screening procedure designed to isolate inappropriate prospective opportunities, and the 'constraint corridor' is a procedure for categorizing the constraints or limitations commonly experienced by entrepreneurs in the same or similar areas of expertise. The purpose of all of these procedures is to assess return objectives, financial resources, risks, and more. Astute evaluations of the resources and the market at each stage of development often lead to useful revisions of business concepts and plans, or to aborting overly risky opportunities before they are set in motion. Evaluations of the market can prevent the establishment of too many similar businesses too close together (Keh, Foo and Lim 2002; Bishop and Nixon 2006).

Many entrepreneurs find the evaluation procedure too costly for the stage of opportunity recognition and avoid it, 'leaving' the evaluation to their intuition and common sense. This is a risky, albeit understandable decision; in order to upgrade this process, a 'peer-judgmental evaluation procedure' could be applied. Entrepreneurs expose their raw data to colleagues who are external to their business, and brainstorm through an evaluative perspective regarding the business's odds of succeeding in light of the data presented; this process is then replicated for their colleagues, while they take on the role of the peer to judge or evaluate their colleagues' business success prospects.

PRACTICAL WAYS OF IDENTIFYING OR EXPLOITING OPPORTUNITIES

There are several research models for identifying, exploiting and evaluating an opportunity; the core backbone of these models is that while identifying an opportunity, the perceived outcome of the entrepreneurial venture should already be visualized; accordingly, the entrepreneur will be able to evaluate the future venture's success or failure, in order to determine the causes of the success or failure and respond appropriately to the business's needs.

Four main practical ways of identifying opportunities, which have been introduced in the entrepreneurship literature, are presented: active search, passive search, fortuitous discovery and opportunity creation (Figure 6.1).

Entrepreneurship scholars have long recognized that individuals can learn to identify opportunities or to improve their ability to do so, and have emphasized five major attributes relevant to such exploitation: (1) creativity – seeing things in new, innovative ways and turning these creative ideas into practice; (2) securing – the ability to pay attention to and preserve new ideas; (3) expanding – acquiring new skills and knowledge, thus increasing the available human resources; (4) exposing – opening oneself up to multiple controlling stimuli (e.g., brainstorming, knowledge sharing); (e) challenging – opening oneself up to new challenges through failure (Amabile 1988; Epstein 1996).

Active search	Opportunity creation
Goal setting, environmental scanning, competitive analysis, strategic planning	The individual is the main source of opportunity. The entrepreneur not only introduces the new product/service, but creates, adjusts or changes the market conditions within which it is sold
Passive search	**Fortuitous discovery**
Opportunities not clearly defined before discovery; passive searches should therefore enhance their learned capabilities and sensitivity to the environment	Entrepreneurial opportunities arise when markets are operating in disequilibrium; alertness allows them to be discovered. Alert individuals discover opportunities that align with their personal knowledge and aspirations

Figure 6.1 *Four means of opportunity identification*

UNIVERSITY INCUBATORS: PROMOTING ENTREPRENEURSHIP IN HIGHER EDUCATION

An *incubator* is a facility that is designed to encourage entrepreneurship and minimize obstacles to new business formation and growth, particularly for hi-tech firms. University incubators provide a nurturing, supportive environment for fledgling businesses. While offering perks such as low-cost rental space, shared office services and equipment, access to capital, and academic as well as business counseling and planning, incubators help new firms survive the initial startup stage.

Business incubators tend to focus on a specific type of company (such as technology, manufacturing, service, minority-owned and so forth). Incubators' objectives vary depending on the type of organization running the incubator.

Prof. Schramm,[3] the President and Chief Executive Officer of the Ewing Marion Kauffman Foundation, was cited as saying that the twin engines of entrepreneurship and knowledge economy lead to many innovations, including new forms of technology, new patterns in society, new demands on the workplace, new modes of living. Universities have been instrumental in developing many of these innovations. Nevertheless, there are different types of incubators in universities and their impact therefore fluctuates: the *university incubators* that aim to develop and transfer new technology; *joint public-private* venture incubators that seek to use the expertise of the private sector combined with access to public funds; *non-profit incubators* which usually focus on creating jobs, diversifying the economy, expanding the tax base and trying to revitalize a community; *privately owned incubators* that exist primarily to turn a profit, and *social incubators* which sponsor environmental, social and cultural initiatives and link the social entrepreneur with the business of design (Von Zedtwitz 2003; Karatas-Ozkan, Murphy and Rae 2005).

University incubator characteristics:

- Spatial infrastructure (office space, equipment).
- Business coaching, mentoring, consulting.
- Handling all the phases of a project, from the feasibility study to prototype realization, including simulation, design testing and definition of the testing set-up.
- Financial support.
- Entrepreneurship promotion among target groups.
- Spreading entrepreneurial culture and the positive image of the entrepreneur.
- Highlighting the benefits of self-employment.
- Providing basic entrepreneurial education.
- A bridge between education and the economy (to accelerate technology transfer between universities and companies).

Students' business incubators. These types of incubators help bridge the gap between academics and real-world entrepreneurial experience in a supportive environment that includes individual advisors and mentors specialized in training sessions, from both the faculty and the business-related and entrepreneurial world. Students receive ongoing coaching, information resources, technical assistance, and access to capital, as well as other support that includes a computer with internet access, use of a phone, fax, copy machine, and more.

Students receive on-the-job training and recognition from competitors and market players and expand their networking. More importantly, relevant networks are created and these play a major role in the entrepreneurial venture's likelihood of survival and success (Conway and Steward 1998; Carayannis and Von Zedtwitz 2005). University incubators add values in the following ways.

97

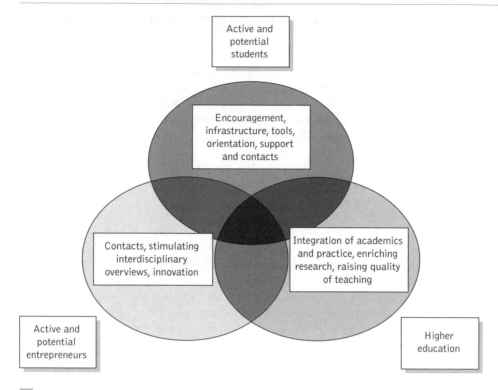

Figure 6.2 *The main roles of incubators for students, entrepreneurs and higher education*

Students:

■ Providing entrepreneurship education to students of all disciplines.
■ Providing more practical-oriented entrepreneurship education.
■ Providing the necessary infrastructure; individual tutoring and mentoring; research and academic support.

Potential students:

■ Encouraging potential students to participate in entrepreneurial programs.

The entrepreneurial realm:

■ Stimulating interdisciplinary teams.
■ Promoting entrepreneurship through well-known entrepreneurs.

Higher education:

■ Integrating the incubators' projects into faculties' study curricula.
■ Reintegrating graduates into the university environment.
■ Enriching faculty members' fields of interest and providing them with the opportunity to be 'hands-on' in the practice.

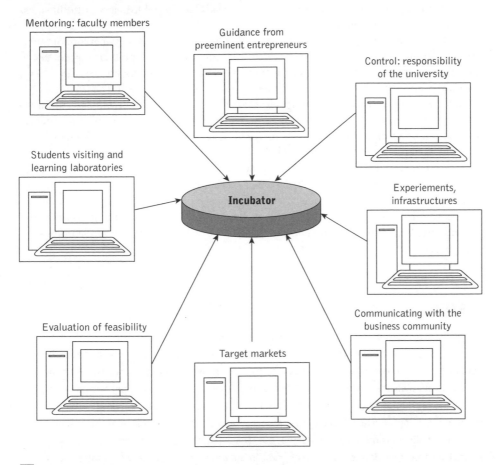

Figure 6.3 *An alternative design of university incubator*

■ Raising the quality of teaching and the curriculum of faculty members in entrepreneurship.
■ Benefiting research and thus cross-border cooperation and interaction in entrepreneurship.

SUMMARY

Entrepreneurial businesses become successful by filling the market's existing needs, interests and insufficiencies. Opportunities to start new businesses that will meet such needs exist everywhere, yet any given entrepreneurial opportunity is not obvious to all entrepreneurs. Some individuals are more sensitive to market needs than others and can identify such opportunities more easily. To exploit opportunities, the entrepreneur should be able to add extra value to the existing identified opportunities, and this is dependent on the 'knowledge corridor' which allows certain individuals, but not others, to recognize certain opportunities. Alertness and prior experience or knowledge of markets, customer problems or their needs advance the process of identification for some individuals.

Most research stresses the need to push individuals to proactively seek new opportunities and evaluate their feasibility. However, empirical evidence shows that entrepreneurs with an ongoing sense of alertness may encounter opportunities 'accidentally' and establish successful business concepts based on such opportunities.

In this chapter, we addressed the differences identified in the literature between opportunity identification, exploitation and creation to enable entrepreneurs and potential entrepreneurs to seek the best type of opportunity recognition for them. Every process of opportunity 'discovery', however, requires a process of information seeking.

An incubator is a facility that is also designed to encourage entrepreneurship and minimize obstacles to new business formation and growth; universities are a helpful means of facilitating the development of innovations, including new forms of technology, new patterns in society, new demands on the workplace and new modes of living.

Additionally, opportunities should be evaluated at each stage of their development, formally or informally, by pursuing investigations of presumed market needs and resources.

By engaging in certain behavioral conducts, such as being alert to the market, to new inventions and developments, by being proactive and accumulating information, by being creative and thinking outside the box, entrepreneurs may find it easier to exploit or create opportunities for their new business.

CASE STUDY 6.1   'GetStarted' Advertising, New Zealand

GetStarted is a three-year-old dynamic business, a form of online advertising enabling and facilitating highly targeted advertising of new businesses and SMEs across private and public sites (portals, hubs, commercial sites, corporate sites, intranets and extranets). GetStarted is typically targeted to novice businesses and SMEs by providing them with a competitive advantage through online promotion 'right from the startup point'. Jackie and Brigitte, two fifty-year-old teachers from Wellington, New Zealand, first launched a business for high-school entrepreneurs in 2000; their business ran for fifteen months, but it never turned a profit and the two decided to close it. However, they developed a new concept in the advertising sphere, which later evolved into the launching of GetStarted.

Jackie was a high-school mathematics teacher with over fifteen years' experience and Brigitte was a remedial teacher assisting underachieving pupils with learning needs on an individual basis. They worked in the same district school for over ten years. Jackie quit her job due to severe differences of opinion with the school principal and suggested that Brigitte join her on an entrepreneurial adventure. Brigitte accepted but retained her job at the school. 'One of the main difficulties we faced in our first business was in locating businesses that would be willing to assist high-school entrepreneurs; we were looking for novice businesses to mentor high-school students in the entrepreneurial process. We believed that it would be a win–win situation; yet novice businesses used poor advertising due to financial constraints at the startup stage. We found it very difficult to locate them,' said Jackie.

The reasons for the first business failure were only partly related to this, but having discovered the lack of advertising in businesses' stratup stage, they developed a practical model to assist young businesses in online advertising. Following the closure of their first business, it was Brigitte who came up with the idea to start a new virtual venture in advertising. Jackie was hesitant, as neither of them had any professional experience in the advertising world. Brigitte's enthusiasm convinced Jackie and they decided to exploit this possibility. Encouraged and supported by some local agencies, they conducted a search among business people in New Zealand of their need for an online advertising forum; the results were inconclusive and could not assist the two in developing a concept to assist those business people. They decided to enlarge their search to Australian business people, but again the results of their search were vague.

At that time, Brigitte had many commitments at the school and almost dropped the whole idea of launching a second business. But one day, on her way to the mall, she came across 'the smallest and most charming, adorable, innovative shop I had ever seen; with a sign at the front door saying, "Sorry, after five years we are closing our boutique."' 'It was a concept boutique focused on products related to "royalty" and included almost anything on that topic, e.g., stationery, kitchenware, furniture, ceremonial clothes, books, letters and much more – all authentic and collected from all over Europe. The owners of this boutique-shop were a retired married couple from Germany who had decided to settle in New Zealand. 'This was the breaking point for me, and I decided to assist them in advertising for free,' said Brigitte. 'I called Jackie and told her that I was completely "in," and that we had our first client. I must admit that Jackie was very disappointed to find out later on that this was pro-bono work.'

They did a tremendous job and the boutique survived; via online advertising they reached clients from all different places in New Zealand and around the world who collected royalty-related products. They both gained experience and knowledge from their pro-bono work and understood that in order to succeed in the business this time, they needed to create their own opportunities. Brigitte started delivering presentations at the school where she worked on the need for advertising and its importance at the business's startup stage for its rapid growth; she invited the students' parents and people from the community to several free presentations at the school, and started to promote the concept of their new business.

Jackie used a different strategy: the 'walk-in'. She visited entrepreneurs who had launched businesses in the prior six months and presented them with the benefits of engaging in virtual advertising at that point in time. Nine months after the launch of GetStarted, Brigitte gathered all her friends and colleagues for a 'professional afternoon tea party' to collect their views and feedback on GetStarted. She asked them to point out the potential constraints they perceived that GetStarted could face and asked those who were already experienced in the entrepreneurial path to describe their entrepreneurial evolution. Jackie made use of the 'devil's advocate' approach by asking one member in each group to present all of the limitations of GetStarted, while the others had to think of solutions to minimize those limitations. The afternoon was a great success and has since been adopted by many other entrepreneurs.

On the firm's third anniversary GetStarted clients received a virtual cake with the number 3 on it and a voucher for free coffee and cake at a well-known coffee-shop chain in New Zealand. Brigitte and Jackie are very proud of their achievements and are developing other strategies to assist their clients in exposing their competitive advantages right from the start.

QUESTIONS FOR DISCUSSION

1   Identify the opportunity-recognition process Brigitte and Jackie conducted for GetStarted; explain its differences from the 'typical model' of opportunity recognition.
2   Is there any connection between Brigitte's and Jackie's career paths and their individual opportunity-recognition processes? Explain the differences between the two in choosing the strategies of opportunity recognition in light of their previous career experience.
3   What is the nature of the opportunity-evaluation process conducted by Brigitte and Jackie? In your opinion, what are the benefits and limitations of such a process for the business's growth?
4   Would you suggest a different opportunity-evaluation process for GetStarted? Explain.
5   Of the five major attributes relevant to opportunity exploitation – creativity, securing, expanding, exposing, and challenging – which do you consider most dominant in the case of GetStarted? Would you recommend emphasizing other attributes as well? Explain.

NOTES

1   Based on the following websites: financial inspiration café, www.financial-inspiration.com/Debbi-Fields-biography.html; Mrs Fields' official website, www.mrsfields.com/.
2   Based on an interview with the author. Some details have been changed to protect his privacy.
3   'The Future of the Research University: Meeting the Global Challenges of the Twenty-first Century', www.kauffman.org/Details.aspx?id=5758.

REFERENCES

Amabile, T.M. (1988) 'From individual creativity to organizational innovation', in K. Gronhaug and G. Kaufmann (eds) *Innovation: A Cross-disciplinary Perspective*, London: Norwegian University Press, 139–66.

Ardichvili, A., Cardozo, R. and Ray, S. (2003) 'A theory of entrepreneurial opportunity identification and development', *Journal of Business Venturing*, 18: 105–23.

Bing, G. (1996) *Due Diligence Techniques and Analysis: Critical Questions for Business Decisions*, Westport, CT: Greenwood Publishing Group.

Bishop, K. and Nixon, R.D. (2006) 'Venture opportunity evaluations: comparisons between venture capitalists and inexperienced pre-nascent entrepreneurs', *Journal of Developmental Entrepreneurship*, 11: 19–33.

Brockner, J., Higgins, E.T. and Low, M.B. (2004) 'Regulatory focus theory and the entrepreneurial process', *Journal of Business Venturing*, 19: 203–20.

Caplan, B. (1999) 'The Austrian search for realistic foundation', *Southern Economic Journal*, 65: 823–38.

Carayannis, E.G. and Von Zedtwitz, M. (2005) 'Architecting gloCal (global-local), real-virtual incubator networks (G-RVINs) as catalysts and accelerators of entrepreneurship in transitioning and developing economies: lessons learned and best practices from current development and business incubation practices', *Technovation*, 25: 95–110.

Christiensen, P., Madsen, O. and Peterson, R. (1994) 'Conceptualising entrepreneurial opportunity identification', in G. Hills (ed.) *Marketing and Entrepreneurship*, Westport, CT: Greenwood Press, 61–75.

Conway, S. and Steward, F. (1998) 'Networks and interfaces in environmental innovation: a comparative study in the UK and Germany', *Journal of High Technology Management Research*, 9: 239–53.

Cooper, A.C., Folta, T.B. and Woo, C. (1995) 'Entrepreneurial information search', *Journal of Business Venturing*, 10: 107–20.

Cooper, R.G. and Edgett, S.J. (2005) *Lean, Rapid and Profitable New Product Development*, Canada: Product Development Institute.

Cope, J. (2005) 'Toward a dynamic learning perspective of entrepreneurship', *Entrepreneurship Theory and Practice*, 29: 373–98.

Corbett, A.C. (2005) 'Experiential learning within the process of opportunity identification and exploitation', *Entrepreneurship Theory and Practice*, 29: 473–91.

Corbett, A.C. (2006) 'Learning asymmetries and the discovery of entrepreneurial opportunities', *Journal of Business Venturing*, 22: 97–118.

Crossan, M.M., Lane, H.W. and White, R.E. (1999) 'An organizational learning framework: from intuition to institution', *Academy of Management Review*, 24: 522–37.

Davidson, P. (2009) *The Entrepreneurship Research Challenge*, Cheltenham: Edward Elgar.

DeTienne, D.R. and Chandler, G.N. (2007) 'The role of gender in opportunity identification', *Entrepreneurship Theory and Practice*, 31: 365–86.

Epstein, R. (1996) *Cognition, Creativity, and Behavior*, Westport, CT: Praeger.

Fiet, J.O. (1996) 'The informational basis of entrepreneurial discovery', *Small Business Economics*, 8: 419–30.

Gaglio, C.M. (1997) 'Opportunity identification: review, critique, and suggested research', in J.A. Katz (ed.) *Advances in Entrepreneurship, Firm Emergence, and Growth*, vol. 3, Greenwich, CT: JAI Press, 139–202.

Gaglio, C.M. (2004) 'The role of mental simulations and counterfactual thinking in the opportunity identification process', *Entrepreneurship Theory and Practice*, 28: 533–52.

Gaglio, C.M. and Katz, J.A. (2001) 'The psychological basis of opportunity identification: entrepreneurial alertness', *Journal of Small Business Economics*, 16: 95-111.

Gartner, W.B., Carter, N.M. and Hills, G.E. (2003) 'The language of opportunity', in C. Steyaert and D. Hjorth (eds) *New Movements in Entrepreneurship*, London: Edward Elgar, 103–24.

Gruber, M. (2007) 'Uncovering the value of planning in new venture creation: a process and contingency perspective', *Journal of Business Venturing*, 22: 782–807.

Hench, T.J. and Sandberg, W.R. (2000) '"As the fog cleared, something changed": opportunity recognition as a dynamic, self-organizing process', paper presented at the Babson-Kauffman Entrepreneurship Research Conference, Babson College, Wellesley, MA, June.

Karatas-Ozkan, M., Murphy, W.D. and Rae, D. (2005) 'University incubators in the UK', *International Journal of Entrepreneurship and Innovation*, 6: 41–51.

Keh, H.T., Foo, M.D. and Lim, B.C. (2002) 'Opportunity evaluation under risky conditions: the cognitive processes of entrepreneurs', *Entrepreneurship Theory and Practice*, 27: 125–48.

Kirzner, I.M. (1973) *Competition and Entrepreneurship*, Chicago: University of Chicago Press.

Kirzner, I.M. (1997) 'Entrepreneurial discovery and the competitive market process: an Austrian approach', *Journal of Economic Literature*, 35: 60–85.

Kor, Y.Y., Mahoney, J.T. and Michael, S.C. (2007) 'Resources, capabilities and entrepreneurial perceptions', *Journal of Management Studies*, 44: 1187–212.

Manigart, S., Wright, M., Robbie, K., Desbrieres, P. and De Waele. K. (1997) 'Venture capitalists' appraisal of investment projects: an empirical European study', *Entrepreneurship Theory and Practice*, 21: 29–43.

McGrath, R.G. (1999) 'Falling forward: real options reasoning and entrepreneurial failure', *Academy of Management. Academy of Management Review*, 24: 13–30.

McGrath, R.G. and MacMillan, I.C. (2000) *The Entrepreneurial Mindset: Strategies for Continously Creating Opportunity in an Age of Uncertainty*, Boston, MA: Harvard Business School Press.

Ronstadt, R. (1988) 'The Corridor Principle', *Journal of Business Venturing*, 3: 31–40.

Schumpeter, J.A. (1934) *The Theory of Economic Development: An Inquiry into Profits, Capital, Credit, Interest, and the Business Cycle*, Cambridge, MA: Harvard University Press.

Shane, S. (2000) 'Prior knowledge and the discovery of entrepreneurial opportunities', *Organization Science*, 11: 448–69.

Shane, S. (2003) *A General Theory of Entrepreneurship: The Individual–Opportunity Nexus*, New Horizons in Entrepreneurship Series, Cheltenham: Edward Elgar.

Shane, S. and Venkataraman, S. (2000) 'The promise of entrepreneurship as a field of research', *Academy of Management Review*, 25: 217–26.

Shaver, K.G. and Scott, L.R. (1991) 'Person, process, choice: the psychology of new venture creation', *Entrepreneurship Theory and Practice*, 16: 23–42.

Shepherd, D.A. and DeTienne, D.R. (2005) 'Prior knowledge, potential financial reward, and opportunity identification', *Entrepreneurship Theory and Practice*, 29: 91–112.

Stewart, W.H., Jr., Watson, W.E., Carland, J.C. and Carland, J.W. (1998) 'A proclivity for entrepreneurship: a comparison of entrepreneurs, small business managers, and corporate managers', *Journal of Business Venturing*, 14: 189–214.

Ucbasaran, D., Wright, M., Westhead, P. and Busenitz, L.W. (2003) 'The impact of entrepreneurial experience on opportunity identification and exploitation: habitual and novice entrepreneurs', in *Advances in Entrepreneurship, Firm Emergence and Growth*, vol. 6, Bingley, UK: Emerald Group Publishing, 231–63.

Venkataraman, S. (1997) 'The distinctive domain of entrepreneurship research: an editor's perspective', in J. Katz (ed.) *Advances in Entrepreneurship, Firm Emergence and Growth*, vol. III, Greenwich, CT: JAI Press, 119–38.

Von Zedtwitz, M. (2003) 'Classification and management of incubators: aligning strategic objectives and competitive scope for new business facilitation', *International Journal of Entrepreneurship and Innovation Management*, 3: 176–96.

Woo, C.Y., Folta, T.B. and Cooper, A.C. (1992) 'Entrepreneurial search: alternative theories of behavior', in *Frontiers of Entrepreneurial Research*, Wellesley, MA: Babson College, 31–41.

Chapter 7

The startup stage

OBJECTIVES

After studying this chapter you will be able to:

■ Trace the phases and related activities in the business at the launching stage.

■ Detect the processes and activities relevant to the launching stage in order to perform the required, essential preparatory tasks and apply them to an existing/planned business.

■ Identify the necessary activities, processes and tools for each of the phases in order to use effective related strategies to accomplish the business's goals.

■ Combine creativity and innovation (the knowledge acquired in prior chapters) with the required activities at the launching stage to develop a strong, vigorous plan for the launching stage.

■ Recognize the Four Ps model that promises relevant differentiation of the new enterprise from those of competitors, right from the launching stage.

■ Assess the fit between the competencies needed for the launching stage and their purposes.

The launching phase of a new enterprise is the entrepreneur's first contact with the nitty-gritty of the business world and the encounter between expectations, dreams and ideals and the actual market rules which can come as a 'reality shock' (Perrow 1963). Such encounters are often totally unexpected, and even when known in theory, they may lead to disappointment and frustration. They may turn into an insurmountable hindrance preventing the entrepreneur from realizing his or her ideas.

Above, we addressed the exploitation of opportunities and conception of visions, and the primary steps toward implementing an idea. Following these two primary steps, the entrepreneur desiring to establish a new venture has to go through a series of steps, or stages, before a newly launched business enterprise can run successfully. To acquaint the founder with the key activities usually encountered during this process, the stages and activities within them are presented, along with the main characteristics attributed to them, and the main competencies needed. By identifying the variety and complexity of these activities, as well as unique aspects of each, the reality shock may be anticipated and the vigorous power of venture creation and growth may turn the inevitable obstacles into successive triumphs (Greiner 1972; Churchill and Lewis 1983; Quinn and Cameron 1983; Miller and Friesen 1984; Kazanjian 1988; Kazanjian and Drazin 1990; Kariv, Filion and Borges 2010).

Launching any new enterprise entails the successful management of a number of different activities during the first stages of its founding. There is, of course, no single clearly defined path of activities that guarantees business success, but recognizing the elements of the activities enables carrying them out *if* and *where* they are relevant to and suit the needs of the specific business (Bird 1992).

Figure 7.1 presents seven core activities (phases) that are likely to pave the way to the successful management of a new venture. Some of the elements dealt with in some of the activities, or stages, may appear during other stages in the same or in another form.

PHASE 1 – DECISION-MAKING

Entrepreneurs make various decisions in their work world, the primary and crucial one being to launch a venture. They then have to decide on every activity, process and method they plan to

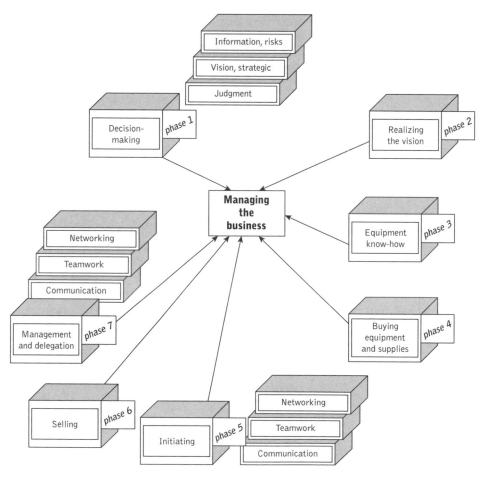

Figure 7.1 *Activities characterizing the creation and operation of a venture*

implement. Some entrepreneurs have no previous experience, in either management or entre-preneurship, and their decisions are made on a trial-and-error basis. Although in the long run, decisions taken and implemented in this way may improve and enhance the venture, there are usually no indications of their efficacy when they are first taken. It is very difficult to predict the eventual results of most decisions as they are usually made in vague or uncertain situations, and often under fluctuating conditions. Mintzberg (1973), in his seminal work *Strategy-making in three modes*, asked: 'How do organizations make critical decisions? And how do they link them together to form strategies?' These important questions are even more relevant to new and small businesses, and they indicate the need for entrepreneurs to address the decision-making process. Even while engaged in dealing with many pressing commitments at the launching stage, entrepreneurs have to take both short- and long-range plans and possible outcomes into consideration when making decisions, and this is something that can, and should, be learned.

Decision-making is the first step in the creation of a new venture, and it is critical and more complex than decision-making in the ensuing phases of the business's evolution. There is an urge to see immediate results and, at the same time, to form stable building blocks for long-term stability and growth. Entrepreneurs of actively running businesses, on the other hand, have already achieved at least some degree of stability and are more concerned with growth, and their decisions are therefore more focused. This can be demonstrated by analogy to learning to ride a bicycle: the novice rider must first learn to balance and keep the bike upright as he or she practices riding, and to avoid injurious falls and crashes. At the same time, the novice rider will try to learn tactics that will enable him or her to continue riding the bicycle for longer distances and in the best, most comfortable and advantageous way (e.g., for health and fitness). A trained and experienced bicyclist, however, is no longer concerned with balance and stability and focuses all or almost all of his or her attention on developing new ways to generate more benefits, perhaps by racing or going on all-terrain bike rides.

There is a long-standing debate among researchers of entrepreneurship surrounding the question of which decision-making model is the best one to adopt prior to and during the launching phase, and which are more suitable in later phases of the business's existence, and various models for rational analysis, creative thinking and intuitive methods have been suggested.[1] Researchers argue that since decisions have to be made during different phases, and over a wide range of managerial concerns, all of which eventually affect the firm's performance, the *way* in which the decisions are made is of the utmost importance. They recommend employing different decision-making models for the business's different activities and processes; for example, adopting rational analysis for processing information, risk analyses and creative thinking for assessment of selling alternatives and business opportunities, and intuitive methods for making decisions about recruiting people and establishing networking.

However, making decisions during Phase 1 should perhaps also include rational analysis models, which are more systematic and reliable, and can be validated; the creative thinking and intuitive methods of decision-making should not be neglected in this phase as they may involve the ideation of new and unexplored perspectives and entail visualizing possibilities from hitherto untried angles. Creativity and intuitive processes, which involve processing relevant ideas and information, may lead to new ideas and perspectives which will act as catalysts and facilitators of efficient and effective decisions (Kamm and Nurick 1993; Zacharakis and Meyer 1998; Gruber 2007; West 2007).

PHASE 2 – REALIZING THE VISION

Most entrepreneurs visualize the configuration and the operational workings of their businesses before they begin its actual step-by-step establishment. At this point their dreams are often quite concrete, and they are confident that they will be realized. Entrepreneurs are enthusiastic not only about the new products or services they have conceived, but about their envisioned process of implementation. The pre-operational visualization often includes prosaic details such as how, when and with whom their ideas will be brought into being, and although there is usually considerable uncertainty and ambiguity at this stage, creative energies and ambition to succeed generate self-confidence and belief in the vision, and these prevail over concerns and fears.

Most entrepreneurs are not only usually quite alone in their endeavor at this point, they also try to be very hands-on and in complete control of every aspect of their business. However, without the more objective views of others, their priorities may be skewed, and without assistance, taking care of urgent but less important matters may lead to overlooking or postponing some important ones, or even failure to take care of them at all. It is therefore important that entrepreneurs delegate some tasks to partners and/or employees, and even to relatives and friends, as doing so may be vital for the realization of the vision.

Communicating with knowledgeable and experienced people within and outside the field of the envisioned venture is a requisite, as are proactive rather than reactive and retroactive activities. Reacting refers to actions taken by the entrepreneur in response to environmental occurrences; these are mostly unplanned actions taken after a situation has already occurred, but they are sometimes part of the entrepreneur's original plan or schedule. Proacting is an active behavior intended to cause something to happen rather than waiting to respond to it after it happens; it involves anticipating a situation and taking affirmative steps to deal with it. Retroacting is the feedback, the assessment of already executed activities.

Entrepreneurs should establish a system of assessment that includes gathering the relevant data and analyzing it as a basis for their mission statement and their concrete plans. Since presently available assessment systems are not always relevant, entrepreneurs should collaborate or consult with people already involved in the field, or with those with past experience in it, for retroactive evaluations. Not only do such collaborations allow for the benefits of objective and non-biased views, they also create opportunities for new ideas and innovations to come into being. Realizing visions entails the Sisyphean work of studying the results of others' experiences and integrating the lessons that can be learned from them into new and creative outcomes. Although some of these outcomes may be revealed in the future as unsatisfactory, or even as total mistakes, they may then be the subject of what-not-to-do lessons for other entrepreneurs on the way to realizing their visions (Hornaday 1992; McFadzean, O'Loughlin and Shaw 2005).

PHASE 3 – EQUIPMENT KNOW-HOW

In every kind of business venture, a certain amount of equipment is necessary. During the earliest stage of venture creation, entrepreneurs should be able to operate the equipment that has been acquired, or at least be knowledgeable about the intricacies of its operation. As their businesses stabilize, the ability to operate the equipment may be left solely in the hands of trained employees, but the entrepreneurs must always keep abreast of the equipment's condition, spare parts, upgrading, and so on. Some entrepreneurs consider learning how to operate their business's equipment not only time-consuming, but also a waste of money, and most prefer to hire experts to both operate and maintain it. In all cases, the entrepreneurs' expertise in everything that has to do with the equipment used in their businesses is of crucial importance, as it enables them to construct their business plans knowledgeably and systematically. The founder of an accounting company who plans to acquire sophisticated software, for example, by ascertaining what different kinds of software are available, what they can and cannot do, how fast they operate, and how much time is involved in training people to use the software, is better able to plan the business and more accurately predict the company's output.

During the first stages of venture initiation, polyvalence – the ability to carry out a variety of tasks in a given field – and the ability to adapt to new technologies are crucial aptitudes. At this stage, entrepreneurs have to cope simultaneously with a large number of tasks and with new, and possibly unfamiliar equipment. When the business is functioning, they must also follow the development of new equipment and techniques related to their enterprise, and acquire those that are likely to improve their product or service. The acquisition of new equipment may entail various adaptations, according to its specific requirements, and may necessitate training or retraining some of the workers and/or hiring new employees familiar with the equipment, as well as an ongoing assessment of the equipment's output and its effects on the business's performance.

PHASE 4 – BUYING

Entrepreneurs buy their equipment and materials at known given prices, and expect to sell their products or services at unknown but profitable prices. However, the true costs of the equipment and materials purchased are not always known, as they can include a considerable number of expenses that are hard to ascertain. For example, an owner of a clothing industry has to calculate the purchase prices of the fabrics, sewing threads, needles, buttons, zippers, etc., and to assess the amounts proportionate to the costs of machinery use and other furnishings, amortization of these articles, employees' wages, rent or mortgage payments, and more. The selling price has to take all of these into account, although some of them are not easy to calculate vis-à-vis the sell-for price of the manufactured or supplied product or service. Moreover, the prices that entrepreneurs pay for the purchased equipment and materials are dependent to a large extent on their knowledge of what is available on the market and on their negotiation abilities.

Since revenues and the future success of the venture are dependent on the selling prices, and these depend to a greater or lesser degree on the purchase prices and other costs of all of the investments, accurate analyses of all of the inputs are essential. The tools for such analyses include asking the right questions, identifying the point of forfeit, etc.; in all of these, assistance, advice and networking can be crucial, and maintaining effective and positive communication with active, experienced entrepreneurs is highly recommended (training, mentorship and counseling are discussed further on in this chapter).

PHASE 5 – INITIATING THE VENTURE

The first steps of the business venture culminate in the initiation phase; it is then that the risky plunge becomes an active enterprise. This is the moment of entrepreneurship in which the vision is realized. A venture is transformed into a 'real business' when the first sale is made, or when some sort of opening event, such as a gathering of partners, investors, potential clients, and friends and relatives, or an open-to-the-public demonstration of what the business offers.

When initiating a venture, it is important to differentiate the new enterprise from those of competitors, usually by stressing its originality. The means used to do this are often called the Four Ps – *product*, *price*, *place* and *promotion* (Figure 7.2), i.e. what is being sold, how much it costs, where or how it can be acquired, and why the consumer should buy it. The price is not only the sum stated on the sticker or invoice: it has much to do with consumers' perceptions of the price, the determination of which is based on pricing strategies. Place is connected with the costs of

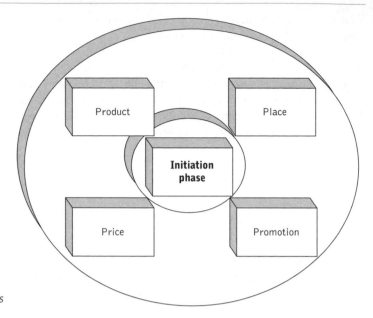

Figure 7.2 *The four Ps*

distribution. Promotion creates awareness and a 'need' for the product, thus persuading the consumer to purchase it (Masurel, Nijkamp and Vindigni 2004).

During the venture's initiation stage, the equipment has to be installed and the staff trained. During this phase, entrepreneurs have to multitask: they must function as all-purpose managers and workers, and deal simultaneously with numerous facets of a large variety of problems and dilemmas. While this should be done according to the prepared plan, which should be followed with forethought and care, the entrepreneur must allow for flexibility when the need arises. Entrepreneurs have often acknowledged that their original business plan was only partially linked to reality and that they were constrained by unforeseen situations that arose to make new decisions on activities and processes that were quite different from the planned ones. When such situations arise, it is important that the diverse elements of the business continue to be managed coherently.

Marketing is an important factor during the initiation stage as it not only promotes sales and builds up the business's reputation, but it also compels the entrepreneur to prioritize and decide which of the significant and representative elements of the business are most important. For example, the owner of a newly opened flower shop (product) located in the center of town (place) must use marketing (promotion) to emphasize the shop's originality and added value (price) in order to differentiate this new shop from those of competitors in the same area. The most significant elements characterizing the new flower shop should ideally be characteristics that are lacking in the other flower shops in the vicinity. Marketing should serve to highlight these characteristics, but they should be very carefully selected, as they will then characterize the flower shop and shape its comparative advantage. The flower shop founder may decide to focus on the free delivery of bouquets within a certain radius, the promise of undamaged and/or very fresh flowers, unusual or exotic blooms, or unique arrangements for special occasions, and so on.

In order to allocate the human and monetary resources needed to ensure the successful launching of the business, entrepreneurs arriving at this stage of their new venture have to learn, through mentors, counseling, and training, how to organize all of the major activities of the initiation.

PHASE 6 – SELLING

During a venture's initiation phase, selling is usually the most difficult and intense activity for all business people, but especially for novice entrepreneurs. Prior to the first sales, feelings of ambiguity and doubt inevitably arise, and although the first trade activities do not guarantee success, the feelings generated by the first sales are encouraging and motivating. Selling, per se, is obviously the purpose of the venture, and good sales mean that the business is succeeding. But above and beyond the monetary aspects, selling the product or services of one's new venture is the indicator par excellence of entrepreneurial success; it raises the fledgling entrepreneur's self-esteem and belief in his or her creativity and competence, and constitutes proof of the capabilities and salesmanship needed to be in business.

Sales at the launching stage should be handled by the entrepreneur. These are not regular sales; they are multifaceted: the entrepreneur is selling not only a product or service, but the idea or concept of a new business. Moreover, the way the sale is carried out exemplifies the owner's professionalism, competence, honesty and integrity. By meeting face-to-face with the clients and making hands-on sales, the entrepreneur/owner can ascertain clients' demands and what they like about the entire purchase – be it the price, the owners' attitude, the quality of the product, or the atmosphere of the venue. The answers to these questions are best obtained by the entrepreneur/owner him or herself.

Entrepreneurs should learn how to ask questions, and to do so proactively: to ask, and to then listen very carefully to the responses, complimentary as well as critical. Asking questions of others in the same field is an inherent part of entrepreneurial life; it is how the pulse of the surrounding business world is measured, and it should be done on a regular basis. Equally important are the comments and reactions of customers, those who bought as well as those who didn't. Competitors' comments should also be listened to and analyzed, as they may lead to improvements in one or more of the four Ps, and can contribute to a better understanding of client demands.

Flexibility is essential throughout the selling process. Profit margins cannot be determined before a sufficiently long period of sales has passed and the results studied, and the entrepreneur/ owner must adopt a very flexible sales strategy in order to adjust to client demand and to the circumstances, so as to stay linked to the market. Profit margin is an indicator of a company's pricing policies and its ability to control costs. Differences in competitive strategy and product mix cause profit margins to vary among different companies.

PHASE 7 – MANAGING THE BUSINESS

Many entrepreneurs working in new areas, as they face the entrepreneurial process for the first time or encounter demands, needs and complexities that are different from those they encountered in their previous businesses, lack well-established and already applied models for managing the particular kind of business envisioned. In such cases, entrepreneurs have to base their plans and strategies, as well as their on-the-spot decisions, not only on others' knowledge and experience, and whatever relevant advice they can obtain from people both within and outside the company, but also on up-to-date information which they must accumulate on an ongoing basis, and on common sense and current experience, which sometimes appears to be a trial-and-error course.

Entrepreneurs have to organize and systemize all their personal or acquired resources and to base them on accepted, practical models in order to manage the business from the very beginning. Those entrepreneurs who leave the management to more advanced stages then find themselves in many difficult situations because they did not standardize their management from the start. The people working in and connected to the business (suppliers, clients, potential clients, investors) need to be able to follow the business management flow, to identify with a certain type of business management and trust it; trusting the managerial behavior means trusting the business's products and services. For example, we sometimes avoid a shop because it looks neglected, and we doubt its products, but when we discover that its owners are trustworthy, we set our previous reservations aside; this is because we have begun to trust the management or the managerial behavior.

The main resource of most entrepreneurs is the people working with them, and most entrepreneurs are inexperienced in managing people. Entrepreneurs have to learn how to turn their employees into teams, and how to motivate them both as individuals and as teams. This should be done by giving each employee specific responsibilities, and a distinct role that is vital to the business's success. This is shown in Table 7.1.

The novice entrepreneur in particular should seek those who can look at his company-in-the-making objectively and offer good advice. Friendly support and encouragement when things are not going exactly as visualized are often forthcoming in such instances, and are a welcome bonus. Employees and potential employees, partners, investors and others who are likely to be within the entrepreneur's networking circle should be selected according to their specific abilities and the complementary information they can provide (Filion, Luc and Fortin 2003). Although while launching their ventures, entrepreneurs function independently and are involved in and responsible for every step of the process, the people around them, along with efficient networking, are crucial factors.

Since in managing a business, a great deal depends on what people working in the business tell people outside the business, networking and communication skills are essential in this phase. Entrepreneurs that are not endowed with a natural aptitude for this should learn or improve the communication skills needed for managing a business. Positive, functional and target-oriented communication is needed to ascertain the competencies of potential associates and to determine

Table 7.1 *Competencies needed and activated during the launching process*

Phase	Competencies needed	'In order to'	Apprenticeship
1 Making decisions	Judgment Caution	Vision	Information risk
2 Realizing the vision	Know-how Constancy Firmness	Take action Carry out plans	Retroaction
3 Equipment Know-how	Polyvalence and multiple competencies	Operate or oversee all domains	Techniques
4 Buying	Intensity Flexibility	Negotiate	Diagnostic
5 Initiating	Differentiation Originality	Arrange	Marketing Management
6 Selling	Flexibility	Adapt	Recognizing the clients
7 Management	Discernment	Build up relationships and team spirit	Holistic perspective

how they can help in the venture creation process. Such communication is important during three stages of the advisor–advisee relationship: first, at the outset, by proactively asking for assistance and/or advice; then, while getting this assistance, to convey recognition of the significance of the assistance for the business's success, along with praise of the advisor's expertise; and, lastly, by asking for the advisor's opinions on how well the entrepreneur utilized the assistance and advice, and how it affected the business. This last step is 'retroacting'; it serves as a learning experience for both advisor and advisee, as both weigh the results of the advice in order to affect future actions (Gumpert 1982; Lipparini and Sobrero 1994).

SUMMARY

While no two entrepreneurial businesses are exactly alike in their development path, some activities are generic and characterize the creation and operation of almost all entrepreneurial businesses. In some cases, a phase may be passed through so quickly that one hardly recognizes it as a distinct phase; in others, a particular phase may last longer, or even drag out for an inordinate length of time. Either way, the overall framework illustrated in this chapter provides a view of the road ahead before and while taking the first steps.

Seven core activities for each of the entrepreneurial business phases are presented in this chapter, representing their unique and characteristic actions and operations. In the first phase, the entrepreneur's focal processes involve decision-making regarding the business's vision, choosing the business strategy, best practices to be implemented accordingly, and deciding on how to acquire the relevant and most reliable information. In the second phase, most activities are conducted around realizing the vision, by communicating it, learning from knowledgeable and experienced people, and being attentive to potential complexities. The third phase is characterized by the entrepreneurs' advancement of their own proficiency in the business's core equipment know-how; moreover, this phase is characterized by polyvalence, which is the ability to carry out a variety of tasks in a given time as well as being proficient in operating the business's core equipment(s), including that equipment which is unfamiliar. In the fourth phase, the most significant core activity is buying the material needed for the business to operate effectively (e.g., equipment, raw material, recruitment of the workforce, purchasing information and services) as a means to promote the selling phase of the business's products and/or services. Phase 5 involves 'initiation'; the typical activities in this phase focus on placing the business in a working system. The sixth phase is focused on the selling activities, one of the most complex and stressful activities that the entrepreneurs will have to go through. The entrepreneur is selling not only a product or service, but also a concept, even when the business does not represent an innovative concept, because the way in which the sale is carried out demonstrates the business concept, along with the entrepreneur's professional knowledge, competence and integrity. The seventh phase – managing the business – addresses the business's long-term management and maintenance, while guaranteeing sustainability of the business's competitive advantage.

CASE STUDY 7.1   Restau.com, Poland

Restau.com is a website that provides up-to-the-minute information on menus, promotions and discounts for restaurants in Warsaw, listed according to location. Restau.com has no stock or inventory, and has no role in the pricing of goods; the site acts only as an intermediary in the ordering process.

Four partners, students who met during their university studies in Warsaw, Poland, had a brilliant idea: 'to establish a highly customized website for providing *something* according to clients' preferences in an area where such a service was still lacking in Poland'. But they had no idea in which area.

The members of the group differed greatly in terms of culture and nationality: Nathan Zawacki and Zarek Duda are Polish, Wayne Burke is British, and Asil Çalık is from Turkey. Zawacki, co-founder, partner and currently the CEO of the company, was the driving force in ultimately choosing food as the area for their website: 'Since we operate in the Polish economy, we had to choose a sector that would not be so vulnerable to economic fluctuations. Food and the internet were well suited,' says Zawacki. The partners' choice of the food sector was not based only on the vagaries of economic crises or fluctuations; Çalık's brother had opened a Turkish restaurant in Warsaw, and they realized that food was a good area for business. And so, Restau.com was launched.

Despite recurring economic crises, and with neither money for investment nor any other tangible resources, the four partners decided that a website could succeed. Since all four were experts in web design and management, they were not concerned about the professional and technical aspects of the website. However, none of them had any training or experience in marketing or financing, and they were concerned about these facets of operating a business. They decided that they would introduce new perspectives to e-commerce; for example, Restau.com does not require that its customers provide their credit card number when ordering, and the form of payment is flexible: users may pay for their orders in any form that the specific restaurant accepts.

This trust in their customers' honesty had positive results in terms of the number of users that entered the website during the business's first stages, and they decided to focus their marketing strategy on word-of-mouth promotion – a very innovative concept for marketing in Poland: 'We knew that if our service was successful, all the users would be talking about it. With no listed clients and no marketing at all, Restau.com achieved three-digit growth in the years 2004–2006. Then, in order to keep up with orders, we decided to increase the number of restaurants [in our listings] in line with the growth of new users,' says Zawacki. Since its soft-launch in 2000, business has increased greatly in terms of value, sales, number of users (clients) and number of employees.

New technologies and novel ways of doing things are greatly appreciated in Poland; its population of young people is growing, and opportunities are sought after and exploited by many companies; cultural symbols are changing, and modernism is 'in'. In order to sustain a competitive advantage in the market, Zawacki and his partners broadened the range of their business's operations. For example, they initiated an interactive satellite connection through which users can order meals while watching television, without having to log into a website or call anyone.

The high cost of the connection needed to transmit the orders is partially covered by monthly membership fees paid by the restaurants participating in the scheme.

When business began to level off, the partners set up a new service: a real-time order-and-dispatch system, which began with more than 110 restaurants. Each order placed with Restau.com is transferred in real time to the respective restaurant; the restaurant immediately transmits the order to the restaurant's own software to ascertain if it can be filled and signals Restau.com with a 'confirmed' or 'rejected' signal. At present, more than 65 per cent of the orders, a very large percentage, are automatically confirmed in this way, and a lot of time is saved for both the restaurants and the clients. The entire order-confirm-and-dispatch process is manageable and scalable, and the cost per order to the client is generally negligible. Restau.com charges the restaurants a small monthly operating fee for this service, the first time it is doing so. The project was a valuable innovation and a beneficial one for the firm's profitability, which continues to rise. A commercial company has shown interest in buying Restau.com.

Their success stimulated the four young partners to look for other innovations; they felt that there were other possibilities with great potential. Their firm grew and they moved to a nice location in Warsaw, hired specialists in marketing and financing, human resources (HR), and administration. They built an infrastructure to categorize their clients (for example, clients who order more than five times from the same restaurant are given a discount on their next order), and an infrastructure for their representatives to support their clients by directly observing the customer's 'history' from their database and assisting the users by providing relevant and matching information, links, graphics, or even guidance according to the user's 'history'. These innovations improved the service level and motivated their clients to use their website.

The four partners are preparing for negotiations involving the sale of Restau.com. Along with their preparations for this, they are continuing with other activities and seeking additional innovations. Based on the same infrastructure and ideas as those of Restau.com, they launched a spin-off company for amusement and recreation events. In their ongoing attempts to sustain their competitive advantage, and to maintain the interest of the commercial company that wants to buy Restau.com, the four partners have begun a new multilanguage tourist-oriented project that provides information about ethnic restaurants.

QUESTIONS FOR DISCUSSION

1 Identify the phases in Restau.com's development that were described in this chapter; then match them with the characteristics, competencies and apprenticeship in Table 7.1.
2 Which phases were the partners most involved in?
3 Which changes in the environment affected the development of Restau.com most?
4 What is the role of innovation in businesses based on e-commerce in general? What was the role of innovation in establishing Restau.com? Explain.
5 Identify the differences in the launching stages of Restau.com and its spin-off.

NOTE

1   Rational analysis models include methods such as SWOT, cash flow projections, balance sheets, balance score cards, income and financial statements, Pareto analysis, grid analysis, force field analysis and many more; intuitive and creative aspects of decision-making include methods and techniques such as creative problem-solving (CPS), the six-hats analysis (De Bono 1999), brainstorming, positive thinking and positive alternatives, Porter's five forces (Porter 1979), and others.

REFERENCES

Bird, B.J. (1992) 'The operation of intentions in time: the emergence of the new venture', *Entrepreneurship Theory and Practice*, 17: 11–21.

Churchill, N.C. and Lewis, V.L. (1983) 'The five stages of small business growth', *Harvard Business Review*, 61: 30–9.

De Bono, E. (1999) *Six Thinking Hats*, Boston, MA: Little, Brown & Company.

Filion, L.J., Luc, D. and Fortin, P.A. (2003) *L'essaimage d'entreprises. Vers de nouvelles pratiques entrepreneuriales*, Montréal: Éditions Transcontinental.

Greiner, L.E. (1972) 'Evolution and revolution as organizations grow', *Harvard Business Review*, 50: 37–46.

Gruber, M. (2007) 'Uncovering the value of planning in new venture creation: a process and contingency perspective', *Journal of Business Venturing*, 22: 782– 807.

Gumpert, D.E. (1982) 'Entrepreneurship: a new literature begins', *Harvard Business Review*, 60: 50–5.

Hornaday, R.W. (1992) 'Thinking about entrepreneurship: a fuzzy set approach', *Journal of Small Business Management*, 30: 12–24.

Kamm, J.B. and Nurick, A.J. (1993) 'The stages of team venture formation: a decision making model', *Entrepreneurship Theory and Practice*, 17: 17–27.

Kariv, D., Filion, L.J. and Borges, C. (2010) 'Emerging strategies and generation gaps among entrepreneurs: differences between baby boomers and generation X', paper presented at 2010 BCERC–Babson College Entrepreneurship Research Conference, Lausanne, Switzerland, 9-12 June.

Kazanjian, R.K. (1988) 'Relation of dominant problems to stages growth in technology-based new ventures', *Academy of Management Journal*, 31: 257–79.

Kazanjian, R.K. and Drazin, R. (1990) 'A stage-contingent model of design and growth for technology based new ventures', *Journal of Business Venturing*, 5: 137–50.

Lipparini, A. and Sobrero, M. (1994) 'The glue and the pieces: entrepreneurship and innovation in small-firm networks', *Journal of Business Venturing*, 9: 125–40.

Masurel, E., Nijkamp, P. and Vindigni, G. (2004) 'Breeding places for ethnic entrepreneurs: a comparative marketing approach', *Entrepreneurship and Regional Development*, 16: 77–86.

McFadzean, E., O'Loughlin, A. and Shaw, E. (2005) 'Corporate entrepreneurship and innovation part 1: the missing link', *European Journal of Innovation Management*, 8: 350–73.

Miller, D. and Friesen, P.H. (1984) 'A longitudinal study of the corporate life cycle', *Management Science*, 30: 1161–83.

Mintzberg, H. (1973) 'Strategy-making in three modes', *California Management Review*, 16(2): 44–53.

Moberg, D.J. and Velasquez, M. (2004) 'The ethics of mentoring', *Business Ethics Quarterly*, 14: 95–122.

Perrow, C. (1963) 'Goals and authority structure: a historical case study', in E. Friedson (ed.) *The Hospital in Modern Society*, New York: Free Press, 112–46.

Porter, M.E. (1979) 'How competitive forces shape strategy', *Harvard Business Review*, March/April: 91–101.

Quinn, R.E. and Cameron, K. (1983) 'Organizational life cycles and shifting criteria of effectiveness: some preliminary evidence', *Management Science*, 29: 33–51.

West, G.P. (2007) 'Collective cognition: when entrepreneurial teams, not individuals, make decisions', *Entrepreneurship Theory and Practice*, 31: 77–102.

Zacharakis, A.L. and Meyer, G.D. (1998) 'A lack of insight: do venture capitalists really understand their own decision processes?', *Journal of Business Venturing*, 13: 57–76.

Chapter 8

Mentorship, coaching and counseling

OBJECTIVES

After studying this chapter you will be able to:

- Understand the importance of implementing training programs for both the entrepreneur's empowerment, relevant skills and knowledge, and the business's management and goal accomplishment.
- Describe the various types of training programs for entrepreneurs (e.g., traditional training, coaching, mentoring, counseling), and distinguish between them so that the relevant program is selected for the business according to its specific needs.
- Underline the main characteristics and core principles of each program: training, mentorship, coaching and counseling.
- Identify the responsibilities and tasks of the provider (trainer, mentor, coach, counselor) and the entrepreneur (trainee, mentee, person being coached or counseled) to establish and maintain trustful relationships and maximize the potential success of the programs.
- Assess the effectiveness of training-related programs (or mentoring, coaching, counseling) employed in the business in light of its objectives and sustainable contribution to the business and the entrepreneur.

It's lonely at the top! A frequently reported experience of entrepreneurs, especially novice ones, is feeling alone in the fray. Entrepreneurs have to make decisions and choose between different options; they have to initiate processes and manage people – and they usually have only their own experience and intuition to guide them, in addition to which they are often operating in unfamiliar environments. They lack the experience and the tools needed to predict the effects of their decisions and activities on their businesses.

Academics, practitioners and governments worldwide are beginning to recognize the role of mentoring and counseling in providing entrepreneurs with support at critical moments of venture creation. From the fledgling entrepreneurs' perspective, acquisition of the necessary business skills and enhancement of acumen to plan, set up and operate their businesses are the most valuable aspects of mentorship or counseling, but such support can also provide feelings of fellowship and colleagueship, and inspire greater confidence in their decisions and activities. The guidelines underlying entrepreneurial support programs stress role modeling, close attention to the entrepreneurs' needs and demands, and intervening only at the entrepreneurs' request. Not surprisingly, support programs for entrepreneurs have been identified as having a positive influence on levels of entrepreneurial activity and on the improvement of the quantity and quality of future entrepreneurs (Birley and Westhead 1993; Alsos and Kolvereid 1998). As a result, the number and type of programs offered throughout the world is on the rise.

Programs for entrepreneurs are goal-based, and depend on the guidance of mentors, counselors and coaches, and on networking, all of which have been shown to have direct, positive results. Entrepreneurship-support programs are based on one-on-one relationships between mentors or counselors and entrepreneurs, in order to find prompt, on-the-spot solutions aimed at increasing the success rate of startup ventures by providing the knowledge and expertise needed to make and implement relevant business decisions. Assistance ranges from teaching the entrepreneur to identify opportunities for new ventures, through new ways of thinking in implementing ideas, to dealing with the unique barriers faced when managing new ventures.

A life-cycle approach that attempts to deal with the evolution of entrepreneurial enterprises, as reflected by the changes in the types of challenges – and consequently the unique needs – that businesses encounter as they mature, is relevant to the support these programs provide. As businesses move through the different phases of their development, managerial needs change, and along with them, the support that is needed. The skills that novice entrepreneurs believe they require, or want to acquire, evolve and change over time. Different support programs that take into consideration different and evolving needs are therefore needed.

In this chapter, we present several different types of support programs for entrepreneurs, explain the differences among them, and suggest the types of programs best suited to different owners' needs (Chrisman and McMullan 2000; McMullan, Chrisman and Vesper 2001; De Faoite et al. 2004).

MENTORSHIP

Mark Twain wrote, 'You cannot depend on your eyes when your imagination is out of focus.' Twain seems to be describing a situation faced by many creative entrepreneurs. Such entrepreneurs need guidance in getting 'their imaginations into focus', as well as in turning their desires and dreams into a functioning business, while exploiting each of the available resources, qualifications and skills they may have or may proactively obtain. This guidance may be obtained through a mentor.

Mentoring is a multifaceted type of facilitation that is open to a broad range of diverse interpretations and applications. A mentor is defined as a 'wise and trusted counselor or teacher'. The origin of the term lies in Greek mythology: Mentor was Odysseus's trusted counselor, the guardian and teacher of his son Telemachus. Today, however, mentoring is viewed mainly as being a role model, an example set by a person who exerts considerable influence over the person being mentored, to the extent that the latter may sometimes be considered the mentor's protégé or dependant. Mentorship is thus often viewed as a relationship. Collin (1979) defines mentoring as a protective relationship in which learning and experimentation can occur, potential skills can be developed, and results can be measured in terms of competencies gained rather than curricular territory covered.

In the context of entrepreneurship, mentoring is aimed at increasing the success rate of startup entrepreneurs by providing them with a more profound knowledge and insights on how they perceive their motivation to become an entrepreneur, what their focus in entrepreneurship is, what they consider to be the driving forces for success, and what the main strengths of their business are. As such, the mentored entrepreneur develops his or her own expertise in making and implementing relevant business decisions.

This is usually done by matching novice entrepreneurs with competent veteran entrepreneurs, senior executives, experienced business people or professionals, but it is also very relevant to active entrepreneurs who want the guidance of a trustworthy and notably successful person in the same or a similar field of enterprise. Mentorship of an entrepreneur is based on the mentor listening to the views and problems of the people he or she is mentoring and sharing his or her own experiences with them in order to provide both support and encouragement. The goals and desired results of the mentoring are usually established by both the mentor and the person being mentored at the start of the relationship, and then amended and modified according to changing needs.

A variety of mentoring programs for entrepreneurs have emerged in the past three decades. All of them deal with the various areas relevant to entrepreneurship, such as management, finance, marketing, competition, intellectual property rights, and so on. Most popular are formal types of mentoring programs, which are affiliated with and financially supported by government agencies or private companies. Most of these are non-academic, and are devoted to entrepreneurship; they incorporate a structured process for matching mentors with their charges according to the mutual interests of the partners, as well as a structured, planned and controlled learning process. A different type of mentorship has evolved in which the selection and matching of the partners is informal and is conducted by the partners themselves. The mentor–mentored matches are made through the growing networking circles and ecosystems within which many entrepreneurs are involved, and where they can find the co-partners most suited to what the person being mentored wants to learn or the mentor wants to impart. Although the learning process in this type of mentorship is thus less formal and less controlled, the trusting relationship and mutual attractiveness of the partners promise its success.

An increasingly large number of reports on research projects and publications on mentorship have begun to appear, mostly in the United States and Canada, Latin American countries (especially Brazil), almost all of the European countries, Asian countries (mainly India and Singapore), and Mediterranean countries (in particular Israel). They report on the beneficial outcomes of mentorship programs for both mentors and the people they are mentoring. In the specific context of entrepreneurship, both former and current mentored people report improved career outcomes, positive professional identity, greater job satisfaction, and higher income across time. The one-on-one, just-in-time (JIT) and goal-based programs characteristic of mentoring have several important offshoots: the one-on-one interaction between mentor and mentored guarantees privacy and confidentiality throughout the process, which allows for a very significant psychological contract between the partners; the JIT intervention's importance lies in its ability to address problems as they arise. The major element of mentoring is that it is a broad and long-range learning process that is continuous, focused on the person being mentored, flexible in learning methods and themes, includes the major elements of a total quality process, is strongly connected to improvement, and comprises mutual respect for the people involved (Scherer, Brodzinski and Wiebe 1990; Bard and Moore 2000; Leonard and Swap 2000; Peterman and Kennedy 2003; Longenecker and Neubert 2005).

Figure 8.1 illustrates the processes (e.g., identifying personal goals in becoming an entrepreneur; identifying competitive strengths, such as professional and personal skills) and the outcomes (e.g., becoming more committed to the role of entrepreneur; ascertaining self-evaluation along the entrepreneurial path) of a mentoring process. With their broad range of interpretations and applications, mentorship programs and styles may vary, but their underlying characteristics and core principles remain the same, as follows:

- The mentor–mentored relationship is based on trust and honesty.
- Mutual respect is the basis of the mentoring process.
- The focus is on the person being mentored – the learner.
- The mentor as role model is the basis of the process.
- The pace is determined by the learner's needs and learning abilities.
- The experience for both mentored and mentor should be rewarding, satisfying and enjoyable.
- Challenging but achievable goals should be set at the beginning of the process.
- The mentorship should be a flexible and open process, adapting to changing situations, demands and constraints.
- The mentoring process has to be monitored for weaknesses and oversights, and a system for correcting them established.
- The mentoring process has to be monitored for its strengths, and a system for sustaining them established.

The success of mentorship depends on both the person being mentored and the mentor. The responsibilities of the the former are as follows:

- To be aware of and to identify and categorize their strengths and weaknesses as entrepreneurs.
- To identify the main vision and goals of their ventures.
- To be proactive in the mentoring relationship: to keep appointments and their time limit, to prepare and ask relevant questions, and to search the mentor's knowledge, etc.
- To be prepared for each meeting, with 'assignments' done, and with notes on the events and experiences since the previous meeting in order to discuss them and to hear the mentor's comments on their way of handling them.

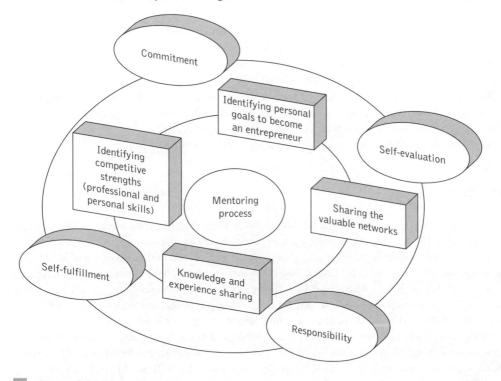

Figure 8.1 *Mentoring process and outcomes*

- To take an active role in sharing entrepreneurial experiences honestly while disclosing the associated reactions and emotions so that the mentor can identify and explain the meanings of those experiences.
- To listen carefully to the mentor's feedback, advice and responses; not necessarily and automatically implementing each one of them, but analyzing their deep meaning and exploring possibilities of using the feedback and advice in the future.
- To be keen to learn from the mentor's experiences.
- To show respect for and appreciation of the mentor and the process.

All active and successful entrepreneurs are ethically obligated to offer their accumulated knowledge to other entrepreneurs, novice or experienced. The benefit of this is mutual, as both sides learn from the experiences of their colleagues and peers. Some, however, can, and should, guide and help others as mentors. Mentors are rewarded by the gratification and fulfillment they experience upon enriching and empowering their counterparts (O'Neill and Blake-Beard 2002; Moberg and Velasquez 2004).

The responsibilities of mentors are:

- To be positive role models.
- To share entrepreneurial knowledge and experiences.
- To both encourage and challenge the person being mentored to succeed both professionally and personally.
- To provide guidance and constructive feedback.
- To have or develop strong interpersonal and leadership skills.
- To be interested in developing and empowering others.
- To be tolerant of the mentored person's different ways and qualities of learning and learning styles.
- To have the patience to repeat things that were not immediately or fully understood.
- To have a positive attitude toward ongoing learning.
- To be able to offer psycho-social support.
- To have technical knowledge in their field of expertise.
- To take responsibility for the learning process: being prepared for each meeting, taking notes during meetings as reminders, being flexible in availability to the person being mentored, and in changing the meeting goals or themes from time to time.
- To be respectful of the person being mentored and the mentoring process.

COACHING

The term 'coaching' is taken from the field of sports, where the coach is the expert in charge of training an athlete or a team. In entrepreneurship, coaching means tutoring and giving instructions in order to improve business performance. Entrepreneurs involved in the launching phase of new businesses tend to focus on the day-to-day issues they encounter and have to deal with immediately, and inevitably lose sight of broader and more distant ones. Through coaching, today's issues and tomorrow's agenda are pinpointed, making it possible to set realistic and feasible goals, while not losing sight of the end goals. Coaching can thus help the entrepreneur find a balance between today's demands and tomorrow's needs. Coaches support, challenge and motivate, they ask questions, and they act as a sounding board for ideas, problems and solutions. Most of all, coaches train for success (Stanworth and Gray 1992; Judge and Cowell 1997; Bonfield 2003; Sherman and Freas 2004; Feldman and Lankau 2005).

Since, as in sports, there are various different tools and methods that promise business success, the main purpose, or goal, of coaching is to identify the entrepreneurs' needs and abilities, and to match them with the best tools and methods, i.e., the ones most likely to lead to success and growth. The interaction between coach and client should enable them to identify the issues that have to be addressed immediately, and to explore different possible tools and ways of dealing with them. It should also allow for reflection on the possible outcomes of the coaching process. Together with their client-entrepreneurs, coaches set goals and timetables and keep records of them; the coaches alert their clients when they see them veering away from the path they have set for themselves. By doing this together, the entrepreneurs learn to monitor themselves and correct unproductive behavior. Coaching has to enable the client-entrepreneurs to identify and tackle the real issues, to manage their important business issues with confidence, and to make the necessary changes for survival and profitability. The entrepreneur has much to gain from a successful coaching relationship. However, this entails prudent choices and learning behaviors. Some of these are listed below.

- The coach should be chosen with care through a trusted person's recommendation.
- The coached person should be clear about what he or she wants to gain from the coaching and should set realizable goals.

Table 8.1 *The coach, mentor, trainer, and counselor*

Coach	Mentor	Trainer	Counselor
Role			
Partner	Role model	Teacher	Advisor
Advocate	Inspiration	Expert	Expert
	Guide	Guide	Guide
Contribution			
Facilitation	Experiences of	Models of methods	Expertise
Support	self-proven methods	and procedures	Experience
Coaching models	Contacts and networks		
Purpose			
To partner with the	To discuss with the	To teach methods,	To advise and to
client in order to	client and show the	procedures, skills,	provide strategies
clarify and to	keys of success	expertise, etc.	for success
achieve goals			
Entrepreneur's objective			
To connect with	To understand and	To develop skills	To use advice,
deep values and	use the mentor's	and proficiency in	expertise, and
desires, create	proven methods	an area of the	strategies for
personal guiding	of success	venture	success
principles, and to	To make contacts		
construct a model	Networking		
for success			
Desired results			
Personal alignment	Increased success by	Increased or	Success in using the
Profound change	implementing the	improved abilities	consultant's advice
	mentor's approach	and proficiency	
	and using new		
	contacts		

- A clear agreement between coach and client should be reached on all facets of the coaching: when it will begin, how long it will last, and its main content and directions.
- The coaching process should spill over into the entrepreneur's life outside work and vice versa: the ability to identify and solve business problems can help in dealing with non-business issues, and vice versa.
- It is important to listen to *all* of the coach's instructions and advice, not just to the easy or achievable ones.
- It takes time to develop the coaching relationship, unlike mentorship in which the mentor listens to the person being mentored and shares experiences with him or her. Coaching is demanding; the coach expects instructions to be followed, and the results reported. Assignments (e.g., preparation of a business plan) are expected to be turned in on time.
- Coaches should have more significant data and knowledge than their clients, and the client-entrepreneurs should verify this. Although it is impossible to do so during a single, first meeting, awareness of this topic is very important.
- Coaching has to be evaluated at pre-set times for progress. Comparison with others being coached by the same or other coaches can provide useful benchmarks.

COUNSELING

Counseling is a domain-specific support system for an entrepreneur or group of entrepreneurs in a specific field; it addresses the managerial and behavioral competencies of entrepreneurs in order to guide them in creating competitive advantages, creating profit and promoting their businesses in general through their personal performance. Counseling offers multiple methods for developing a business, and attempts to provide entrepreneurs with the means to succeed. Counselors are usually professionals, and experts in the specific areas in which they are counseling; entrepreneurs seeking counseling should therefore identify the exact area in which they want counseling. The areas in which counseling can be helpful are varied: economic efficiency; strategic vision; optimization; IT management; HR efficiency; reconciling personal and professional lives, and so on.

There are different types of counseling, and they can take place in various frameworks:

- On a one-on-one basis – a counselor with expertise in the designated field addresses the client's specific needs (e.g., how to start a business or expand an existing one, packaging a loan application, writing a business plan).
- Training programs – courses for a group of several prospective or current business owners for the same purpose or for compiling comprehensive solutions for their businesses; such programs focus on the necessary organizational skills to get a business off the ground or to achieve business growth.
- Seminars – stand-alone colloquiums or discussion groups for several entrepreneurs to help them deal with specific obstacles or to clarify topical issues.
- Workshops – experts on specific business issues, such as marketing, financing, legal structures, insurance, sales, and more.

Counselors may have one or more of the following strengths: active attentiveness to the clients' needs; objective analysis of the dilemmas and problems presented; a grasp of complicated circumstances in new subject ranges; ability to compile solutions customized to the specific requirements and needs of the client or group of clients. Entrepreneurs should be aware of the strengths of different counselors, and inquire about or assess them before their final decision on the counselor best suited to their needs. The outline below illustrates the flow of the selection process for a suitable counselor.

Step 1. Asking questions about past experiences in the counselor's field of expertise:
- Ascertain successful and unsuccessful results and the reasons for both.

Step 2. Preparation and presentation of a 'sample' dilemma you have encountered recently. Listen carefully to how the counselor treats it, and if possible take notes:
- Does he or she ask additional insightful questions, or 'jump to conclusions'?
- Does he or she try to understand the situation in depth, or propose general 'textbook' answers?
- Is the counselor showing the benefits as well as the costs of the proposed solutions to the dilemma, or just focusing on the benefits?
- Evaluate the simplicity versus complexity of the analysis and the responses of the counselor to the presented dilemma; a counselor who complicates a simple situation may not be what the entrepreneur needs at the launching stage.
- Follow any 'extras' the counselor may offer (e.g., up-to-date knowledge, benchmarking, new practices, examples from leading companies in the relevant field, examples of some best practices, etc.).

Step 3. Discussing the potential relationship with the counselor:
- How does he or she envisage the counseling relationship? Ask specifically about the envisioned process, foreseen results and benefits, realistic odds of achieving goals.
- What happens in situations of disagreements between counselor and client?
- How available will the counselor be?
- What are the main elements of the psychological contract? Why and how are they significant?

Step 4. Analyzing the interaction with the counselor in terms of:
- Sense of personal trust in the counselor.
- Professional confidence in the counselor.
- The client-entrepreneur's enthusiasm toward starting the counseling sessions.
- The expectations that these sessions will help in achieving the planned goals.

Step 5. 'Talking business' about the duration, costs and conditions of the counseling:
- Ascertain the duration and underlying rationale of the counseling process; why the proposed length is required, what tasks the client needs to fulfill, and how long it might take in order to achieve the planned goals of the counseling, etc.
- Ascertain the cost of the counseling and how it is calculated (per working hours, per active sessions, per results, etc.).
- Establish an outline for a confidentiality contract.

Step 6. Benchmarking:
- It is important to meet other recommended counselors prior to making the final selection.
- Ask colleagues and people you trust for their views and impressions of their counselors in order to make a comparative assessment.
- Clients' comparisons of the services they receive, and the 'discovery' that their own counselor is providing different services, may be frustrating and may even damage the counseling process. A prior assessment of different counselors' potentials and methods may establish their 'equity model' (Adams 1965) in advance.

- It is imperative to decipher the main evaluative parameters for a successful counselor.
- Try to consolidate the decision regarding the choice of a counselor based on rational and emotional considerations.

Step 7. Making the decision and being self-confident about it.

Step 8. Continually assessing the counseling process and personal progress in view of having used the counselor's suggestions:
- During the counseling process, assess the effectiveness of the counselor's suggestions vis-à-vis the results achieved.

There are different types of counseling:
- *One-on-one basis* — a specialist training and counseling on a one-on-one basis in strong relation to the client's needs (such as how to start a business, expanding an existing business, packaging a loan application, or writing a business plan).
- *Training programs* — courses assisting a small group of several prospective or current business owners gathered for the same purpose: compiling a comprehensive solution for their businesses. These programs are focused on familiarizing the clients with the needed organizational skills to guide business growth or to get a business off the ground.
- *Seminars* — stand-alone colloquiums or discussion groups for several entrepreneurs to help them deal with predefined stumbling blocks or instruct them on specific matters related to entrepreneurship.
- *Workshops* — practical sessions led by experts on a variety of specific business issues that include marketing, financing, legal structures, insurance, sales, and more.

Counseling for entrepreneurs can also be found on the internet,[1] in many local areas, community business-development corporations, local departments for business assistance, and small and medium-sized governmental business associations or institutions[2] (Chrisman 1989; Bechard and Toulouse 1998).

SUMMARY

Entrepreneurs' learning, training and support practices are very important factors in a business's potential success at each stage of its evolution, and entrepreneurs should actively seek either practical support of immediate value or mental support to elevate their confidence in their own capability to turn their vision into a business. Short- and long-term learning and support practices are effective for both the business outcomes (survival, profitability, innovation) and processes (strategic management, decision-making, recruiting processes); yet entrepreneurs should learn to identify which format of learning and support best suits their business's needs and demands, mark out their possible courses of action and promote their business. Entrepreneurs should also decide upon the 'role' of the 'guide' (e.g., mentor, coach, counselor) they wish to engage, according to their own preferences and the business's needs; some individuals would prefer a mentor because he or she inspires them by providing them with opportunities to experience the entrepreneurial reality, rather than just learning skills, yet they should take into consideration the business's needs according to its stage. For example, at the startup stage, while negotiations with investors and banks are at stake, for some entrepreneurs, especially novice ones, a coach may be of more assistance in the training and promotion of negotiation and communication skills.

Assistance can cover many aspects of the business's launch, management and growth; specifically, assistance in analyzing the business's life cycle may be critical for entrepreneurs, to be able to delineate the actions that need to be taken, the skills, processes and practices needed to deal with each phase in the cycle of the business. Entrepreneurs may then 'use' training and learning tools to turn their vision into reality. Assistance in selecting an entrepreneurial path, reorganizing thoughts and ideas on how to launch and manage a business, or encouraging entrepreneurs by providing them with positive reinforcement and feedback may also be of high importance for many entrepreneurs. However, by relying too heavily on preconceived notions and established behaviors formed through experiential learning, entrepreneurs may fall into 'learning traps' in which they continue to rely on fixed rather than flexible situational 'truths'. To avoid the risk of becoming dependent on a mentor, coach or counselor, entrepreneurs need to analyze the training practices they are engaged in and choose those strategies that apply and with which they can identify. The guidance of mentors, coaches or counselors may ease the difficulties faced by entrepreneurs, but the entrepreneurs themselves must remain independent and able to function in flexible, free surroundings.

Two case studies are offered for comparison.

CASE STUDY 8.1   Rutujit Jindal, India

Rutujit Jindal, an active university professor, works independently as a paid mentor. He specializes in mentoring hi-tech startups in product development of both software and hardware. Jindal refrains from calling the mentorship sessions he conducts a 'job', as he sees them as a mission, and he refers to his clients as 'mentees'. 'As a scientifically minded academic, and a member of society, I enjoy doing this. I discovered how much young startup entrepreneurs need a guide or mentor and decided to contribute my knowledge and experience. A mentor has to be a person with more experience and wider exposure than entrepreneurs in the general area of their chosen business, but has to advise and guide the people he mentors in the right direction without being overbearing. Along with the experience and field knowledge, a mentor also brings his network of connections to the entrepreneurs,' says Jindal.

Jindal's mentorship sessions were free of charge at first, but he soon realized that when the people being mentored paid, they were more committed: 'It was too easy for the young entrepreneurs, with so many urgent and important things to deal with during the first stages of their venture creation, to miss a session or two. But when they have to pay, they make appointments and come to speak with me on a regular basis,' he explains. Jindal doesn't seek 'clients' – they come to him on their own – but he follows the people he mentors after the completion of the mentorship sessions: 'The companies I mentored are doing well and they keep coming back for advice; therefore, one can indirectly infer that the process we followed has been effective.'

Jindal's mentoring sessions are not pre-structured; they focus on the mentored's current needs. He prefers to 'flow with the mentee' and to let the discussion between them direct them, rather than plan a specific topic to be dealt with. Jindal considers such talk an expression of thoughts and emotions that spring forth from both their conscious and unconscious minds, and believes that the mentor's role is to enable this expression, and then to help the people being mentored to look deep within themselves and discover the inner resources and strengths needed to carry out their plans. 'To me, mentoring is akin to the role of a father initiating a grown-up son or daughter into the family enterprise. You must have experience and integrity in order to inspire trust and a certain amount of awe and reverence – but you must be approachable as well,' he concludes.

Jindal's mentorship sessions can take place anywhere: in an office, park, or restaurant, as well as at any time, and session duration is also flexible. Jindal wants the people he mentors to feel at ease, and meets with them from time to time 'to hold in-depth discussions, mostly on sticky and confusing points'. He explains that as a mentor, he has the advantage of being able to look at things objectively, because he is not part of their executive team, and then, 'if at the end of the discussion, I have helped them resolve the problem, or enabled them to get a clearer picture, or have steered them on a plan of action to secure the sought-after goal, I feel I have done my job . . . In most such discussions, I have found that my non-attachment with the executive part of the company is my biggest strength in trying to bring objectivity to the table. Of course, my experience of dealing with similar situations in the past helps tremendously.' Jindal then sums up: 'As a mentor, I always try to do two things: to help my mentees see things more clearly when they are confused, and to raise their spirit with all kinds of encouragement when the chips are down.'

Jindal did not plan to be a mentor. He explains his path to mentorship as an outcome of his incredible life. Jindal was born and brought up in one of the most backward parts of rural India. He grew up without any modern conveniences, not even electricity, and he remembers going with his mother and little sisters to wash their clothes in the river, as well as those days when there was no food on the table. But he did not feel unfortunate; in fact, he loved his life and the place he lived in. Jindal, however, was one of the few people in his village who could read and write, and due to his intelligence and determination, he was allowed to study in the best schools in the region. One of these schools was a two-hour walk from his home, but Jindal walked to school and back every day. At school Jindal was a quiet leader and extremely successful in his studies, especially in mathematics and the sciences; his teachers trusted him and his classmates wanted his friendship. Despite the difficult conditions of his life, Jindal was a determined student: he completed his studies, was accepted at the best schools, and was finally admitted to one of the best colleges in India, in Kharagpur. He then studied at one of the top universities in the United States, where he received a Ph.D. in nanotechnology.

'In the course of twenty years, I experienced a life that spanned about two centuries on this earth! The sheer spectrum of my life experience in terms of living, education, cross-cultural exposure, and competing at all levels has been incredible. In short, it is almost like I have seen it all. But I did not realize this myself until I started mentoring. It is this huge resource that I draw upon and bring to the table as a mentor,' says Jindal. Almost always optimistic by nature, Jindal says that his optimism, his upbeat mannerisms and his pep talks have a 'lifting' effect on the people he mentors: it raises their spirits and gives them strength when they are feeling down. His pep talks, however, are not just designed to motivate; they are an expression of his strong convictions and spiritual strength.

Jindal's mentorship technique is semi-diagnostic, his thinking is scientific and methodical, and he always tries to bring objectivity to confusing or sticky issues. He usually parameterizes a business problem in order to pinpoint it and thus gain insight into possible paths for its resolution. His method is greatly appreciated by the people he mentors. Jindal sums up his mentorship as follows: 'It has meant giving confidence to the investors, almost as a third party. You must be very attentive to anything your mentees say or even do, be alert and assist them – stimulate their own ideas.'

CASE STUDY 8.2   Consiglio, a mentorship company, Italy

Paterina Cammarata, of Verona, Italy, is the new owner and CEO of Consiglio, a family enterprise that provides counseling and mentoring services for the business sector in Italy. Cammarata took over only nine months prior to the events described below and was still attending counseling sessions with a family-business specialist to ensure the best possible succession; she was also attending courses in mentorship offered by the regional center of entrepreneurship.

Cammarata's parents, Ruth and Claude, founded Consiglio in 1970, shortly after they moved to Rome from London. Her mother is still in charge of some of the business's financing but Claude, who conducted most of the mentorship programs until very recently, was injured in a skiing accident and is unable to continue doing so.

Paterina Cammarata was raised in the family business and earned an MBA from a university in Italy. She worked at Consiglio for more than ten years, mainly in marketing, but also in counseling. In her counseling sessions, she was very structured, well organized and always fully prepared, never depending on luck or intuition. Cammarata, who relies on knowledge and objective information, and has very pragmatic ideas, was highly thought of by her clients.

When Cammarata took over the business, she became its CEO and was unable to continue with the counseling sessions. However, since she loved and was successful in counseling, she decided to replace her father by assuming the responsibility for the mentoring programs. Since most of Consiglio's business consisted of workshops and counseling programs, mentoring enabled her to be hands-on in managing the business and still keep professionally up-to-date.

Consiglio is a highly organized and well-structured company; it has seven different departments, each headed by a director, and staffed by well-trained, professional team members, all very committed to their jobs. Mentoring is the company's main department, and it is headed by Abu Rahim, Consiglio's most senior employee and Claude's best friend. Consiglio is well known in Italy for the high quality of its programs and services – as well as for the high prices it charges for them. Those who attend mentorship programs are mostly CEOs or very high-level managers (middle-level managers are usually directed to the company's counseling programs). The mentoring department functioned very smoothly and was the company's most cost-effective department until Claude's accident; Rahim was responsible for the marketing, and Claude conducted the mentoring sessions.

But, as changes began to occur at Consiglio, Cammarata felt that she did not have Rahim's full cooperation; he was still treating her as a little child and was not willing to accept her professional authority. When Cammarata noted that sales in the mentoring department had declined, Rahim rejected her concerns. He told her that he 'was in the business long before she was born' and that she was not the one to tell him whether the marketing had slowed down in his department. He also reproached her for her 'wrong attitude' toward the active 'mentees' and said that this was probably the reason for the decline in the mentoring department. After hearing this criticism, Cammarata decided to conduct a survey among Consiglio's clients. The results showed very positive attitudes and a high level of satisfaction with Consiglio's professional programs and services, but only moderate satisfaction with its service orientation. She decided to focus on this aspect of the business as the main objective for the coming year.

Cammarata could not figure out why sales in the mentoring department had declined, while in all the other departments they had stayed at the same level or increased. She consulted her father, but he took Rahim's side and was very adamant that she hire an outside specialist for the mentoring activities.

During her search for a mentoring specialist, Cammarata continued to conduct mentoring sessions. One of the people she was mentoring, a manager in one of Italy's most successful food chains, called Cammarata 'my Guru', and another, a well-known ship owner, was cited in an Italian daily newspaper as saying that he 'would not dare to reach any decision prior to hearing my mentor's [Cammarata's] advice'. Paterina Cammarata was neither a role model for these experienced business people nor could she share her entrepreneurial or life experiences with them. She was, however, very strong in providing constructive feedback and was not afraid of confronting the people she was mentoring with the reality of the situation – and she was valued for that. As CEO, Cammarata oversaw all of Consiglio's departments and she tried to solve the mentoring department's problem by moving one of the company's best program developers from counseling to mentoring, but sales continued to decline.Cammarata happened to meet the owner of a chain of drugstores selling natural medicines who had just immigrated to Italy, where he wanted to open several more drugstores. She told him about Consiglio's mentoring programs and he expressed great interest in such guidance as he wanted to facilitate his business activities in what was a new environment for him. A few weeks later, Cammarata discovered that Rahim, to whom she had given the drugstore owner's contact details, had not followed up on contacting him. Unwilling to turn to her parents yet again, or to confront Rahim with this, and tired of the arguments and the negative atmosphere in the mentoring department, she decided to establish a separate marketing path for Consiglio's mentoring activities, without involving Rahim. The new mentoring department began to flourish; applications and sales rose, and the clients were very satisfied.

Cammarata continues to study at the regional center for entrepreneurship. She feels that her professional training and the experience she has gained have raised her mentoring sessions to a much higher level.

QUESTIONS FOR DISCUSSION

1   What are the differences between Rutujit Jindal's and Paterina Cammarata's mentoring approaches?
2   What are the main sources of the differences between Jindal's and Cammarata's mentoring?
3   How did the life experiences of the two mentors affect their approaches to mentoring?
4   Jindal's and Cammarata's approaches to mentoring are very different. Analyze the effects of a conflicted environment and a benign one on a mentor's approach. To what degree, in your opinion, does a mentor's environment influence the effectiveness of the mentoring?
5   What are the pros and cons of being both a CEO and a mentor simultaneously?
6   How would you advise Jindal and Cammarata to continue developing their businesses? Explain.

NOTES

1   Business information centers can be found at different locations: India, www.ediindia.org/itec.asp; the Netherlands, www.nino-leiden.nl/about.aspx; Singapore, www.ace.org.sg/Contact/index.asp; the United States, www.dba.state.va.us/virginia/center/default.asp?SECTION_ID=19; SCORE, counseling to America's small businesses, www.score.org/business_toolbox.html; the worldwide Larta, www.larta.org/governments.asp, and many more.
2   The International Labour Organization, www.ilo.org/public/english/employment/skills/career/index. htm, with categorization by continents and countries.

REFERENCES

Adams, J.S. (1965) 'Inequity in social exchange', in L. Berkowitz (ed.) *Advances in Experimental Social Psychology*, New York: Academic Press, 267–99.

Alsos, G.A. and Kolvereid, L. (1998) 'The business gestation process of novice, serial and parallel business founders', *Entrepreneurship Theory and Practice*, 22: 111–14.

Bard, M. and Moore, E. (2000) 'Mentoring and self-managed learning: professional development for the market research industry', *International Journal of Market Research*, 42: 255–75.

Bechard, J. and Toulouse, J. (1998) 'Validation of a didactic model for the analysis of training objectives in entrepreneurship', *Journal of Business Venturing*, 13: 317–32.

Birley, S. and Westhead, P. (1993) 'A comparison of new businesses established by "novice" and "habitual" founders in Great Britain', *Small Business Journal*, 12: 38–60.

Bonfield, H. (2003) 'Executive coaching is not just for big companies', *British Journal of Administrative Management*, 36: 18–19.

Chrisman, J.J. (1989) 'Strategic, administrative, and operating assistance: the value of outside consulting to pre-venture entrepreneurs', *Journal of Business Venturing*, 4: 401–19.

Chrisman, J.J. and McMullan, E.W. (2000) 'A preliminary assessment of outsider assistance as a knowledge resource: the longer-term impact of new venture counseling', *Entrepreneurship Theory and Practice*, 24: 37–53.

Collin, A. (1979) 'Notes on some typologies of management development and the role of mentors in the process of adaptation of the individual to the organization', *Personnel Review*, 8: 10–14.

De Faoite, D., Henry, C., Johnston, K. and van der Sijde, P. (2004) 'Entrepreneurs' attitudes to training and support initiatives: evidence from Ireland and The Netherlands', *Journal of Small Business and Enterprise Development*, 11: 440–8.

Feldman, D.C. and Lankau, M.J. (2005) 'Executive coaching: a review and agenda for future research', *Journal of Management*, 31: 829–48.

Judge, W.Q. and Cowell, J. (1997) 'The brave new world of executive coaching', *Business Horizons*, 40: 71–7.

Leonard, D. and Swap, W. (2000) 'Gurus in the garage', *Harvard Business Review*, 78: 71–82.

Longenecker, C. and Neubert, M.J. (2005) 'The practices of effective managerial coaches', *Business Horizons*, 48: 493–500.

McMullan, E.W., Chrisman, J.J. and Vesper, K. (2001) 'Some problems in using subjective measures of effectiveness to evaluate entrepreneurial assistance programs', *Entrepreneurship Theory and Practice*, 26: 37–54.

Moberg, D.J. and Velasquez, M. (2004) 'The ethics of mentoring', *Business Ethics Quarterly*, 14: 95–122.

O'Neill, R.M. and Blake-Beard, S.D. (2002) 'Gender barriers to the female mentor–male protege relationship', *Journal of Business Ethics*, 37: 51–64.

Peterman, N.E. and Kennedy, J. (2003) 'Enterprise education: influencing students' perceptions of entrepreneurship', *Entrepreneurship Theory and Practice*, 28: 129–44.

Scherer, R.F., Brodzinski, J.D. and Wiebe, F.A. (1990) 'Entrepreneur career selection and gender: a socialization approach', *Journal of Small Business Management*, 28: 37–44.

Sherman, S. and Freas, A. (2004) 'The wild west of executive coaching', *Harvard Business Review*, 82: 82–90.

Stanworth, J. and Gray, C. (1992) 'Entrepreneurship and education: action-based research with training policy implications in Britain', *International Small Business Journal*, 10: 11–24.

Chapter 9

Planning and managing an entrepreneurial venture

OBJECTIVES

After studying this chapter you will be able to:

- Identify the potential advantages of the planning process for the business's success, competitive advantage and sustainability.
- Assess the traditional written business plan through a different lens and compare it to other planning alternatives; understand that the business plan is not a stand-alone tool and consider the planning alternatives as appropriate options.
- Use the major themes of planning processes to establish and then continually assess the business's goals, communicate the business's goals to the related communities, and lead the business toward achievement of those goals.
- Realize the importance of the value statement, the mission statement and the break-even analysis and trace how these work in the business context.
- Combine 'unusual' processes in planning (e.g., creativity, innovation, intuition and emotion) to gain a more flexible and dynamic business and individual capabilities in the face of a changing environment.

New businesses around the world face a greater chance of failure than of success, yet potential success for such businesses can be angled in the new business's favor with effective planning, adequate capitalization, and effectual management (e.g., clarifying the business goals, setting priorities, ensuring that the relevant information, workforce proficiency, marketing initiatives, etc. fully support the business objectives), among others. Due to the great importance of entrepreneurial businesses to the market, it is of particular interest to identify the factors that contribute to the performance of such firms. Planning may be one of those factors. In fact, planning is inherent to the principles of organization theory, suggesting that planning before taking action improves the quality of business actions, processes and development. Planning is an important precursor to actions mostly because it provides a framework within which subsequent action takes place, thereby facilitating the achievement of goals. It allows the business to speak with 'one voice' so that all of the business's activities are fully integrated and consistent, and it helps unify the employees and strengthen the business's focus on meeting its core objectives (Ansoff 1980; Latham and Locke 1991; Ansoff and Sullivan 1993; Shaw, Brown and Bromiley 1998).

BUSINESS PLANNING AND BUSINESS PERFORMANCE

Detailed planning can benefit those engaged in the development of a new venture in three ways: (1) it allows for faster decision-making by identifying missing information without first requiring the commitment of resources; (2) it provides the tools for managing resource supply and demand in a manner that avoids time-consuming bottlenecks; and (3) it identifies the actions needed to achieve the broader goals in a timely manner, and makes it easier to correct deviations from the stated goals. Strategic planning encompasses numerous key factors for the running of a successful business, including garnering the relevant information, gaining a deeper and broader understanding of the market and the environment, and reducing the uncertainties that inevitably accompany the founding of a business. Most research in entrepreneurship reveals a positive relationship between strategic planning and businesses performance in terms of survival, turnover growth, employment growth, and reputation. The main implications are that planning helps firms identify risks and opportunities in the marketplace and plan for actions in due time, both of which increase the chances of success. There are several planning instruments that are aimed at achieving these goals (Vesper 1980; Ackelsberg and Arlow 1985; Sexton and Van Auken 1985; Perry 2001).

MISSION STATEMENT

A mission statement is defined in entrepreneurship research as the guide to a new firm's current and future goals, its decision-making processes and its mode of operations. The mission statement is considered the basis on which both overall strategy and the more specific functional strategies are built. From the outsiders' point of view, it is a statement of the firm's purpose and its *raison d'être*: it defines the business's present and short-range goals, as well as the firm's aims for the more distant future. A firm's success is often ascribed to the mission statement, and business managers often consider it to be the agent that contributes most to their firm's effectiveness by getting everyone focused on common objectives and pulling together in the same direction.

In order to turn the goals presented in a mission statement into goals shared by all those concerned and affected, it has to be communicated to them. When a firm's core values and its objectives are known and acknowledged, all of those who are involved, directly and indirectly, know what is expected of themselves and of each other. Some mission statements are composed collaboratively and are thus known and acknowledged from the outset. In addition, the teamwork involved in composing them allows everyone to identify with the same goals, promotes conflict reduction, prevents errors, provides feedback on both the internal business processes and external outcomes, and creates a more effective and bonded team.

Rigby (1994) and Abrahams (1999) carried out studies of a large number of mission statements from all over the world (mostly from the United States), and came up with several practical suggestions for how to formulate them.

- Mission statements should focus on five crucial aspects of the firm: people, service, capacity, technology and support systems.
- Mission statements should announce the firm's presence and communicate its purpose to all those related to it in any way (e.g., clients, the community). This can be done through direct

communication (mail, phone, internet), announcements (newspapers, posters in public places), or both. In some organizations, a handsomely printed and framed mission statement is hung on a wall in a central and visible place.

- Mission statements are best drafted collaboratively. When a mission statement is drafted by a team that includes owners, managers and employees, the ideas generated, the viewpoints discussed, and the camaraderie shared during the composition process promote shared expectations and behaviors, as well as emotional commitment (El-Namaki 1992; Collins and Porras 1996; Wickham 1997; O'Gorman and Doran 1999; Talbot 2003; Toftoy and Chatterjee 2004).

VALUE STATEMENT

A mission statement can include or follow a statement of values. Such a statement specifies the ethical and professional principles that the owners and their management teams and employees have in common and will endeavor to put into practice. These values should guide the owners and their teams in how to perform their work cooperatively and ethically. It is important to nurture values that represent the business, its aspirations, and its plans for the future. By reinforcing its key sources of competitive advantage, value statements can pave the way and form a solid basis for the mission statement. Value statements can have various forms, such as codes of conduct or codes of ethics, and they may emphasize corporate philanthropy and corporate citizenship.

In a study on structuring organizational value statements, Wenstøp and Myrmel (2006) identified the six most frequently cited American core values: integrity, honesty, respect, diversity, openness and fairness. The fast-food chain McDonald's, however, focuses on QSCV – quality, service, cleanliness, and value; IBM emphasizes dedication to every client's success – 'It's innovation that matters' – and trust and personal responsibility in all relationships; SAIC, a leading systems, solutions and technical services company, emphasizes technical and professional excellence, customer success, ethics and integrity, entrepreneurial freedom with responsibility, culture of ownership, and importance of the individual (Osborne 1996; Goyder 1999).

Many websites are dedicated to tutoring entrepreneurial businesses in writing a value statement 'that works', and advise entrepreneurs to think about the following questions:

- What need(s) does the firm fulfill?
- What is the firm's revenue model?
- What problem(s) is the firm facing at present?
- How is the firm unique and what is its unique selling proposition?
- What are the firm's economic/financial goals?
- What are its goals vis-à-vis the community?
- What type of company does the entrepreneur visualize and want to create?
- Where is the company going? What products/services/industries do the owners plan to venture into in the future?
- What is the owner's five-year strategy?
- Are there any plans to sell internationally, build an online store, franchise the business, build partnerships, develop additional products, sell the company or go public?
- What is the entrepreneur's exit strategy?

The answers to these questions delineate the nature, social function, competencies, developments and visions of the business.

135

WRITING A MISSION STATEMENT

- List the organization's core competencies, unique strengths and weaknesses.
- List the organization's primary internal and external customers by type and by importance to the firm's sales.
- Review how each customer relates to each of the organization's strengths. If possible, ask them for their opinions.
- Write a one-sentence description of each customer's evaluation and combine any that are essentially the same.
- List the sentences in order of importance to the organization's vision, if one exists.
- Ask your customers if they would want to do business with an organization with that vision.
- Ask your employees if they understand, support, and can act on the mission statement.
- Ask your suppliers if it makes sense to them.
- Incorporate feedback from customers, employees and suppliers.
- Refine all of the information gathered into statements that clearly articulate the company's vision.
- Publish it. Post it in public places. E-mail it to all concerned.

REDEFINING THE FIRM'S GOALS

As entrepreneurial firms develop and grow, and the original and familiar settings change and become irrelevant, the owners may experience 'reality shock'. When this occurs during the startup stages, the entrepreneurs are more tolerant of uncertainties and contingencies and, in fact, have usually taken their potential appearance into account. But when firms are more stabilized, and have established systems and procedures that are functioning well and producing results, reality shock is likely to be both disruptive and obstructive. In such situations, the owners have to reassess and recalculate both their primary goals and their operative functions. Firms tend to change their goals throughout the different stages of their business life and adjust them in light of the changing needs of all those involved with the firm (i.e., clients, owners, partners, investors, suppliers, etc.), and in response to the environment's varying demands (Cunningham and Lischeron 1991; Woo, Cooper and Dunkelberg 1991; Matthews and Dagher 2007).

In order to reassess the firm's situation, the underlying mission statement has to be examined and new goals set in view of this assessment. This is described in Table 9.1.

MAIN THEMES IN BUSINESS PLANNING

Most business researchers and practitioners admit that there is a difference between planning a business and a business plan. During the first stages of a business's creation, entrepreneurs must plan, examine forecasts and set objectives, although these are not necessarily incorporated into a formal and structured business plan. A business plan is only one of a wide range of organizational tools. Entrepreneurs should use the tools that best fit their needs and are user-friendly for them. Some entrepreneurs consider a business plan an overly structured tool that does not suit their entrepreneurial characteristics; others use it as a general outline for their thoughts and ideas but not as a practical tool for their own use; still others consider a business plan an effective tool for certain specific topics (e.g., marketing, pricing), but not for others. Since entrepreneurs are, in

Table 9.1 *Reassessing a firm's operations and setting new goals*

Reassess past performance	Define new goals
Examine the firm's activities in light of results and financial state: are they still relevant?	Adjust the objectives to the changes in available resources and in the environment
Identify the organization's nature: is it the same as originally planned?	Review your statements with others within and outside the firm to assure consistency and mutual support
	Modify your statements to meet changing conditions and priorities
Clarify the organization's declared purpose and goals: are they still being pursued?	Construct an updated rationale for organization design, processes, resources, etc.
	Adapt your objectives directly to these organizational goals and strategic plans
Assemble feedback about goals and actual progress: does the feedback show discrepancies?	Quantify and target the results; goals should always be measured and verified
Examine the standards of assessment of the firm's processes, employees' accomplishments, sales, marketing, advertising, etc.: are they still relevant?	Establish performance reports and milestones that measure progress toward the goals

general, characterized by intuition and spontaneity, along with a proclivity toward unplanned behavior, each has to find and employ the business plan that best suits him or her.

During the first stages of a business's creation, most entrepreneurial firms focus on recognizing and exploiting opportunities and on tools for managing the conditions of high uncertainty and limited information that they often encounter. During the next stages of the entrepreneurial firm's development, when it is functioning in an orderly fashion, the firm needs effective tools for managing such affairs as competition, profits, clients, and so on, and still remain competitive and successful. Each firm has to find the tools that work for it, and adapt them to the specific needs and developmental stage of the business; although different tools (e.g., business plans, gap analyses, financial analyses, benchmarking, etc.) may be needed at different stages, some may be useful or adaptable for other stages.

Business planning is crucial; entrepreneurs should have a good grasp of the workings of the environment and the market; they have to acknowledge the rules of the game and adjust their strategies accordingly. Some entrepreneurs find it easier to plan by discussing their goals with a mentor or counselor rather than by formatting them according to a structured business plan.

The next section deals with the use of business plans in the management of existing firms; it is meant to introduce the entrepreneur to tools that may be very effective when used as the basis for organizing the objectives, resources and results of the firm. For a new or existing business, the business plan is not a stand-alone tool; it has to be used together with other strategic tools such as SWOT analyses, marketing plans, cash flow plans, financial projections, and so on. Most of all, it has to be used creatively and with common sense (Hormozi et al. 2002; Meers and Robertson 2007).

BUSINESS PLANS FOR ESTABLISHED FIRMS

It is not only the cash-starved startups that need business plans; they are useful at all stages of a company's existence. Many business plans are formed by and for companies that are long past the startup stage: they may be valuable tools for established but growing or expanding companies in presenting goals and prospects to potential investors, suppliers, possible customers, and others. Business plans may be needed for any of a variety of reasons (e.g., to guide a firm's management and staff in carrying out new projects; to guide retailers weighing the prospects of mergers; to manage mergers; to deal with rapid growth; to set priorities when planning changes; to capture new clients; to deal with difficulties and contingencies).

Business plans may be helpful in getting debt or equity financing; in promoting relationships with joint venture partners and large customers, suppliers, and distributors; for providing strategic guidance, operating tactics and objectives; for furnishing a standard against which to judge future business decisions and results; for evaluating strengths and weaknesses and identifying viable alternative strategies; for establishing the operational and financial structure of a management buy-out. The reasons for forming or updating business plans are also diverse: a new financial situation relevant to the company; significant changes in the market, such as shifting client tastes, changes in regulations, fluctuations in the purchasing climate; development of new products, technologies or services; changes in management; structural changes in the company due to rapid growth; a successful exit, etc. Put differently, a business plan can be used as a map that suits the needs of any firm, at any stage, under any situations encountered, and for any player involved in the firm.

Researchers in the field of entrepreneurship stress the importance of an effective business plan to a firm's performance. An effective plan organizes the firm's goals and objectives, its equipment and other assets in an optimally efficient configuration to improve operations and to achieve the firm's goal(s). Some researchers regard effective business plans as the difference between success and failure (Delmar and Shane 2003; Wright et al. 2004).

There are many types of business plans, and they can differ widely in length and appearance, in the details that are dealt with, and in the emphases they place on different aspects of the business. All, however, tend to have a large number of elements in common, some of which appear in virtually all business plans and in business planning in general:

- *Milestones* – deadlines and budgets set for completing specific actions, in order to track and measure both past and future conformity to the plan.
- *Cash flow analysis* – sources and amounts of past and projected financing, past and projected monthly expenses and revenues.
- *Priorities* – ongoing and planned projects and activities are weighted for their degree of importance and urgency, in order to ensure that the most pressing ones are dealt with first, and the less exigent ones deferred.

Examples of a firm's priorities in terms of importance and urgency are shown in Table 9.2.

A promising way to begin constructing a business plan is through a deep analysis of the company from both inner and outer perspectives. A comprehensive strategic planning tool for this purpose is the SWOT analysis, which is used to pull back the curtain and see what may lie behind it. SWOT stands for *strengths*, *weaknesses*, *opportunities* and *threats*: strengths and weaknesses often relate to internal factors dealing with core competencies and resources that are under the firm's control; opportunities and threats are often external factors that are beyond the firm's immediate control. SWOT analysis helps categorize these factors by asking pertinent questions about the firm's performance and its environment.

Table 9.2 *Importance and urgency matrix*

	Urgent	Not urgent
Important	A *Important/Urgent* Deadline-driven tasks Daily chores Demanding problems Crisis management Delayed field operations Daily care of livestock Last-minute financing Last-minute repairs Paying past-due bills	B *Important/Not urgent* Preparation and planning Crisis prevention Deadline-avoiding activities Timely field operations Work with consultants Marketing Skills improvement
Not important	C *Not important/Urgent* Interruptions Minor pressing tasks Certain phone calls Certain meetings Certain mail Certain salespeople Certain repairs and clean-up	D *Not important/Not urgent* Likable things, but not necessary for the company Time wasters Junk mail Many phone calls

Strengths (internal):
- What does the company do well?
- What are its assets?
- What advantages does the company have over its competitors?

Weaknesses (internal):
- Why is the company for sale?
- What is being done badly?
- Why is it losing money?
- How might a change in ownership affect the staff?

Opportunities (external):
- What have the competitors missed?
- What are the emerging needs of the customers?
- What can this company do better?

Threats (external):
- Are the company's competitors getting stronger?
- Will a change of ownership be perceived negatively by vendors and customers?
- Does the company have cash to fund research and development?
- Will it be possible to retain key employees after the sale?

Examples of SWOT analyses can be accessed at: Bplans.com;[1] Smart Draw;[2] Startups,[3] and many other websites.

BREAK-EVEN ANALYSIS

There are several different ways of calculating break-even points, but certain core elements must be included in all such analyses. To compare the business's costs and revenues, the owner has to make accurate forecasts of all costs and sales. There are both *fixed* and *variable* costs.

- *Fixed costs* are those not directly related to the level of production or output; they are the same regardless of production, levels of efficiency and sales. They include startup costs such as machinery, equipment and furniture, rent, insurance, technology, administration expenses, and R&D. Fixed costs may change with time, for example, as a result of R&D. Therefore, costs should be reassessed from time to time in order to form the most accurate financial analysis in the future.
- *Variable costs* fluctuate according to the level of production. They include output-related inputs such as raw materials, direct labor, fuel, and revenue-related costs such as commissions. There are three kinds of variable costs: *direct*, *indirect*, and *semi-variable*.
    - Direct variable costs are those that are directly attributed to the production costs of a particular product or service. Raw materials and the wages of those working on the production line are examples of direct variable costs.
- *Indirect variable costs* are not directly attributable to production but do fluctuate with output. These include depreciation (e.g., machine hours), maintenance and certain labor costs.
- *Semi-variable costs* are largely related to the overall scale and complexity of the business. For example, when a business has relatively low levels of output and/or sales, it may not have costs associated with HR management or a fully resourced finance department. However, as the scale of the business grows, for example, in output, number of people employed, and number and complexity of transactions, more resources are required. If production rises suddenly then some short-term increase in warehousing and/or transport may be required. Under these circumstances, we say that part of the cost is variable and part fixed (Welsh and White 1981; Zacharakis 1997; Ho and Wong 2007).

SETTING PRICES

When setting prices, the entrepreneur has to differentiate between the prices for items bought in bulk and those bought as single units. Prices are usually set according to a 'cost-based pricing' formula that calculates cost per unit, and setting the price as that amount plus a predetermined profit margin. This approach is considered risky since it allows competitors who can make the product at lower cost to easily undercut this price. The entrepreneur also has to determine how many units have to be sold to meet a profit goal by using cost-based pricing. Sometimes there are considerations for setting prices other than those based only on costs (Bond 1986; Ballantine, Cleveland and Koeller 1993; Baker, Marn and Zawada 2001).

Business owners should be familiar with the different techniques for calculating prices:

- *Premium pricing* – setting a high price that implies exclusivity of the products/services, and is useful where a serious competitive advantage exists.
- *Penetration pricing* – setting a low price in order to gain entry to the market; once this is achieved, a different pricing method is used.

- *Psychological pricing* – addresses the customer's reactive rather than rational decision-making; e.g., most customers perceive $4.99 as in the '$4 range' rather than in the '$5 range'.
- *Promotional pricing* – a very attractive, particularly low price, often an 'introductory' one, is offered.
- *Product-line pricing* – in assembly-line types of services, such as a car-wash or a self-service cafeteria, the prices reflect the benefits of non-individualized service.
- *Geographical pricing* – different prices in different parts of the country, according to external, environmental factors that affect the purchasing power of the general population of the area.

WHAT SHOULD ENTREPRENEURS LOOK FOR?

Planning is beneficial for entrepreneurs in several respects, especially in that it minimizes the initial time-consuming process of deciding how and where to allocate their available resources, and does so without losing sight of the goals established in the original plan. Figure 9.1 illustrates the main themes that entrepreneurs have to consider in order to collocate their goals in a systematic way, and to avoid being sidetracked by other activities that may interfere with achieving those goals. Suggestions for doing so are also listed in the diagram (Armstrong 1982; Robinson 1984; Shrader, Mulford and Blackburn 1989; Ansoff 1991).

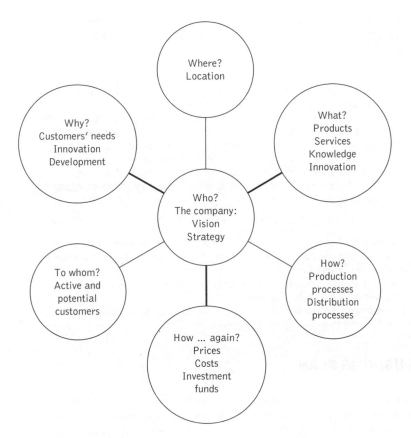

Figure 9.1 *The main themes in planning*

The main themes, with the associated issues to consider, may be listed as follows.

Main themes	Matters and questions to consider
Company Who are we?	Consider the business strategy for creating a legal entity. How will the initial ownership be divided among founders? What is the history and past performance of the business?
Product What are we selling?	What products and/or services does the business offer? Why should people buy these products/services? What are the benefits of these products/services? How much will it cost to deliver these products?
Process How are we selling it?	Focus on certain target market segments, certain products or services, and specific distribution avenues. Forecast the company's sales and the cost of sales – through experience, by asking people, reading documents and market analyses, using intuition, etc.
Customers Who are we selling to?	Who are the main and peripheral targeted clients? What are the market's characteristic needs and trends? What is the nature of the business's industry? What and how much competition does the business face? (Some entrepreneurs include measures and figures that allow for a market forecast.)
Distribution How do our products/ services reach the customers?	How will the business's products/services reach the customers: website, postal service, sales representatives, retail sales, etc.? What kind of distribution channel should be used: direct distribution channel – from manufacturer to consumer, one-stage distribution channel – from manufacturer to retailer to consumer, traditional distribution channel – from manufacturer to wholesaler to retailer to consumer? Outline the various companies, people, or technologies that will be involved in the process of getting the product or service to the company's customers.
Financing What are the set-up costs, and investments?	Describe the financial strategy and how it supports the company's projected growth. Some entrepreneurs find it useful to include analyses that show risk as a matter of fixed versus variable costs. Calculate the break-even point – when the company's total in sales or revenues equals its total expenses. Think about: projected profit or loss; cash flow; balance sheets.

TWO TYPES OF BUSINESS PLAN

- *The miniplan.* A miniplan is a useful tool during the first stages of a business. It may be used to quickly test a business's concept or to measure the interest of a potential partner or minor investor. It usually consists of a few pages that briefly describe the concept, financing needs, marketing plan and financial statements, projected income and cash flow.

■ *The working plan.* A working plan serves an entrepreneurial company during the more advanced stages of its establishment. It is a detailed document containing adequate and reliable data, facts and figures, and is a necessary tool for the staff responsible for managing the company's business. A working plan may also serve as the basis of plans for the company's activities and may very easily be turned into a presentation of the vision and future plans for investors, potential partners, potential franchisors, etc.

The main factors to be dealt with when constructing a business plan were described above. The items below comprise a checklist of the subjects to be dealt with in the business plan; the amount of attention given to each topic is dependent on the type and scope of the business and on the character and objectives of each individual entrepreneur (Fry and Stoner 1985; Sahlman 1997).

ELEMENTS OF A BUSINESS PLAN

■ Executive summary.
■ Introduction to the company: major events, resumes of key persons, financial history, major customers, principal suppliers, insurance policies, bank documents, etc.
■ Vision.
■ Main products and/or services.
■ Marketing strategies: sales goals, public relations, economic and industry environments, customer profiles, trends, marketing channels, sales tactics, pricing, etc.
■ Competitors and competitive advantages and weaknesses.
■ Development plan.
■ Operations and management plan: advisory and management teams, support structures, human resources, policies, standard operating procedures, etc.
■ Financial plan: revenue projections, break-even analysis, credit, cash flow projection, balance sheet projection, insurance, taxes, etc.
■ Future plans: growth/expansion plans, investment funds needed, detailed budget, repayment options, etc.

REFLECTIONS ON THE PLANNING PROCESS: A NEW PERSPECTIVE ON BUSINESS PLANS

Confucius, a Chinese philosopher who has deeply influenced Asians' thinking and way of life (206 BCE–220 CE), has been quoted as saying: 'When it is obvious that the goals cannot be reached, don't adjust the goals, adjust the action steps.' In line with this philosophy, planning via a structured, rigid business plan means restricting the business's operation to a pre-planned path. A burgeoning group of researchers, including Louis Jacques Filion and Claude Ananau (2009), have criticized the concept of a traditional business plan by stressing that it exposes the business to potential risk: the business is expected to follow the action plan that has been written in advance while it faces a different 'reality' (e.g., environment, clients, investors, competitors, etc.) that may differ, sometimes contradict, the 'reality' addressed in the written business plan. Clients' and users' interests and tastes may change over time or under new circumstances; new competitors may emerge; investors may become interested in different undertakings, and global economic situations often fluctuate. Therefore, any assumptions made in the business plan about 'reality' risks being misleading for business operations.

A different set of plans needs to be considered, one that can be established in a changing, dynamic world, rather than basing the business operations and processes on a traditional business plan. Confucius was further quoted as saying: 'There are three methods to gaining wisdom. The first is reflection, which is the highest. The second is limitation, which is the easiest. The third is experience, which is the bitterest.' This quote indicates how the planning process for an entrepreneurial business should be developed. Setting up limitations, a set of 'dos and don'ts', is the easiest way to plan and subsequently manage a business; however, a business based on such limitations may not necessarily grow or be sustainable. In fact, studies continually show that basing a business's actions on mainly avoiding things that are 'beyond its scope' may help manage the business in the short term but not in the long run. As such, planning by limitation may provide the business with short-term survival by following a written plan that addresses very specific circumstances of a very specific 'reality', but when 'reality' changes, the business plan becomes obsolete.

Reflection, on the other hand, is the highest level of thinking according to Confucius, and thus of planning. Using a reflective process means planning by cognitively confronting different, alternative situations; honing in on the challenges and hindrances the business may encounter; questioning what has already been achieved in the business; analyzing and learning from that which was not successful at accomplishing the goals, and looking at the situation with a different lens. Reflective processes force entrepreneurs to tackle ambiguity and uncertainty in the planning phase, thereby training and equipping them to effectively cope with uncertain situations that may be encountered in the future.

Unlike traditional business plans, a reflective process allows planning by thinking, observing and learning on an ongoing basis rather than following instructions written in a business plan. Reflection in planning provides the freedom to decide differently at any time or stage, instead of compelling the business to 'fit' the written plan. Typical written business plans are not sufficiently adapted to the contingencies that characterize the startup phase and do not, therefore, address different possible scenarios for the business, nor do they provide alternative tools for coping with various difficulties that may confront the business. They lack the dynamic spirit and vibrant action that typifies entrepreneurial businesses, more closely resembling a case study scenario, as they essentially concentrate on a main situation with few alternative forecasted situations, and develop action plans around these. Thus traditional business plans give entrepreneurs the illusion that 'everything is under control': entrepreneurs do not see the value of developing alternative tools, means and thinking strategies to cope with unexpected situations. In this sense, business plans are easier to follow. Once the business plan is written, it reduces the entrepreneur's responsibility in terms of continually rethinking, reconsidering and reassessing the business's activity. At the stages at which business plans are developed and written, entrepreneurs are usually deeply involved in launching and managing their startups, and lack the time to rethink the processes that their business is going through. A written business plan pretends to encompass whole activities and scenarios, thus giving the entrepreneur the needed 'quiet' to focus on real things. However, the reflective planning processes actually give the entrepreneurs the needed 'quiet' by empowering them and bolstering their self-confidence and by facilitating the crafting of their own ways of achieving their goals, even when environments and markets change.

Business plans and the dynamic environment

Turbulent and dynamic environments force businesses to constantly re-examine their playing fields; businesses regularly strive to maintain a competitive advantage in new playing fields.

A new playing field exposes the business: its services, goods, information, customer service and other processes become transparent to actual and potential clients, investors, competitors and suppliers via the internet and benchmarking, data-mining business-based companies, etc. Basing its planning on a rigid business plan means restricting the business's ability to adjust to the changing, dynamic environment, and risking stagnation; and by virtue of this transparency, everyone will know about it.

Business plans do not do a good job of addressing contingencies: when writing a business plan, it is impossible to predict the many kinds of potential barriers that the business may face in the future. Business plans do not tell the entrepreneur how to fix the business if something goes wrong: under unexpected circumstances, entrepreneurs have to rely on their intuition, 'feelings' and 'senses' to cope with these unforeseen difficulties. Since the environment – the playing field – of entrepreneurial businesses is unpredictable and ambiguous, while the business plan deems it to be stable, a rigid business plan is futile for entrepreneurial businesses. Entrepreneurs should revitalize the use of reflection, learning from experience and employing their intuition in order to create a relevant planning process for their business.

Business plans and entrepreneurial characteristics

Entrepreneurs are characterized as innovators, creative, intuitive and proactive beings who possess a risk-taking spirit. Many studies show that entrepreneurs are restless: they experience constant inconveniences which trigger their entrepreneurial action. These studies state that in fact, when individuals are in a 'comfortable phase', they may be less enthused and stimulated by things around them; their creative and proactive activity may decline. It is common knowledge that individuals tend not to attempt change in a comfortable and familiar environment.

The traditional written business plan provides the illusion that the business is sitting on stable ground, thus leaving limited space for risk-taking or for searching for creative solutions to cope with the unknown. As such, the trigger for an entrepreneurial action – the uncomfortable phase – diminishes. Entrepreneurs are no longer expected to employ creativity or proactivity or take risks, which means that their most significant strengths are no longer relevant under the restrictions of a rigid business plan (Biggadike 1979; Hoy and Carland 1983; Begley and Boyd 1987; McClelland 1987; Bird 1989; Shane, Locke and Collins 2003).

In addition, a traditional business plan gives entrepreneurs a process that they may find difficult to follow. Many entrepreneurs have admitted to writing a business plan but not acting accordingly, because they are unable to follow rigid, well-planned instructions. Most of them are more free-minded, open to experiences and resentful of planned actions (Ahmed 1985; Allinson, Chell and Hayes 2000; Hisrich, Langan-Fox and Grant 2007; Chell 2008; Gupta and Fernandez 2009; Zhao, Seibert and Lumpkin 2010).

An efficient business plan should allow for more flexibility and room for adjustment, in line with the entrepreneurial characteristics and spirit. Entrepreneurs need to plan by reflecting, thinking, doubting 'reality', experiencing trial-and-error situations, and learning from their experiences. Entrepreneurs are usually impassioned by such challenges, and these types of planning processes suit their qualities and personality.

Generation Y. Born between 1982 and 1995, this is the cohort of the population filling the labor market today. 'Generation Y-ers' make up about 25 per cent of the US population and in some countries this percentage is even higher. In contrast to their precedents, the Baby Boomers and Generation X-ers, Generation Y-ers appreciate a work–life balance, leisure time and being their own boss. They therefore thrive in a workplace that is flexible and informal and offers freedom from rules, workplace regulations, work hours, etc. They are typified as being more independent, self-motivated and self-sufficient than the former generations: they ultimately expect work to be fun (Howe and Strauss 1992; Krug 1998; Kupperschmidt 2000; Zemke, Raines and Filipczak

2000; Karp, Fuller and Sirias 2002; Lancaster and Stillman 2002; Raines 2003; Davis, Pawloski and Houston 2006; Tulgan 2006; Zaslow 2006; Seaton and Boyd 2007; Cennamo and Gardner 2008; Gursoy, Maier and Chi 2008; Kariv, Filion and Borges 2010).

There is a real mismatch between what the young generation wants and what business plans can offer. In their study on Generation Y, Ananou and Masson (2009) constructed a grid showing this generation's major characteristics and work-related preferences in relation to the main entrepreneurial business characteristics in the twenty-first century. The authors showed that teamwork, being a citizen of the world, cultivating knowledge and mind, and protecting one's independence are the most important characteristics for the Generation Y entrepreneurs and that these characteristics suit twenty-first-century business characteristics – flexibility, innovation, a nonconformist structure and user-friendliness. The authors concluded by suggesting that planning should be effected by innovative and creative tools and concepts, and that the concept of the traditional written business plan, based on a stable and predictable environment, should be revised.

Planning should facilitate the entrepreneur's launching process and subsequent business activities and practices. Planning should be crafted around the strengths of today's entrepreneurs by stimulating their intuition, creativity and open-minded thinking.

FINALIZING THE PLANNING PROCESS: THE STRATEGIC PLAN

After all of the relevant information has been amassed and thoroughly considered, and combined with a realistic understanding of the company's strengths and weaknesses, the entrepreneur should develop a *strategic plan*. This plan addresses the entrepreneur's decision to enter the market, and deals with how to do so successfully. He or she may decide to compete head-on with other businesses in the best markets; target a market as yet untouched by competitors; or search for different favorable opportunities in other countries. Since finalizing the business plan entails identifying several alternative approaches, when other opportunities arise, or problems occur, various options will be readily available; the advantages, disadvantages and overall chances of success that have been listed for each alternative will enable settling on a plan with the greatest potential for success.

Guidance in forming a business plan can be obtained by attending courses offered by government agencies, state commerce departments or private organizations, or by taking part in a network and asking for assistance. Self-study software and books, many of which contain models of business plans, may be referred to. Additional examples can be found on the web at: businessknowhow,[4] morebusiness,[5] startupventuretoolbox,[6] and vfinance.[7]

Guidance and assistance can also be obtained by hiring a specialized consultant. When this avenue is chosen, certain documents will have to be prepared and presented to the consultant (Reid 1990; Pine and Gilmore 1998; Lim, Lee and Tan 2001). Most of these are listed below:

- *Personal résumés:* work history, educational background, professional affiliations and honorary memberships, special skills.
- *Financial statements:* personal assets and liabilities.
- *Credit reports:* business and personal reports from suppliers or wholesalers, credit bureaus and banks.
- *Copies of leases:* all agreements currently in force between your company and a leasing agency.
- *References:* letters of recommendation attesting to the firm's reliability and reputation, and to its being worthy of being considered a good risk.
- *Contracts:* all business contracts, both current and terminated.

■ *Legal documents:* all legal papers pertaining to the firm's legal structure, proprietary rights, insurance titles, etc.

PLANNING BY 'IPA' – AN ALTERNATIVE APPROACH

Revising the concept of business plans does not imply totally discarding the planning process, which may serve as a basis for the organizational and industry-related actions in some businesses. Revising the concept means considering, in addition to or instead of the traditional written business plan, other possible means of planning and simulating potential pitfalls and the business's consequent responses. It also means considering planning in different phases, in contrast to traditional business plans, by reconsidering (1) the input, e.g., the business's capabilities, expertise, entrepreneur's characteristics, and the environment in which the business exists; (2) the planning process – questioning, reflecting and rethinking, and learning from experience, and (3) the action plans.

By accepting a planning process that is intentionally incomplete and leaves room for adjustment and reconsideration, creative and innovative initiatives find a place in the business and the 'inconveniences' that stimulate creativity, proactivity and risk-taking return to the entrepreneurial undertaking.

Figure 9.2 demonstrates an alternative model for planning, according to the Input–Planning process–Action plan (IPA).

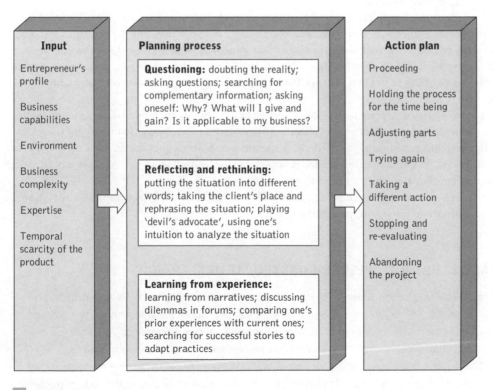

Figure 9.2 *The IPA planning process*

SUMMARY

Although controversial in research and practice, many practitioners perceive planning as fundamental and crucial to an entrepreneurial business's effective management and to performance that has a significant impact on the business's sustainability. Some consider it the backbone of the business's success, as it assists in organizing the business's goals, objectives, tangible and intangible resources and assets in an optimally efficient configuration. Such planning enables the entrepreneur to construct realistic business goals and develop effective processes to achieve those goals.

Yet, some other researchers and entrepreneurs consider intuition rather than planning to be most important in achieving business success. According to the research, a limited number of entrepreneurial businesses craft and implement formal business plans; some craft such plans but then quickly abandon them. Thus planning should take different forms, enabling entrepreneurs to pick those forms that best match their business goals, as well as their business routines. Engaging in a rigid business plan while the business is unprepared may be a waste of time and money and most frustrating for the entrepreneur, while crafting an intuitive plan for a business that needs to stabilize its activities may also be unsuitable and discouraging. Planning should therefore match the business's and entrepreneur's inputs.

Practical, but also flexible planning tools are recommended when a business is starting from scratch, in times of crisis or when the business needs to change, adjust or eliminate some of its practices, i.e., at its turning points. While not rigid or inflexible, planning can be a useful tool to overcome such complex situations. In times of ambiguity or very rapid environmental changes, planning may be the secure and stable anchor, by directing the entrepreneur toward the goals he or she is attempting to achieve.

By encouraging a reflective, intuitive outlook in the planning realm, entrepreneurs will not only be able to follow their planning processes, because these will better suit their own intuitive spirit, but they will also profit from being more qualified at handling the unexpected situations encountered by their business. An IPA model exemplifies how entrepreneurs can plan by using an ongoing reflective process that sharpens their responsiveness to any unforeseen situations.

In a nutshell, business plans may typically consist of documents containing data, facts and figures on the business, but also of intuitive, reflective processes that foster questioning, rephrasing ideas or learning from testimonials and others' experiences. A strategic plan focuses on successful penetration into a competitive market and is imperative for the business's performance and success, and in determining the firm's competitive advantage.

In research, planning has been proven to be effective, but it should be accompanied by common sense and intuition in the entrepreneurial realm.

CASE STUDY 9.1   NEIGER-CONSTRUCTEURS, FRANCE

Rita, Eliane and Jerome Neiger are two sisters and a brother living in a rural area near Nancy, in France. As children, they worked on their parents' large farm, but they went on to study and all three became university graduates. Both Eliane and Jerome are married, and each has two children. Until November 2002, they worked as employees in their chosen professions.

Shortly before Christmas 2001, Rita, an aviation engineer, was informed that due to personnel changes in her company she would be dismissed. She loved her work but, unable to find another suitable position in her region, she accepted a job offer from a Romanian entrepreneur, a builder who worked half of each month in France and half in Romania. Since the job entailed working half of each month in Romania, her family encouraged her to search for other opportunities in the region. After being jobless for a long time, Rita decided to take the offer. She had to learn about building materials, and construction equipment and procedures, since her engineering experience had been in aviation, but she acquired the relevant knowledge easily and relatively quickly. She worked long hours and blogged many professional web-related networks not only to expand her knowledge in the field, but also to build a relevant professional network. Rita adjusted very quickly and successfully to the job, which she found to be very fulfilling, and the owner of the company was very satisfied with her work.

Some months later Jerome had to leave his job as well, and since he had previously worked in construction, he suggested that he and Rita launch their own business in this field. Although Rita loved her job, she was exhausted from the traveling and decided to be a partner in her brother's business. Eliane left her job as a teacher and joined her siblings as third partner.

Neiger-Constructeurs was launched in November 2002. Their first client, who was familiar with Rita's capabilities from her previous job, wanted to carry out extensive construction work in a new neighborhood in Nancy. The founders felt they had made a great start, but as they were about to complete their only construction job for their only client, and although their work was to the client's complete satisfaction, no other clients had appeared.

None of the three knew anything about marketing, promotion or advertising; they had expected that word-of-mouth reports in their area would bring jobs, but this was not happening. Rita and Eliane attended a business planning course and adopted several points they learned there, which turned out to be very beneficial for their business in the long run. They soon realized that most of the people in the largely rural area near Nancy were not the customers Neiger-Constructeurs was looking for, and their first structured step was to design their target market. They consulted Rita's former employer and some of his clients, as well as bloggers on construction websites, all of whom advised them not only to concentrate on building for businesses rather than for private clients, but to focus on small businesses, as the big ones usually engaged large and well-known construction companies. The second step was to segment their services; they decided to concentrate on prefabricated construction, a technology that was used mostly for mini-storage buildings and steel self-storage units. Rita, who is very organized, set milestones, defined each of the co-founders' responsibilities, and specified the company's budget limits.

When advertising in the newspaper, on flyers in people's mailboxes and in jingles on the radio failed to bring the hoped-for results, the Neigers decided to advertise and brand their business through professional websites. This was successful, and they now have several clients and a number of others who are interested. Their construction business is not yet stable, and is far from the break-even point, but the co-founders are determined to continue with Neiger-Constructeurs's activities. They are confident that they will succeed.

QUESTIONS FOR DISCUSSION

1 Identify the wrong steps taken by the Neigers in the first stages of their venture creation.
2 How did being an employee in a company prior to launching their own business affect the Neigers' first steps as business owners?
3 Identify the main themes of the business plan that the Neigers implemented after attending a business planning course. How did this promote Neiger-Constructeurs?
4 Outline a miniplan for Neiger-Constructeurs that can facilitate the stabilization of their business.

NOTES

1 At www.bplans.com/ma/swotanalysis.cfm.
2 At www.smartdraw.com/examples/view/index.aspx?catID=.Examples.SmartDraw.Marketing_Charts.SWOT_Analysis_Diagrams.
3 At www.startups.co.uk/SWOT_analysis.YV9tqyc.html.
4 At www.businessknowhow.com/Startup/businessplanning.htm.
5 At www.morebusiness.com/templates_worksheets/bplans/amt2.brc.
6 At www.startupventuretoolbox.com/Business%20Plan%20Advisor.htm.
7 At www.vfinance.com/.

REFERENCES

Abrahams, J. (1999) *The Mission Statement Book: 301 Corporate Mission Statements from America's Top Companies*, Berkeley, CA: Ten Speed Press.

Ackelsberg, R. and Arlow, P. (1985) 'Small businesses do plan and it pays off', *Long Range Planning*, 18: 61–7.

Ahmed, S.U. (1985) 'nAch, risk-taking propensity, locus of control and entrepreneurship', *Personality and Individual Differences*, 6: 781–2.

Allinson, C.W., Chell, E. and Hayes, J. (2000) 'Intuition and entrepreneurial behaviour', *European Journal of Work and Organizational Psychology*, 9: 31–43.

Ananau, C. and Masson, M.A. (2009) 'La génération Y et l'entrepreneuriat', in L.J. Filion and C. Ananou (eds) *De l'intuition au projet d'entreprise*, Montréal: HEC Montréal Presses, 209–25.

Ansoff, H.I. (1980) 'Strategic issue management', *Strategic Management Journal*, 1: 131–48.

Ansoff, H.I. (1991) 'Critique of Henry Mintzberg's "The design school": reconsider the basic premises of strategic management', *Strategic Management Journal*, 12: 449–62.

Ansoff, H.I. and Sullivan, P.A. (1993) 'Empirical support for a paradigmic theory of strategic success behaviors of environment serving organizations', *International Review of Strategic Management*, 4: 173–204.

Armstrong, S.J. (1982) 'The value of formal planning for strategic decisions: review of empirical research', *Strategic Management Journal*, 3: 197–212.

Baker, W.E., Marn, M. and Zawada, C. (2001) 'Price smarter on the net', *Harvard Business Review*, 79: 122–7.

Ballantine, J.W., Cleveland, F.W. and Koeller, C.T. (1993) 'Profitability, uncertainty, and firm size', *Small Business Economics*, 5: 87–101.

Begley, T.M. and Boyd, D.P. (1987) 'Psychological characteristics associated with performance in entrepreneurial firms and smaller businesses', *Journal of Business Venturing*, 2: 79–93.

Biggadike, R. (1979) 'The risky business of diversification: a bold approach can make all the difference in new ventures', *Harvard Business Review*, 57: 103–11.

Bird, B.J. (1989) *Entrepreneurial Behavior*, Glenview, IL: Scott, Foresman and Company.

Bond, E.W. (1986) 'Entrepreneurial ability, income distribution, and international trade', *Journal of International Economics*, 20: 343–57.

Cennamo, L. and Gardner, D. (2008) 'Generational differences in work values, outcomes and person-organisation values fit', *Journal of Managerial Psychology*, 23: 891.

Chell, E. (2008) *The Entrepreneurial Personality: A Social Construction*, 2nd edn, New York: Taylor & Francis.

Collins, J.C. and Porras, J.I. (1996) 'Building your company's vision', *Harvard Business Review*, 74: 65–78.

Cunningham, J.B. and Lischeron, J. (1991) 'Defining entrepreneurship', *Journal of Small Business Management*, 29: 45–62.

Davis, J., Pawloski, S. and Houston, A. (2006) 'Work commitments of baby boomers and gen-exers in the IT profession: general differences or myth?', *Journal of Computer Information Systems*, spring: 43–9.

Delmar, F. and Shane, S.A. (2003) 'Does business planning facilitate the development of new ventures?', *Strategic Management Journal*, 24: 1165–85.

El-Namaki, M.S. (1992) 'Creating a corporate vision', *Long Range Planning*, 25: 25–30.

Filion, L.J. and Ananaou, C. (2009) *De L'intuition au projet d'entreprise – Une nouvelle approche pour la conception de projets d'affaire*, Montreal: HEC Montreal Presses.

Fry, F.L. and Stoner, C.R. (1985) 'Business plans: two major types', *Journal of Small Business Management*, 23: 1–7.

Goyder, M. (1999) 'Value and values: lessons for tomorrow's company', *Long Range Planning*, 32: 217–24.

Gupta, V. and Fernandez, C. (2009) 'Cross-cultural similarities and differences in characteristics attributed to entrepreneurs: a three-nation study', *Journal of Leadership and Organizational Studies*, 15: 304–18.

Gursoy, D., Maier, T.A. and Chi, C.G. (2008) 'Generational differences: an examination of work values and generational gaps in the hospitality work force', *International Journal of Hospitality Management*, 27: 448–58.

Hisrich, R., Langan-Fox, J. and Grant, S. (2007) 'Entrepreneurship research and practice: a call to action for psychology', *American Psychologist*, 62: 575–89.

Ho, Y.P. and Wong, P.K. (2007) 'Financing, regulatory costs and entrepreneurial propensity', *Small Business Economics*, 28: 187–205.

Hormozi, A.M., Sutton, G.S., McMinn, R.D. and Lucio, W. (2002) 'Business plans for new or small businesses: paving the path to success', *Management Decision*, 40: 755–63.

Howe, N. and Strauss, W. (1992) *Generations: The History of America's Future, 1584 to 2069*, New York: Harper Perennial.

Hoy, F. and Carland, J.W. (1983) 'Differentiating between entrepreneurs and small business owners in new venture formation', in J.A. Hornaday, J.A. Timmons and K.H. Vesper (eds) *Frontiers of Entrepreneurship Research*, Wellesley, MA: Babson Center for Entrepreneurial Studies, 180–91.

Kariv, D., Filion, L.J. and Borges, C. (2010) 'Emerging strategies and generation gaps among entrepreneurs: differences between baby boomers and generation x', Paper presented at 2010 BCERC Babson College Entrepreneurship Research Conference, Lausanne, Switzerland, 9–12 June 2010.

Karp, H., Fuller, C. and Sirias, D. (2002) *Bridging the Boomer Xer Gap*, Palo Alto, CA: Davies-Black.

Krug, J. (1998) 'Understanding Generation X', *Journal of Management in Engineering*, 14: 18–19.

Kupperschmidt, B. (2000) 'Multigeneration employees: strategies for effective management', *Health Care Manager*, 19: 65–76.

151

Lancaster, L.C. and Stillman, D. (2002) *When Generations Collide: Who They Are. Why They Clash. How to Solve the Generational Puzzle at Work*, New York: HarperBusiness.

Latham, G.P. and Locke, E.A. (1991) 'Self-regulation through goal setting', *Organizational Behavior and Human Decision Processes*, 50: 212–48.

Lim, G.H., Lee, K.S. and Tan, S.J. (2001) 'Gray marketing as an alternative market penetration strategy for entrepreneurs: conceptual model and case evidence', *Journal of Business Venturing*, 16: 405–27.

Matthews, S.W. and Dagher, G.K. (2007) 'Need for achievement, business goals, and entrepreneurial persistence', *Management Research News*, 30: 928–41.

McClelland, D.C. (1987) 'Characteristics of successful entrepreneurs', *Journal of Creative Behavior*, 21: 219–33.

Meers, K.A. and Robertson, C. (2007) 'Strategic planning practices in profitable small firms in the United States', *Business Review, Cambridge*, 7: 302–8.

O'Gorman, C. and Doran, R. (1999) 'Mission statements in small and medium-sized businesses', *Journal of Small Business Management*, 37: 59–66.

Osborne, R.L. (1996) 'Strategic values: the corporate performance engine', *Business Horizons*, 39: 41–7.

Perry, S.C. (2001) 'The relationship between written business plans and the failure of small businesses in the US', *Journal of Small Business Management*, 39: 201–8.

Pine, B.J. and Gilmore, J.H. (1998) 'Welcome to the experience economy', *Harvard Business Review*, 76: 97–106.

Raines, C. (2003) *Connecting Generations: The Sourcebook for a New Workplace*, Menlo Park, CA: Crisp Publications.

Reid, D.M. (1990) 'Where planning fails in practice', *Long Range Planning*, 23: 85–94.

Rigby, D.K. (1994) 'Managing the management tools', *Planning Review*, 22: 20–5.

Robinson, W.L. (1984) 'Management and ethical decision-making', *Journal of Business Ethics*, 3: 287–92.

Sahlman, W.A. (1997) 'How to write a great business plan', *Harvard Business Review*, 75: 98–108.

Seaton, L.J. and Boyd, M. (2007) 'The organisational leadership of the post baby boom generation: an upper echelon theory approach', *Academy of Entrepreneurship Journal*, 13: 69–78.

Sexton, D.K. and Van Auken, P. (1985) 'A longitudinal study of small business strategic planning', *Journal of Small Business Management*, 23: 7–15.

Shane, S., Locke, E.A. and Collins, C.J. (2003) 'Entrepreneurial motivation', *Human Resources Management Review*, 13: 257–79.

Shaw, G., Brown, R. and Bromiley, P. (1998) 'Strategic stories: how 3M is rewriting business planning', *Harvard Business Review*, 76: 41–4.

Shrader, C.B., Mulford, C.L. and Blackburn, V.L. (1989) 'Strategic and operational planning, uncertainty, and performance in small firms', *Journal of Small Business Management*, 27: 45–61.

Talbot, M. (2003) *Make Your Mission Statement Work: Identify Your Organization's Values and Live them Every Day*, Oxford: Oxford How-to Books.

Toftoy, C.N. and Chatterjee, J. (2004) 'Mission statements and the small business', *Business Strategy Review*, 15: 41–4.

Tulgan, B. (2006) *Managing the Generation Mix*, 2nd edn, Amherst, MA: HRD Press, Inc.

Vesper, K.H. (1980) 'New venture planning', *Journal of Business Strategy*, 1: 73–5.

Welsh, J.A. and White, J.F. (1981) 'A small business is not a little big business', *Harvard Business Review*, 59: 18–28.

Wenstøp, F. and Myrmel, A. (2006) 'Structuring organizational value statements', *Management Research News*, 29: 673–83.

Wickham, P.A. (1997) 'Developing a mission for an entrepreneurial venture', *Management Decision*, 35: 373–81.

Woo, C.Y., Cooper, A.C. and Dunkelberg, W.C. (1991) 'The development and interpretation of entrepreneurial typologies', *Journal of Business Venturing*, 6: 93–115.

Wright, M., Lockett, A., Pruthi, S., Manigart, S., Sapienza, H., Desbrieres, P. and Hommel, U. (2004) 'Venture capital investors, capital markets, valuation and information: US, Europe and Asia', *Journal of International Entrepreneurship*, 2: 305–26.

Zacharakis, A.L. (1997) 'Entrepreneurial entry into foreign markets: a transaction cost perspective', *Entrepreneurship Theory and Practice*, 21: 23–39.

Zaslow, J. (2006) 'Baby Boomer managers struggle with mentoring', The Wall Street Journal Online. Available at <http://208.144.115.170/columnists/movingon/20030606-movingon.html> (accessed 15 March 2007).

Zemke, R., Raines, C. and Filipczak, B. (2000) *Generations at Work: Managing the Clash of Veterans, Boomers, Xers, and Nexters in Your Workplace*, New York: AMACOM, 1–151.

Zhao, H., Seibert, S.E. and Lumpkin, G.T. (2010) 'The relationship of personality to entrepreneurial intentions and performance: a meta-analytic review', *Journal of Management*, 36: 381–404.

Chapter 10

Management skills in the entrepreneurial realm

OBJECTIVES

After studying this chapter you will be able to:

■ Understand the importance of professional management in the typically unstable entrepreneurial business to efficiently and effectively navigate it toward its goals.

■ Distinguish between management skills, leadership skills and entrepreneurial-related skills, in order to fill in the 'missing expertise' in the business.

■ Identify the unique skills that managers of entrepreneurial businesses need to engage, unlike managers in established and non-entrepreneurial businesses, and use these skills to ensure management targeted toward a sustainable, competitive advantage.

■ Master the key factors unique to managing people and operations in entrepreneurial businesses.

■ Establish an underlying conception among the business's staff that professional management is one of the most important strategic assets for the businesses.

■ Distinguish between types of leadership and their uses in entrepreneurial businesses.

■ Be more proficient at managing entrepreneurial teams by prompting employees' commitment, creativity and enthusiasm.

■ Assess management quality in entrepreneurial businesses.

MANAGERIAL SKILLS IN ENTREPRENEURSHIP

Entrepreneurship is sometimes introduced as an undertaking that is embarked upon in the uncertainty produced by the presence of many and diverse individuals, talents, characteristics and ideas; thus management of entrepreneurial ventures must navigate these uncertainties in manageable, responsible ways, to allow the venture to reach its goals and achieve advantages over its competitors (Pfeffer and Salancik 1978; Reynolds et al. 1994; Honig 1998). Such complex management is far different from the 'traditional' models of management in well-established businesses.

In general, management is typically seen as a well-structured process that deals with carrying out tasks such as planning, organizing, leading, coordinating and controlling in order to attain certain objectives. On the other hand, management in entrepreneurial businesses is unique in that it consists of some aspects that are typical of novice or small businesses, such as emotionality, team building, fostering 'startup motivation', and managing without clear hierarchies, processes or administration, among others. Moreover, in the entrepreneurial realm, management is best carried out by people who are naturally skilled or trained to function in predetermined structures, as these are probably more prevalent in entrepreneurial ventures. Such people may possess relatively limited entrepreneurial characteristics, but they need to be the best promoters of business success and competitive advantage. Such challenges push entrepreneurial businesses to develop and then preserve the entrepreneurial dynamics that enable the entrepreneur to manage the business effectively.

Differences between entrepreneurship and professional management, in both skills and styles, are well documented in entrepreneurship research. The orientations and mindsets of entrepreneurs have also been found to differ significantly from those of professional managers, and entrepreneurship and management are increasingly being considered as separate features of entrepreneurial ventures.

Entrepreneurs are characterized as being creative, innovative, restless, and willing to take risks; professional managers are characterized as capable of organizing tasks and directing others through regulations, norms and procedures; and since professional managers see maintaining the company as their main goals, they are generally wary of risk-taking.

In new and emerging businesses, the founders of the enterprises often have, or acquire, the necessary entrepreneurial characteristics of innovation, creativity, passion to create, proactivity and risk-taking; however, once the business begins to function, the nature of the firm's needs changes. Businesses are said to develop through stages that parallel those of human development: at each stage different challenges arise and must be dealt with. It is not unusual for entrepreneurs to be disinterested in or inexpert at handling certain managerial challenges that are needed when the businesses are set up and functioning. Entrepreneurs often lack sufficient managerial skills to help their firms make critical life-cycle transitions, and are sometimes poor at supervising staff, managing routine problems, or maintaining the ongoing business processes. Although some entrepreneurs may have adequate managerial skills, they are motivated mainly by an inner drive to exploit opportunities, create and innovate, while managers, by both their nature and their training, are more directed to organizing the efficient operation of the enterprise. However, entrepreneurial enterprises are generally small when they are first founded, and their management is usually handled by the founding entrepreneurs themselves. Ownership of a business also tends to create elitist attitudes and self-orientation, and this might prevent the entrepreneurs from seeking and obtaining the managerial skills best suited to their businesses' needs. Moreover, the elitist attitudes and self-orientation that often already exist or develop in the entrepreneur's character often work against their seeking and obtaining the managerial expertise needed to ensure their businesses' success. Differences in business success measures, at least at the micro-level dimension of analysis, depend on the ability of firms to adapt internal structures and processes to available opportunities and external constraints, and such adaptations depend on the actions of the firm's leader, usually the entrepreneur. Effective managerial skills are thus critical in assuring the success of entrepreneurial ventures.

There are thus specific sets of managerial skills that are better suited to entrepreneurial businesses than to well-established firms, because they are flexible and take into account the dynamics of entrepreneurial businesses as they evolve and develop from one stage to the next.

MANAGERIAL SKILLS RELEVANT FOR DIFFERENT STAGES OF BUSINESS DEVELOPMENT

Research and field studies carried out in entrepreneurial and startup enterprises have documented the widespread and well-known phenomenon of initially successful new entrepreneurial firms declining and, sooner or later, failing. The prevalence of this phenomenon raises questions as to the ways and means discovered and utilized by successful startup businesses to help them weather the storms of rapid growth.

Many entrepreneurs are unprepared for the rigorous organizational demands of rapid growth. As firms mature, the loose and informal management styles that led them to success at the startup stage become inadequate. The original systems become strained, profits decline, and the entrepreneurs are constrained to employ managers who are experienced or trained in the use of various different managerial styles and behaviors that can answer the changing demands of the business. Although the management of a developing enterprise can be successfully carried out by the entrepreneur, and/or by managers specifically recruited for this purpose, the transition from a humble startup to a professionally managed firm is a radical change. Such a transition is essential, but it is preferably weathered without sacrificing the unique spirit that inspired the company's founding in the first place. The ability to do so is one of the main secrets of entrepreneurial businesses' survival, sustainability and success.

The purpose of professional management is to ensure that relevant behaviors are adopted during the different stages of a firm's founding and development, thus increasing the likelihood of success in achieving planned goals. Managerial skills and behaviors, such as acquiring a deep knowledge of a product or service, obtaining feedback from customers, or adapting to changes in the market, are required, to varying degrees, at each stage of the business's development (Calori and de Woot 1994; Sykes and Dunham 1995; Clegg, Ibarra-Colado and Bueno-Rodriquez 1999; Wyer, Mason and Theodorakopoulos 2000; Mankins 2004).

ENTREPRENEURIAL MANAGEMENT

Some traditional management models spawned in the last century are considered by some leading researchers in entrepreneurship as strategically less aligned with the demands of a twenty-first-century global knowledge-based economy, and in particular do not correspond to the entre-preneurial business's potential of achieving a competitive advantage in this century's dynamic marketplace. Many traditional management principles (e.g., Taylorism, Theories X/Y, Management by Objectives, Re-engineering) focus on maximizing operational efficiency toward superior performance. Today, there is a need for principles that will create adaptability by encouraging human creativity and innovation, and empower employees to cope with frequently unknown, risky, unstable and unpredictable environments. Entrepreneurial businesses face challenges and threats, including lack of adequate capital, scarcity of funds, underestimation of financial risks, unrealistic estimates of borrowing potential, imitation or duplication of products, ideas or strategies by new and/or existing competitors, uncommitted clients who turn from one supplier to another because of price differences, service orientation, or product variety, unstable and non-durable customer tastes. Furthermore, entrepreneurial businesses need to be managed toward a sustainable advantage, which is the key to long-term competitive success. An over-systematized, stringently organized, fixed management model therefore does not correspond to such complex needs and constraints.

Unlike their counterparts in well-established ventures, managers of entrepreneurial businesses should engage in a more innovative style of management, by tightly associating all of the business's processes and activities to its vision and goals, correspondingly employing a flexible, adaptive management style by providing the employees with sufficient autonomy to think outside the box, and act dynamically and innovatively.

Such a management strategy should focus on developing a shared vision that is approved by the employees, then following widely accepted activities that reflect the business's vision and are closely allied with the business's values, goals, aims, purposes and culture, at the outset. To do so, the manager needs to develop a management approach that will treat each employee as an entrepreneurial business owner. By being part of the process, employees are prompted to create and transform the vision into product, services, and money; they are more enthusiastic and committed to the business goals and mission, and more easily identify their unique role in the business and their own ways of achieving the business's goals (Hamel 2000).

As shown in Figure 10.1, the management of entrepreneurial businesses functions on flat hierarchical structures that use a swarm of small self-managed teams, thereby avoiding power distinctions and power-related behavior. Unfiltered communication flow between the manager and the employees or team members, or between the business teams themselves, is necessary, and

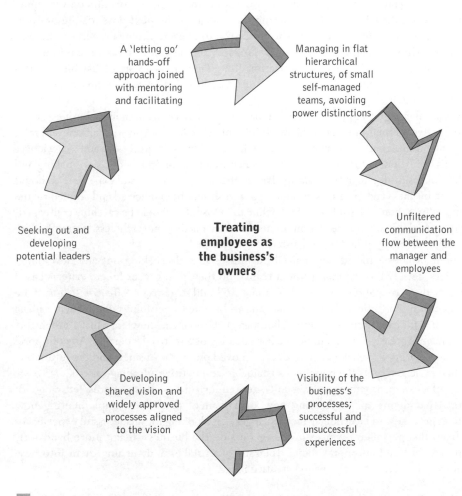

Figure 10.1 *Management principles of entrepreneurial teams: prompting employees' commitment, creativity and enthusiasm*

THE PROCESS-ORIENTED PERSPECTIVE

such flat structures may facilitate it. Such communication is mainly associated with a non-judgmental atmosphere, which is a platform for encouraging the questioning of well-established 'truths', continually testing current practices, uncovering then questioning the firm's principles that act as the business's anchors, and sharing different insights on the so-called firm ground the business stands on. Some current examples illustrate the benefits of such flat hierarchical structures and unfiltered communication. Mark Zuckerberg, the founder of Facebook,[1] presented his own belief regarding flat, almost 'unnoticeable' hierarchical structures: he chose to locate his work desk in the same ground space with his teams, rather than work in a separate space symbolizing the difference in hirearchy between them; Zuckerberg has been quoted as saying that he feels more connected to his teams, and that this allows for fertile synergic processes. Moreover, he is inherent in the teams' successful and unsuccessful experiences and these dynamics are one leading source of both learning from experience and innovating in an attempt to explore different ways of managing these experiences the next time they appear. The co-founders of Google,[2] Sergey Brin and Larry Page, developed their idea and then the business through an innovative, unorthodox management philosophy of 'organizational revolution', including turning 'the office into a playground', reducing bureaucracy, providing all workers with a high level of autonomy, encouraging people to share their ideas and considering these ideas as the next potential innovation, recruiting the best people, the 'go-getters' who are driven to make the company successful. They believe in extra benefits for their employees, such as Yoga, Pilates and the best restaurants in-house, as part of a trusting and efficient communication flow. Their philosophy of flat hierarchical structures symbolizes a revolutionary climate, a culture that stimulates creativity, innovative ideas, autonomy and proactivity.

Visibility is another highly important factor in managing today's entrepreneurial business: team members, regardless of their position or hierarchical rank, should be involved in all relevant facts surrounding the business and its environment. Visibility of all business processes and experiences develops a sense of belonging to the business and encourages autonomous decision-making and accountability for results for all individuals involved in the business. Successful experiences should be visible in the business and even its surroundings, and should be publicized and studied by the management; failures should be studied as well, while their visibility should be carefully controlled, so that it will not inhibit any further autonomous decision-making; nevertheless, accountability and responsibility for poor or faulty results should be enforced.

Management processes in entrepreneurial businesses include seeking out and developing potential leaders, selected by the management teams and their peers according to criteria based on ability rather than credentials, such as: their ability to build sustainable, effective teams, to be practical and committed to the business's goals, and to be able to get things done. Such criteria should be modified for each business's culture, but managers should acknowledge that a sustainable business advantage is greatly dependent on the continuance of effective leadership. Any temporal gap in leadership, for instance, when one leader has moved out of the business and the future one has not yet been selected, puts the business's sustainable competitive advantage at risk.

Finally, an effective management process in entrepreneurial businesses requires 'letting go' of the traditional paradigms and embracing new management principles, implementing new management approaches, and learning from the fringes, i.e., looking for unsuccessful experiences that come from the 'peripheral' voices inside or outside the business; being more hands-off, providing more trust and autonomy, being tolerant of mistakes and turning them into new opportunities via the business participants' creative ideas.

MANAGEMENT AND THE RESOURCE-BASED VIEW

In recent years, the resource-based view (RBV) has been developed to explore the internal core competencies and assets of a business that can create barriers for competitors and provide the business with a sustainable competitive advantage (Barney 1991, 2001; Amit and Schoemaker 1993; Peteraf 1993). Sustainable competitive advantage means creating a business's 'economic value' with its own internal resources; this enables the business to generate more value to its customers than competitors can, and positively contribute to the business's performance and success. Such internal resources can be classified as financial, human, and physical, as well as the entrepreneur's managerial and personal traits.

Penrose (1959), who first proposed the concept of the RBV, recognized the unique importance of managerial capabilities and behavior for the business's sustainable competitive advantage and success. According to his view, management quality greatly depends on the entrepreneur's traits and background, which by being valuable, rare, imperfectly imitable and imperfectly substitutable resources, are the most influential strategic assets for the business. The business's concurrent resources influence managerial perceptions and behavior and reciprocally, managerial perceptions influence the acquisition of new resources. Management that embraces innovative and creative combinations of internal resources may be open to new opportunities, resource investments, products and contracts that are the essence of the potential competitive advantage (Wernerfelt 1984; Barney 1986, 1991; Pfeffer 1994; Dollinger 1999).

Taken a step further, with today's dynamic markets and rapid technological advances, only businesses that build new resources and strategic assets that best fit the customers' demands or needs and build new assets on an ongoing basis will generate a sustainable competitive advantage. This means that managers of entrepreneurial businesses are the pillars of a business's competitiveness and growth. They should create internal structures and processes that will be flexible and adjustable, and will eventually produce new internal resources and assets that will create long-lasting competitive advantages.

The RBV has been criticized for not emphasizing *how* the superior strategic assets are to be achieved (Hamel 2000; McGuinness and Morgan 2000; Priem and Butler 2001). The following dynamic capability (DC) approach fills this gap by being focused on *how* the management of entrepreneurial businesses creates mechanisms to facilitate the creation of new, distinctive and hard-to-imitate advantages. By acting as a buffer between a business's internal resources and the dynamic business environment, dynamic capabilities allow the business to adjust its resource mix and thereby maintain a sustainable competitive advantage that might otherwise become rapidly eroded. Management toward flexibility, adjustment and innovation is thus a key factor in operating the business in a rapidly changing environment (Pisano 1994; Grant 1996; Teece et al. 1997; Zahra 1999; Eisenhardt and Martin 2000; Makadok 2001; Elliott 2003).

LEADERSHIP IN THE ENTREPRENEURIAL REALM

Schumpeter (1934) describes an entrepreneur as an individual who is not reluctant to fight back, to succeed, to conquer, all with a joy of creating and of getting things done; he or she 'seeks out difficulties, changes in order to change, and delights in ventures' (Schumpeter 1934: 93–4).

These characteristics correspond to a large extent with those attributed to leaders; thus entrepreneurs, as leaders, affect the performance of their employees and top management teams toward creating the conditions for success. In entrepreneurial businesses, the leadership abilities of the person(s) managing the business are highly significant in both promoting the business employees' commitment to the business goals, and encouraging proactive, autonomous, high-quality work (Haleblian and Finkelstein 1993; Hambrick 1994; Finkelstein and Hambrick 1996; Finkelstein and Boyd 1998; Judge et al. 2002; Herrmann and Datta 2005). The most prominent models for leadership that apply to the entrepreneurial context are described in Table 10.1.

Personality traits and psychological capacities, which are found to be correlated with leaders' traits and behaviors, participants' performance and the business's success (Cunningham and Lischeron 1991; Littunen and Storhammar 2000; Rauch and Frese 2000; Korunka et al. 2003; Beugelsdijk 2007). Among such traits are the need for achievement (McClelland 1961), an internal locus of control, extraversion, openness to experience, pleasantness, and conscientiousness which includes self-discipline, striving for achievement and emotional stability (Littunen 2000; Rauch and Frese 2000; Korunka et al. 2003; Beugelsdijk 2007). Bass and Avolio's (1994) well-established model includes characteristics such as self-awareness, transparency, a high standard of moral and ethical conduct and balanced processing; while Luthans' (2002) renowned model addresses confidence, hope, and resilience. Having the in-built characteristics to lead the business and teams guarantees a competitive advantage for the entrepreneurial business, and is considered a valuable, rare, imperfectly imitable and imperfectly substitutable resource which is one of the most significant strategic assets for the business (Barney 1986, 1991; Goldberg 1990; Barrick and Mount 1991; Pfeffer 1994; Avolio 1999; Dollinger 1999; John and Srivastava 1999).

Transformational leadership. The goal of the transformational leader is to inspire employees to share the business's vision, by increasing their awareness of task importance and value, getting them to focus on their teams and the business's goals at the outset, rather than their own interests, and activating their higher order needs. Entrepreneurs who engage in the transformational leadership style rise above their self-interest and short-term goals, and by exhibiting hard work, employees come to share the leader's goals and values to transcend their self-interest and accomplish the mission.

In the context of entrepreneurial businesses, several prominent characteristics represent a transformational leadership style 'that works'. The first is being able to build and maintain trust between leaders and employees; the second is the leader's ability to challenge and inspire the employees by appealing to what is right and what needs to be done, thereby providing the impetus for all to move forward with him or her through shared goals. The third characteristic addresses intellectual stimulation, which affects the subordinates' generation of creative ideas, while the fourth addresses framing the business process and dynamics by connecting the vision with the employees' role and allowing the employee to foresee the 'big picture', thus deepening their understanding of the business's challenges and threats; the fifth point addresses providing the employees with individual coaching, mentoring and growth opportunities that match and fulfill their need for self-actualization, self-fulfillment, and self-worth; this naturally propels the employees to further achievement and growth (Bass 1960, 1997; Burns 1978; Lowe, Kroeck and Sivasubramaniam 1996; Kotter 1999; Dong and Yammarino 2001).

Transactional leadership. This style is based on a transaction or exchange of something of value that the leader possesses or controls and that the employee wants, in return for the latter's services; i.e., reward or punishment that is contingent upon performance. Despite much research highlighting its limitations, transactional leadership is still a popular approach for many leaders, although it is more representative of a style of management than of leadership per se. Its basic assumptions lie in employees' reaction to reward and punishment, specifically that coming through a clear chain of command; as such, the prime purpose of subordinates is to do what their supervisors tell them to do.

This leadership style could be very relevant to the entrepreneurial realm, mainly in the first stages of the venture creation, when more uncertainty, vagueness and ambiguity characterize the business environments. Having a clear idea of the dynamics and structures of the business, including

Table 10.1 *Application of some leadership models to the entrepreneurial realm*

Leadership model	Contributors	Application to entrepreneurship
Personality traits and psychological capacities	McClelland 1961; Bass and Avolio 1994; Cunningham and Lischeron 1991; Littunen and Storhammar 2000	Managing entrepreneurial businesses by leadership-related characteristics guarantees the business's competitive advantage, e.g., internal locus of control, extraversion, openness to experience, striving for achievement, self-awareness, transparency, a high standard of moral and ethical conduct, confidence, hope, and resilience
Transformational leadership[a]	Bass 1960, 1997; Burns 1978; Kotter 1999; Lowe, Kroeck and Sivasubramaniam 1996	Being able to: ■ Build and maintain trust between leaders and employees ■ Challenge and inspire the employees by appealing to what is right and what needs to be done ■ Provide intellectual stimulation ■ Frame the business process and dynamics by connecting the vision with the employees' role ■ Provide the employees with individual coaching, mentoring and growth opportunities that fulfill their needs
Transactional leadership[a]	Bass 1985, 1990; Bass and Avolio 1990, 1994; House and Podsakoff 1994; Yammarino and Bass 1990	At the first stages of the venture creation, by: ■ Developing clear dynamics in the business including reward and punishment systems ■ Providing the employees with full responsibility for the missions allocated to them ■ Ongoing job training and education
Task-oriented leadership	Likert 1961, 1967; Blau and Scott 1962; Hersey and Blanchard 1977	A clear design and definition of the employees' tasks can be very effective in times of close deadlines and crisis situations, and especially at the launching stage
Participative leadership	Vroom and Jago 1988; Bass 1990; Bowen and Lawler 1995; Cole, Bacdayan and White 1993; Harber, Marriot and Idrus 1991; McGrath 1984	■ In more established phases of the entrepreneurial business, participative leadership can be very relevant by facilitating the participation of the employees in decision-making processes ■ In entrepreneurial businesses, most employees are very involved in the business processes; thus it is important to develop participative leadership ■ Development of informal systems in the business would facilitate the participation of employees in decision-making processes ■ Improved communication, conflict resolution, and a calm and positive atmosphere evolve through a participative style

Note: a The best practices of today's leadership in entrepreneurial businesses comprise both transformational and transactional styles.

reward and punishment systems, facilitates the employees' adjustment in the business. In addition, the transactional style is associated with providing the employee or team with full responsibility for the work or missions allocated to them, which in essence constitutes ongoing job training and education. When leaders reward for success and offer praise for exceeding expectations, while punishing for failure or applying some kind of corrective action for performing below expectation, this has the potential to empower the employee or team and move the business forward.

The relationship between transactional and transformational leadership is complementary and very relevant to the dynamic environment often experienced by entrepreneurial firms, and the best practices of today's leadership in entrepreneurial businesses comprise both transformational and transactional styles. In light of the ambiguous, fluctuating environment, it seems a necessity for leaders and employees to steep in the same core values and energize themselves to tackle the complex challenges encountered by entrepreneurial businesses together; and when the connection between the leader and the employees is trusting and positive, their energy is focused on achieving the best results with less oversight, because the leader has articulated the target goal in a way that all of the business's participants will accept and support (Bass 1985, 1990; Waldman, Bass and Einstein 1987; Bass and Avolio 1990, 1994; Yammarino and Bass 1990; House and Shamir 1993; House and Podsakoff 1994; Yukl 1994; Bycio, Hackett and Allen 1995; Den Hartog, Van Muijen and Koopman 1997).

The task-oriented leadership style focuses on the task and the business goal; leaders embracing this style put all of their effort into functions aimed at carrying out tasks and are committed to planning, organizing and coordinating activities related to those tasks. As such they are responsive in providing the necessary help, equipment and technical assistance for their employees to adequately carry out the business's tasks (Likert 1961, 1967; Blau and Scott 1962; Hersey and Blanchard 1977).

Task-oriented leaders structure and define their and their employees' timetables and additional arrangements, as well as the business's policy and regulations around its tasks and goals. One major disadvantage of this leadership style rests in the managers' tendency to keep a close eye on their employees and constantly verify the fulfillment of their planned goals. Consequently, the employees are most likely to exhibit increasing dependence on such leaders, effectively nullifying their initiative and creativity. Nevertheless, in the entrepreneurial realm, in times of close deadlines and crisis situations, especially in the launching stage, the clear design and definition of subordinates' tasks can be very effective and efficient for the business's development as well as for profits and competitive advantage.

The *participative leadership* style addresses managers that share their decision-making process with other members of the business (e.g., Vroom and Jago 1988), encourage their subordinates to take on responsibilities in their work, reward ideas or behaviors aimed at innovation and creativity, and help increase personal interactions between team members, mutual obligation and responsibility. In more established phases of the entrepreneurial business, participative leadership can be very relevant as it efficiently guides the leader's efforts toward motivating and facilitating the participation of subordinates in decision-making and in the performance of new ideas; however, it is a time-consuming style and is ineffective in times of pressure.

In the context of entrepreneurial businesses, especially SMEs that are typified by a small number of participants who are all typically very involved in the business processes, it is important to develop a participative style of leadership to engage the employees around the business vision and mission; crafting informal systems in the business will facilitate the employees' participation in decision-making processes. By engaging in a participative style of leadership, improved communication and conflict resolution processes, as well as a calmer and more positive atmosphere develop (McGrath 1984; Bass 1990; Harber, Marriot and Idrus 1991; Cole, Bacdayan and White 1993; Bowen and Lawler 1995).

CASE STUDY 10.1   Lewin Law Firm, California

Father and son David and Danny Lewin manage a family business in Los Angeles, California, the Lewin Law Firm, in which they became partners. David founded the firm in the 1980s with his late brother Saul, who died two years ago, and with Saul's wife Geraldine, who still works part-time in the firm. The Lewin Law Firm provides legal counseling and representation in commercial law, mainly to hi-tech startups and established firms, in matters regarding joint ventures, investments, intellectual property, patents, trademarks and copyrights, among others. Approximately 80 percent of the firm's clients are recent immigrants from Israel or Israeli investors, entrepreneurs and business people requiring the firm's services in LA.

The Lewin Law Firm has fifty employees, thirty-five of whom are lawyers or law students. The rest comprise an administrative staff of marketing, advertising and social entrepreneurship professionals. David Lewin's father was a well-known judge in Israel before his recent retirement. He moved to LA to be with his sons and is an honorary consultant in the firm, as well as the main influence on his grandson Danny's decision to go to law school. Danny was a free-spirited adolescent who could not find his way and spent a few years back-packing in the countries of Southeast Asia. He had no plans for academic studies of any kind, but his bond with his grandfather led him to change his mind. With poor high-school grades, it was very difficult for him to find a place to study law; he moved to the east coast of the United States where a university accepted him 'conditionally', and he completed his studies successfully.

David and his late brother Saul had been perfect partners. David was the moving spirit: he invented new things, negotiated with clients, made effective contacts, and become well known in the local Jewish community; he managed the staff, financing and marketing, and was excellent at delegating work, yet remained very hands-on. Saul was the academic spirit: he read everything, kept up to date in the latest legal matters and had the right answer for every legal question; he was the knowledgeable person in the company. The brothers got along very well and the firm's management was carried out efficiently. Members of the staff used to tell the brothers that 'whenever one of you starts to say anything, the other immediately knows what he is intending to say'.

David oversaw the firm's recruiting processes. He believed that a firm is its employees, and often told his staff that they were the firm's 'showcase'. He was attentive to his staff's well-being and safety and devoted time and money for training and courses, and for company celebrations: the entire staff and their families were hosted at an annual barbeque for which Saul's wife Geraldine prepared all of the food. David treated his staff like family, providing financial assistance or legal counsel whenever needed. Saul, who was excellent in managing efficient and practical discussions, was in charge of the lawyers' Monday morning meetings during which he updated them on the latest rulings, verdicts and rules.

Salaries at Lewin Law Firm were high, but the staff worked very hard. Promotion within the firm was according to known standards, which enabled each member of the staff to work toward them. Employee loyalty was widely known – employees did not leave the Lewin Law Firm.

Danny's entry as a partner was long expected by the staff, especially after Saul's sudden death. They all knew David's handsome elder son and they were happy for David when Danny graduated from law school and became a partner. David, like his father, was a decisive educator, and the partnership was conditional on Danny's paying for his share of the business, and he maintained several jobs to earn the money to do so. Danny was not equipped to replace Saul in his role in the firm and was put in charge of the firm's HR management. Danny was very dedicated to his new responsibilities. In order to strengthen his authority, he initiated various changes intended to improve the firm's performance. He started to manage the HR 'by the book'; for example, the administrative staff was required to record actual hours worked; the system of flexible work hours was cancelled in order to provide better service to the clients; the Monday morning staff meetings were rescheduled to after-work hours; and the company's annual barbeque was shelved since Geraldine could no longer manage the food preparations and Danny thought that they shouldn't 'spend money to feed the staff'.

The redesign of the company's personnel and procedural structures led to complaints, a drop in motivation, and an overall unpleasant and unhealthy work atmosphere. In addition, four administrative staff employees quit the firm, and two very senior lawyers, who had served the company for more than ten years, resigned.

QUESTIONS FOR DISCUSSION

1   What are the main differences between David's and Danny's managerial behaviors?
2   What are the main sources of the employees' complaints? How can you explain the resignation of two senior lawyers?
3   Which management style – David's, Saul's or Danny's – was best for Lewin Law Firm? Explain.
4   Match each of these managerial styles to the stage of the business to which it is best suited.
5   Which management changes would you suggest the partners carry out in order to improve the atmosphere and increase their employees' motivation?

THE NEW VENTURE TEAM

It is well documented that today, businesses are typically launched by teams rather than by individuals and the prevalence of entrepreneurial teams is an emerging economic reality. Entrepreneurial teams, more than a single 'hero',[3] have diversified skills and competences, a wider social network base, additional social capital and resources; as such, teams have an advantage over 'a one-man show' in increasing the business (Fiet et al. 1997; Ensley et al. 1999); in addition, venture capital firms rarely consider proposals of businesses based on individuals and favor those that come from teams.

Entrepreneurial teams are considered the 'heart of entrepreneurship' and businesses owned by teams (partners) are typically more successful than those based on one individual in terms of survival, longevity, profitability and sales (Kamm and Shuman 1990; Cooper and Daily 1997).

From a process-oriented standpoint, team members have synergistic effects on one another, and they positively influence the firm's performance through brainstorming and inspirational interactions designed to achieve shared goals; team members are considered to be committed to each other and to the firm's interests, and they transmit their enthusiasm to each other. Entrepreneurial teams have positive effects on the survival rates of their firms (i.e., partnerships versus individual firms), on the quality of social interactions and on clients' satisfaction. In fact, venture capital firms favor proposals received from team-based ventures as they have better track records (Timmons and Gumpert 1982; Timmons and Bygrave 1986; Kamm and Shuman 1990; Katzenbach 1997; Li and Hambrick 2005).

There are many forms of teams in the entrepreneurial realm, for example: founding and pre-startup teams, consisting of individuals who envisioned the initial idea for the business; teams brought into a venture in its early phases who then become the backbone of the business in its subsequent stages; managerial teams in entrepreneurial businesses; R&D teams; teams of employees in specific departments; virtual teams; and even external teams such as advisory boards or Mastermind teams, among others.[4] Most of the team members share certain common interests, yet have other, individual interests. Team members work interdependently in the pursuit of common goals and the venture's success; each individual member is accountable to the entrepreneurial team and to the venture as a whole.

Commitment, friendship and positive inspiration are the main characteristics of entrepreneurial team members; they are manifested in team members' behavior, and in high degrees of mutual trust, candor, cooperation, brainstorming, and interaction (Francis and Sandberg 2000; Zahra, Yavus and Ucbasaran 2006).

Teams that effectively manage their entrepreneurial businesses are typically illustrated by a pool of potentially corresponding competitive practices: each team member has strengths that balance others' weaknesses. The members of entrepreneurial teams need to gather regularly, discuss their shared goals, determine tactics, and devote their utmost energy to achieving the team's and business's goals. Each member's energy contributes to cumulative team energy.

The entrepreneur has to ensure that the gathering events remain stimulating – fun events and not all-out warfare. The 'six sigma' model[5] for effective team management suggests that the more managers and team members understand the team dynamics, the better the team's collective performance is likely to be.

In order to constructively manage their team dynamics, entrepreneurs have to:

- Identify the natural forces at play and search for the 'real' team dynamics.
- Determine whether the team's major forces are acting for shared or personal interests.
- Recognize the social and informal roles of the members of the team (leaders, innovators, curators, facilitators, etc.).
- Apply interventions to maximize the effect of the team dynamics.

Teams are likely to perform better when entrepreneurs provide them with:

- Feelings of acceptance, recognition and support from management.
- Encouragement to interact socially with others in the workplace.
- Self-managed responsibilities, although controlled by the firm's management.
- Opportunities to take part and be involved in related programs, projects, or teams.
- Empowerment to make decisions regarding their work.
- Roles, job-related duties and tasks that represent their authority and power over their work in the team.
- Goals, objectives, and understood and mutually accepted expectations.
- Recognition that mistakes or lapses are an inherent part of the performance of any job and that occasional lapses will not be penalized.
- A true learning atmosphere at the firm and team levels.
- Access to needed information.

165

- Visibility.
- The needed resources.
- Continuous challenges.
- Time and support to foster innate creativity and innovations and to share innovative ideas training.

A GLIMPSE INTO ENTREPRENEURIAL TEAMS

Managing entrepreneurial teams is a complex undertaking. Studies in management address this complexity by stressing the exclusive needs, tastes and desires of the individuals incorporated in a team, their different forms, phases and speeds of development, and the complex dynamics typifying teams as a whole.

Table 10.2 adapts Bruce Tuckman's Forming–Storming–Norming–Performing model to the entrepreneurial realm, and uses it as a basic framework to understand team development in entrepreneurial ventures. The first stage of team development, which is pertinent to both entrepreneurial and employee teams involved in the launching process of the venture, is characterized by enthusiasm and eagerness to start the business. Although the aims, missions and tasks have not been constructed and the tasks have therefore not yet been assigned to the individuals who will execute them, the vision exists and leads the team's performance and dynamics. Personality traits and motivations are crucial factors in the team's success at this stage. However, despite much variation, a mutual interest in the core issues of the business binds the team together. Teams at this stage are dynamic, no structured division of labor has been crafted and the atmosphere is typically joyful and optimistic. The next stage is more structured in terms of the team's tasks and responsibilities, essentially because partners, investors, clients and suppliers require a structured framework for their work. However, the teams are now characterized as 'stormy', encountering conflicts and disagreements. At this stage, team members are building and shaping their roles in the team and defending their expertise, unique abilities and knowledge by establishing their territory, imposing their ideas and initiatives. This is an important stage in the development of the teams and the entrepreneurial business, and it reflects the dilemmas which are typical in such businesses: this stormy stage enables the teams to brainstorm and discover new and innovative solutions for the difficulties they are facing and discussing, but also for other, sometimes potential, difficulties which have not yet emerged, but for which potential solutions are raised by the team's discussions of the conflicts and dilemmas.

One very unique team issue in entrepreneurship regards entrepreneurial teams that have previously been through the venture process together and may feel less of a need to bring in additional members. This is because they have either experienced problems with bringing in new members in the past who did not possess the required skills for the venture, or are concerned about losing control of the team, the work or the business.

Take the case of Jean-Paul from Bordeaux, France, an entrepreneur who founded a private IT research and services company that offers research reports for software development, IT services and e-business solutions – the business was launched by Jean-Paul, the entrepreneur, and a committed team of employees consisting of five IT experts, Jean-Paul's colleagues from university, who were deeply involved in the launching and development of the business. Two years after the business was launched, only one member of the team remained employed in the company. The team encountered difficult times in the second stage of the business's development, even though Jean-Paul was selected by two different funds and received money for the business, which was therefore stable and secure in terms of survival. The interrelationships were simply difficult to

Table 10.2 Stages of team development in the entrepreneurial realm

Stage	Team development	Dependence on the founder/entrepreneur	Group communication
Pre-startup	*Forming*. When ideas pop up, usually in highly unstructured environments, members are learning about each other. Members attempt to identify tasks, how to accomplish them and proactively take on multiple tasks, roles and responsibilities. The situation is unstructured and there is no clear understanding of what information is needed. Participation is hesitant	Very high in every aspect of the business and the team	Formal, hesitant
Seed	*Storming*. Team members come up with ideas through debates on how to proceed with the task Members feel the need to more clearly construct the purpose of the task, task priorities, and roles and responsibilities Members are eager to influence each other with their ideas, and power struggles may arise Members compromise to enable the business to progress, often by competition, bringing about frustration and the formation of 'cliques' Unrealistic, overambitious goals are established	Very high in challenging the founder on organizational structure and priorities	Formal and informal, squabbling, negative
Startup/ launching stage (work as a team starts)	*Norming*. The members establish clearer and accepted tasks, roles and responsibilities Members start to work as a team in terms of participatory behavior and group agreement More members are committed to their team, and trust and unity increase More members accept the team's norms and roles and the other members' needs and demands Members are freer to identify the other members' strengths Members attempt to patch up previously stormy relationships	High in having the founder's feedback and coaching. As most members trust their peers, they 'move' to a higher dependence on their team members	More informal, more positive, more trust

Table 10.2 cont'd

Stage	Team development	Dependence on the founder/entrepreneur	Group communication
Development	*Performing.* This stage is characterized by high levels of: Goal orientation, interpersonal relations, independence, motivation, knowledge and competence of team members Teams know the what, why and how of the task they are executing High level of respect in the communication among team members Team expects delegation of tasks instead of instruction/assistance Members gain insight into personal and interpersonal processes; constructive self-change occurs A great deal of work is accomplished Team becomes capable of diagnosing and solving problems	Moderate as team members are independent and have sometimes reached a stage at which their expertise surpasses that of the founder/ entrepreneur	Informal, well known, an internal client-supply dynamic, trustful and respectful. Sometimes feels like a family
Growth or 'exit', mergers or acquisitions	*Adjourning.* Happens when project has been completed Members move out of the group after project goal achievement Everyone can move on to new things Achievement celebrated Members have difficulty, as they have developed close working relations with other team members	A correspondingly dependent–independent relationship: the members are professionally and organizationally independent yet in encountering a new and ambiguous situation, they may become more dependent on the founder/ entrepreneur	Informal and formal, complicated and based on each member's ability to cope with changes and ambiguity

Source: Adapted from Bruce Tuckman's Forming–Storming–Norming performing model, one of the most well-known models for team development.

manage: the team members opposed the recruitment of new employees, they were intolerant of each other's ideas, and they criticized one another's performance and work. Consequently, they released themselves from the business and went their own way.

The next stage in a team's development represents the 'quiet after the storm' and is shaped through the arrangements which have been established and accepted by the team's members in their attempts to overcome the stormy phase. Some teams establish a formal division of labor; others agree on giving each other space, and some settle on more intense communication, such as weekly update meetings, while still others settle on role rotations. The last stage represents the well-structured and well-known phase of the team, which functions like a well-oiled machine: the team members are independent and self-motivated, and each is familiar with his or her role, responsibilities and tasks in the team and in the business. This stage is typically characterized by shared interests and mutual relationships among team members. However, entrepreneurs should not consider this stage as the ultimate, best and final phase of team development; rather, they should make an effort to inspire and challenge the team in order to prevent burnout, exhaustion or undesirable turnover of team members.

Team cultures. Many entrepreneurial businesses work, or plan to work, in international environments, but people from different countries and cultures behave differently. Studies consistently provide empirical evidence of differences in the way people in different cultures think, feel, and act in business, even though human instinct leads us to treat others based on how we operate in our own culture. Peter Drucker (1985, 1999)[6] has been quoted as saying that company cultures are like country cultures; therefore, entrepreneurs should not try to change them. Instead, they should work with what they have. In the current era of emerging international entrepreneurial businesses, establishing culture-related teams is critical to a business's performance and outcomes.

The research in entrepreneurship broadly distinguishes between national cultures, which differ mostly in their values, which are then translated to differences in practice; the models developed by Hofstede on national dimensions[7] provide interesting insights into the national cultural differences by introducing a model with the five following dimensions: the Power-Distance Index is the extent to which the less powerful members of organizations and institutions accept inequality in the business's distribution of power; this dimension affects the team's performance in terms of tolerance of different types of power distribution in the team related to career prospects, benefits, visibility and prestige. Individualism versus collectivism is the degree to which individuals are integrated into groups or are independent and have sole responsibility for their outcomes; some societies, such as Canada and the United States, are characterized by an individualistic culture while others, such as Israel and Arab states, are more collectivistic. The Uncertainty-Avoidance Index deals with a society's tolerance for uncertainty and ambiguity; it ultimately indicates to what extent a culture programs its members to feel at ease in structured versus unstructured situations. Masculinity versus femininity refers to the distribution of roles between the genders; the assertive pole has been called 'masculine' and the modest, caring pole 'feminine'. Long-term versus short-term orientation is based on studies which were conducted in the 1990s after finding that Asian countries had a strong link to Confucian philosophy and that they acted differently from Western cultures in terms of values. This dimension is associated with a respect for tradition, fulfilling social obligations versus a respect for the business's needs, strategic considerations and rational goals (Hofstede 2001, 2004).

A national-oriented culturally diverse work force has been found to be beneficial for entrepreneurial businesses in a variety of ways, but achieving diversity is not always easy, nor is maintaining an effective culturally diverse workforce in entrepreneurial businesses.

SUMMARY

Management, leadership and teamwork are significant elements in the success of entrepreneurial businesses; some leading theories (i.e., RBV and the DC approach) consider team management to be the leading business resource, which maintains the business's goals. The traditional models of management and leadership do not provide the business with a strategic 'best fit' to the demands of the twenty-first century's global and dynamic economy, and new models and strategies are required to handle uncertainties and changing demands encountered by today's entrepreneurial businesses. A mix of models is needed to handle the entrepreneurial navigation process, for example, participative leadership combined with a task-oriented style or with transactional leadership. Such 'merging' of styles illustrates the dynamics needed for the new manager-leader-entrepreneur and demonstrates the prerequisite for flexible and adaptive management in order to navigate the entrepreneurial business toward success. Such mixes should be embedded in the formal and informal systems in order to facilitate the participation of subordinates in decision-making, the stimulation of creativity, and motivation.

Managing teamwork in teams or partnerships is much more complex, and challenging, in entrepreneurial businesses than in established ones; moreover, entrepreneurial workforces in most countries are becoming increasingly diverse, and many businesses operate in the international arena. As such, a wide range of backgrounds need to be managed and navigated and diversity should be at the center of effective teamwork management.

AT A GLANCE 10.1   The entrepreneurial team: the Center of Entrepreneurship, Canada (First Nation)

A group of fourteen entrepreneurs of First Nation communities in Canada attended a course in venture creation in northern Ontario. The group studied and acquired many tools and strategies in the areas of marketing, advertising, financing and managing entrepreneurial business. Their final project was to interview a successful First Nation entrepreneur and to ask him or her about his or her key to success. Duma, one of the students, interviewed Eagle, an entrepreneur in the field of adventure tourism in Canada. Eagle shared his experience, but most of all he expressed his deep gratitude to his team for the success of his business, Canoe River: 'Our business is to offer our guests, our Canoe River clients, an experience in our way of life, of living along the rivers and among the forests of our land. We are proud to share our stories,' says Eagle.

Duma. What motivated you to start this business?

Eagle. Owning my own business has always been my dream. We decided to enter tourism to honor our history and ancestors. Nearly 7,000 years ago, our grandfathers carved out a life in this rugged land and created a culture that has managed to survive until today – the Europeans came only 400 years ago . . . Canoe River is the original First Nations tourism facility to depict our ancient people's way of life.

Duma. Did you consult your family prior to launching Canoe River in 2004?

Eagle. Oh yes! This is the wonderful thing in our community – we share everything! Our thoughts, decisions, dilemmas and teamwork. I first consulted my father, who gave me his blessing; then we consulted some very important people in the community. They provided me with many practical stories and historical details that facilitated the construction of the concept. They all told me that they would assist with the first investment in Canoe River. They also promised to have their grandchildren work in Canoe River, in the construction and design of the place, as guides, and in the administration. After that we announced it to our community, and we got lots of support.

Duma. Would you have gone on with your dream if you had not received your community's blessing?

Eagle. It would have meant that I would have had to go against them. I might have tried to convince them, for the benefit of our history and heritage; but if I had not obtained my father's blessing I would not have proceeded with it. I was an employee in a dry-cleaning shop for many years . . . I guess you would still find me there . . .

Duma. At what point did you say to yourself, 'Canoe River is a success!'?

Eagle. There was no such point. Establishing the concept of Canoe River was very demanding. My team and I went to each one of the families in our communities and collected stories, memoirs and historical paraphernalia; it took around three months. We then had the various items copied for us, and kept the originals for the museum: we had to use copies for the hands-on experiences. Luckily one woman in our community is a poet and she provided us with many relevant details for Canoe River. We have a painter in our community who helped us a great deal. We then had many difficulties in terms of formalities, and we had to find professional people for the design and concept. Preparations lasted a very long time. If I hadn't had my team, Canoe River would not have been launched. We did everything – and I mean everything – from cleaning the reserve, constructing canoes, designing and sewing the costumes, cleaning the trash and feeding the animals. But we all had to study the guide's role, and take care of the formalities, etc. My success is this team. Everybody was engaged in everything.

Duma. You mention your team a lot . . .

Eagle. Yes, Canoe River's growth is due to our teamwork. Our team includes our youth, some of whom are university students, artists, lawyers, teachers. Most are engaged part-time in the reserve and help in everything: they weren't asked to take part in it, but they wanted to help. We are a permanent team of twelve people and around twenty more who come to the reserve to help. When we planned Canoe River, they were all equally involved in everything in the reserve's establishment, and they were all trained by our people to be guides. So they are all accredited to be the guides as well as to do anything else that needs to be done here.

Duma. Who are your main clients?

Eagle. Mostly families from Canada who wish to experience the lives of the First Nations for one or two days. They 'live' our traditional life, sleep in original tents, feed our animals and experience the preparation of our traditional food – all of which is done with one of our guides.

Duma. What do you do when your clients complain about your services?

Eagle. Once a French family came to the reserve after traveling a great distance, but they came after closing. Our front desk receptionist would not let them in and the man was furious. I was away just then, but other people from the team were there and they supported our receptionist and tried to convince the family to come back the next day. The family did not come back, but we decided to treat it as a case study of how we should handle clients' demands while providing them with the best possible service. We held a team meeting, which lasted three hours, and came up with a mission statement on our values and vision. It was stimulating.

We were once faced with the case of a young visitor who treated our animals brutally and the guide had to stop him. The guide then asked to set up a team meeting to discuss such situations. That introduced us to the Center of Entrepreneurship. We sent some of the team to attend a course on stress management and leadership. Then, those that attended the course taught what they had learned to the other team members, and this has helped us all a lot.

Duma. What is your main piece of advice for young entrepreneurs who want to succeed?

Eagle. Choose your team; train them; involve them in your business processes; maintain them by feedback; make them feel that it is their business too. You will harvest the fruits of this effort by gaining a wonderful, cheerful atmosphere. And above all, motivate them to choose entrepreneurship. Three young members of our team have already expressed their will to launch their own businesses; and I plan to treat them as my community treated me – I'll help financially and in every other way that I can.

NOTES

1 Facebook, http://il.youtube.com/watch?v=1CGF00VIxB8&feature=related.
2 Google, http://il.youtube.com/watch?v=aOZhbOhEunY&feature=related; At http://il.youtube.com/watch?v=zIx5F0vbjB4; http://il.youtube.com/watch?v=JV2HcNta1gU&feature=related.
3 Entrepreneurs have been dubbed 'heroes' by Dell, whose campaign highlights the entrepreneurial heroes, PreWeek, 11 September 2009, www.prweekus.com/Dells-new-campaign-highlights-entrepreneur-heroes/article/148641/.
4 Among others, www.passionforbusiness.com/articles/mastermind-group.htm; www.speakernetnews.com/post/mastermind.html; www.learningfountain.com/mastmind.htm.
5 At www.isixsigma.com/.
6 One of the most influential writers and management consultants, author or co-author of numerous publications. See also www.druckerinstitute.com/.
7 At www.geert-hofstede.com/.

REFERENCES

Amit, R. and Schoemaker, P. (1993) 'Strategic assets and organizational rent', *Strategic Management Journal*, 14: 33–46.

Avolio, B.J. (1999) *Full Leadership Development: Building the Vital Forces in Organizations*, Thousand Oaks, CA: Sage.

Barney, J. (1986) 'Types of competition and the theory of strategy: toward an integrative framework', *Academy of Management Review*, 11: 791–800.

Barney, J. (1991) 'Firm resources and sustained competitive advantage', *Journal of Management*, 17: 99–120.

Barney, J. (2001) 'Is the resource-based view a useful perspective for strategic management research? Yes', *Academy of Management Review*, 26: 41–56.

Barrick, M.R. and Mount, M.K. (1991) 'The big five personality dimensions and job performance: a meta analysis', *Personnel Psychology*, 44: 1–26.

Bass, B.M. (1960) *Leadership, Psychology, and Organizational Behavior*, New York: Harper and Brothers.

Bass, B.M. (1985) 'Leadership and performance beyond expectations', New York: The Free Press.

Bass, B.M. (1990) *Bass and Stogdill's Handbook of Leadership: Theory, Research, and Managerial Applications,* 3rd edn, New York: Free Press.

Bass, B.M. (1997) 'The ethics of transformational leadership', in *Kellogg Leadership Studies Project,* Transformational Leadership Working Papers, The James MacGregor Burns Academy of Leadership.

Bass, B.M. and Avolio, B.J. (1990) *Multifactor Leadership Questionnaire*, Palo Alto, CA: Consulting Psychologist Press.

Bass, B.M. and Avolio, B.J. (1994) *Improving Organizational Effectiveness Through Transformational Leadership*, Thousand Oaks, CA: Sage Publications.

Beugelsdijk, S. (2007) 'Entrepreneurial culture, regional innovativeness and economic growth', *Journal of Evolutional Economy*, 17: 187–210.

Blau, P.M. and Scott, W.R. (1962) *Formal Organizations: A Comparative Approach*, San Francisco: Chandler Publ. Co.

Bowen, D.E. and Lawler III, E.E. (1995) 'Empowering service employees', *Sloan Management Review*, 36: 73–84.

Burns, J.M. (1978) *Leadership*, New York: Harper & Row.

Bycio, P., Hackett, R.D. and Allen, J.S. (1995) 'Further assessments of Bass's (1985) conceptualization of transactional and transformational leadership', *Journal of Applied Psychology*, 80: 468–78.

Calori, R. and de Woot, P. (1994), *A European Management Model,* New York: Prentice-Hall.

Chowdhury, S. (2005) 'Demographic diversity for building and effective entrepreneurial team: is it important?', *Journal of Business Venturing*, 20: 727–46.

Clegg, S.R., Ibarra-Colado, E. and Bueno-Rodriquez, L. (1999) *Global Management: Universal Theories and Local Realities,* Thousand Oaks, CA: Sage.

Cole, R.E., Bacdayan, P. and White, B.J. (1993) 'Quality, participation and competitiveness', *California Management Review*, 35: 68–81.

Cooper, A.C. and Daily, C.M. (1997) 'Entrepreneurial teams', in D.L. Sexton and R.W. Smilor (eds) *Entrepreneurship 2000*. Chicago, IL: Upstart Publishing, 127–50.

Cunningham, J.B. and Lischeron, J. (1991) 'Defining entrepreneurship', *Journal of Small Business Management*, 29: 45–61.

Den Hartog, D.N., Van Muijen, J.J. and Koopman, P.L. (1997) 'Transactional versus transformational leadership: an analysis of the MLQ', *Journal of Occupational and Organizational Psychology*, 70: 19–34.

Dollinger, M.J. (1999) *Entrepreneurship, Strategies and Resources*, 2nd edn, Englewood Cliffs, NJ: Prentice-Hall.

Dong, I.J. and Yammarino, F.J. (2001) 'Perceptions of transformational leadership among Asian Americans and Caucasian Americans: a level of analysis perspective', *Journal of Leadership and Organizational Studies*, 8: 3–21.

Drucker, P. (1985) *Innovation and Entrepreneurship: Practice and Principles*, New York: John Wiley & Sons.

Drucker, P. (1999) *Management Challenges for the Twenty-first Century*, New York: Harper Paperbacks.

Eisenhardt, K. and Martin, J. (2000) 'Dynamic capabilities: what are they?', *Strategic Management Journal* , 21: 1105–21.

Elliott, H. (2003) 'SHRM best-practices and sustainable competitive advantage: a resource based view', *Otago Management Graduate Review*, 1: 43–57.

Ensley, M.D., Carland, J.C., Carland, J.W. and Banks, M. (1999) 'Exploring the existence of entrepreneurial teams', *International Journal of Management*, 16: 276–86.

Fiet, J., Busenitz, L., Moesel, D. and Barney, J. (1997) 'Complementary theoretical perspectives on the dismissal of new venture team members', *Journal of Business Venturing*, 12: 347–66.

Finkelstein, S. and Boyd, B. (1998) 'How much does the CEO matter? The role of managerial discretion in the setting of CEO compensation', *Academy of Management Journal*, 41: 179–99.

Finkelstein, S. and Hambrick, D. (1996) *Strategic Leadership: Top Executives and Their Effects on Organizations*, St. Paul, MN: West.

Francis, D.H. and Sandberg, W.R. (2000) 'Friendship within entrepreneurial teams and its association with team and venture performance', *Entrepreneurship Theory and Practice*, 25: 5–26.

Goldberg, L. (1990) 'An alternative "description" of personality: the Big-Five-Factor structure', *Journal of Personality and Social Psychology*, 59: 1216–29.

Grant, R.M. (1996) 'Toward a knowledge-based theory of the firm', *Strategic Management Journal*, 17: 109–22.

Haleblian, J. and Finkelstein, S. (1993) 'Top management team size, CEO dominance, and firm performance: the moderating roles of environmental turbulence and discretion', *Academy of Management Journal*, 36: 844–63.

Hambrick, D.C. (1994) 'Top management groups: a conceptual integration and reconsideration of the "team" label', in L.L. Cummings and B.M. Staw (eds) *Research in Organizational Behavior*, Greenwich, CT: JAI Press, 171–214.

Hamel, G. (2000) *Leading the Revolution*, Boston, MA: Harvard Business School Press.

Harber, D., Marriot, F. and Idrus, N. (1991) 'Employee participation in TQC: an integrative review', *International Journal of Quality and Reliability Management*, 8: 24–34.

Herrmann, P. and Datta, D.K. (2005) 'Relationships between top management team characteristics and international diversification: an empirical investigation', *British Journal of Management*, 16: 69–78.

Hersey, P. and Blanchard, K.H. (1977) *The Management of Organizational Behaviour*, Upper Saddle River, NJ: Prentice Hall.

Hofstede, G. (2001) *Culture's Consequences: Comparing Values, Behaviors, Institutions, and Organizations Across Nations*, 2nd edn, Thousand Oaks, CA: Sage Publications.

Hofstede, G. (2004) *Cultures and Organizations: Software of the Mind*, 2nd edn, New York: McGraw-Hill.

Honig, B. (1998) 'Who gets the goodies? An examination of microenterprise credit in Jamaica', *Entrepreneurship and Regional Development*, 10: 313–34.

House, R.J. and Podsakoff, P.M. (1994) 'Leadership effectiveness', in J. Greenberg (ed.) *Organizational Behavior: The State of the Science*, Hillsdale, NJ: Erlbaum, 45–82.

House, R.J. and Shamir, B. (1993) 'Toward the integration of transformational, charismatic, and visionary theories', in M.M. Chemers and R. Ayman (eds) *Leadership Theory and Research: Perspectives and Directions*, San Diego: Academic Press, 81–107.

John, O.P. and Srivastava, S. (1999) 'The Big-Five trait taxonomy: history, measurement, and theoretical perspectives', in L.A. Pervin and O.P. John (eds) *Handbook of Personality: Theory and Research*, vol. 2, New York: Guilford Press, 102–38.

Judge, T.A., Bono, J.E., Ilies, R. and Gerhardt, M.W. (2002) 'Personality and leadership: a qualitative and quantitative review', *Journal of Applied Psychology*, 87: 765–80.

Kamm, J.B. and Shuman, J.C. (1990) 'Entrepreneurial teams in new venture creation: a research agenda', *Entrepreneurship Theory and Practice*, 14: 7–17.

Katzenbach, J.R. (1997) 'The myth of the top management team', *Harvard Business Review*, 75: 82–91.

Korunka, C., Frank, H., Lueger, M. and Mugler, J. (2003) 'The entrepreneurial personality in the context of resources, environment, and the startup process – a configurational approach', *Entrepreneurship Theory and Practice*, 28: 23–42.

Kotter, J.P. (1999) *John P. Kotter on What Leaders Really Do*, Boston, MA: Harvard Business School Press.

Li, J.T. and Hambrick, D.C. (2005) 'Factional groups: a new vantage on demographic faultlines, conflict and disintegration in work teams', *Academy of Management Journal*, 48: 794–813.

Likert, R. (1961) *New Patterns of Management*, New York: McGraw-Hill.

Likert, R. (1967) *The Human Organization: Its Management and Value*, New York: McGraw-Hill.

Littunen, H. (2000) 'Entrepreneurship and the characteristics of the entrepreneurial personality', *International Journal of Entrepreneurial Behaviour and Research*, 6: 295–309.

Littunen, H. and Storhammar, E. (2000) 'The indicators of locus of control in the small business context', *Journal of Enterprising Culture*, 8: 343–60.

Lowe, K.B., Kroeck, K.G. and Sivasubramaniam, N. (1996) 'Effectiveness correlates of transformational and transactional leadership: a meta-analytic review of the multifactor leadership questionnaire literature', *Leadership Quarterly*, 7: 385–425.

Luthans, F. (2002) 'The need for and meaning of positive organizational behavior', *Journal of Organizational Behavior*, 23: 695–706.

Makadok, R. (2001) Toward a synthesis of the resource-based and dynamic-capability views of rent creation', *Strategic Management Journal*, 22: 387–402.

Mankins, M.C. (2004) 'Stop wasting valuable time', *Harvard Business Review*, 82: 58–65.

McClelland, D.C. (1961) *The Achieving Society*, Princeton, NJ: Van Nostrand.

McGrath, J.E. (1984) *Groups: Interaction and Performance*, Englewood Cliffs, NJ: Prentice-Hall, Inc.

McGuinness, T. and Morgan, R.E. (2000) 'Strategy, dynamic capabilities and complex science: management rhetoric versus reality', *Strategic Change*, 9: 209–20.

Penrose, E. (1959) *The Theory of the Growth of the Firm*, Oxford: Blackwell.

Peteraf, M. (1993) 'The cornerstones of competitive advantage: a resource-based view', *Strategic Management Journal*, 14: 179–91.

Pfeffer, J. (1994) 'The cornerstones of competitive advantage: a resource-based view', *Strategic Management Journal*, 14: 179–91.

Pfeffer, J. and Salancik, G.R. (1978) *The External Control of Organizations: a Resource Dependence Perspective*, New York: Harper & Row.

Pisano, G.P. (1994) 'Knowledge, integration, and the locus of learning: an empirical analysis of process development', *Strategic Management Journal*, 15: 85–100.

Priem, R.L. and Butler, J.E. (2001) 'Is the resource-based "view" a useful perspective for strategic management research?', *Academy of Management Review*, 26: 22–40.

Rauch, A. and Frese, M. (2000) 'Psychological approaches to entrepreneurial success: a general model and an overview of findings', in C.L. Cooper and I.T. Robertson (eds) *International Review of Industrial and Organizational Psychology*, vol. 15, Chichester, Sussex: Wiley & Sons, 100–35.

Reynolds, P.D., Storey, D.J. and Westhead, P. (1994) *Frontiers of Entrepreneurship Research*, Wellesley, MA: Babson College.

Schumpeter, J.A. (1934) *The Theory of Economic Development*, Cambridge, MA: Harvard University Press (first published in German in 1911).

Sykes, H.B. and Dunham, D. (1995) 'Critical assumption planning: a practical tool for managing business development risk', *Journal of Business Venturing*, 10: 413–24.

Teece, D.J., Pisano, G. and Shuen, A. (1997) 'Dynamic capabilities and strategic management', *Strategic Management Journal*, 18: 509–33.

Timmons, J.A. and Bygrave, W.D. (1986) 'Venture capital's role in financing innovation for economic growth', *Journal of Business Venturing*, 1: 161–76.

Timmons, J.A. and Gumpert, D.E. (1982) *The Insider's Guide to Small Business Resources*, New York: Doubleday & Company, Inc.

Vroom, V.H. and Jago, A.G. (1988) *The New Leadership: Managing Participation in Organizations*, Englewood Cliffs, NJ: Prentice-Hall.

Waldman, D.A., Bass, B.M. and Einstein, W.O. (1987) 'Effort, performance, and transformational leadership in industrial and military settings', *Journal of Occupational Psychology*, 60: 177–86.

Wernerfelt, B. (1984) 'A resource-based view of the firm', *Strategic Management Journal*, 5: 171–80.

Wyer, P., Mason, J. and Theodorakopoulos, N. (2000) 'Small business development and the "learning organization"', *International Journal of Entrepreneurial Behaviour and Research*, 6: 239–59.

175

Yammarino, F.J. and Bass, B.M. (1990) 'Long-term forecasting of transformational leadership and its effects among naval officers. Some preliminary findings', in K.E. Clark (ed.) *Measure of Leadership*, Greensboro, NC: Center for Creative Leadership.

Yukl, G. (1994) *Leadership in Organizations*, 3rd edn, Englewood Cliffs, NJ: Prentice-Hall.

Zahra, S.A. (1999) 'The changing rules of global competitiveness in the twenty-first century', *Academy of Management Executive*, 13: 36–42.

Zahra, S.A., Yavus, R.I. and Ucbasaran, D. (2006) 'How much do you trust me?: The dark side of relational trust in new business creation in established companies', *Entrepreneurship Theory and Practice*, 30: 541–59.

Chapter 11

Marketing

OBJECTIVES

After studying this chapter you will be able to:

- Explain the concept of the marketing process and its different perspectives in today's highly competitive markets.
- Distinguish between marketing purposes and activities targeted to startups and the established stages.
- Justify Porter's model of the forces involved in developing a competitive advantage for the business, and adopt its principles for an existing/planned business.
- Construct a marketing plan that will provide entrepreneurs with important and most significant information about the market.
- Conduct market research that will give the entrepreneur an opportunity to discover new ideas and possibilities, and to get feedback from people who are not involved in the business on its products/services.
- Understand what positioning and segmentation mean; develop a positioning process as a competitive strategy.

Many entrepreneurial businesses consider their entrepreneurial orientation to be the backbone of their future business success. This orientation is reflected in the business's degree of risk-taking and proactiveness with respect to developing new products and services, building new competencies, and capitalizing on emerging opportunities. Yet, an entrepreneurial orientation is not sufficient to sell products and services, and the most important driver of business growth is marketing. Specifically, marketing is needed in using the entrepreneurial business's resources and capabilities to identify and meet customers' new needs, as well as satisfy their latent needs to better differentiate the business's products and services.

Marketing is an organizational function and a set of processes for creating, communicating and delivering value to customers and for managing customer relationships in ways that benefit the organization and its stakeholders.

Marketing is not only an ongoing activity for entrepreneurs: it is one that involves various combinations of marketing techniques and strategies. Porter (1980), in his seminal theoretical work on strategy which included marketing for fast-growing businesses, argued that an entrepreneurial business should carry out a differentiation strategy, and should do so in either of two ways: broadly, by targeting a large market, or more narrowly, by focusing on a particular segment of the market. Using Porter's framework, many well-known researchers (e.g., Ireland and Hitt 1997; Baum, Locke and Smith 2001) found that vis-à-vis entrepreneurial businesses, marketing strategies such as adopting a 'first to market' product strategy, differentiation through high quality or innovation, differentiation through emphasizing quality over low cost, or diversification, strongly promote positive financial returns.

Marketing techniques and practice include product development and improvement, pricing and re-pricing, special sales, public relations, advertising, packaging, distribution and development of new promotional campaigns, among others. All of these are based on the entrepreneurs' (1) understanding of the customers' needs; (2) promise of value for the customer; (3) communicating this value to the target market, and (4) facilitating acquisition of the products and/or services. Simply stated, marketing is everything entrepreneurs do in order to bring their products and/or services to the notice and into the hands of potential customers.

Persuading people to spend money for products and/or services is a highly complex endeavor in today's highly competitive markets, where almost anything can be sought, and often found, cheaper. When familiar products are updated or of higher quality, and hence costlier, customers become suspicious and selective; the marketing of these products has to convince the customers that they are worth the additional cost. A major strategy in marketing, and one that is particularly relevant in entrepreneurial practice, is the establishment of a *competitive advantage*; consumers are offered greater value for their money, either by means of a lower price for a product or service, or by means of higher quality or greater benefit, which justifies the higher price (Porter 1998). In order to create and maintain a competitive advantage, entrepreneurs have to be thoroughly acquainted with their competitors' products and services, and to offer a better or more worthwhile counterpart (Ramaswamy, Gatignon and Reibstein 1994; Slater and Narver 1995; Becherer and Maurer 1997; Baker and Sinkula 2005).

A model of the forces affecting the establishment of a competitive advantage in entrepreneurial firms, developed by Porter, includes: (1) potential entrants that may be a threat; (2) suppliers' and customers' bargaining power; and (3) the threats of substitute products or services. Several techniques may be used effectively for establishing a competitive advantage:

- *Differentiation*. The selection of one or more criteria used by buyers in a market, and then uniquely positioning the business to meet those criteria; customers are given clear reasons for preferring the given product over others. For example, Mercedes-Benz offers its customers excellence: elegance and very high standards in comfort, design, mechanical functions, and many more. These luxury cars are highly priced, yet Mercedes-Benz is not only one of the most prestigious and valued car companies in the world, it also sells many cars.
- *Cost leadership*. The objective is to become the lowest cost producer in the industry. This technique is usually associated with large-scale businesses offering fairly standardized, non-differentiated products that are perfectly acceptable to a large number of customers. Many fashion clothing shops in malls use cost leadership to attract clients.
- *Differentiation focus*. The focus is on a limited but unique segment of the market, usually one with specific and/or special needs or demands. The products and/or services offered are

clearly different from those of competitors targeting a broader group of customers. The important consideration for businesses adopting this marketing strategy is to ensure that there are a sufficient number of potential customers with these different needs or demands, and that these are not being met by existing competitors. Baby shops and educational programs for children with learning disabilities are examples of business that may use this marketing technique.

■ *Cost focus*. The emphasis is on the lower cost of products similar to those of a featured and higher priced market leader but acceptable to a sufficiently large target market. For example, many imitators produce and sell products very similar to the plastic kitchenware originated by Tupperware.

ESTABLISHING A CONCEPT

Marketing is more than simply selling a product. It is based on selling a concept that plays to consumers' unvoiced question: 'What will this product do for me?' It is based on potential customers' needs and demands combined with their *perceptions* of what the product can do for them, and their readiness to purchase it even when it is clearly unsuitable. Various experiments examining the placebo-treatment effect have demonstrated how strongly patients' perceptions of the medication they believe they are receiving affect their moods and even the actual state of their medical problem. This effect is mirrored in that of customers who buy a concept. For example: customers' perceptions that a particular brand of a specific cosmetics firm is the best, most effective anti-aging face cream will believe that it is making their skin look younger and will purchase only that firm's products, without even considering those of any other firms that produce face creams with the same functions.

Entrepreneurs who aspire to turn their products into a concept must first identify the needs of potential clients by performing a drill-down of the perceptions of products similar to those they are about to sell. In order to do this, entrepreneurs have to first examine their internal, subjective view of their own products and then move to the external, detailed phase (Phase 4 in Table 11.1). Entrepreneurs must be aware of and open to customers' reactions to and evaluations of the product, possibly by allowing themselves to 'become the customer'. This may enable them to assess the product's qualities objectively and provide a key to marketing it within the context of customers' wants or needs, the problems the product may solve, or the elements in need of improvement.

In order to establish and maintain their competitive advantage and the 'concept', entrepreneurs have to be constantly aware of social and economic trends, governmental regulations, and cultural influences (FitzRoy 1993; Chrisman, Chua and Steier 2002; Alsaaty 2006).

Table 11.1 *Building a concept: understanding customers' perceptions*

	General view	Detail view
Internal: entrepreneur's view	*Phase 1* Entrepreneurs are enthusiastic about their product; the high value they place on it is based on their own assessment. They may not recognize any weaknesses in their product and may also be unwilling to listen to negative feedback. Their enthusiasm is affected by the long and arduous path that led to producing the product. Their enthusiasm and hard work lead them to expect the reward of a successful product	*Phase 2* Entrepreneurs move to an objective and more detailed analysis of the strengths and weaknesses of their product and an assessment of its valuation in the industry. Their assessments are nevertheless still based on their own views and analyses
External: customers' views (active and potential)	*Phase 3* Entrepreneurs become interested in customer feedback on their product, but at a superficial rather than an in-depth level. They are open to 'general impressions' but are not ready to make any corresponding changes	*Phase 4* Entrepreneurs are more confident about their product and are therefore willing to have detailed information about its strengths and weaknesses and how these translate to the customers' willingness to spend money on them. They may plan on how to improve their product accordingly

CASE STUDY 11.1   e-HK.Flowers, Hong Kong

Fai Yang is the owner of e-HK.Flowers, Hong Kong. The company specializes in web-sourcing for deliveries and shipping of special flower bouquets from Hong Kong to any place in the world. Orders can be placed through the internet or through e-HK.Flowers' website.

Fai Yang and his wife Hua launched their first flower shop in Victoria City, Hong Kong in May 2000: 'My wife and I were born and raised in farming areas in China. My wife's father was a florist, known for his traditional bouquets of autumn flowers. My wife learned how to design flower bouquets from her father, but also graduated from a flower designing program at a university in Beijing. Our house was always full of flowers and bouquets,' says Fai Yang. Business in the couple's first flower shop went very well. They had no business plan or any specific marketing strategies, but Chinese people love flowers and don't need special occasions to buy them, the shop was centrally located, and people passing down the street came in and bought flowers. Three years later, Fai Hua became ill and was unable to work. Fai Yang had to run the shop by himself. Meanwhile, other flower shops, attractive and vividly decorated, sprang up all over. For these and other reasons, sales dropped dramatically; Fai Yang had only a small number of customers, those who had bought his bouquets in the past and appreciated the high quality of his work. He was about to close the shop but, as a last resort, he attended a management course given by a government association and was matched with a mentor to assist him.

However, busy attending to his family problems, Fai Yang was unable to devote the time and energy needed to follow his mentor's suggestions on how to recover his business. Fai Yang's mentor Claire, an experienced British mentor who had been living with her husband in Hong Kong for five years, was an enthusiastic mentor, and she was determined to help him save his business: 'I have met many entrepreneurs that wanted to give up their business when things did not work out, and I am challenged by these people. I try to provide them with as many strategies as possible to help them restore their businesses. Fai Yang was going through a family crisis, but his four kids were dependent on his income. I told him that he could not afford to lose his business or to have a smaller income from it. In fact, anyone seeing Fai Yang's flower bouquets would not let him close his business – it was art, pure art!' exclaims Claire.

One night, after a mentoring session with Claire, which was held in the shop, a well-dressed European man came to the shop's door. Just as Fai Yang was about to tell him that the shop had been closed for business for hours, Claire signaled him not to turn the man away and asked the man how they could help him at such a late hour. The man told them that he had been looking for hours for a florist that could deliver a traditional bouquet to his wife in the UK the next day, which was their anniversary; he explained that he was on a business tour and had missed their celebration but wanted to send her special flowers. Fai Yang started to apologize, explaining very kindly that they did not provide overseas deliveries, but Claire stopped him and told the man that they would be able to make such a delivery, but that it would cost a lot of money due to the late hour and the extra work it would entail. Relieved to find a florist that would deliver the bouquet, the man was willing to pay any price. Claire asked for, and Fai Yang received, triple the usual price. While Fai Yang was designing and arranging the bouquet, Claire arranged the delivery. Three days later the man entered the shop with a handwritten letter of thanks: Dear Florists, I postponed my departure for my next business meeting in Taiwan in order to personally give you this thank-you note. A long-distance relationship can be difficult at times, and due to my business trips, I sometimes barely see my wonderful wife . . . But the bouquet I sent her was so beautiful that she couldn't stop crying. She told me on the phone that it was obviously made with love . . . I know that you had to work long into the night to make this delivery happen, and it apparently arrived fresh and undamaged. I am delighted to have found a florist in Hong Kong specializing in overseas deliveries as I come to Hong Kong frequently and often need such a service. Again I want to express my sincere thanks to you both for handling my request in so professional a manner. Sincerely yours, Dr. Aaron Milliner.

Fai Yang then realized that as Hong Kong attracted more and more foreign business people and investors, the need for overseas deliveries would also increase. It was a turning point for him. He hired a web specialist to build an attractive website, quickly designed and made up twenty beautiful flower arrangements, and hired a special photographer to prepare photographs of them for the website. (He planned the photography session for the day before the Buddha's birthday holiday so that the bouquets that he prepared would be bought and not go to waste.) While the website was still being constructed, Fai Yang personally called the human resources (HR) staff of as many international companies as he could find on the internet, informed them about his service, and sent his website address. He also published Dr. Milliner's testimonial on his website.

In May 2006, Fai Yang launched e-HK.Flowers. He continued to work closely with Claire to get her feedback on his rebuilt business and her suggestions for further possibilities. At this point, Claire was more concerned than Fai Yang about turning his storefront business into an e-business: ordering and pricing are difficult over the internet and some people are uneasy about online credit payments – but by then, Fai Yang was determined to turn his flower shop into an e-business.

Fai Yang's seventeen-year-old daughter Mei helped him in the design and creation of the bouquets, and then came up with the idea of designing traditional baskets of fruits and sweets as well, to which Fai Yang readily agreed. He hired employees to make local deliveries and to manage the marketing.

Fai Yang is presently working very closely with a quality-control specialist who checks the contents of every flower bouquet and fruit basket prior to consignment. The entire process of creating a bouquet or basket is depicted on e-HK.Flowers' website: the flower farms, design process, order documentation, quality control, consignment, etc. Details on security and privacy are also provided, and there is an e-address for inquiries. Fai Yang now has students who work in shifts to maintain the website.

Fai Yang's prices are high – but so is the quality of his merchandise.

QUESTIONS FOR DISCUSSION

1   What were Fai Yang's marketing techniques in his first flower shop? Can you explain why sales were dropping?
2   What are Fai Yang's major marketing techniques in e-HK.Flowers?
3   Discuss the strengths and weaknesses of Fai Yang's marketing choices in e-HK.Flowers.
4   What is your opinion regarding Claire's concerns about turning Fai Yang's flower shop into an e-business? Explain.
5   Is Fai Yang depending on one major competitive advantage or is he strategically developing more than one? How is he differentiating e-HK.Flowers?
6   Construct a marketing plan for e-HK.Flowers.

MARKETING PLAN

With regard to his inventions, Thomas Edison said: 'I never perfected an invention that I did not think about in terms of the service it might give others . . . I find out what the world needs, then I proceed to invent.'

Following the gist of Edison's maxim, marketing means focusing on the outcome, in this case producing and selling something that fulfills consumers' needs or demands. To do this requires planning. Thus, before becoming consumed with entrepreneurial zeal – and possibly investing one's life savings in a new and untested venture – smart entrepreneurs have to be smart marketers; they have to invest time and thought into identifying potential consumers of the product they propose to sell, and into figuring out how to reach them effectively. Without a plan for doing this, entrepreneurial dreams are merely wishful thinking.

A marketing plan can be viewed as a map for success; its purpose is to enable a forecast of the future by carrying out a study of the past. This study examines what people have done, and from that it extrapolates what people *might* or *are likely to* do in the future. The first step in planning is therefore researching the past. Both are imperative features of the map-making process (Pavia 1991; Ashill, Frederikson and Davies 2003; Atherton and Sear 2004; Chakravorti 2004; Covin and Miles 2007).

Three main themes in marketing planning are *where*, *when* and *who*. The answers to these three questions comprise the framework of the marketing plan.

A carefully researched and objectively examined marketing plan can provide venture entrepreneurs with important information about the market in several ways:

■ *It provides a better understanding of the industry* and sector in which the business operates and of the 'role' of the business's products/services in this industry.

For example, when launching a pizza restaurant in a suburban shopping center and exploiting the niche that was missing among the existing 'pizza joints' – an authentic and more sophisticated Italian pizza – the role of such a restaurant is determined. Accordingly, the matching market strategy to be applied is differentiation or differentiation focus.

■ *It allows for identification of the target market* – the people most likely to buy the product or services that the business offers.

Entrepreneurs should determine why customers would want to buy their product and/or service, that is, what their particular products/services offer. To do this, it is essential to be able to differentiate between the features and benefits of the product/service. A feature is a characteristic of a product/service that automatically comes with it. While certain features are valuable and can certainly enhance the product, benefits are usually what motivate people to buy.

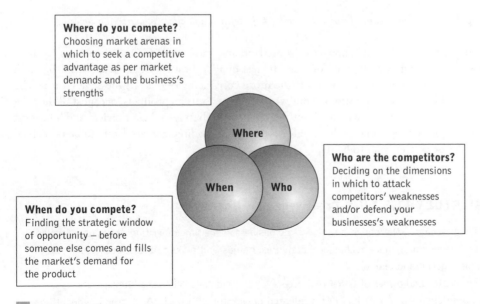

Where do you compete?
Choosing market arenas in which to seek a competitive advantage as per market demands and the business's strengths

When do you compete?
Finding the strategic window of opportunity – before someone else comes and fills the market's demand for the product

Who are the competitors?
Deciding on the dimensions in which to attack competitors' weaknesses and/or defend your businesses's weaknesses

Where

When   Who

Figure 11.1 *Three main themes in marketing planning*

183

Sometimes, however, what are considered benefits by the entrepreneur are not identified as benefits by the customers. Take, for example, healthy chocolate bars: the entrepreneur may consider their benefit to be the way to a healthier life but for the customer, the benefit lies in that it is a *chocolate* health bar which tastes good.

By recognizing what their product and/or service has to offer, and what will entice customers to buy it, entrepreneurs may be able to identify the characteristics of their potential market. They can then segment that market. For example, the potential customers of dietetic, 'healthy' chocolate bars may be sports enthusiasts, overweight people, people on a diet program for health reasons, diabetics, people who are aware of artificial ingredients, etc.

- *It allows for identification of the competitors*. Entrepreneurs should also identify their competitors' strengths and their place in the market, and try to determine why their competitors are successful in selling their products.

One technique for determining competitors' strengths is to 'research' their success, i.e., to find one or two successful firms in the same industry and interview their customers and, if possible, their employees, and go around the firms as a customer or visitor. Information may sometimes be found on the internet. Such quasi-research may bring to light the strengths, and the weaknesses, of the particular firm, or of the field of enterprise in general.

- *Careful planning* makes it possible to predict distribution costs, and to establish a pricing scale and product positioning. To be able to sustain a competitive advantage, the products have to be affordable.

Entrepreneurs should address questions such as: How cost effective will it be to introduce the product to the market? Which market is the most suitable for this product? Is it easy to imitate the product? Can the sale of the product at the proposed 'affordable' price turn a profit? Does the product have proprietary protection (i.e., copyrights, trademarks or patent)?

- *It enables the entrepreneur to focus on a simple, well-defined and effective marketing concept*.

For example: two stationers' shops are located on the same street. One advertises itself as 'Cheapest on the High Street'; the other as 'Highest quality, best service, cheapest on the High Street.' The first advertisement is probably the more convincing one, as its message is clear. The second one is likely to raise questions about why a business sells its products 'cheapest' if they are 'highest quality' products, as well as about the connection between 'best service' and 'cheapest prices'. Multiple concepts may be both unfocused and misleading, and are likely to be perceived as unreliable, or as 'too good to be true'.

CASE STUDY 11.2   U-R-Creativeee . . ., Norway

U-R-Creativeee . . ., Norway, is a two-year-old business at the time of writing. It designs, develops and facilitates tailor-made techniques, activities, games and tasks to assist business groups in their managerial and teamwork.

The creator and owner of U-R-Creativeee . . . is Ingrid Aas. When she launched the business she had no clients at all: 'I had just graduated university with an M.A. degree in educational programs development. I loved the subject, and I knew I could do it well. One of my father's clients had to move to Sweden for two years and offered me the use of his perfectly designed and equipped office, totally free of charge. It was the chance of a lifetime! So I went into business with only an office. I had to build up a client base, but most of all I wanted to build up a loyal client base that would provide me with a regular supply of interesting work,' she says.

Aas didn't know where to start: she had no contacts, she seemed (and was) very young, and she felt that her young age and lack of experience led people to not 'take her seriously'. She could not even find a way to introduce herself properly to potential clients. 'I was making non-stop telephone contacts and having meetings with potential clients, and meanwhile I was developing materials for workshops and business celebrations. I wasn't sure whether the client would stimulate the development of the material or whether the creative material that I developed would attract customers, so I was trying to do both at the same time; and I guess that this was a mistake,' she says. 'I asked my parents and my friends and neighbors to tell me about anyone they thought might be interested in my services. My first client, the tenant of a friend's parents, came after four months; he was looking for creative ideas for the celebration of his construction business's first anniversary. I took the project on and produced a magnificent celebration party, but this was not a connection that would bring other clients. My business was still unstable, and I had to approach everyone all over again. I was very uneasy doing that,' says Aas.

However, Aas learned a lot from this one experience; she decided to turn down clients who would neither use her services again, nor lead to connections with other potential customers. Although she still had no clients and was desperate for work, she was well aware of the trap she could fall into; determined to create her own niche, she turned down requests to plan children's birthday parties, family celebrations and so on. Realizing that she had to differentiate her company, she decided to specialize. She turned down customers requiring services that she was not planning to provide, although she had all the tools to do so. It was not an easy decision, but she was persistent.

Six months after launching U-R-Creativeee . . ., and still with only the rare customer, she decided to turn to an area in which her expertise could play to her advantage. She went to schools, introduced herself and her relevant accreditation (an M.A. in educational programs development) and offered workshops to enhance teachers' creativity and innovative thinking and their combination. This proved to be a success: 'My work with teaching staffs expanded, and many schools now offer me projects; my clients trust me and the service I provide . . . And I was fulfilled by the challenges, because I had to address a diverse range of topics,' she adds.

However, Aas still wanted to reach the private sector and business people; she was excited about how teams and managers in the business world manage their work lives, and she was convinced that they needed her services. She contacted businesses and introduced herself, along with a record of her experience and her clients' testimonies. 'What I do is highly niched and cutting-edge; people are only now being introduced to the concept of creativity within organizations, so I have to not only sell, but also to educate. People hear about my work through word-of-mouth, and it is often set up quite informally, which sometimes makes getting people to sign contracts for the work a bit uncomfortable.'

Aas's planning process targeted the private sector for customers: 'I constructed a marketing plan and determined my target market. My business strategy was to network in order to establish relationships, which would then supply me with work. I did this by sending out form letters describing my work, attending events, and, in general, maintaining ongoing contacts with potential clients.' Her first client from the private sector was the manager of a large company that bottles water for export. He wanted her to organize creativity enhancement and teamwork promotion workshops for 180 employees, in groups of ten.

Today, Aas differentiates her U-R-Creativeee. . .'s services by focusing on innovation. Her company now offers various different customized workshops: *Creativity Bits*, which are based on 'warmers and energizers to ignite and connect teams', and which are found to be very effective in keeping energy and motivation high in professional teams; *Creativity Chips*, which help managers 'run more productive meetings by increasing team involvement and cohesiveness whilst creating a fun work environment'; *Creative Kick-offs*, 'designed for meetings and conferences where there is a need for a group to interact and perform quickly'; *Fast Foodies*, sessions for increasing innovative and creative thinking, and so on. Aas's market research indicated that her services could be beneficial for groups at different levels in various businesses; they are both unique and adjustable; activities can be modified to suit highly dissimilar groups – from unskilled factory workers to bankers and university academics.

A client's testimonial of one of Aas's workshops is quoted in her brochure: 'It was like going out of the box. The sessions opened our minds and allowed for creative flair; we were able to go to work the following day and make a change. Our major benefits were in getting to know "the people behind the people" and in finding the creative parts of ourselves. We found both new friends and soul-mates and new aspects of ourselves. The team found the sessions insightful and useful, as individuals discovered more about each other's motivations and ways of working. This helped the group understand how to work together effectively as a successful team. It was inspiring and exciting.'

Aas describes her vision today: 'I want to continue to build a base of key clients with whom I enjoy working and with whom working is fun and beneficial for both sides – a base that will assure me a stream of interesting and well-paid projects. I want to build a solid reputation as a niche provider of creative solutions for building great teams, and that offers the best and most suitable service for my clients.'

QUESTIONS FOR DISCUSSION

1   In marketing terms, why did Ingrid Aas face difficulties in getting clients when she began her new business?
2   What was the turning point in Aas's business? Explain.
3   Do you think Ingrid Aas should be more selective with her target market? What might be the benefits and costs of such a target market?
4   What is unique about U-R-Creativeee . . .? How did Ingrid Aas differentiate her business?
5   Define and describe U-R-Creativeee. . .'s competitive advantage.
6   Which marketing strategy is Ingrid Aas applying?
7   What would you suggest that she do next in order to expand her business?

CONSTRUCTING THE MARKETING PLAN

The major components that should be included in a marketing plan are:

- *A mission statement* – in which the objectives and standards of the business are declared.
- *The business's objective* – the three W's: *what* the entrepreneur wants to do, *when* he wants to do it, and *how*, i.e., what are the business's resources?
- *Market analysis* – the findings of the research about various factors of the market environment in relation to the product, including legal, social, political, economic, and technological considerations.
- *Target audience* – the active and potential customers and how they can they be reached.
- *Competitive analysis* – the existing and latent or developing competitors and how the competitors' products compare with those of the entrepreneur; the advantages of the entrepreneurs' business, including plans for keeping these advantages.
- *Action plan* – defining the best route to reach the customers, i.e., advertising, public relations, specific programs and promotions of interest to the community, sales strategies, incentive programs for representatives, and more.

MARKET RESEARCH

Market research is first and foremost the opportunity to look outside the business to identify factors that may affect its success, as described in Phase 4 of the evolutional model for understanding customers' perceptions (Table 11.1). Conducting market research provides an opportunity to discover other ideas and possibilities, and to evaluate feedback on the products/services of the business and others like it. Market research is more than the collation and analysis of raw data; it is an in-depth examination of the observations made through a valid data-gathering process. The research should be carried out according to several general methodological rules:

- *Focus*. The focus should center on one or two topics that the entrepreneur is interested in having information about, e.g., the target market; segmentation of potential clients; segmentation of active clients; statistics about the consumer; habits of different segments of the active and potential clients, etc.
- *Hypothesizing*. For example, an entrepreneur launching a shop for women's and children's clothing can hypothesize that the target market consists mainly of mothers, who usually take their children with them when they go shopping; therefore, complementary services for kids are required, etc. Intuition may play a large role in hypothesizing.
- *Listing information* gathered from 'active clients' and from 'potential clients' about what they 'like' and what they 'dislike' about the business's products/services.

Data may be gathered easily and at little cost by making on-site inquiries. For example, entrepreneurs may politely ask their active clients questions about the product they are buying and the service. The motivation for asking can be explained tactfully, e.g., as 'research to improve my company's service', or the inquiries may be framed as 'small talk'.

Listing the replies, and then sorting them according to satisfaction and non-satisfaction with your products/services. The responses are likely to fill information gaps regarding clients' motivation to buy, their consumer habits, etc.

Noting the sub-topics in order to identify pertinent and valuable information; for example, whether or not most of the active clients consider the prices satisfactory, or whether they consider the product a luxury that they cannot afford, etc.

Identifying non-clients, such as family, friends, neighbors and even casual acquaintances, and asking them questions in order to ascertain their reasons for not availing themselves of the business's products/services. The questions should relate to why they don't purchase or use the company's products/services; what would motivate them to buy or use such products/services; whether they do so elsewhere, and why. The replies should be sorted and listed in the same satisfaction/non-satisfaction way as for active clients.

- *'What does it mean?'* All of the gathered information should be examined in order to transform it from raw data to meaningful data (e.g., the data indicate that 55 percent of the active clients are mothers and about 80 percent of these mothers have children under the age of five; most of the other 45 percent are young women, etc.). The entrepreneurs should then ask themselves the meaning of the segmentation: How do the products/services benefit these groups more than others? Why aren't the products attractive to other groups? Friends and reliably knowledgeable people may be asked what they think this means; hearing different points of view enhances one's understanding of the issues.

Awareness of changing trends: support for what may be new trends and how they may affect the business's products/services is invaluable. Discussing the information with knowledgeable people and hearing their ideas and views can enhance the entrepreneur's understanding of the issues.

- *'What next?'* A combination of the information and analyses gained from the market research, along with experience, tacit knowledge, intuition and instincts, and imagination and creativity, can contribute to the development of a plan to enhance the business's profits (e.g., build a baby-sitting and play area for kids in the store so that their mothers/buyers can shop without hindrance; develop attractive complementary products for kids that their mothers will buy; attract the young women-buyers by offering coupons, price reductions and special sales, etc.)

Focusing on the strategies relevant to the information derived from the research is important, but so, too, is openness to adjust, change, and add according to the 'reality feedback'.

- *Searching for more knowledge.* Things should not be allowed to simply 'happen'. It is necessary to take control, look for more information, and find the best possible practices for the business. Other people who are experienced in marketing, or a mentor or counselor, can be asked what they would do, and an ongoing awareness of feedback can be utilized for making business decisions.

The results of such market research may support entrepreneurs' initial feelings about their businesses, but they can also negate them. In either case, they are confronted with reality (Treacy and Wiersema 1993; Stokes 2000; Wilson and Stokes 2004).

POSITIONING

Positioning is a competitive strategy that addresses the role of an entrepreneurial business from the customers' point of view, and compares it to that of the competitors. In order to build an effective positioning stance – which is, essentially, the business's image – entrepreneurs should answer basic questions about their businesses: what it does best, what is unique about its products/services, what its strengths and weaknesses are, and so on (Cooper, Willard and Woo 1986; Anon. 1996; Andersen and Winn 2004).

The main elements in positioning are:

- *Pricing.* Pricing should match the image of your business (e.g., high-quality products should cost more that low-quality products).
- *Quality.* It is critical to have well-produced, quality-controlled products; entrepreneurs should back their quality claims with customer-friendly guarantees, warranties, and return policies.
- *Professionalism.* The founder and/or the leading people in the entrepreneurial business's team should have a high level of the specific expertise needed in the firm; this includes in-depth knowledge of the relevant subject matters, ability to control the processes of producing the firm's products/services and assuring their continued quality. They should be proficient in providing knowledgeable and reliable answers to clients, experienced in correctly itemizing orders for supplies and equipment, and competent in negotiating with stockholders and investment institutions' management.
- *Service.* Entrepreneurs should offer the added value of customer service and support; and their products/services should be customized and personalized.
- *Distribution.* Getting the goods to the clients on time, undamaged, fresh, etc., is an important part of positioning; entrepreneurs should find the best ways to get their products/services to their customers.
- *Packaging.* Packaging makes a strong statement and entrepreneurs should assign a budget for sturdy and attractive packaging.

A useful strategy for positioning a business is structured around a comparison with competitors and highlighting advantages as shown in Figure 11.2.

Who are a business's main competitors?

- *Imitators* – Entrepreneurs who replicate the successful product/service and sell it at a lower price.
- *Inventors* – Entrepreneurs who grow by exploiting their technological superiority and creating new products/services at the right time and for the right customers.
- *Insiders* – Former employees who learned entrepreneurial strategies and business practices and then decided to go into the same or a similar business on their own, and to become entrepreneurs themselves. They are a special threat to their former entrepreneur-employers because they are in the same niche and intimately familiar with its characteristics and its workings.
- *'Illuminators'* – Entrepreneurs who recognize gaps in the market sooner and more clearly than their competitors, and fill them first.

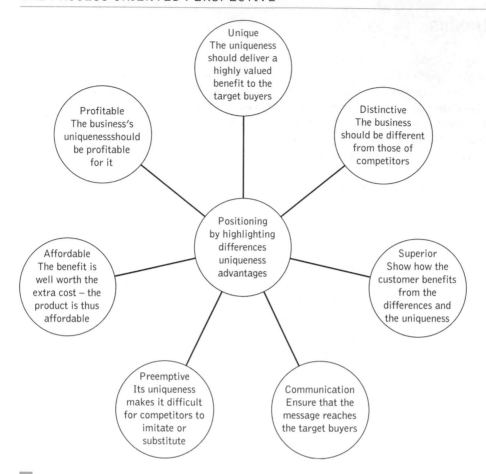

Figure 11.2 *Positioning by comparing with competitors' products and/or services*

SEGMENTATION

Market segmentation is the process of identifying sectors or divisions of the population with similar characteristics, interests, needs or demands, each of which may constitute a specific target clientele. Criteria for customer selection might include demographic characteristics (e.g., age, income, gender, marital status, family size, occupation, education, income, nationality), psychological and sociological traits (e.g., lifestyles, activities, interests, social class), customer behavior (e.g., frequency of purchases, sensitivity toward prices, levels of desired quality), and so on.

Kotler, Ang and Tan (1999) describe three essential steps for marketing management: market segmentation, market segment targeting, and design and implementation of a marketing mix. The crucial importance of market segmentation is in the possibility of designing the right products or services for the targeted potential customers and the best and most effective ways to reach them, which is possible only after they and their special characteristics and shopping preferences have been identified (Prokesch 1993; Davidson 2005).

MARKETING MANAGEMENT

Different types of marketing strategies are suitable for the general population or for various different segments of it:

- *Mass marketing or undifferentiated marketing* – The focus is on providing basic and universally acceptable goods/services for the general population.
- *Product-variety marketing or differentiated marketing* – Several market segments are targeted and separate and different offers are designed for each segment according to its needs, tastes, and resources.
- *Target marketing or concentrated marketing* – Large share of a few sub-markets.

(Cahill 1997; Bond and Fink 2003; Hedaa and Ritter 2005)

Regardless of the population or segment at which the marketing is directed, several important things should be kept in mind while mapping a marketing strategy:

- *A clear goal* – Determining the goal and then establishing a step-by-step process for reaching it by achieving objectives.
- *Constancy* – Focusing on what is necessary to achieve the defined objectives and, in the long run, the goals.
- *Openness* – Being open to unexpected occurrences, considering them challenges rather than threats, and managing them by being flexible, but focused on the goal. It is a misconception to believe that the entrepreneur can control the entire process and outcome of the marketing activities: anything that involves other individuals is likely to have some unpredictable turns. Entrepreneurs should acknowledge this and be prepared for it. If the plan of action does not go as arranged, a different way – still leading to the defined goal – can be implemented.
- *Focus* – Focusing on specific groups of potential customers who share common characteristics is efficacious; it is easier to monitor the response of a defined target population while building in-depth knowledge of their profile and developing an environment of trust.
- *Consistency* – Both active and potential clients build trust more easily with entrepreneurs who abide by their marketing promises. For example, announcing a price reduction one day and renouncing it the next day – even if another, better deal is offered – is a lack of consistency in marketing behavior, and clients are likely to consider the business or the products/services, and hence the entrepreneur, undependable and/or untruthful.
- *Positioning* – A convincing perceptual location that allows the entrepreneur to create an effective image is an important and convincing marketing tool; the entrepreneur should achieve the best possible positioning for his or her product/service in the marketplace.
- *Active marketing* – Ongoing publicity, in different forms, is essential. The media, such as newspapers, yellow pages, radio, and outdoor billboards should be exploited; flyers and direct mail are also sometimes suitable. Online advertising, a business website that provides descriptions of the available products and services, introducing the team and their expertise, and testimonials from satisfied customers, etc. may be effective. Depending on the nature of the business, entrepreneurs can: seek sponsorships; proactively arrange meetings with potential clients, partners, suppliers, etc.; offer professional talks in their field of expertise to the local community; publish articles on their projects and successes in business publications and in local newspapers; circulate business cards among people, and establish and maintain an effective, lasting professional network.

CASE STUDY 11.3   Olive Oil Production, Malaysia

Fatima, Maha, Abia, Is'ad, Jinan and Maryam are the six co-founders of Olive Oil Production, in Malaysia. The six women, from diverse backgrounds, became acquainted only shortly before they created their venture. Abia, for example, had studied in London and Jinan in the United States, while Fatima had lived for five years in China when her husband worked there as a miner. During the two years prior to their business startup, the six women lived in the same neighborhood and were full-time housewives and mothers; they became acquainted when they all came to the same school to pick up their children at the end of the day.

On *Eid Al-Adha*, one of the most important Moslem holidays, Fatima invited some friends and neighbors to a celebration at her home. Among them were the other five women who became her partners in Olive Oil Production. It was on that occasion that the idea of an entrepreneurial business evolved. As they socialized, they chatted about work and job opportunities, and expressed their desire to work and to be independent.

They noticed that Fatima had around thirty large containers of olive oil in the backyard, and when she showed them the oil, and they tasted it, they said it reminded them of 'home'. Fatima told them that making olive oil was her hobby, and that she had all the necessary equipment for doing so in a shed out back. She had developed her own techniques and produced oil in different flavors and textures. There were three very large olives trees and some sacks of unripe olives in the backyard. Fatima said that her husband did not allow her to sell the oil or the olives, so she stored them and gave them as gifts to friends and family.

The following day, Abia asked Fatima if she would consider launching an olive oil production venture; Abia had some money that her late husband had left her and she was ready to invest it in such a business. Fatima's husband did not agree to this, but Abia was very enthusiastic about it and reminded Fatima about their chat and how they had all expressed a desire to be independent. When she realized that the timing wasn't right for the venture, she suggested that Fatima join her at the Malaysian Entrepreneurship Development Center, which Fatima did, with considerable enthusiasm. At the center, the women acquired many useful tools and techniques on business management and this encouraged Fatima to reconsider Abia's idea. At the center, they also met Maha and her daughter Jinan; Jinan was an MBA graduate from an American university and both she and her mother had been 'shopping around' for some entrepreneurial ideas. They were interested in launching a restaurant in their neighborhood shopping center but, again, there was opposition to any business enterprise, in this case from Janin's father, Maha's husband. The six women became more and more excited about the idea of launching a business of oil production, and they discussed it continually.

Abia took the first pragmatic step: she rented a storeroom and hired a truck to transport Fatima's machinery and bags of olives there. Maha had told them that she was an expert in making marinated pickles. The six women went to the market, bought the necessary products, and began to work. Fatima planned a structured division of labor and each of the women had a defined task in the oil or marinated pickles production. Jinan was responsible for marketing, Abia for financing, Fatima was the 'general manger' and assigned the work tasks, and Maha oversaw the marinated pickles work. Fatima's and Maha's husbands were not aware of their wives' activities in their entrepreneurial business.

Marketing was problematic: the partners had asked Jinan to refrain from turning to potential clients who were acquainted with Fatima or Maha or their husbands; she had to sell not only some edible products, but a 'concept', and she had to establish a competitive advantage. She decided to find manufacturers willing to buy their oil directly, and thus avoid very high brokerage costs. She had no deep knowledge of the market or its needs, but was convinced that oil 'is always a needed ingredient in the kitchen, like bread and butter', and she was also aware of the success of boutique olive oil enterprises in other places in Malaysia and, in fact, worldwide. She encouraged her partners with her positive attitude and her conviction that their product would penetrate the market successfully.

Jinan decided to position the business as an efficient firm, with many workers, all of whom are shareholders in the company. A Chinese manufacturer and a local manufacturer were interested in their olive oil and business began to improve. Some supermarkets in neighboring areas were also interested in their merchandise but Fatima was afraid to take any chances, and the women turned these stores down. This was the partners' first conflict: half of them voted for selling to neighborhood stores, and the others, concerned that Fatima's and Maha's husbands might discover their business, voted against.

Olive Oil Production's sales increased. The Chinese manufacturer recommended their business to several restaurants, and they, as well as several other clients, bought their oil and pickles directly. Abia was now unable to manage the financing alone and decided to outsource it. This led to the partners' second crisis, as some of them were against an 'outsider' being privy to such a sensitive matter. The outsourcer did not get along well with the partners, and they decided to discontinue working with her. The women had many complaints about Abia's management, as they expected her to take more responsibility for the financing. Relations did not improve, and the atmosphere was fractious.

The partnership survived for two years, until the numerous conflicts among the women brought it to a dead-end and they decided to split: Abia, Fatima and Maha continued to run Olive Oil Production, and the others decided to take different routes. Abia conducted a small-scale market segmentation of manufacturers who were potential customers or overseas partners and came to the conclusion that overseas partnerships would enable easier and more efficient control and monitoring of sales. After six months of negotiations with manufacturers and business people overseas, Abia succeeded in establishing partnerships with Vietnamese, Thai and Philippine commercial companies. The companies invested in the production process and in a very attractive retail shop. At Abia's suggestion, the three partners placed the old oil-making machinery in the front of the shop as a trade-symbol. They also turned it into their company's logo, featuring it in their advertisements and on their invoices. People soon became familiar with their attractive and evocative symbol.

The next step in the revival of their business was the hiring of a marketing team. The team recommended that they diversify, and Fatima started to produce bath and cosmetic oils, which they sold in handsome containers. Malaysian women adored their products, the marketing expanded, and Olive Oil Production's products penetrated the Chinese market. But along with their success, their family problems also grew: both Fatima and Maha divorced their husbands with lawsuits from members of their families. They both emigrated to China. Fatima and Maha remain financially involved with Olive Oil Production but do not deal with daily operational affairs; Abia manages the headquarters in Malaysia, and Jinan has asked to come back into the business.

QUESTIONS FOR DISCUSSION

1   Describe the different types of marketing the partners used at different stages of their business venture, from launch to multinational. Explain the main differences between them.
2   Classify the strengths and weaknesses of Jinan's marketing attitudes and how they affected Olive Oil Production's outcomes at that time.
3   Identify the differences between Jinan's and Abia's marketing thinking and activities.
4   What would you suggest that Abia and Jinan do next in marketing terms? Explain.

INTELLECTUAL PROPERTY

Creative inventions, innovations and technological developments, as well as symbols, images and designs, are found throughout the entrepreneurial market; and each of these is considered the intellectual capital of its first creator. Intellectual property (IP) comprises inventions, trademarks, industrial designs, utility models, appellations of origin, integrated circuits, topographies, copyrights, know-how, trade secrets, proprietary technology, unique or specifically developed talents, skill and knowledge, training processes and methods, customer lists, distribution networks, quality management systems, and many more. Most of these are protected by patents.

IP is thus an asset that is legally protected on a national basis. IPs are protected by a set of rules that permit their inventors or creators to work without threat of imitation; the inventors/creators are thus able to recover research and development costs through a competitive advantage. For most technological inventors, setting up a new business requires practical and domain knowledge which they lack, such as of patent investigation, technology licensing and transferring, commercialization of the patent, industrial information collection, and operations involvement, among others. They therefore need massive support from experts, mainly those in academic entrepreneurship, to provide them with critical knowledge about the industry and the market. These experts, however, may not be proficient in the technological concepts or procedures of the invented knowledge, and this may hinder the commercialization process. There is a growing exchange between entrepreneurs/inventors and their networks toward more involvement and acquiring more proficiency in the IP-based process, to be able obtain maximal value from IP rights.

The conventional view of property rights in both the law and economics literature follows the 1967 work by Harold Demsetz, which viewed property rights as 'tools for internalizing externalities'. Demsetz argued that property rights emerge when the benefits of internalization outweigh their costs; that is, when the good of concentrating benefits and costs on owners so they deploy resources more efficiently outweighs the bad of the transaction costs associated with recognizing those rights. The effects of IP protection have been thoroughly dealt with in the legal and economic literature (McAdam and Marlow 2007; De Castro, Balkin and Shepherd 2008; Lichtenthaler 2009).

As a protected asset, IP has vast economic value: it grants exclusivity to the business, the technology and the resulting products, allowing entrepreneurs to further research and develop those products without worrying about their technologies being stolen, imitated or infringed upon by other businesses with greater resources. The fundamental values of a business's IP are that it can be sold, licensed, exchanged or gifted, and its owners can prevent its unauthorized use or sale. In addition, it compels the larger companies, while partnering with or investing in small startups, to legally gain access to the technology and resulting products, thus protecting the startup business from forced acquisition or takeover by the larger, wealthier businesses.

The general perception is that the service sector is less dependent on IP rights (IPR), because its services are less amenable to patenting: they are of an intangible nature, making it difficult to prove that they are innovative and should be protected. Nevertheless, several businesses in the service sector have developed technologies or innovative applied systems, e.g., financial businesses, media production, information technology. Innovation and inventions are as important in the service sector as they are in science, research and academia-related businesses, as they provide a source of competitive advantage for the business, both locally and overseas. Services are becoming increasingly global and their output is being traded across borders. This is leading to an increase in potential forms of innovation but also in the need to protect them from, for example, unfair competition through acquisition of the business's knowledge. Some innovations may be readily copied, preventing the owner from earning sufficient profits from it. Employee transferability and relocation may also put the business at risk for transferal of its unique knowledge, trade secrets and copyrights, among others. At the same time, clients purchase mainly goods and services whose origins are known: they look for trademarks and brand names, thereby indirectly forcing businesses to protect their innovative creations.

While IPR incorporate a variety of regulatory policies designed to enhance the functioning of businesses and encourage their innovative creations, they also pose some problems that need to be taken into consideration. Entrepreneurs must thoroughly evaluate the benefits versus costs of IP for their business. While IPR enable businesses to integrate and join forces with other businesses or providers of similar or complementary goods/services for R&D, benchmarking and other organizational, competitive or economic purposes, it should be noted that the process involved in getting the IP license is long and costly, and entrepreneurs need to consider the pros and cons of engaging in this process.

In short, businesses should strive to achieve a balance in IPR, in order to develop new content and benefit from the innovation but also to ensure adequate access at a reasonable cost.

There is a general consensus that IP protection has important implications for the creation of new firms and for competition between existing ones: the enforcement of trade secret laws, including prevention of the spread of tacit knowledge and inevitable disclosure rules, is positively and directly related to the rates of startups. Thus legal protection of IP at the national level increases the number of firms and the level of competition in a given country.

Like owners of tangible property such as buildings, vehicles and stores, inventors have the right to prevent the unauthorized use or sale of their 'property', that is, their creations. However, compared to owners and makers of tangible goods, people whose work is essentially intangible face more difficulties in earning a living if their claim to their creations is not respected; due to the difficulties they face in relying on legal regulations to protect their work, they turn to IPR to prevent others from harvesting the fruits of their labor.

In the long run, IPR (Elias and Stim 2000; Miles, Munilla and Covin 2004) are beneficial not only for the creators, but also for consumers, local and global economies, and various other 'players' involved in the inventions, as shown in Table 11.2.

Academic and scientific entrepreneurship and IPR. Academic entrepreneurship is based on the intellectual assets developed by people working in, or in collaboration with academic institutions. In the United States, Canada, Israel and several European countries, academic entrepreneurship is on an upward trend. Inventors are striving to both create value for their inventions and achieve their personal goals; for this reason, in recent decades, almost all research universities in North America and Europe have established technology transfer offices to commercialize their IP. The offices serve as facilitators for inventors, and other suppliers of innovation involved in the process

Table 11.2 *Benefits and beneficiaries of IPR*

The entrepreneur
- It encourages inventions, creativity and innovation.
- It safeguards intellectual property.
- It provides a framework for the transfer of technology by contributing to increased confidence and transparency in transactions.
- It acts as a means for the commercialization of inventions and their transfer to productive use, which can benefit the inventor.

Community/customers
- It provides the community with the fruits of inventive and innovative activity, of higher performance and higher quality goods.
- It gives an incentive for the creation of new technology, resulting, *inter alia*, in new products, inventions and employment- and commerce-related opportunities.

The local economy
- It promotes investment by guaranteeing against unauthorized use of inventions or patents, thus safeguarding those who take risks and invest in developing the items from the prototype stage to mass production.
- The patent system contributes to economic growth, by developing the conditions for the economic and commercial use of inventions.
- It is an instrument of commercial and industrial planning and strategy.
- The patent system is a long-term investment in infrastructure for development of the national technology market.
- It is a policy instrument that encourages the development of original technological capabilities by providing an incentive to local inventors.
- It develops the locality by more developed research and R&D.

The global economy.
- It widely broadcasts new ideas and technologies, by creating a global database of new inventions and new technologies.
- It contributes to the creation of an environment that facilitates the successful industrial application of inventions and new technology.
- It provides a legal framework that encourages investment, including that from foreign countries.

(i.e., universities, scientists, research centers, spin-offs) to obtain commercial knowledge transfers of IP through licensing.

Licensing IP at the university level can result in additional revenue for the university, employment opportunities for university-based researchers and graduate students, and local economic and technological spillovers through the stimulation of additional R&D investment and job creation.

As different people and bodies involved in academic and scientific inventions have different interests, it is essential to obtain IPR licensing so that the invention process can proceed.

Firms and entrepreneurs seek to commercialize university-based IP for profit. When innovation is a key source of competitive advantage, it is critical to maintain proprietary control over these technologies. Therefore, firms typically wish to secure exclusive rights to university-based technologies. Speed is another major area of concern, since firms and entrepreneurs often seek to establish a 'first mover' advantage.

The *university administrators* generally regard themselves as the guardians of the university's IP portfolio, which can potentially generate revenue. Therefore, they are anxious to market university-based technologies to companies and entrepreneurs, although they will often protect them 'too well' and slow down the commercialization process, either so as not to be accused of 'giving away' profitable funded technologies, or to protect the researchers that have generated the innovations.

Academic scientists seek the rapid dissemination of their ideas and breakthroughs through publications in the highest ranking scholarly journals, presentations at leading conferences, and submission of proposals to research grants.

Faculty members seek pecuniary rewards which can be put back into their research to pay for laboratory equipment, research assistance, graduate students, etc. Some faculty researchers who perform little research or do not get sufficient academic recognition may also have research contracts with companies that can generate possibilities for joint-venture spin-offs (Jensen and Thursby 2001; Zucker and Darby 2001; Di Gregorio and Shane 2003; Jensen, Thursby and Thursby 2003; Siegel, Waldman and Link 2003; Siegel, Westhead and Wright 2003; Siegel et al. 2003; Chapple et al. 2005; Clarysse et al. 2005; Debackere and Veugelers 2005; Lacetera 2005; Lockett et al. 2005; O'Shea, Allen and Chevalier 2005; Van Looy, Callaert and Debackere 2006).

SUMMARY

One of the strongest convictions in marketing is that it contributes to business performance and sustainability substantially more than any other organizational strategy. In the context of entrepreneurship, this conviction is even more compelling, as success depends on the customers' perception of the products and services offered by a business as the highest value proposition available in that market; thus entrepreneurial businesses must create constructive, mutually beneficial exchange relationships with their customers to build this perception, thereby ensuring an advantageous market position and competitive advantages. This is the core of marketing. While entrepreneurship means leveraging innovation to create products, processes, and strategies that better satisfy customer needs, marketing is the constant pursuit of opportunities to create additional value for the customers through innovation of the business products, processes, and strategies (Covin and Miles 2007).

To do so, entrepreneurs should master the marketing-plan process and determine, through market analysis, the various factors of the market that are related to their product and services (e.g., legal, economic, and technological considerations), identifying their active and potential customers, and defining the best route to reach those customers, as well as identifying their competitors. In addition, entrepreneurs should enhance their business by positioning (i.e. using a strategy that addresses the role of their entrepreneurial business from the customers' point of view), and compares it to that of their competitors. Finally, they need to conduct market segmentation to identify sectors or divisions of the population with similar characteristics, interests, needs or demands, each of which may constitute a specific target clientele.

Today, many entrepreneurial businesses are exposed to imitation and duplication; thus as part of an all-inclusive marketing management they need to protect their intellectual property by patent.

CASE STUDY 11.4   Vetery-Tekuno, Korea

Dimon Li, a twenty-four-year-old biology student at Seoul University, was in the process of developing a special apparatus for measuring vital signs, such as blood pressure, body temperature, pulse, and heart and respiration rates, of animals in emergency situations. The device is very important as animals, especially very large ones, may become wild when in pain, and measuring these signs is almost impossible unless they are anesthetized.

Li had been working on this invention for four years and had been joined by his American friend and collaborator, John, an expert in IT and a website designer. The two friends were planning to establish an inclusive website on animals in emergency situations, with tips, tools and information on how to treat them. The website would also feature the new apparatus and thus facilitate its penetration into the market. Li looked for similar sites on the internet and realized that such a website was lacking in Korea and probably in other countries as well. He also conducted benchmarking and did some market research by inquiring among veterinarians, pet doctors and staff members of veterinary surgical clinics regarding the possible purchase of such an apparatus and obtained very encouraging results.

Li's professor warned him to be very careful about advertising the apparatus in this way, and suggested that he get IP protection prior to establishing the website or launching a business; he also encouraged Li to search for investors in order to speed up the development process, as Li had nearly completed his first prototype.

The complicated and time-consuming measures and bureaucratic procedures for acquiring IP protection were daunting. Li was inexperienced and had no idea of how aggressive the patent world was. He began the IP protection formalities but did not give them high priority: 'As in many other countries, people in Korea face serious obstacles in getting IP protection, and above all there is a huge lack of IP awareness, as well as both inadequate laws and ineffective enforcement mechanisms. I had neither the time nor the resources to address these issues. Things were going along fine, and I couldn't figure out why it was so important and what would I gain from it. Mostly, it was very annoying. My mentor kept asking me how the IP procedures were coming along, and not wanting to disappoint him, I went through the entire procedure. I owe him a lot; if I had not completed all the paperwork and procedures, I would have lost the investment and the profits of four years of R&D,' he admits.

John had a friend, an industrialist from New York, who wanted more information about the apparatus and how it works in order to consider cooperation with Li in the future. He sent a representative to conduct a patent evaluation to assure the patent's validity based on its underlying technological quality. Li, innocent and totally inexperienced in such matters, disclosed a great amount of information without any signed formality on confidentiality. A few weeks later, John told Li that his friend would not take part in the business as the report did not convince him that the patent's quality was valid and consistent.

Li continued his search for investors, and the apparatus was ready to be marketed when his professor showed him an article in a scientific journal describing exactly the same apparatus and procedures that Li had invented. Li's IP formalities were almost complete, but his IP protection was at risk in light of this sudden development. John sent the article to his industrialist friend, who, it turned out, had suspected the man he had sent to investigate the apparatus of presenting him with a flawed report, but he had preferred to simply drop the matter rather than check up on the man and his company. However, when he received the article from John he felt he had to do something. First, he encouraged Li to speed up the IP formalities in Korea; then he tried to contact the reporter of the article in order to locate the company that had so quickly developed a virtually identical apparatus.

The industrialist had the means and the connections – and the will – to trace the man. Li: 'It was like an action movie. Everything was going so fast that it felt out of control. John was constantly on the phone with his friend from the States, and we were all running against the clock. And then we got the IP protection.'

Li launched Vetery-Tekuno shortly thereafter, and it is now in an 'exit process', having caught the interest of a well-known company. Li still does not know who wrote the article about the same apparatus in the scientific journal, or whether his idea was imitated or stolen during the development process. He is, however, aware of the importance of IP protection and proactively encourages all inventors to make sure that they acquire such protection.

QUESTIONS FOR DISCUSSION

1   Describe IP protection in your country in terms of awareness, legislation, mechanisms and enforcement.
2   How do you think inventors can best be encouraged to acquire IP protection: training, advertising, enforcement?
3   Explain which way would be best for inventors in your country.
4   Is Dimon Li's initial attitude toward IP protection characteristic of your country's inventors?

REFERENCES

Alsaaty, F.M. (2006) 'Case study: a young entrepreneur going global', *Business Review*, 6: 178–86.

Andersen, M. and Winn, J. (2004) 'Anglo American College in Prague: positioning for growth', *International Journal of Entrepreneurship and Innovation*, 5: 276–91.

Anon. (1996) 'Finding new positions: the entrepreneurial edge', *Harvard Business Review*, 74: 65–6.

Ashill, N.J., Frederikson, M. and Davies, J. (2003) 'Strategic marketing planning: a grounded investigation', *European Journal of Marketing*, 37: 430–61.

Atherton, A. and Sear, L. (2004) 'Generating orders and winning new business: how owners and managers of small businesses describe and approach their market development and marketing activities', *International Journal of Entrepreneurship and Innovation*, 5: 255–65.

Baker, W.E. and Sinkula, J.M. (2005) 'Environmental marketing strategy and firm performance: effects on new product performance and market share', *Academy of Marketing Science*, 33: 461–75.

Baum, J.R., Locke, E.A. and Smith, K.G. (2001) 'A multidimensional model of venture growth', *Academy of Management Journal*, 44: 292–303.

Becherer, R.C. and Maurer, J.G. (1997) 'The moderating effect of environmental variables on the entrepreneurial and marketing orientation of entrepreneur-led firms', *Entrepreneurship Theory and Practice*, 22: 47–58.

Bond, E.U. and Fink, R.L. (2003) 'Customer satisfaction and the marketing–quality interface', *Journal of Business and Industrial Marketing*, 18: 204–19.

Cahill, D.J. (1997) 'Target marketing and segmentation: valid and useful tools for marketing', *Management Decision*, 35: 10–13.

Chakravorti, B. (2004) 'The new rules for bringing innovations to market', *Harvard Business Review*, 82: 58–67.

Chapple, W., Lockett, A., Siegel, D.S. and Wright, M. (2005) 'Assessing the relative performance of university technology transfer offices in the UK: parametric and non-parametric evidence', *ResearchPolicy*, 34: 369–84.

Chrisman, J.J., Chua, J.H. and Steier, L.P. (2002) 'The influence of national culture and family involvement on entrepreneurial perceptions and performance at the state level', *Entrepreneurship Theory and Practice*, 26: 113–31.

Clarysse, B., Wright, M., Lockett, A., van de Velde, E. and Vohora, A. (2005) 'Spinning out new ventures: a typology of incubation strategies from European research institutions', *Journal of Business Venturing*, 20: 183–216.

Collins, J.C. and Porras, J.I. (1996) 'Building your company's vision', *Harvard Business Review*, 74: 65–78.

Cooper, A.C., Willard, G.E. and Woo, C.Y. (1986) 'Strategies of high-performing new and small firms: a reexamination of the niche concept', *Journal of Business Venturing*, 1: 247–61.

Covin, J.G. and Miles, M.P. (2007) 'Strategic use of corporate venturing', *Entrepreneurship Theory and Practice*, 31: 183–207.

Davidson, S. (2005) 'Grey power, school gate mums and the youth vote: age as a key factor in voter segmentation and engagement in the 2005 UK general election', *Journal of Marketing Management*, 21: 1179–92.

De Castro, J., Balkin, D.B. and Shepherd, D.A. (2008) 'Can entrepreneurial firms benefit from product piracy?', *Journal of Business Venturing*, 23: 75–90.

Debackere, K. and Veugelers, R. (2005) 'The role of academic technology transfer organizations in improving industry–science links', *Research Policy*, 34: 321–42.

Demsetz, H. (1967) 'Towards a theory of property rights', *American Economic Review*, 57: 347–59.

Di Gregorio, D. and Shane, S. (2003) 'Why do some universities generate more start-ups than others?', *Research Policy*, 32: 209–27.

Elias, S. and Stim, R. (2000) *Patent, Copyright and Trademark: An Intellectual Property Desk Reference*, 4th edn, Berkeley, CA: Nolo Press.

FitzRoy, F.R. (1993) 'Small firms and entrepreneurship: an East West perspective: a review article', *Small Business Economics*, 5: 239–44.

Hedaa, L. and Ritter, T. (2005) 'Business relationships on different waves: paradigm shift and marketing orientation revisited', *Industrial Marketing Management*, 34: 714–21.

Ireland, R.D. and Hitt, M.A. (1997) 'Performance strategies for high-growth entrepreneurial firms', in P.D. Reynolds, W.D. Bygrave, N.M. Carter, P. Davidsson, W.B. Gartner, C.M. Mason and P.P. McDougall (eds) *Frontiers of Entrepreneurship Research*, Babson Park, MA: Babson College, 90–104.

Jensen, R.A. and Thursby, M.C. (2001) 'Proofs and prototypes for sale: the licensing of university inventions', *American Economic Review*, 91: 240–59.

Jensen, R., Thursby, J. and Thursby, M. (2003) 'Disclosure and licensing of university inventions: the best we can do with the s**t we get to work with', *International Journal of Industrial Organization*, 21: 1271–300.

Kotler, P., Ang, S. and Tan, C. (1999) *Marketing Management – An Asian Perspective*, Englewood Cliffs, NJ: Prentice-Hall.

Lacetera, N. (2005) 'Multiple missions and academic entrepreneurship', Mimeo, MIT.

Lichtenthaler, U. (2009) 'Strategic planning in open innovation systems: how to develop an out-licensing strategy', *International Journal of Intellectual Property Management*, 3: 386–95.

Lockett, A., Siegel, D., Wright, M. and Ensley, M. (2005) 'The creation of spin-off firms at public research institutions: managerial and policy implications', *Research Policy*, 34: 981–93.

McAdam, M. and Marlow, S. (2007) 'Building futures or stealing secrets?', *International Small Business Journal*, 25: 361–82.

Miles, M.P., Munilla, L.S. and Covin, J.G. (2004) 'Innovation, ethics, and entrepreneurship', *Journal of Business Ethics*, 54: 97–101.

O'Shea, R., Allen, T. and Chevalier, A. (2005) 'Entrepreneurial orientation, technology transfer, and spin-off performance of US universities', *Research Policy*, 34: 994–1009.

Pavia, T.M. (1991) 'Using marketing models in strategic planning', *Long Range Planning*, 24: 59–68.

Porter, M.E. (1980) *Competitive Strategy*, New York: The Free Press.

Porter, M.E. (1998) 'Clusters and the new economics of competition', *Harvard Business Review*, 76: 77-90.

Prokesch, S.E. (1993) 'Battling bigness', *Harvard Business Review*, 71: 143–4.

Ramaswamy, V., Gatignon, H. and Reibstein, D.J. (1994) 'Competitive marketing behavior in industrial markets', *Journal of Marketing*, 58: 45–56.

Siegel, D.S., Westhead, P. and Wright, M. (2003) 'Assessing the impact of science parks on the research productivity of firms: exploratory evidence from the United Kingdom', *International Journal of Industrial Organization*, 21: 1357–69.

Siegel, D.S., Waldman, D.A. and Link, A.N. (2003) 'Assessing the impact of organizational practices on the productivity of university technology transfer offices: an exploratory study', *Research Policy*, 32: 27–48.

Siegel, D.S., Waldman, D.A., Atwater, L. and Link, A.N. (2003) 'Commercial knowledge transfers from universities to firms: improving the effectiveness of university–industry collaboration', *Journal of High Technology Management Research*, 14: 111–33.

Slater, S.F. and Narver, J.C. (1995) 'Market orientation and the learning organization', *Journal of Marketing*, 59: 63–75.

Stokes, D. (2000) 'Entrepreneurial marketing: a conceptualisation from qualitative research', *Qualitative Market Research*, 3: 47–54.

Treacy, M. and Wiersema, F. (1993) 'Customer intimacy and other value disciplines', *Harvard Business Review*, 71: 84–94.

Van Looy, B., Callaert, J. and Debackere, K. (2006) 'Publication and patent behavior of academic researchers: conflicting, reinforcing or merely co-existing?', *Research Policy*, 35: 596–608.

Wilson, N.C. and Stokes, D. (2004) 'Laments and serenades: relationship marketing and legitimation strategies for the cultural entrepreneur', *Qualitative Market Research*, 7: 218–27.

Zucker, L.G. and Darby, M.R. (2001) 'Capturing technological opportunity via Japan's star scientists: evidence from Japanese firms' biotech patents and products', *Journal of Technology Transfer*, 26: 37–58.

Chapter 12

Financing the entrepreneurial venture

OBJECTIVES

After studying this chapter you will be able to:

- Recognize the 'how, what and when' of financing an entrepreneurial business: e.g., how to raise capital, what the funding sources are, when it is most suitable to use each of the financial sources, how to maximize value in a growing venture, how to forecast financial performance and cash flow.
- Identify the various financial resources available for entrepreneurial activities and evaluate their relevance to the business by recognizing their pros and cons for the different stages of the business.
- Understand the flow in entrepreneurial businesses: i.e., assembling resources, combining them to build a resource platform that will yield distinctive capabilities, assessing their long-term and sustainable availability to the business.
- List the business's needs for the purpose of choosing the best-suited financial resources, and distinguish between needs for initial financing and venture growth capital.
- Recognize the role of networking for the most valuable financial information and for locating the relevant, available financial resources.
- Recognize the major processes in managing the business's financial operations.
- Understand the role of factoring for immediate cash funding while experiencing long billing cycles that put a strain on cash flow, and understand the actions of factoring.
- Distinguish the key competitive issues facing the entrepreneurial business while buying and selling a business, including research, due diligence and pricing.

THE HOW, WHAT AND WHEN OF FINANCING THE VENTURE

Financing is an important input for every business, especially in its first stages: it enables smooth running of the daily and long-term operations, as well as asset acquisitions, expert recruitment, and the development of marketing and distribution channels. In the early stages, businesses are typically constrained in terms of liquidity, and most entrepreneurs are continually concerned about their finances; their businesses are typically not yet profitable, and they may have a fear of 'running out of dry powder'. Entrepreneurs in the first stages of these emerging ventures cover their fear of the demanding capital-raising marathon by presenting propitious but sometimes unrealistic business plans to potential investors. Entrepreneurs therefore need to develop skills that are relevant to financing their ventures.

Some of the initial and basic questions faced by entrepreneurs include: how to raise capital for the new venture; what the pros and cons are of each of the sources of capital, as well as their availability and reliability; how to maximize the value in a growing venture in terms of valuation, structuring investments in the entrepreneurial setting, investment staging; how to forecast financial performance and cash flow. Entrepreneurs should be well acquainted with the art of negotiation, and need well-established knowledge on using and managing financial modeling, working capital, fixed versus variable costs, and cash flow versus accounting, among other things. Most entrepreneurs, however, are either not experienced or lack the relevant knowledge to manage their financial or potential financial sources, and they may end up choosing unsuitable sources of financing, managing incongruous negotiation processes with investors and banks, or disregarding some critical techniques and tools that may assist them in raising money for their ventures.

Capital is an umbrella term for the critical and valuable assets for the business such as human, social and financial capital. Financial capital is defined as an economic asset consisting of personal and general funds. Personal funds include an entrepreneur's personal savings, financial assistance from family and friends, or bank loans based on personal guarantees, whereas general funds consist of seed funding from a developmental agency, government loans and grants, or funds from business angels or venture capital firms. Existing research shows that entrepreneurs tend to rely on personal sources of finance both at the startup stage and as the principal source of initial capital in the following stages of the business (Sullivan 1991; Kelly and Hay 1996; Mason and Harrison 1997; Gompers and Lerner 2001; Wang and Sim 2001; Hindle and Lee 2002; Wright, Pruthi and Lockett 2005; De Clercq et al. 2006; Villalonga and Amit 2006; Mason 2009).

One major problem with choosing unsuitable financial sources has to do with risk: entrepreneurs must understand that any decision they consider has an inherent level of associated risk. Some of the risks that they face are not unique to entrepreneurial markets but others may be, particularly those concerning issues such as penetration costs of products and potential returns, potential buyers, promotional programs, billing, pricing, IT systems, and so on. Avoiding or mitigating exposure to risks is impossible; however, they may be offset by acknowledging diverse financing strategies. Moreover, entrepreneurs' inexperience sometimes causes them to over-emphasize short-term expenses or immediate costs: for example, entrepreneurs that are renting or buying a plant for their business may take into account only the rental costs and ignore additional, indirect or attached costs (local amelioration, municipal taxes and other expenses). In such a case, the financial analysis will be lacking and consequently, their choice of types of financial sources may be unrealistic (Bruno and Tyebjee 1985; Schwienbacher 2007).

In order to turn risks into opportunities and needs into strengths, entrepreneurs need to be able to estimate the firm's financial needs. Two main factors are essential to this estimation: (1) the net cost of the investments in the long term and (2) the assets in the short term.

Moreover, entrepreneurs should be able to conduct benchmarking research on the costs and expected expenses, using information from colleagues, suppliers and printed materials. Validating the financial analysis, as well as enriching it by including a variety of different items – even those that might be considered marginal or irrelevant may assist in matching financial sources to the firm's needs. However, some financial terms need to be understood prior to searching for financial sources:

203

- *Return on investment (ROI)*. The entrepreneur invests capital in a particular combination of assets, from which the company generates sales. Those sales cover the costs of operation and hopefully, will produce a profit.

The return, i.e., the profit from an investment, is divided by the cost of the investment; the result is dependent upon what is included as returns and costs, and it may vary across entrepreneurial businesses (Lusch, Harvey and Speier 1998). It is expressed in the following versatile and simple ratio:

- *Internal rate of return (IRR)*. This measure is commonly referred to in the venture capital industry, and includes a concurrent assessment of actual cash flow (see example in Table 12.1) and the value of unrealized investments held in a fund portfolio. A fund's IRR is sometimes measured after the fund has finally been wound up and no unrealized investments remain. If the risks are equal, investments with higher IRRs pay better when comparing the net expected returns over the useful life of a project being reviewed by management to the funds spent on that decision (or project) (Cohan and Unger 2006).
- *Assets*. Assets are subdivided into current and long-term assets to reflect the ease of liquidating each asset. From a finance perspective, these assets are the revenue generators.
- *Current assets*. Any assets that can be easily converted into cash within one calendar year (e.g., cash money-market accounts, accounts receivable, funds parked in near-term instruments earning interest, funds tied up in inventory and notes receivable that are due within one year's time).

Table 12.1 *The cash flow statement*

	Jan.	Feb.	Mar.	Apr.	May.	Jun.	Jul.	Aug.	Sep.	Oct.	Nov.	Dec.
Source of funds												
Beginning cash												
Sales/income												
Sale of assets												
Customer deposits												
Loans												
Contributed capital												
Available cash												
Salaries												
Other operating expenses												
Loan payments												
Capital expenditures												
Tax payments												
Total cash out												
Net cash flow												

■ *Fixed assets.* The long-term base of the business's operation (e.g., equipment, machinery, vehicles, facilities, IT infrastructure and long-term contracts), all of which the firm has invested in to conduct business (George 2005).

■ *Cost of capital.* This is the true cost of securing the funds that the business uses to pay for its asset base. Ando, Hancock and Sawchuk (1997), for example, used the before-tax rate of return on capital, adjusted for inflation, to estimate the cost of capital; Jog (1997) computed the weighted average costs of debt and equity on an after-tax basis for 714 Canadian firms grouped into twenty-two industrial sectors. This 'financial cost of capital' constitutes only part of the 'user cost of capital', the latter being a broader and more economically complete concept.

■ *Weighted average (between debt and equity) cost of capital (WACC).* The firm's true annual cost for obtaining and holding on to the combination of debt and equity that pays for the fixed asset base.

■ *Risks.* Two basic approaches in risk and risk control are accepted in the entrepreneurial realm; both refer to how the capital market can affect the firm and how the firm can control its potential risks in this context. One is the principal agent approach, referring to the use of comprehensive contracts, and the other, the incomplete contract approach, which deals with active involvement in venture management (Hart 1995). Entrepreneurs must always decide whether the risk premium of additional potential return is commensurate with the additional risk costs that come with choosing that investment project (Jensen and Meckling 1976; Bourgeois and Eisenhardt 1998; Harvey and Lusch 1995; St-Pierre and Bahri 2006). Due diligence may help in managing potential risks (see example in Table 12.2).

Table 12.2 *Due diligence: main topics*

Topic	Examples
Organization and good standing	The business's minute book, including all minutes and resolutions of shareholders and directors, executive committees, and other governing groups The business's organizational chart The business's list of shareholders and number of shares held by each
Financial information	Audited financial statements for the past three years, together with auditors' reports The most recent unaudited statements, with comparable statements from the prior year Auditors' letters and replies for the past five years Any projections, capital budgets and strategic plans
Physical assets	A schedule of fixed assets and their locations A schedule of sales and purchases of major capital equipment during the last three years
Real estate	A schedule of the business's locations Copies of all real-estate leases, deeds, mortgages, title policies, surveys, zoning approvals, variances or use permits
Intellectual property	A schedule of domestic and foreign patents and patent applications A schedule of trademarks and trade names A schedule of copyrights A description of important technical know-how A description of methods used to protect trade secrets and know-how

Table 12.2 *Continued*

Topic	Examples
Employees and employee benefits	A list of employees, including positions, current salaries, salaries and bonuses paid during the past three years, and years of service Résumés of key employees The business's personnel handbook and a schedule of all employee benefits, and holiday, vacation and sick-leave policies
Licenses and permits	Copies of any governmental licenses, permits or consents
Environmental issues	Environmental audits, if any, for each property leased by the business A listing of hazardous substances used in the business's operations A description of the business's disposal methods A list of environmental permits and licenses
Taxes	Federal, state, local, and foreign income tax returns for the past three years State sales tax returns for the past three years Any audit and revenue agency reports Any tax-settlement documents for the past three years
Material contracts	A schedule of all subsidiary, partnership, or joint-venture relationships and obligations, with copies of all related agreements All loan agreements, bank financing arrangements, lines of credit, or promissory notes to which the business is a party Any options or stock purchase agreements involving interests in other companies The business's standard quote, purchase order, invoice and warranty forms
Product or service lines	A list of all existing products or services as well as those under development Copies of all correspondence and reports related to any regulatory approvals of any of the business's products or services A summary of all complaints or warranty claims A summary of results of all tests, evaluations and other data regarding existing products or services and those that are under development
Customer information	A schedule of the business's twelve largest customers in terms of sales and a description of those sales for a period of at least two years Any supply or service agreements A description or copy of the business's purchasing policies A description or copy of the business's credit policy
Litigation	A schedule of all pending litigations A description of any threatened litigations Copies of insurance policies that may provide coverage for pending or threatened litigation
Insurance coverage	A schedule and copies of the business's general liability, insurance claims history, personal and real-estate property, product liability, errors and omissions, key man, directors and officers, workers' compensation, and other insurance
Professionals	A schedule of all law firms, accounting firms, consulting firms, and similar professionals engaged by the business during the past five years
Articles and publicity	Copies of all articles and press releases relating to the business within the past three years

Source: Modified from FindLaw for small businesses, at http://smallbusiness.findlaw.com/business-forms-contracts/be3_8_1.html; the Kauffman Foundation, at www.kauffman.org/; AllBusiness, at www.allbusiness.com/business-finance/equity-funding-private-equity-venture/81-1.html.

Table 12.3 illustrates the major components that should be taken into account when listing the firm's needs for the purpose of choosing the best-suited financial sources. The cash flow statement shows estimated cash inflows and outflows for the business, on a monthly basis. It is simple to operate and important for controlling the business's financing. It allows entrepreneurs to compare the original or planned statement with the actual one, in order to gauge the likely results of moving forward with plans.

Before entering into the financing process, some general key steps need to be taken, as illustrated in Figure 12.1.

Table 12.3 *The principal components of the firm's needs in terms of initial financing*

Long-term
■ Land and construction, including local improvements
■ Equipment and machinery
■ Working materials
■ Transferable material and furniture
■ Startup costs (incorporation, judicial costs, marketing research, credits, and more)

Short-term
■ Startup cash and stock
■ Reservation of capital and assets

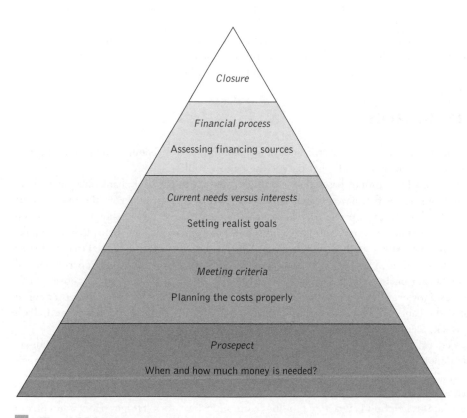

Figure 12.1 *General key steps in the financing process*

- The *prospect* addresses questions regarding when and how much money is needed for the firm, what it will be used for, and how long the entrepreneur thinks the financial assistance will be needed.
- *Meeting criteria* means planning the costs properly: rather than either overestimating or underestimating the financial requirements needed to properly capitalize the business, the preparation of financial projections in the business plan is essential.
- *Current needs versus interests* are the realistic goals that should be set; this is the first step in financing management that entrepreneurs should determine – the scope and size of their business. Rather than simply jumping into the idea of starting a business without understanding what the business really entails, goals need to be set with respect to the financial requirements of multiple issues – i.e., management know-how and technological skills, HR requirements, among others – in the short and long term.
- *Financial process.* Financing a small business is not a lock, stock and barrel proposition. For many entrepreneurs, no single source will finance their entire operation and they need to look at financing as the sum of their business's parts. The ideal financing source is one that provides the longest payback period, carries the lowest interest rates, requires little or no collateral and demands no personal liability, but such sources are very difficult to find. Thus a financial process is needed that emphasizes assessment of the different sources of financing and their pros and cons.
- *Closure* is the stage at which the sources of financing are chosen. This should be decided upon with full knowledge of what the financing sources entail, what the entrepreneurs' obligations to and participation in such financing sources and processes are, and how to best manage such sources.

By obtaining detailed information on operations and finances, entrepreneurs may better understand their business's needs and make them more attractive to investors. The due-diligence checklist (Table 12.2) addresses some major topics that should be assessed and documented.

FINANCIAL SOURCES

- *Family and friends.* At the very early stages of any startup, entrepreneurs tend to raise money from relatives, colleagues and other people they know well.
- *Banks.* The bank loans money based on the business's ability to pay back: banks are more likely to finance businesses that have greater value to minimize their risks. From the bank's point of view, lending to entrepreneurial businesses is a complex and challenging task since entrepreneurs (i.e., the borrowers) have more information about their firms than the banks have, as entrepreneurs usually do not disclose all important information related to their firm's business transactions. Furthermore, many entrepreneurs lack the skills to prepare financial statements and business plans, and this amplifies the risk of loaning to entrepreneurial businesses. However, when professional management practices are run in an entrepreneurial business, the bank will be more willing to loan money to that business (Colombo and Grilli 2007; Beck, Demirgüç-Kunt and Maksimovic 2008; Le and Nguyen 2009).
- *Grants.* Federally funded programs mandate that certain agencies set aside part of their budgets to fund fledgling high-tech companies with interesting inventions they want to commercialize (e.g., Small Business Innovation Research grant (SBIR); government grants for women and minority-owned businesses). Competition for this money is steep, and as such, if such a grant is received, it is helpful in attracting funding from other investors (Holger, Henry and Strobl 2008).

■ *Angels.* Angel investors enable the business to acquire venture capital from individual investors who are looking for companies that exhibit high growth prospects, have a synergy with their own business or compete in an industry in which they have succeeded. Early-stage companies with no revenues or established companies with sales and earnings can use this source, but they must be ready to relinquish some control of their business. Most important, to successfully accommodate angel investors, the entrepreneurs should be ready to provide them with an 'exit' through an initial public offering (IPO) or buyout by a larger firm (Steier 2000; Bruton, Chahine and Filatotchev 2009; Wiltbank et al. 2009).

■ *Bootstrapping.* Bootstrapping market entry is a viable model involving launching a business on a low budget, including outsourcing the work, renting rather than buying equipment and bartering for services; this is when entrepreneurs have great faith in their idea and they want to give up any equity, or when they have taken on a small amount of seed financing, just enough to get them into the market. The benefits of bootstrapping are in the speed of raising capital and generating revenue, flexibility in 'taking the time' to learn the entrepreneurial process and modify the business's operations accordingly, efficiency and capital preservation, by using money in a more disciplined manner, tracking expenses carefully, and spending only on the most efficient tactics.

■ *Venture capital.* This is a type of private equity capital typically provided by professional, outside investors to new, high-potential-growth companies in the interest of taking the company to an IPO. Venture capitalists pool their money with additional funds from institutional investors (e.g., pension funds, endowments and foundations), and these investors become 'limited partners' in the firm's funds. Typically, venture funds have a life span of approximately ten years: during the first several years, they invest in promising new companies that then become part of the firm's portfolio; over the course of the fund's life, these companies are treated for acquisition or to go public at a premium of the total amount invested ('exit') (Sahlman 1990; Gompers and Lerner 1999; Jeng and Wells 1998).

■ *Initial public offering (IPO) and sellout.* When private firms move to public ownership, they can either do so through an IPO or a sellout. In an IPO, a private firm generally sells off a portion of its outstanding equity, but the previous owners retain significant ownership and control of the public corporation. IPO investors, on the other hand, take a significant risk when they invest in a business whose worth has yet to be revealed in the marketplace. Sellout is a transaction in which a public company generally buys all of the outstanding shares of a privately held business. Both sellout and IPO firms benefit from access to public debt and equity markets, from liquidity of ownership for managers and investors, and from the possibility of linking management and employee compensation to traded securities (Deeds, Decarolis and Coombs 1997; Mulherin and Boone 2000; Certo, Daily and Dalton 2001; Brau, Francis and Kohers 2003; Certo 2003; Certo et al. 2003).

OBTAINING VENTURE AND GROWTH CAPITAL

Several sources of funding and financial alternatives are pertinent for entrepreneurs; they vary in their content, suitability and uses, as well as in their supply process. All businesses know that financing is vital to their present and future success; however, some entrepreneurs – inexperienced ones or those lacking knowledge on the benefits and shortcomings of the different options – may obtain less than optimal forms of financing. To help entrepreneurs in their bootstrapping (i.e., finding the best way to run and nurture their business strategically and securely), Table 12.4 summarizes the different sources of financing.

Table 12.4 *Summary of the different sources of financing*

What is it?	Appropriate for	Best used	Supply
Angel investors			
Entrepreneurs who make high-risk investments in small companies. Some angel-backed companies go on to receive venture funding, become publicly traded companies and industry leaders. In this way, angel investing strongly complements the role of venture capital	Early-stage companies with no revenues; or established companies with sales and earnings. To successfully accommodate angel investors, a company must also be able to provide an 'exit' for these investors in the form of an eventual public offering or buyout from a larger firm	For funding early-stage, fast-growing entrepreneurial firms, which are ultimately responsible for nearly all job creation	Large. The more technology-driven an area's economy is, the more abundant these investors are
Banks			
Commercial loans, typically carrying fixed interest rates and monthly or quarterly repayment schedules, and including a set maturity date	Intermediate-term loans and long-term loans exist. Established small to medium-size enterprises (SMEs) that can leverage sound financial statements and substantial down payments to minimize monthly payments and total loan costs. Term loans require collateral and a rigorous approval process but can help reduce risk by minimizing costs	For construction; major capital improvements; large capital investments, such as machinery; working capital; purchases of existing businesses	Abundant but highly differentiated. The degree of financial strength required to receive loan approval can vary tremendously from bank to bank, depending on the level of risk the bank is willing to take on

Every venture fund has a net asset value or the value of an investor's holdings in that fund at any given time; therefore, evaluating which financial option best suits the business is difficult. This decision takes considerable investment knowledge and time on the part of the entrepreneur and on the part of the investors, as each company is given a valuation that is agreed upon between the venture firms when invested in by the venture fund(s). In subsequent quarters, the venture investor will usually keep this valuation intact until a material event occurs to change the value (Fiet 1996; Mullins 2004; Cumming 2005; de Bettignies and Brander 2007).

Some entrepreneurs may therefore seek to delegate this decision to an investment advisor or so-called 'gatekeeper'. This advisor will pool the assets of its various clients and join together entrepreneurs and the best options for them with the shorter funding-process cycles. Some websites can facilitate these decisions.[1]

NETWORKING AND FINANCIAL INFORMATION

The success of a new venture often depends on an entrepreneur's ability to establish a network for the mobilization of financial resources. One of the most important key benefits of networks for the entrepreneurial process is the access they provide to information and advice, which may lead to better financial resources for the business.

In the uncertain and dynamic environments under which entrepreneurial activity occurs, resource holders, such as potential investors, 'angels', etc., are likely to seek information that helps gauge the underlying potential of a venture, while entrepreneurs seek ways to reduce risks associated with their business process by associating with investors. Access through a network to venture capitalists and professional service organizations, for example, is an important means of tapping into key market information and establishing financial ties (Freeman 1999). Moreover, when an entrepreneurial business is recognized and appreciated by more well-regarded individuals and organizations associated with that entrepreneur in the same networks, it will lead this business to effective and subsequently beneficial financial resource exchanges; in support, there is some empirical evidence that high-tech businesses with prominent strategic alliance partners are able to go public faster and at higher market valuation (Stuart, Hoang and Hybels 1999; Calabrese, Baum and Silverman 2000).

Studies in entrepreneurship have also documented that entrepreneurs consistently use networks to get ideas and gather information that will facilitate their search for financial resources, entrepreneurial opportunities, or a niche (Birley 1985; Smeltzer, Van Hook and Hutt 1991; Singh et al. 1999; Hoang and Young 2000), for example, in organizing and managing a supportive angel or informal investor networks.

The reliance on networks is not constrained to the startup stage. Entrepreneurs continue to rely on networks for business information, advice, and problem-solving, with some contacts providing multiple resources (Johannisson et al. 1994); effective networks have also been found to affect both survival and financial performance of entrepreneurial businesses (Gimeno et al. 1997; Bruderl and Preisendorfer 1998; Honig and Davidsson 2000). Trustworthy ties with suppliers, competitors, distributors, customers, or financial organizations can be important as conduits of information and know-how and can lead to reliable information flow, advice and beneficial business exchange (Brown and Butler 1995; Deeds, Mang and Frandsen 1997; Stuart, Hoang and Hybels 1999; Higgins and Gulati 2000; Shane and Cable 2001).

MANAGING THE FINANCIAL PROCESS

Once the source of financing has been decided upon and the selection has been made, entrepreneurs need to maintain it and manage it. Six major tips for managing the business's financial operations are provided (Shepherd, Armstrong and Levesque 2005; Sørheim 2005).

- *Follow up on the financial operations of the business.* Entrepreneurs should have control over their financing by following up on their business's financial operations daily – costs, sales, turnover, and more. In the computerized era, such follow-up is simple and attainable. Once a month, a larger follow-up should be performed for the other financial elements, such as loans, long-run payments, unfixed payments, long-run sales, and more.
- *Always leave a margin for financial tactics.* The margin for financial tactics has two purposes – security, in case there are unexpected costs, and as a reserve, when a feasible opportunity becomes available and the ongoing cash flow may not be enough to exploit it. For example, the initial purchase of a particular raw material might be at the bottom of an entrepreneur's priority list but then unexpectedly, this raw material becomes available for sale at a reduced price. Such a margin may assist the entrepreneur in purchasing it.
- *Proceed step by step.* It is recommended that the business be launched step by step, and that the sources of financing be used over several months rather than all at once. This has several advantages: first, it decreases the financial risk; second, it allows the gradual establishment of credibility; and third, if the first steps are well managed, better conditions will exist for subsequent steps.
- *Prevention is better than recovery.* Entrepreneurs should proactively gather information on potential financial funding. Acknowledging the nature of the potential problems connected to each financial source means envisaging how to plan operations accordingly and preparing a plan that may prevent some of the potential problems. This is much more highly recommended than preparing a plan for recovery because things have gone wrong.
- *Sign an agreement with the stockholders.* Confidence is the key factor in deciding which funds to select for the business. In order to ensure such confidence, a set of rules should be established and signed by the players. Topics such as the engagement of both sides for the business's interests, rules regulating how to 'go public' or sell the business, partitioning of profits, among others, should be discussed and regulated in a contract (Brown 1992).
- *Insurance policy.* The secret of an entrepreneurial business's success relies for the most part on a very limited number of team members who are the business's 'key people'. Insurance companies offer policies for these 'key people'; the business is generally designated as the recipient of these policies and, when needed, the insurance company covers the business.

THE USE OF FACTORING

Factoring[2] is a financial service that allows a business to liquidate outstanding receivables to a financial institution called a Factor for immediate cash funding; in essence, the firm sells its accounts receivable invoices to a factoring firm, which pays a percentage of the invoices immediately. Factoring is not a loan. It enables the preservation of financial leverage to take on new debt, the purchase of capital equipment or the paying off of delinquent obligations.

The factoring company buys the invoice from the entrepreneur 'today' for a cash amount that is less than face value and then later collects the full amount from the entrepreneurs or their customer(s) when the receivable is due. If the entrepreneurial business sells products or services to other businesses on credit, factoring receivables can eliminate the long billing cycles that put a strain on the entrepreneurial business's cash flow.

Many business owners use factoring to improve their cash flow, probably because unlike traditional bank financing, factoring relies on the financial strength and credit worthiness of the customer(s) rather than the entrepreneur. Moreover, factoring can be used as much as the entrepreneur wants or needs it. However, the value assigned to the account depends on the age of a receivable: a more current invoice will pay more, while accounts receivable that are over ninety days old are typically not financed. Factoring comes at a price and it should only be considered after a thorough evaluation of all available financing mechanisms.

Businesses experiencing long billing cycles that put a strain on their cash flow or that, despite increasing sales, suffer from complicated or ineffective management of receivables and payables; entrepreneurs spending too much time collecting from slow-paying customers and not enough time building up the business, and those entrepreneurs that feel very stressed by their financial state, among others, may benefit from factoring. With factoring, the main benefits come from:

- *Passing off collections* by outsourcing the management of accounts receivable to another company that may direct their resources to the core target-oriented activities, i.e., marketing, selling, more efficient production pace, improved planning, etc.
- *Quick financing*, a quick form of cash: this is most beneficial to businesses experiencing a cash crunch.
- *Releasing capital* that is often tied up in inventory and turning it into working capital.

For novice entrepreneurial businesses, factoring may be beneficial in several dimensions. First, improving customer–supplier relationships by outsourcing the payment procedure to a different company results in retaining clients, and even attracting new clients who will have heard of the simplified money-collection procedure. Second, during their very first stages, many entrepreneurial businesses are very strict with their cash flow and need to manage their expenses very carefully; factoring, like any other outsourcing service, reduces administrative costs and thus redirects critical resources to marketing and production. Third, since entrepreneurial businesses are not experts in money collection, factoring businesses – in essence, the experts – can collect the money more efficiently and therefore potentially improve receivable turn around and improve the entrepreneurial business's accounting.

On the down side, the factoring industry is not as strictly regulated as banking. Entrepreneurs must spend the necessary time investigating the companies they are working with, inspecting contracts and negotiating discount rates. In addition, this is a costly financial service: a 5 percent discount fee and other charges exceed the interest on bank credits or loans. As such, entrepreneurs should thoroughly consider their need for factoring, by addressing the following questions.

Survival and opportunity

- Is the money needed for the company's survival (i.e., without it, it might face bankruptcy)?
- Is the money needed for financing an opportunity?

Strategy

- How does this financing strategy match up with the business plan?
- Is the business ready for more money and expansion?

- What are the current conditions in the economy and industry?
- Is now a favorable time to finance?

Alternatives

- Has the entrepreneur explored other possible sources of small-business financing?
- Has the entrepreneur mapped the strengths and weaknesses of each possible source of financing relative to factoring and based his or her decisions upon these comparisons?

FACTORING IN ACTION

1 *Identifying the customer for factoring.* Credit is established on the customer whose invoices you wish to factor. Entrepreneurs should provide the customer's details and the amount they wish to factor for that customer. Credit is pulled and a monthly limit is established for that customer; sometimes, for new customers, the credit-validation service is free to the client (the entrepreneur); free credit checks are a significant benefit of factoring for entrepreneurs, encouraging them to use factoring for as many new customers as possible.

2 *Generating invoices for products.* Entrepreneurs should complete their business transaction as usual, and generate an invoice for products delivered and/or services rendered for the customer.

3 *Sending invoice for factoring.* Entrepreneurs send the original invoice to the factoring company along with proof of product/service delivery, normally received from the customer. Invoices eligible for factoring are those that are payable by other businesses or governments.

4 *Verification.* Factoring companies verify that the products have been received and/or services rendered.

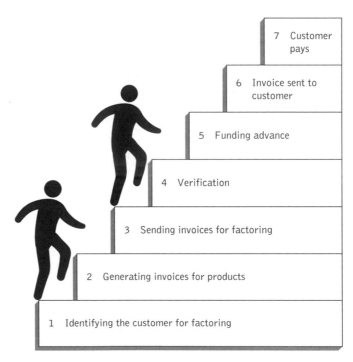

Figure 12.2 *Factoring in action: practical steps*

5   *Funding advance.* Entrepreneurs receive an immediate advance payment wired to their business banking account. The advance is usually between 80 percent and 90 percent of the original invoice amount.

6   *Invoice sent to customer.* Factoring companies send the invoices to the entrepreneur's customers; the customers then send their payment to the factoring company.

7   *Customers pay.* When the payment is due and the customer pays the invoice, the entrepreneur's business will receive the remainder of their advance payment minus the factor fee (the discount rate).

In the competitive and unpredictable market faced by entrepreneurial businesses, factoring appears as a newly developed financial form, providing entrepreneurs with flexible, updated and probably simplified solutions for situations characterized by cash flow shortages or financial uncertainty of the entrepreneurial business. Factoring reduces the entrepreneur's need to borrow money or to use bank services in order to offer credit terms to customers; it is a budding alternative financial form that is becoming known and used by more and more businesses (Thakur 1999; Soufani 2000; Zahra, Neubaum and Huse 2000; Burkart and Ellingsen 2004).

BUYING AND SELLING A BUSINESS

One way to reduce financial risks in launching a new venture, as opposed to a startup, is to buy an existing business that has already demonstrated an ability to successfully operate at a profit. From a financing perspective, buying an existing, established business is much easier in terms of securing capital from lenders than starting one from scratch.

If the business has a positive cash flow, a proven track record and perceived stability, it becomes easier to secure affordable acquisition financing. An existing business should already have a solid customer base, an experienced management team with proven practices and established systems. Even if the business is not yet profitable, the entrepreneur's strengths may lend themselves perfectly to turning it into a viable business (Joseph, Nekoranec and Steffens 1993; Osborne 1993; Bing 1996; Bhide et al. 1999; Haigh 2007).

The advantages and disadvantages of buying an existing business are listed in Table 12.5.

Research

When purchasing a small business, the buyer will want to learn everything he or she can about that business before signing the purchase agreement. Thorough and focused research, careful planning and following the advice of professional counsel are key to avoiding problems related to buying an existing business. Negotiating a reasonable amount of time to transition from the current management and bring in specific expertise in mergers and acquisitions before the letter-of-intent stage is reached can also help avoid some of the pain associated with new management for the staff, suppliers and customers, among others. In other words, seek the advice and guidance of business finance experts, a lawyer and a certified accountant before beginning the search for an acquisition target.

However, in order to do this effectively (i.e. buy the right business), a thorough investigation of the business's historical performance is needed — its operations, current status, the staff and management, competition, the industry and its future potential. Once this analysis has been completed, you will then have to determine how the business measures up with your skill, expertise and leadership.

Table 12.5 *The advantages and disadvantages of buying an existing business*

Advantages	Disadvantages
■ Much lower risk of failure ■ Business generates cash flow from day one ■ Proven business concept and processes ■ Proven products, services, marketing and sales strategies ■ Established customer base providing referrals and references ■ Established suppliers ■ Trained employees already in place ■ Immediate credibility and perception of success ■ Seller likely to lend support and may assist with financing ■ Easier to secure affordable financing to complete the acquisition	■ The initial purchasing cost: as the business concept, customer base, brands, and other fundamental work are already in place, the financial cost of acquiring an existing business is usually greater than that of starting one from the ground up ■ Hidden problems associated with the business and receivables that are valued at the time of purchase, but later turn out to be non-collectable ■ Costs, procedures and time invested in changing or adapting the existing business's already known strategy, marketing, credibility and perception of success into your own planned goals and strategies to achieve these ■ Other transfer costs such as consultants, lawyers, accountants and valuation specialists ■ The time and travel required to research available opportunities and hidden problems associated with the business and receivables that are valued at the time of purchase but later turn out to be non-collectable ■ Acquired businesses lose 5–10 percent of their customers in the first year after the sale

Due diligence

'Due diligence' refers to the information-gathering process buyers perform prior to committing to the purchase of a business. From a seller's perspective, due diligence is similar to a background check designed to reveal any hidden liabilities or problem areas within the company. Due diligence preparations need to be made as early as possible to avoid delays in the selling process; these should be very well organized and constructed, as an attempt to conceal potential liabilities can open the door to litigation later on.

Due diligence may assist the buyer in avoiding the following:

■ Discovering that the purchase price of the business is too high.
■ Misunderstandings as to the type and condition of the business being bought.
■ Fluctuating or miserable financial situations.
■ Management problems.
■ Pending lawsuits.
■ Contingent liabilities.

Selling a business

Selling a business is also a complex undertaking, as it involves several necessary steps that may assist in ensuring the best deal possible.

There are many reasons entrepreneurs report selling a business, but most are driven by an attempt to maximize profit or the investment. Each motivation is expected to give rise to a different selling strategy that will optimize the profitability of the selling process.

Some of the main motivations for selling a business are presented in Figure 12.3.

Pricing a business

- Value of tangible business assets.
- Value of intangible business assets.
- Sale prices of comparable businesses.
- Industry formulas.
- Market demand.
- Personal needs.
- Type of buyer.
- Terms of payment.
- Appraisals.
- Putting it all together.

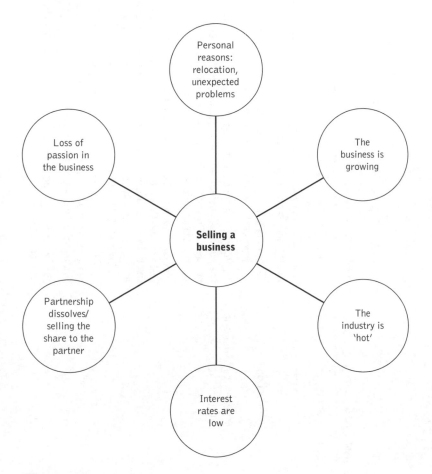

Figure 12.3 *Motivations for selling a business*

Table 12.6 Steps and stages in the selling process

Step	Stage	Content
1	Self-assessment	Assess your reasons for wanting to sell the business. You have to be sure about your decision because once it is made, there is no turning back
2	Valuation	Discerning a fair and objective price for your company will require you to calculate its worth based on one or more generally accepted methods of business valuation
3	Determine a realistic price range	To figure out a range that is realistic, you can use one of several methods, e.g., base the price on the value of the business's assets, and add in a sum for the goodwill the business has developed; see how much comparable businesses in your industry and locale have recently sold for; use an industry formula, such as, a value based on the number of units sold annually or a multiple of average earnings
		Tax consequences. Taxes can take a huge bite out of the money you receive for your business. It pays to know just how big that bite will be – and try to lower it, most likely with the help of a CPA or other tax expert. The tax bill will be influenced by two key factors: how your business is legally set up and whether you are selling the assets or the entity. Sales of all sole proprietorships and almost all partnerships are asset sales. So are the sales of many corporations and limited-liability companies
4	'Get ready'	When you sell a business, there are usually things that need to be done to prepare it for sale and make it presentable to potential buyers. Potential buyers will want to examine assets such as buildings and equipment firsthand, as well as the business's financial statements
		Entrepreneurs should prepare a packet of financial information that accurately reflects the financial condition of their business

5	Consult professionals	Consult with accountants, lawyers, an appraiser and another business owner who may make additional suggestions regarding valuation and preparation. The advance work should be performed by the entrepreneur as it provides a deeper understanding of, and broader perspective on the selling process
6	Screen potential buyers	Not everyone who expresses interest in your business will be a serious buyer. Some people shop for businesses like others window shop for shoes. The problem is that showing your business to potential buyers takes time. Rather than waste your time with insincere customers, it is much better to screen buyers in advance and only meet with those who seem truly serious
		Seek potential buyers. Reach out to a pool of potential buyers. This often includes putting ads in newspapers and trade publications, and on business-sale websites. Entrepreneurs may want to engage a business broker to reach more buyers, or to keep plans from going too public too fast. Expect to pay a substantial commission
7	Negotiate your deal	In working out the terms of the sale, some key issues include whether you will sell the business entity or just its assets, what assets you want to keep, and how the buyer will pay you
8	Sign a sales agreement	The selling process should be in writing, and the agreement should list and value the assets the buyer is purchasing, list any contracts the buyer is assuming, and include protections that ensure that you will get paid the full sale price
9	Finalize the sale	*Plan for the closing.* The closing is the meeting at which you transfer the business to the buyer. To reduce last-minute hassles, make a checklist of all the papers you and the buyer will need to bring – everything from the documents and money associated with the transfer to your alarm codes, keys, and customer lists
		Once a deal has been negotiated it is up to the attorneys and lenders to finalize the sale. All you have left to do is sign a few papers and ride off into the sunset

SUMMARY

Every entrepreneurial business longs to make better valuations, choose the right financing sources, avoid costly pitfalls and determine the best financial strategy for sustainability and growth. Yet entrepreneurs are often unqualified in identifying, choosing or evaluating the financial processes that will best fit their businesses; moreover, they consider the process of financing the business a one-dimensional 'assignment' to be accomplished. This chapter shed light on the multidimensional phases of financing the business by associating it to financial management, networking, the psychological aspects of using factoring and of buying and selling a business. It also drew attention to financing as a process that evolves with the business's needs; it is an all-encompassing process that requires skills, including absorbing information from the external environment, planning, making decisions, negotiating, and taking risks.

Financing an entrepreneurial business is an exclusive aspect that requires professional and specialized assistance, and entrepreneurs should engage professionals to assist them in managing the finances of their business properly, especially in entrepreneurial businesses, which are typically more vulnerable than well-established ones. However, they should also be proactive and in control with respect to their business's financial status. A robust understanding of the financial sources they can use, the importance of due diligence or the use of factoring, for example, may facilitate their financial short- and long-term decisions; eventually, entrepreneurs, and not their accountants, should make the strategic decisions for the business's financing.

CASE STUDY 12.1   Retirement villages, Russia

Forty-eight-year-old Kiril Sadovnichy has been an entrepreneur since 2001. He owns five luxury villages for the elderly in Russia. He was born in a quiet township beneath Mount Elbrus, near the border of Georgia and at the age of twenty-seven moved to Chicago, Illinois, where he studied education at the university and then worked in a private school for more than four years.

Sadovnichy developed the concept and managed his first retirement village in a beautiful new twenty-five-acre locale in the very center of the Valdai Hills on the banks of the beautiful Valdai Lake. He developed his concept and the subsequent business model as the 'ultimate choice for luxury living in active adult housing'; he visualized the village to contain the most prestigious, independent living residences in Russia, and provide diverse activities and services to its clients. He planned for the vast majority of his potential purchasers in the village to be those who had not yet retired, but had imminent plans to do so, by assuring them, while they were still independent, that they would be 'in good hands': as they got older and faced more health- and age-related problems, they would not need to look for assistance as it would be available to them in the village.

Sadovnichy is very successful today but the beginning of his entrepreneurial journey was very difficult; in fact, he almost renounced his idea and concept. Sadovnichy returned from Illinois following a painful divorce, and he planned to maintain an identical job in Russia, since he knew he was successful at teaching and guiding children; still, he had always been internally driven to have a business of his own. During the first months of his return to Russia, he was unemployed and lived from his savings; he even decided to go back to the United States to his previous job. It was on his way to his parents' house, by train, that he came up with the idea of developing a luxury village for the elderly in Russia; he shared his idea with his parents, who were very supportive and proposed some assistance from their relatives and friends in their home township.

The next morning, Sadovnichy contacted some real-estate agencies in his parents' township, as well as construction contractors; in two weeks, he had crafted a business plan for the village for the elderly as he visualized it. At this seed stage, he used his personal savings, a severance package from his prior job in Illinois, cash raised as a loan from his parents' friends and members of their township, and some more money that he borrowed from two different banks in Russia and the United States, and purchased a locale near this township, situated on expansive grounds, with views of the surrounding woods and mountains and which was able to provide luxury housing for forty senior households. Without any engineering plans, or the necessary authorizations, he started the construction of the village, eagerly anticipating its progress. In the meantime, he was also giving English lessons to the children in his parents' township, studying from books and websites on geriatric needs, conducting research by interviewing the elderly population in his parents' township on their needs and dreams, and working very hard to receive the needed authorizations for the construction.

He designed a tight business plan which forced him to pay for the real estate in cash, to pay the contractor in cash every month according to a formula he had developed, and to pay back his bank loans on a monthly basis. At that time, Sadovnichy said he was eating only twice a week, at his parents' house: he did not spend money on food elsewhere. One day, while things seemed to be going well with the loan payments and the construction was progressing, he received a letter from his ex-wife in the United States with a lawsuit; he had to attend court in the United States, where he lost the case; consequently, his debts greatly exceeded his financial abilities; he was desperate. He returned to Russia and knew he had to find a solution; with regret and sorrow he decided to sell the almost fully constructed village he longed for. He had no time as the banks were very demanding, and he therefore applied to an international real-estate association for assistance.

In a short time, a sixty-five-year-old American businessman expressed interest in the site and in Sadovnichy's concept. He bought the site for a good price, which left Sadovnichy with some extra money after paying off all his debts. Sadovnichy decided to exploit this opportunity by suggesting to the American that they partner on another village with the identical concept. The American researched Sadovnichy in depth and decided to accept and subsidize another village, under two conditions: first, he wanted 80 percent of the benefits as well as full control over the village; second, he expected profits by eighteen months' time; if the business would not be profitable, Sadovnichy would have to pay him half of the money he had already put into the project. Sadovnichy was so confident in his idea's novelty and feasibility that he immediately agreed. They bought land in the Valdai Hills and engaged the same contractors that had worked on Sadovnichy's first village, and were thus experienced in the project. Very optimistic and enthusiastic with the construction's progress, Sadovnichy turned his effort to locating potential customers, but he had a very hard time finding any; meanwhile, thirteen months had passed and he had five months left to show his partner some profits.

Assisted by a mentor, he sent proposals on topics related to geriatric housing to some governmental granting agencies and received a grant consisting of a very large sum of money which allowed him to proceed with the marketing process. Through this grant, he became acquainted with some wealthy Jewish people who were interested in moving into the village for the elderly as a community. In the seventeenth month of his contract with his partner, Sadovnichy sold 75 percent of the residences in the village. The other 25 percent were very easy to sell, as people had heard about the village through word of mouth and were interested in purchasing a residence. After a very short time, when monthly cash flow was at the break-even point but the profit was still very low, Sadovnichy's partner lost interest and abandoned the partnership. The residents of the village were satisfied yet very demanding, and Sadovnichy was determined to satisfy their needs, as he realized that they represented his future marketing power; however, he did not have enough money to satisfy all of their demands. He tried to get a line of credit from a commercial bank as revenues were gaining momentum, but without much success. He was again looking for more money and decided to track investors overseas.

After a long search, has found an Israeli of Russian origin who was interested in collaborating with him in this business; this Israeli had been separated from his family for a long time and it took them a long time to reunite; he was interested in assisting the elderly population in Russia. He too had rigid financial conditions for a partnership that Sadovnichy agreed to. It took Sadovnichy three years to show profits from the village. The Israeli partner encouraged Sadovnichy to duplicate the success of the village in other locations in Russia: he had large and active networks that he was willing to use for the business's growth. In the next two years, the two partners purchased, constructed and managed four villages all over Russia, all luxurious and specifically intended and designed for the more high-status independent and active elderly population in Russia. Sadovnichy experienced liquidity difficulties for two more years resulting from his tendency to constantly innovate the concepts, equipment and activities in the villages; his internal funds (profits and lines of credit) were insufficient to support the development of assets and internal capabilities necessary for growth. At this point, he was seeking to raise another external round of capital from investors. As he was willing to let go of some control and he was flexible, his relationships with these investors were fruitful and the capital was used to substantially ramp up existing operations and move the business into a significant position in the retirement housing market in Russia. The Israeli partner is now looking for opportunities to expand their business to other countries.

QUESTIONS FOR DISCUSSION

1   Identify the sources of financing that Sadovnichy used in the different phases of his business(es)' development and explain the advantages and disadvantages of using these sources with regard to the business phase.
2   Suggest a financing source to cope with liquidity difficulties other than relying on external investors, and indicate its advantages and disadvantages in comparison to external investors.
3   Address the six characteristics of managing the financial process and identify the one(s) most typifying Sadovnichy's management conduct. Explain your answer.
4   How would you categorize Sadovnichy's first partner and second partner (e.g., entrepreneur, founder, investor, co-partner, etc.)? What are the main differences between these partners in engaging in this venture creation and management?

5   What is the role of networking in the entrepreneurial processes that Sadovnichy and his partners went through? Analyze the benefits of their use.

6   What should Sadovnichy do next in order to financially sustain and grow his business? Address as many aspects of financing the business as possible.

AT A GLANCE 12.1   Qtech, Singapore

'Learn from lions when you attack; learn from tigers when you seek food [expanding customer base]; learn from zebras when being attacked; learn from deers how to escape the lions . . .' says Hillal Alam, founder and owner of Qtech Nanosystems. Alam has had to cross several hurdles – since 2005 when he first launched Qtech – on the way to his current business which is estimated to be worth roughly US$250 million and employs ten team members. This is a true story about raising money in the early stages of a business: Alam founded Qtech Nanosystems in 2005 in Bangalore, India and in 2006 in Singapore. Qtech's main expertise is in nanodynamics, with a focus on nanopositioning technology and the development of related nanomaterials. For the years 2007/2008, Alam's plan was to tap into Malaysia or Taiwan and the United States. Nanopositioning and nanodynamics were Alam's M.Sc. research (Precision Engineering) topic, and he decided to further develop this technology to move ahead of the global leaders. He managed a small software firm in Bangalore for a while, prior to launching Qtech. Alam supports another small software company which he founded in 2001.

Qtech developed relatively quickly from an incubation firm in India in terms of product innovations, R&D, number of patents – from none to two, and six others pending, growth in the number of employees, changes in its products – from nanopositioners to various ultra-precision products, and an increase in the number of clients.

Starting with the help of some friends and family members, Alam had a tough road ahead as he was a recent graduate without a single dollar to his name; the only backing was from his parents and friends, who supported him morally and, to a certain extent, financially. Alam describes the stages he went through as follows: 'Step 1: I collected a few thousand US dollars from parents and friends and added my meager savings'; as a free thinker who was always attempting to innovate something and bring it to the market, he developed the technology, then showcased the product to incubators and investors along with the business plan. Step 2, according to Alam, was focused on building technology and prototypes, then coordinating the rental and use of manufacturing and testing facilities (these infrastructures cost millions to billions of US dollars). 'I executed my design and fabricated a few prototypes to show to customers in the first half of the year,' explains Alam. The next step was finding the manpower and training them, maintaining a low attrition rate, creating awareness among customers and with these setups, and bringing in funds. Then, says Alam, 'in step 3, a few customers bought the technology and I collected their feedback for comparison against the year 1 performances of the world's leaders and followers. Step 4 consisted of rectifying the issues with our innovative ideas and filing patents (around ten at that point), and redesigning them to place our product's performance on par with the world leaders or between the first and second competitors in year 2. Up until then we were using our own funds from various sources.'

In 2006, India was focused on software and service sectors. Venture capitalists knew only about software and the government was not aware of nanotechnology (and had no plans to promote nanotech startups). The infrastructure was scattered all over the country and it was difficult to coordinate with them. Manpower shortage was another big problem as all of the bright students were going into software, irrespective of their Master's topics. Getting support from the government in terms of funding and grants in India failed. 'Relocating to Singapore,' continues Alam, 'was step 5: in year 3, we were talking to big customers and R&Ds for cash flow after we managed to raise the first round of funding on a milestone basis. We are now at step 6: we are in the process of trying to position our company between numbers one and two, and next year we want to emerge on top. We are approaching Singapore's government for grants to take it ahead before attracting VCs.'

NOTES

1   Business.Com, www.business.com/directory/financial_services/venture_capital/; Enterprise Ireland, www.enterprise-ireland.com/Grow/Finance/Seed_Capital_Scheme.htm; London Business School, 'Financing the Entrepreneurial Business' programme, www.london.edu/financeprogrammes/feb. html; Seed Capital Denmark, www.seedcapital.dk/; Seed Capital Partners, www.seedcp.com/html/welcome.html; Vfinance Inc., www.vfinance.com/; Removing Obstacles to Cross-border Investment by Venture Capital Funds, European Commission expert group report, 30 March 2007, http://ec.europa.eu/enterprise/entrepreneurship/financing/publications_documents.htm.

2   Factoring is also known as accounts receivable financing, accounts receivable factoring, or accounts receivable funding.

REFERENCES

Ando, A., Hancock, J. and Sawchuk, G. (1997) 'Cost of capital for the United States, Japan and Canada: an attempt at measurement based on individual company records and aggregate national account data', in P.J.N. Halpern (ed.) *Financing Growth in Canada, Industry Canada Research Series*, vol. 8, Calgary: University of Calgary Press, 71–133.

Beck, T., Demirgüç-Kunt, A. and Maksimovic, V. (2008) 'Financing patterns around the world: are small firms different?', *Journal of Financial Economics*, 89: 467–87.

Bhide, A., Sahlman, W., Stancil, J., Rock, A., Nevens, M. and Summe, G. (1999) *Harvard Business Review on Entrepreneurship*, Cambridge, MA: Harvard Business School Press.

Bing, G. (1996) *Due Diligence Techniques and Analysis: Critical Questions for Business Decisions*, Westport, CT: Quorum Books.

Birley, S. (1985) 'The role of networks in the entrepreneurial process', *Journal of Business Venturing*, 1: 107–17.

Bourgeois, L.J. and Eisenhardt, K.M. (1998) 'Strategic decision processes in high velocity environments', *Management Science*, 34: 816–35.

Brau, J., Francis, B. and Kohers, N. (2003) 'The choice of IPO versus takeover: empirical evidence', *Journal of Business*, 76: 583–612.

Brown, B. and Butler, J.E. (1995) 'Competitors as allies: a study of entrepreneurial networks in the U.S. wine industry', *Journal of Small Business Management*, 33: 57–66.

Brown, G.A. (1992) 'Are profits deserved?', *Journal of Business Ethics*, 11: 105–14.

Bruderl, J. and Preisendorfer, P. (1998) 'Network support and the success of newly founded businesses', *Small Business Economics*, 10: 213–25.

Bruno, A.V. and Tyebjee, T.T. (1985) 'The entrepreneur's search for capital', *Journal of Business Venturing*, 1: 61–75.

Bruton, G.D., Chahine, S. and Filatotchev, I. (2009) 'Founders, private equity investors, and underpricing in entrepreneurial IPOs', *Entrepreneurship Theory and Practice*, 33: 909–28.

Burkart, M. and Ellingsen T. (2004) 'In-kind finance: a theory of trade credit', *American Economic Review*, 94: 569–90.

Calabrese, T., Baum, J.A.C. and Silverman, B. (2000) 'Canadian biotechnology start ups, 1991–1997: the role of incumbents' patents and strategic alliances in controlling competition', *Social Science Research*, 29: 503–34.

Certo, S.T. (2003) 'Influencing initial public offering investors with prestige: signaling with board structures', *Academy of Management Review*, 28: 432–46.

Certo, S.T., Daily, C.M. and Dalton, D.R. (2001) 'Signaling firm value through board structure: an investigation of initial public offerings', *Entrepreneurship Theory and Practice*, 26: 33–50.

Certo, S.T., Daily, C.M., Cannella, A.A. and Dalton, D.R. (2003) 'Giving money to get money: how CEO stock options and CEO equity enhance IPO valuations', *Academy of Management Journal*, 46: 643–53.

Cohan, P.S. and Unger, B. (2006) 'Four sources of advantage', *Business Strategy Review*, 17: 9–14.

Colombo, M. and Grilli, L. (2007) 'Funding gaps? Access to bank loans by high-tech start-ups', *Small Business Economics*, 29: 25–46.

Cumming, D.J. (2005) 'Agency costs, institutions, learning, and taxation in venture capital contracting', *Journal of Business Venturing*, 20: 573–622.

de Bettignies, J. and Brander, J.A. (2007) 'Financing entrepreneurship: bank finance versus venture capital', *Journal of Business Venturing*, 22: 808–32.

De Clercq, D., Fried, V.H., Lehtonen, O. and Sapienza, H.J. (2006) 'An entrepreneur's guide to the venture capital galaxy', *Academy of Management Perspectives*, 20: 90–112.

Deeds, D.L., Decarolis, D. and Coombs, J.E. (1997) 'The impact of firm specific capabilities on the amount of capital raised in an initial public offering: evidence from the biotechnology industry', *Journal of Business Venturing*, 12: 31–46.

Deeds, D.L., Mang, P.Y. and Frandsen, M. (1997) 'The quest for legitimacy: a study of biotechnology IPO's', in P.D. Reynolds et al. (eds) *Frontiers of Entrepreneurship Research*, Wellesley, MA: Center for boat and sinking the boat: a conceptual model of entrepreneurial risk', *Journal of Marketing*, 50: 58–70.

Fiet, J.O. (1996) 'Fragmentation in the market for venture capital', *Entrepreneurship Theory and Practice*, 21: 5–20.

Freeman, J. (1999) 'Venture capital as an economy of time', in R.Th.A.J. Leenders and S.M. Gabbay (eds) *Corporate Social Capital and Liability*, Boston, MA: Kluwer Academic Publishing, 460–82.

George, G. (2005) 'Slack resources and the performance of privately held firms', *Academy of Management Journal*, 48: 661–76.

Gimeno, J., Folta, T.B., Cooper, A.C. and Woo, C.Y. (1997) 'Survival of the fittest? Entrepreneurial human capital and the persistence of underperforming firms', *Administrative Science Quarterly*, 42: 750–83.

Gompers, P.A. and Lerner, J. (1999) *The Venture Capital Cycle*, Cambridge, MA: MIT Press.

Gompers, P.A. and Lerner, J. (2001) *The Money of Invention: How Venture Capital Creates Wealth*, Cambridge, MA: Harvard Business School Press.

Haigh, J. (2007) *Buying and Selling a Business: An Entrepreneur's Guide*, London: Piatkus Books.

Hart, C. (1995) 'The power of internal guarantees', *Harvard Business Review*, 73: 64–73.

Harvey, M.G. and Lusch, R.F. (1995) 'A systematic assessment of potential international strategic alliance partners', *International Business Review*, 4: 195–212.

225

Higgins, M.C. and Gulati, R. (2000) 'Getting off to a good start: the effects of top management team affiliations on prestige of investment bank and IPO success', Working paper.

Hindle, K. and Lee, L. (2002) 'An exploratory investigation of informal venture capitalists in Singapore', *Venture Capital: An International Journal of Entrepreneurial Finance,* 4: 169–77.

Hoang, H. and Young, N. (2000) 'Social embeddedness and entrepreneurial opportunity recognition; (more) evidence of embeddedness', Working paper.

Holger, G., Henry, M. and Strobl, E. (2008) 'Grant support and exporting activity', *Review of Economics and Statistics,* 90: 168–74.

Honig, B. and Davidsson, P. (2000) 'The role of social and human capital among nascent entrepreneurs', Paper presented at the annual meeting of the Academy of Management, Toronto, Canada.

Jeng, L.A. and Wells, P.C. (1998) 'The determinants of venture capital funding: evidence across countries', *Journal of Corporate Finance,* 6: 241–89.

Jensen, M.C. and Meckling, W.H. (1976) 'Theory of the firm: managerial behavior, agency costs and ownership structure', *Journal of Financial Economics,* 3: 305–60.

Jog, V. (1997) *Investing in Canada: Estimation of the Sectoral Cost of Capital in Canada and Case Studies for International Comparisons, Financing Growth in Canada,* Calgary: University of Calgary Press.

Johannisson, B., Alexanderson, O., Nowicki, K. and Senneseth, K. (1994) 'Beyond anarchy and organization: entrepreneurs in contextual networks', *Entrepreneurship and Regional Development,* 6: 329–56.

Joseph, R.A., Nekoranec, A.M. and Steffens, C.H. (1993) *How To Buy a Business,* Chicago, IL: Dearborn, a Kaplan Professional Company.

Kelly, P. and Hay, M. (1996) 'Serial investors: an exploratory study', in P.D. Reynolds, S. Birley, J.E. Butler, W.D. Bygrave, P. Davidsson, W.B. Gartnor and P.P. McDougall (eds) *Frontiers of Entrepreneurship Research,* Wellesley, MA: Babson College, 344–58.

Le, Ngoc T.B. and Nguyen, T.V. (2009) 'The impact of networking on bank financing: the case of small and medium-sized enterprises in Vietnam', *Entrepreneurship Theory and Practice,* 33: 867–87.

Lusch, R.F., Harvey, M. and Speier, C. (1998) 'ROI: the building blocks for successful global organizations in the twenty-first century', *European Management Journal,* 16: 714–28.

Mason, C.M. (2009) 'Public policy support for the informal venture capital market in Europe: a critical review', *International Small Business Journal,* 27: 536–56.

Mason, C.M. and Harrison, R.T. (1997) 'Business angels in the UK: a response to Stevenson and Coveney', *International Small Business Journal,* 15: 83–90.

Mulherin, J.H. and Boone, A.L. (2000) 'Comparing acquisitions and divestitures', *Journal of Corporate Finance,* 6: 117–39.

Mullins, J. (2004) 'Entrepreneurial gold mines', *Business Strategy Review,* 15: 2–4.

Osborne, R.L. (1993) 'Why entrepreneurs fail: how to avoid the traps', *Management Decision,* 31: 18–21.

Sahlman, W.A. (1990) 'The structure and governance of venture-capital organizations', *Journal of Financial Economics,* 27: 473–521.

Schwienbacher, A. (2007). 'A theoretical analysis of optimal financing strategies for different types of capital-constrained entrepreneurs', *Journal of Business Venturing,* 22: 753–81.

Shane, S. and Cable, D. (2001) 'Social relationships and the financing of new ventures', Working paper.

Shepherd, D.A., Armstrong, M.J. and Levesque, M. (2005) 'Allocation of attention within venture capital firms', *European Journal of Operational Research,* 163: 545–64.

Singh, R.P., Hills, G.E., Lumpkin, G.T. and Hybels, R.C. (1999) 'The entrepreneurial opportunity recognition process: examining the role of self-perceived alertness and social networks', Paper presented at the 1999 Academy of Management Meeting, Chicago, IL.

Smeltzer, L.R., Van Hook, B.L. and Hutt, R.W. (1991) 'Analysis and use of advisors as information sources in venture startups', *Journal of Small Business Management,* 29: 10–20.

Sørheim, R. (2005) 'Business angels as facilitators for further finance: an exploratory study', *Journal of Small Business and Enterprise Development,* 12: 178–91.

Soufani, K. (2000) 'Factoring and UK small business', *Journal of Small Business and Entrepreneurship*, 15: 78–89.

Steier, L. (2000) 'Entrepreneurship and the evolution of angel financial networks', *Organization Studies*, 21: 163–93.

St-Pierre, J. and Bahri, M. (2006) 'The use of the accounting beta as an overall risk indicator for unlisted companies', *Journal of Small Business and Enterprise Development*, 13: 546–61.

Stuart, T.E., Hoang, H. and Hybels, R. (1999) 'Interorganizational endorsements and the performance of entrepreneurial ventures', *Administrative Science Quarterly*, 44: 315–49.

Sullivan, M.K. (1991) 'Entrepreneurs as informal investors: are there distinguishing characteristics?', in N.C. Churchhill, W.D. Bygrave, J.G. Covin, D.L. Sexton, D.P. Slevin, K.H. Vesper and W.E. Wetzol (eds) *Frontiers of Entrepreneurship Research*, Wellesley, MA: Babson College, 456–68.

Thakur, S.P. (1999) 'Size of investment, opportunity choice and human resources in new venture growth. Some typologies', *Journal of Business Venturing*, 14: 283–309.

Villalonga, B. and Amit, R. (2006) 'How do family ownership, control and management affect firm value?'. *Journal of Financial Economics*, 80: 385–417.

Wang, C.K. and Sim, V.Y.L. (2001) 'Exit strategies of venture capital-backed companies in Singapore', *Venture Capital: An International Journal of Entrepreneurial Finance*, 3: 337–58.

Wiltbank, R., Read, S., Dew, N. and Sarasvathy, S.D. (2009) 'Prediction and control under uncertainty: outcomes in angel investing', *Journal of Business Venturing*, 24: 116–33.

Wright, M., Pruthi, S. and Lockett, A. (2005) 'International venture capital research: from cross-country comparisons to crossing borders', *International Journal of Management Reviews*, 7: 135–65.

Zahra, S.A., Neubaum, D.O. and Huse, M. (2000) 'Entrepreneurship in medium-size companies: exploring the effects of ownership and governance systems', *Journal of Management*, 26: 947–76.

Chapter 13

Managing rapid and sustainable growth

OBJECTIVES

After studying this chapter you will be able to:

■ Recognize that management of an entrepreneurial business is one of the owner's major responsibilities for survival and sustainability.

■ Understand that sustainable development of an entrepreneurial business requires thorough, careful management and monitoring processes.

■ Acknowledge the different processes for keeping the business rolling by identifying the stages of development for entrepreneurial businesses, acknowledging the characteristics of each stage and subsequently fitting the most suitable management processes to each stage.

■ Discern between the different practices – inside and outside the business – to reach sustainable development for the business, and for both expanding the knowledge and deepening the know-how of managing an entrepreneurial business.

■ Explain the role of education and learning in managing and sustaining entrepreneurial businesses in terms of knowledge transfer, developing concepts on entrepreneurship that will eventually meet the 'ideal' specifications of entrepreneurship, develop core skills and teach different problem-diagnosis and opportunity-exploitation methods.

■ Assess and evaluate the effectiveness of academic and non-academic programs for the development of skills and capabilities that will improve entrepreneurs' managerial competence.

■ Realize the role of the advisory board as a major driving force behind the long-term success of entrepreneurial businesses, in offering direction, advising and assisting the business in networking, mentoring and setting limits, among others. Understand what 'going public' means; stress its benefits and risks and the required obligations entrepreneurs must address in order to successfully complete this stage.

■ Acknowledge the role of relevant, ongoing networking processes (via the internet, face-to-face, professional networks) for business publicity, coverage, finding potential contacts and maintaining existing ones, benchmarking and learning from others' experiences, barter relations, among others.

Today's global hyper-competition and business interdependency have brought about rapid and extensive changes in the entrepreneurial environment, e.g., faster flow – and overflow – of information, easier but less personal communication, higher specialization, more complex internal organization, etc. As a result, businesses now find themselves in a continuous cycle of adjustment in order to meet the environmental demands and compete with other businesses – at a quicker pace and through the use of more complicated tools and methods. Managing rapid growth and sustainability has become a bona fide expertise for those that have developed or acquired it, thereby ascertaining their business's competitive advantage. Such expertise relies on three strategic driving forces: intellectual capital, the business's continuous and rapid capacity for adaptive change, and use of the most up-to-date technologies and processes at the business level.

However, each of these driving forces, like most of the processes managed in entrepreneurial businesses, may be more or less dominant at different stages of the business's development. In the following, we illustrate the main characteristics of each stage of entrepreneurial business development and the best practices at each of these stages for business sustainability (Sadler-Smith et al. 2003; Habbershon 2006).

PLANNING THE ESTABLISHED VENTURE

Planning plays an important role in any business venture at any stage, and businesses continually attempt to develop and implement a winning strategy, which they consider the pathway to achieving the goals they planned for their firms. In fact, strategic planning can make the difference between a business's success and failure.

Unlike the planning of a business's first steps, at seed and startup, typified by a strategic plan for establishing a customer base and a market presence along with tracking and conserving cash flow, or searching for financial resources, planning at the more advanced stages focuses on planning and managing for growth. This may include managing people, projects, growth strategies, competitive strategies and international opportunities. Managerial strategies are most important during these growth stages of the established venture (Kariv 2008).

One of the owners' major responsibilities at these advanced stages consists of running the enterprise at a sustainable and profitable level, which entails programs for keeping the 'business's wheels' in motion. Such programs should be designed in full accordance with the involved players, since they are the business's most valuable resource; they are the people who will actively promote and bring about its success. A strategic program designed by the owners according to their visions and wishes alone, and not understood or accepted by the relevant participants, is highly likely to fail.

As described earlier in this book, during the first stages of venture creation, entrepreneurs analyze the environment, their active competitors, and the needs of potential clients. However, as the business grows, it is essential to form a plan that will enable them to clarify and sharpen their vision and their strategy, and to translate these into action; this is the basis of management strategy.

A new venture's mission statement is its prime managerial tool: it rallies the business's players around the main goals of the business and constitutes the guidelines that underlie effective business management, and, thus, achievement of the planned goals. The relevant parts of the mission statement should be communicated to all of the players who are directly or indirectly related to the business (i.e., employees, customers, suppliers), and acknowledged by them.

Most people tend be more supportive of organizations whose values are known to and accepted by them, and mission statements may thus lead to, or enhance, trusting relationships. Since some

229

of the players may not have the same or similar expectations from the business, the entrepreneurs' mission statements define them, as well as the firm's financial objectives and its resources. Table 13.1 illustrates the players' different expectations with respect to the firm and how these can be translated into a winning mission statement (Hay, Verdin and Williamson 1993; McGrath and Keil 2007).

THE STAGES OF DEVELOPMENT IN AN ENTREPRENEURIAL BUSINESS

The traditional stages of development for entrepreneurial companies are: the seed or concept; the startup; the first, second, and third stages; the harvest. The following provides a brief description of each (Cooper 1981; Siegel, Siegel and MacMillan 1993; Van Stel, Carree and Thurik 2005).

Seed or concept

This is the wild-eyed, incurably optimistic, inventor stage. There is an idea, sometimes a cognitively well-organized concept; however, there is no prototype, no management and no team. Entrepreneurs at this stage are the professionals, and they are therefore less likely to address market research or available resources, and they are not considering competitors or potential clients'

Table 13.1 *Objectives and their incorporation into a mission statement*

Actors	Expectations from the business	Objectives to be developed into a mission statement based on the expectations
Employees	Job satisfaction Motivation Salary Job security	Promoting an environment that encourages new ideas, high-quality workmanship, and professional achievement Treating employees honestly and fairly, and ensuring fair pay and equal opportunities for employment and advancement
Customers	Price Quality	Placing the highest priority on the quality, promptness, and competitiveness of the products/services Monitoring and responding to changes in clients' needs and demands, and to their levels of satisfaction, and considering them important
Shareholders and business partners	Shares of profits	Preserving and enhancing the company's profits, growth and reputation Doing the utmost to provide shareholders a fair return on investment Fairness and professionalism in all business dealings and honoring commitments to business partners
Suppliers	Honesty and good faith in the purchase process	Selection of suppliers and subcontractors who will adhere to the stated ethical standards and commitment to quality products and services
Communities	Environmental protection from pollution and ecological disturbances	Responsibility to respect the laws and customs of each community in which we live and conduct business will be of prime importance

needs. This is the stage of unbridled enthusiasm, with entrepreneurs dedicating their time, energy and money to developing the concept.

This stage is generally characterized by limited financial resources: traditional venture-capital firms will not fund businesses at this stage because the risk is too high. Entrepreneurs therefore use their personal financial resources, personal savings, or loans from family and friends.

Best practice. Performing a market assessment. At this stage, entrepreneurs are usually certain that they know their target market, but they must ascertain it: whenever they come across information that deviates from their expectations (e.g., the expected target market is not anticipating such a product/service; there are much more robust market segments that are willing to buy the product/service, etc.), they should adjust their idea to the clients' demands, or search for the 'right' clientele that will buy their original idea. Market research is critical (Robinson and Pearce 1986).

Startup

When a prototype has been developed or the service has been discussed with potential customers, the business has entered the startup stage. At this stage, the business is more established: it usually consists of a management team or person (usually the founder), and professional and administrative people or teams. In terms of processes being undertaken, the market analysis is being refined and the entrepreneurs have a stronger feel for the potential clients' demands and needs; they may also hone a strategic plan for the next steps, and they are putting their all into raising funds. At this stage, more traditional venture-capital firms may show an interest, assuming that patentability or proprietorship, and marketability have been proven. The main threat at this stage is in finding it impossible to implement a business founded on the innovative idea, due to shortage of money or inapplicability of the prototype.

Best practice. Establishing the product's manufacture and initiating sales; proactively searching for the right segment of potential clients and convincing them of the product/service's competitive advantage (Terpstra and Olson 1993; Jokioinen and Suomala 2006).

First stage

When a business's main product has proven to be manufacturable and saleable, or customers have used the service it provides, it has entered the first stage. The most characteristic processes at this stage are a sustainable initial management team, a more refined marketing strategy and, in response to difficulties encountered up until this stage, adjustments in the plan, strategy and fund-raising processes. At this stage, traditional venture-capital firms are more interested in investing; however, more financing is needed to maintain production and to support initial marketing efforts.

The business is attempting to achieve market penetration and initial sales goals, to get close to breaking even, and it therefore increases productivity, reduces unit costs, and builds the sales organization and distribution system. The main threat is insufficient funding, which, at this stage, is the main factor in firms' failure.

Best practice. Establishing the HR, recruiting the needed workers based on their skills and abilities, and promoting them accordingly; stabilizing the management, and setting up guidelines or a plan that will serve as the baseline for leading the business successfully into the next stages (Bouwen and Steyaert 1990; Blumentritt, Kickul and Gundry 2005).

Table 13.2 Management at each of the firm's development stages

Firm's stage	Firm's objectives	Management style	Managing finance and assets	Managing people/teams	Managing marketing
Concept creation	Inventing an idea Envisioning unique products, services or knowledge creation	Informal Entrepreneurial style Innovative Visionary	Managing own sources of financing Searching for government grants or assistance programs Searching virtually and/or via existing networks for sources of financing	'One-man show' Acting swiftly by managing the 'big picture' and leaving details for later Task orientation Sharing thoughts, ideas and concerns with others, e.g., partners, family members, friends	Undeveloped, lack of identity and brand awareness Identifying potential clients' needs Planning variety, pricing, production speed, marketing channels Virtual networks
Launching the venture	Identifying market needs Establishing a competitive niche Concretizing the vision through the creation of a business platform Production	Leadership Entrepreneurial style Collectivity – everybody for everything Intuitive – directing energy to guide people toward practical solutions	Managing own sources Due to negative balance, searching for financial assistance from friends, relatives, banks Non-conservative cash and financial management	Creating an honest and credible environment Treating employees as assets that require investment rather than control Developing harmonious interpersonal relationships	Forecasting environmental changes Monitoring the competition, managing low market acceptance, potential loss of customers/vendors Viewing the work and business as challenging and exciting Prototypes of products used for marketing (distribution of a limited number of free samples to potential customers, for example)

Stabilization – surviving the first year	Expanding revenues Quality consciousness Expanding the channels to capture more customers Solidifying repeat customers	Managing by walking around (being in the thick of things) Flexibility along with management by objectives Management by information systems – managers depend on data generated within the business to help them increase efficiency and inter-relatedness Management by interaction – of mental, emotional, physical and spiritual spheres, and creating an empowered, high-energy, highly productive workforce	Stabilization of relationship with banks, use of leasing, government grants, assistance programs Seeking to minimize risks and tolerate the mundane Managing the marginal bank balances Emphasis on sales versus profit Expanding human resources (HR) practices; recruiting 'external' forces through the use of objective criteria to manage certain processes in the business	Effective and supportive communication Coaching and mentoring employees People and task orientation Founders should provide 'space' and acceptance for decision-making and choices of the functioning managers by empowering and supporting them Recruiting experts Influencing people through the use of logic, facts and reason	Quality – the name of the game Service – the name of the game Coping with product or service complaints or failures Coping with greedy, existing or emerging competitors
Rapid growth	Maintaining a realistic perspective Balancing today's resources, needs and demands with tomorrow's resources, needs and demands	Management by decision models Management by exceptions Management by matrices and/or objectives – managers study charted variables to discern their inter-relatedness, probable cause and effect, and available options	Negotiating new partnerships Benefiting from institutionalized trust in the business's stability Managing expenditures	Managing multiple intrapreneurs, experts, highly motivated employees Managing conflicts between formal versus informal processes, 'traditional' versus innovative processes, and between veterans' and newcomers' approaches	Broadening the lines International orientation Managing competitors' 'knock-offs' Managing customers' complaints Restructuring a strategic market plan

Table 13.2 *Continued*

Firm's stage	Firm's objectives	Management style	Managing finance and assets	Managing people/teams	Managing marketing
Expansion	Financing growth Maintaining employee control, loyalty and commitment Maintaining customer loyalty	Management by coaching and development Management by organizational development – managers constantly seek to improve employee relations and communication	Managing financial profits Capital markets Joint venturing Coordinating operating plan with financial conditions Controlling the R&D while supporting it Allocating money for disaster-recovery plans	Preserving the leading people and/or teams, those contributing most to the business Empowering teams and delegating Providing and documenting formal, consistent feedback on people's performance and results Improving decision-making processes/systems	Enlarging the shrinking market share Relating marketing expenses to sales targets Forming key account programs
Maturity	Controlling expenses Productivity Global penetration Managing market niches	Management by work simplification Management by consensus Managing the firm as 'a family' – employees are treated as experienced, loyal experts, even though they may be burned out, exhausted or even unmotivated. Management through	Sustaining periods of negative cash flow Managing capital budget	Managing the reduced communication and interaction between functional units Controlling unhealthy competition for power and other negative politics-related issues Remotivating the leading employees and teams Integrating skills and abilities for a common goal	Evaluating the profitability of the marketing channels Assessing advertising and promotion effectiveness Emphasizing the well-known existing accomplishments Basing marketing on loyal customers' satisfaction rates; references on reliable products

Innovation or decline				
Drive change or the organization may die Innovate or lose market shares	involvement, visibility, and empowerment is critical Management for survival – like a captain saving the ship from sinking	Identifying hidden costs, e.g., 'weak' products often consume a disproportionate amount of management time and money; storage space is expensive; adjusting processes in different aspects involves expenses that should be monitored For each product, analyzing its trends in market size, market share, process, costs, and profits and making decisions regarding its financial raison d'être Financing innovative practical ideas – carefully and reasonably, according to concurrent financial conditions	Actively involving all levels of the organization in innovation Motivating the leading persons in the firms Supporting and encouraging brainstorming and breakthrough ideas	Identifying shifts in consumer tastes, and/or increased domestic and foreign competition Marketing the aging products in a new, updated package

Second stage

At this stage, businesses are breaking even; but the business is still not stabilized and the break-even state is a very vulnerable one. However, internal processes, such as marketing, are becoming more established; management systems are becoming more sophisticated, and sales, assets and liabilities are being developed. Businesses at this stage need to obtain working capital to expand marketing, accounts receivable, and inventory. More sophisticated and second-round venture-capital financing is required; the founders and investors are forming plans for the harvest. The main threat at this stage is cash flow management.

Best practice. Achieving consistent profitability by adding significant sales and back orders, expanding sales from regional to national or even international markets (Reynolds and Lancaster 2006).

Third ('mezzanine') stage

The business's processes are well established, are being applied and are working effectively. Most businesses at this stage should prepare for 'the harvest'. The business is working on all cylinders, and it is under a great deal of pressure to demonstrate second- and third-generation products, increase profitability records, improve the balance sheet, and firmly establish market share and penetration.

At this stage, the business may need to obtain 'bridge' or 'mezzanine' financing to carry increased accounts receivable and inventory prior to harvest. The major threat is in being unable to identify the 'right' timing for the harvest; staying in the same place, at this stage and in the face of a competitive market, means falling back.

Best practice. Increasing market reliability, beginning export marketing, putting second-level management in place, beginning the process of 'dressing up' the company for harvest (Lafuente and Salas 1989).

The fourth stage, the 'harvest'

The business is sorting out its options, including going public, being acquired, selling out, or merging. Misidentifying the timing and taking the wrong risks are the main threats. Acquiring information and getting feedback from others is critical at this stage.

SKILLS DEVELOPMENT FOR RAPID GROWTH: ACADEMIC AND NON-ACADEMIC PROGRAMS

The synergy between entrepreneurship practice and education/research was recognized and illustrated by Cherwitz and Darwin (2005), who argued that the best entrepreneurs are intellectual entrepreneurs – scholars who take risks and grab opportunities, discover and create knowledge, innovate, collaborate, and solve problems in any number of social realms. Researchers echoing Cherwitz's view have stated that the best teachers and researchers are the intellectual entrepreneurs, who create new information, new ways of thinking and new ways of seeing their particular discipline.

While there is general agreement that these relationships are valuable, there are still gaps in educators' and researchers' knowledge regarding the ways in which entrepreneurship programs should be amended and adjusted for a variety of players – the direct and indirect clients of academic programs in entrepreneurship. Potential and active entrepreneurs' needs, community demands, labor market trends, and the global entrepreneurial environment all need to be taken into account (Birdthistle, Hynes and Fleming 2007; Pittaway and Cope 2007).

The OECD Centre for Entrepreneurship, SMEs and Local Development, which organized and hosted the 2005 Conference on Entrepreneurship and Higher Education,[1] provides statistics showing the global trends of higher education programs in entrepreneurship. Its most significant findings are presented in Table 13.3.

THE NEW VENTURE AND SUSTAINABLE DEVELOPMENT

Michael Jordan, one of the greatest NBA basketball players of all time, said: 'I play to win, whether during practice or a real game. And I will not let anything get in the way of me and my competitive enthusiasm to win.' Like Jordan, any business starts in order to win, to achieve success. However, sustainable development is difficult to achieve and requires thorough, careful management and monitoring processes. Enthusiasm, self-confidence on the buisness's products or services and entrepreneurs' determination are the backbones of a business's sustainable development, yet these cannot be of much assistace if the entrepreneur is not managing the business toward growth and development. There are several generic recommendations that can be applied in different businesses and different countries and cultures; these may assist entrepreneurs to reach a sustainable development:

- Entrepreneurs should seek out positive and beneficial relationships with key stakeholders.
- They have to involve employees in the identification of current practices relevant to their business's goals, products, services and environments in order to maintain the employees' high motivation, and brainstorm with individuals experiencing the business from different perspectives (such as managers, founders, salespeople, etc.).
- They should communicate the business initiatives that have already been developed and successfully implemented.
- They should develop an awareness of customer expectations from the business in terms of their focus and treat these expectations as benchmarks.
- They should innovate, yet target cost-effective initiatives.
- They should foresee and analyze estimations of how much money customers will be willing to spend for the business's products and services.
- They should familiarize themselves with competitors' practices (e.g., implementation, marketing, advertising, benefits, etc.).
- They should ask for advice – ask suppliers, investors, competitors and clients for alternative solutions and ideas regarding the business's focus, sometimes by hiding the real aim of their questions.
- They have to continually analyze the probability of implementing new, friendly processes, practices and products, rather than only triumphing over past successes.
- They should gather data from other entrepreneurial businesses on products or services which are related or similar to their own in order to distribute this information to clients, suppliers and investors. Other businesses' benefits may echo the stakeholders' benefits of using such products or services.
- They should seek out practical know-how for implementation in their own businesses.
- They should provide access to professional advice that can help the business implement new processes.

Table 13.3 *Recent international trends in higher education programs in entrepreneurship*

Recent trends in academia	Results in the labor market
Entrepreneurship education has been growing dramatically over the past few years and this growth is expected to continue	*Micro level.* Upgrading of entrepreneurial knowledge and best practices *Macro level.* Higher recognition of entrepreneurship; better acknowledgment by the academic institutions of other entrepreneurial markets' characteristics through exchange of ideas (research, books, visiting professors, exchange students)
Entrepreneurship courses remain primarily elective	*Micro level.* Entrepreneurs adapting the managerial, financial, organizational, etc. (according to the courses taken) practices they have learned to their entrepreneurial venture will most likely experience the mismatch between these practices and their entrepreneurial venture's needs. This might perpetuate the limited time for new venture survival *Macro level.* Overall perceptions of entrepreneurship as a 'division' in the management/business/technology, etc. disciplines will be preserved, and will restrict this field's autonomy Most students consider the technological courses more important and disregard the statistics showing that bankruptcy is the result of lacking or faulty entrepreneurial practices, rather than technological failure
Entrepreneurship education still tends to be offered in stand-alone courses, rather than being integrated into the curriculum	*Micro level.* The entrepreneur lacks the broad perspective of entrepreneurship and its different and diverse relationships with the labor market, the employment system, the active organizations and the competitors, among others *Macro level.* The market players perceive entrepreneurship as a 'stand-alone' phenomenon – particularly banks and financial institutions, advertising and promotion companies and employment agencies – all of which tend to work with active and corporate firms and 'ignore' entrepreneurial firms until they can provide evidence-based success. By that time, however, most entrepreneurial firms are not as dependent on the players as they were at the creation stage, when they fell short in terms of getting such assistance
Lack of critical mass of entrepreneurship faculty, research and course materials	*Micro level.* Since most academic institutions that provide academic programs in entrepreneurship target them to undergraduates, the entrepreneurial overview remains very basic among potential and active entrepreneurs. Professors and Ph.D. students find it very difficult to advance in an academic career in entrepreneurship and consider it a complementary field of research; the academic journals in entrepreneurship are rated relatively low, especially in comparison to the management or business administration journals *Macro level.* The status of entrepreneurship will diminish Professions that are accredited in academia, and taught within a solid theoretical framework, even those that are newly established and fueled by research, grants, and other academia-related dynamics, are the highly prestigious ones

International networks among faculty members who teach entrepreneurs are limited	*Micro level.* Transnational entrepreneurship will be neglected by local entrepreneurs; the relevant networks, as well as knowledge of how to construct relevant networks, will be missing for potential and active entrepreneurs
	Macro level. Networks through academia are valuable for international research and advancement in any field, from both academic and applied points of view. Limited networks mean decreases in both aspects
Few innovative teaching approaches are being tested across borders	*Micro level.* Traditional teaching and 'more of the same' will be a major factor in causing students to avoid these programs. Moreover, as entrepreneurship involves innovation, a corresponding teaching model should be implemented
	Macro level. Less innovative knowledge is transferred across borders and this limits the development of teaching in this field, as well as the trans-border exchange of students and future entrepreneurs
Insufficient training in the teaching of entrepreneurship	*Micro level.* Less trained potential entrepreneurs will join the market: they will be more likely to commit the same errors as those before them, thereby exposing their venture to the same pitfalls. Training could help them avoid at least some of these threats
	Macro level. More stories of bankruptcy and failure will emerge in the entrepreneurial market. In the long run, this could affect the entrepreneurial market by either turning it into an unprofessional one or reducing its size, as more firms will fail and less potential entrepreneurs will be willing to take the risk of creating a new venture
Constructive cooperation between academic institutions and external players is still limited	*Micro level.* Students will find it difficult to 'locate' entrepreneurship in the wide-ranging business environment and will doubt the importance or even feasibility of implementing the methods which have been taught; only 'real' evidence can reduce such doubts
	Macro level. Limited contact between academia and the community in the entrepreneurial context will isolate both from their surroundings and will complicate their further cooperation

THE ROLE OF EDUCATION IN ENTREPRENEURSHIP

Figure 13.1 describes the main required concepts and skills that should be included in the academic curriculum for entrepreneurship education (Katz 1991; Solomon and Fernald 1991; Heinonen 2007).

Develop a paradigm of entrepreneurship

Entrepreneurship has been used in a variety of contexts and it covers a broad range of interchangeable meanings and situations. In the absence of a universally accepted and applicable definition, most researchers are likely to settle for the nearest conceptual representation of entrepreneurship and adopt it, or adapt it to their own specific empirical needs. In their quest for conceptual and contextual clarity, the role of education is to construct an increasing number of definitions, models and representations of entrepreneurship by combining forces with students, active entrepreneurs in the community as well as overseas, professionals, researchers in the field,

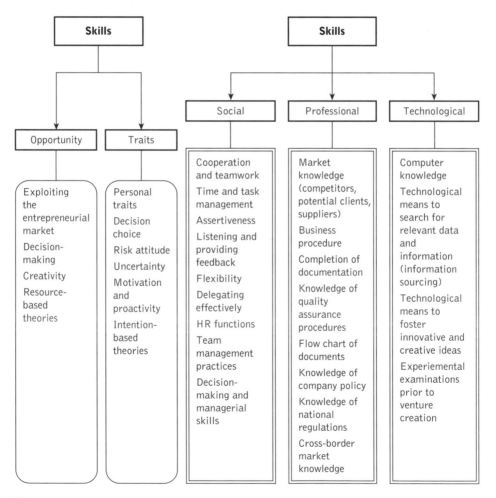

Figure 13.1 *Skill development and conceptualization for successful entrepreneurship*

and other interested parties. Using these methods, there is higher likelihood that an entrepreneurial paradigm will be developed that will meet the 'ideal' specifications of entrepreneurship (Matlay and Westhead 2005).

Transfer knowledge

International and comparative knowledge as well as cross-national knowledge are imperative for the field of entrepreneurship. The diversity of entrepreneurship features and processes raises the need for continually updated information on new trends and innovative inventions in the entrepreneurial realm. Moreover, because several researchers have described entrepreneurship as being 'in its adolescence' (i.e. it is still in the formation and adjustment stages), it is vital to maintain a constant flow of existing knowledge in order to learn from these experiences and existing trends. Such knowledge enables players in the entrepreneurial field to construct a solid academic and practical framework for entrepreneurship.

Shift problem-solving and analytical-thinking education to innovation, creativity and perceptual-skill development

Successful entrepreneurs are pragmatists. They tend to respond to experiences gained from practical environments and move quickly to embrace problem-solving solutions that they have learned through doing. On the other hand, they are also barrier breakers, practitioners of art-based management techniques; as such they can easily adapt to any new, unexpected situation. There is a need for higher education curricula to include material that is oriented toward training entrepreneurs in creativity and forecasting. The recognition that key entrepreneurial functions, such as creativity and innovation, are more art than science, and that they therefore require an alternative set of operational tools, is relatively novel in entrepreneurial research and practice and should be advanced (Chia 1996).

Teach problem diagnosis and opportunity exploitation

Entrepreneurship curricula have matured to the point that they provide a sound conceptual framework for would-be entrepreneurs; however, students typically lack the experience necessary to understand the implications of what they have learned, especially with respect to post-startup issues. They are not prepared to deal with the startup and post-startup problems they encounter. Diagnosis of such problems, identification of the solutions that 'work' and opportunity exploitation are the building blocks of successful entrepreneurship, as they refer to ongoing learning. However, neither problem diagnosis nor opportunity exploitation is trivial; they both involve costs and potential benefits and the ability to deal with these needs to be developed through school programs. Potential entrepreneurs should be able to typify the major problems they face and the mistakes they tend to make, and acknowledge that these do not simply 'occur' but in fact represent a malfunction (see Burton and Obel 2004). Potential entrepreneurs should also be able to identify the situations–opportunities–benefits relationship typical to their ventures and the related time window. Echoing Peter Drucker (1985), we argue that entrepreneurs must specify exactly what the opportunity consists of, its source and its target market. Events become opportunities and their impacts become benefits in a very specific time window; once that window closes, the opportunity is lost, and the benefit expires accordingly (Morris 1998). On the other hand, we might detect the opportunity but fail to respond to it. Here, there is definitely a cost and no benefit. In practice, the loss of one opportunity may give rise to another (Corbetta, Huse and Ravasi 2004;

Davidsson 2004; Blackburn and Smallbone 2008; Brush, Manolova and Edelman 2008; Hjorth 2008; Lasch and Yami 2008; Schmude, Welter and Heumann 2008).

Develop skills

Develop core skills (initiative, confidence), business skills (financial and market recognition), and motivational skills (aspiration for entrepreneurship, establishing the driving forces toward entrepreneurship, stimulating the entrepreneurial spirit).

Henry, Hill and Leitch (2005a, 2005b) debate the merits and drawbacks of intervention programs in entrepreneurship and address the question of whether entrepreneurship can, in fact, be taught. Comparing eight training programs for entrepreneurs in different places in Europe and using several subjective and objective methodological analyses and in-depth interviews, they come to the conclusion that personal skills are insufficient for the generation of entrepreneurial behavior, as are general skills. Rather, a combination of personal, transferable and business skills is needed. These are learned skills that should be taught on an enduring basis and personalized to the extent that entrepreneurs can adjust them to their business's needs. Combinations of core skills appear to be the key to entrepreneurial success.

Use practice in educational programs and facilitate the learning process

Entrepreneurs require a wide portfolio of skills and a significant knowledge base, in order to support the startup stage as well as the management and development of their new ventures; most of the necessary set of entrepreneurial skills is gained from specific vocational training and courses provided by non-academic schools and institutions in the private sector. A great opportunity exists for entrepreneurs to draw upon specific practices from the performance world and gain efficiencies. Considering that both endeavors thrive upon strong skills in collaboration, communication and resource management, their common ground deserves additional exploration. Certainly, the greater business community could benefit by further exploring the interrelationship between the worlds of the entrepreneur and the artist.

Skills developed in academic programs

Entrepreneurship requires varied skills. Most innovative products and services stem from either personal intuition or existing needs as identified by an individual; or from the knowledge acquired in subject-oriented schools (technology, computer, education, pharmaceutics, nursing, tourism, agronomy, etc.). In the latter, potential entrepreneurs come up with their innovative ideas from the knowledge they obtained at academic institutions; for example, students of education might develop a long-distance learning technique for children with special needs; those from nursing schools might invent a comfortable, safe technique for chronic home-bound patients to inject themselves;[2] students of tourism may come up with a user-friendly website sorted by location and activity for people interested in taking trips; and students of psychology might invent an emotion-oriented (or 'affective') computer program proposing scientifically valid representations of those aspects of emotional states that appear to be relevant for a number of use cases.[3] However, having these interesting ideas does not ensure success; in fact, lack of specific skills related to entrepreneurship decreases the likelihood that these ideas will be implemented in practice and stand the test of time.

An entrepreneurial way of thinking or spirit is also required, as traditional concepts and narrow-minded thinking cannot advance entrepreneurship.

AT A GLANCE 13.1   Profguide, Brazil

In the fall semester of 2007, Prof. Eduardo Machado from Brazil and his partner, Alexandre Silva, founded a professional firm providing development and career guidance for professionals, mostly at market entry level. Prof. Machado's firm provides market information to universities, so that they can transfer it through their websites to their students. As a professor in management, Machado expects that the information obtained via the website will stimulate more case studies for new courses in entrepreneurship and management at his university.

The motivation to combine academics and entrepreneurship came from Machado's experience as a teacher at the university: 'I worked for two years as a university professor, and many students came to ask my advice on how to develop their professional careers – which career path to take and how to reach their career goals', Machado explains. 'They all expected a profitable and fulfilling career but did not know how to achieve it. At first, I was very surprised by their inquiries, since I was under the impression that these students were attending management and entrepreneurship courses because they had already decided to become managers or entrepreneurs. In fact,' Machado realized, 'they were still "shopping".' 'As the requests for advice kept coming,' continues Machado, 'I tried to assist the students by searching for information on career avenues. It was then that I discovered that most of the information on jobs in Brazil could be obtained via advertisements in the media or career counselors, but that both of these sources were mostly paid for by commercial companies. As such, they could be very effective for people who knew what they were searching for, but were unsuitable for young people, particularly students, who were still exploring different career options. Moreover, the information that could be obtained from these sources was incomplete, sometimes even out of date', claims Machado.

As a professor in the business department, Machado acknowledged the motivation to 'have a look around' at the market level rather than just study inside the 'ivory tower' – and he encouraged it. In recognizing more and more of his students' doubts, ambiguities and lack of objective sources for information regarding their future careers, Machado turned to his colleague Alexandre Silva, the owner of a headhunting company for more than ten years, for advice. Their conversation evolved into a partnership in an independent center dedicated to assisting students and professionals in their career decisions. Initially, their vision for the center was to provide real solutions for the actual problems students face with respect to choosing a career.

The two decided to collect and organize the most up-to-date, objective information on career offers in and outside of Brazil and sell it directly to the universities, as a service that the universities could then provide to their students. The partners then decided that the information should be backed up by the right business competencies: 'Offering information on management positions when students had not yet developed any managerial abilities would be ineffective and frustrating for the students; eventually it would act against the center's main goals, as the students would figure out that their abilities and competencies are not relevant to the jobs being offered', says Machado. The partners therefore decided to also offer services on career guidance for professionals, as well as to assist their clients in developing the relevant abilities for the jobs being offered.

243

Machado conducted very rigorous market research with a specialized company, and collaborated with a software house for the website. The main concern was in selling a brand-new idea, especially to academic institutions which may see these services as a threat to their authority. Moreover today, according to Machado, Brazil's economy and culture are making it quite difficult to run a business, in terms of laws, high taxes and governmental intervention; and the anticipated success of their partnership was still at stake. At the moment, the partners are using personal funds and leveraging their first contracts with alliances. Unemployment rates are high, and jobs are limited and difficult to find – Machado and Silva see this as an opportunity that should be exploited. 'By targeting the "right" clients, it should definitely become a win–win solution', concludes Machado.

A HARVEST STRATEGY

This is a plan for getting the best value out of a business, mostly in terms of the business's outright sale. This strategy is used in the last stage of an entrepreneurial business, when its end may be near. It is at this point that the company may decide to sift through and sort out its options, i.e., going public, being acquired, selling out or merging. There are several other harvest strategies that allow entrepreneurs to retain ownership of their businesses in a less risky way, calling for sharply cutting investments in assets, labor or other costs of a slow-moving product line or business, and producing higher profits to fund expansion in other areas. However, super premium-value combinations are not a product of luck or timing. Rather, they are the result of an ongoing, long-term strategic planning process, rooted in an understanding of buyers' motivations and behaviors, and in the acquisition of expertise in the process of creating value to meet their expectations.

An idea that started out as a dream has 'suddenly' become an entrepreneurial reality; the next challenge is to create a different idea, and begin implementing it – but this time with much more experience, by avoiding some of the lapses, miscalculations or misjudgments that were made in the former process – with a pocket full of money (Dushnitsky and Lenox 2005; Neves 2005).

NON-ACADEMIC INTERVENTION FOR ENTREPRENEURS

A vast number of small business and entrepreneurship training institutions around the world are offering non-academic comprehensive training programs geared toward the local business community. Among the organizations providing such support are: governmental centers, agencies of commerce, international agencies, regional governmental and non-governmental organizations, entrepreneurial-based organizations, centers for innovation or technology, industrial associations, cooperative centers and even religious centers, non-profit as well as private centers, and continuing-education non-academic programs in cooperation with academic institutions.

The target clients of these programs represent a wide-ranging population of potential or active entrepreneurs: students, young entrepreneurs, refugees, handicapped people and those with special needs, self-employed people, partners, manufacturers, exporters, consultants, academia members, and members of governmental organizations in the field of entrepreneurship.

These programs' basic mission is to respond to their clients' needs by providing training and extension services. However, some entrepreneurs may not be able to identify their needs, and require training in some general entrepreneurial-oriented issues. Most of the programs focus on developing the skills needed to put ideas into practice, developing managerial skills, developing and maintaining entrepreneurial attitudes, developing programs in financing entrepreneurship, and follow-up counseling, sometimes for the first year or two of a new small enterprise's operation, depending on the program. These programs are transferred via training, formal knowledge, simulations, case study analyses and counseling, to heterogeneous groups or specifically to the personnel involved in small enterprises, sometimes on a one-on-one basis. A considerable number of topics have been covered and field projects carried out over the years and their volume continues to grow. The most popular themes dealt with by these programs are financing, marketing, managerial skills, beneficial networking, and communication skills; some programs focus on creativity and innovation.

These programs have a large potential for entrepreneurship and assume that the local community will eventually benefit. However, it is clear that management training programs for entrepreneurs and small-business personnel are poorly received by many entrepreneurs. Several reasons are assumed to explain this: the programs are usually designed by people in ministries and public agencies that promote small enterprises, and they are therefore not relevant, use a 'different language' and are not up-to-date; they are costly and considered to be most effective in the first stages of the venture creation. Paradoxically, it is in these specific stages that the founders are most vague about their financing and they therefore prefer to invest their money in more visible, needed functions than in training. Additionally, the difference between strategic, long-term planning and practices and ad hoc, short-term practices is not straightforward in the first stages of the venture creation, and training is categorized as a practice whose results may be observable only after a while, and even then they are vague and uncertain. The time that needs to be invested in such training programs could be devoted to advancing the business, especially in the early stages of the venture creation when the founder's involvement is critical.

Research in this field shows that well-planned training, conducted by trainers who are familiar with the conditions of small-enterprise management, which is practice-oriented and well received by entrepreneurs, will be perceived as practical and useful by the local business community, and a solid response from the entrepreneurs will follow.

The issues of the cost-effectiveness of training, the training methods that give the best results and the successful methodologies that are learner-based have created several different programs in entrepreneurship (Hytti and O'Gorman 2004; Lerner, Menahem and Hisrich 2005).

EVALUATION AND EFFECTIVENESS OF ACADEMIC PROGRAMS

Evaluating the performance and relevance of entrepreneurship education programs is a difficult and highly subjective task, because the conceptualization and contextualization of entrepreneurship education is confounded by many intervening variables:

- According to Dana (1992) and Gartner and Vesper (1994), the number and variety of entrepreneurship programs has expanded considerably in the past two decades, and the diversity and heterogeneity of the sector is matched by the growing rhetoric that complements the tremendous growth in entrepreneurship education offerings at the primary, secondary and university levels. In the United States, the expansion of entrepreneurship courses has been fueled by students' and accreditation bodies' dissatisfaction with general business education. The same can be said for Europe, Asia, Australia, New Zealand and Canada.

- Another major difficulty in assessing the effectiveness of programs in entrepreneurship is the variety of professional bodies of knowledge in the entrepreneurship curriculum. This produces ambiguous approaches toward meeting entrepreneurs' needs and thus to difficulties in developing academic curricula that will satisfy those specific needs.
- Clear definitions of entrepreneurship in local and global contexts are lacking and thus the appropriate programs and incentives may not be put in place for various types of organizations.
- These difficulties are even more salient in an international context: most curriculum designers deal with the 'what' and 'how' in a local context, while entrepreneurial labor markets have developed into transnational ones. As such, global rather than local knowledge and entrepreneurial practices should be established in higher education. Best practices in entrepreneurship in one place differ from those in another, and the mission statements of academic programs in entrepreneurship from universities around the globe highlight these differences. While some focus on technopreneurs with an emphasis on starting a new business venture, writing a business plan and pitching to investors (Singapore, Brazil), others concentrate on acquiring entrepreneurial skills and business knowledge (China); some emphasize mentoring, getting the first major customers and making the first international market entries (Asian countries), and others focus on identifying and exploiting international business opportunities (Austria, Denmark, France), or promoting the entrepreneurial market (Canada, United States); still others concentrate on gaining perspective on the level and growth of entrepreneurship education in Europe, identifying trends and understanding the training and development needs of faculty teaching entrepreneurship (European counties). These differences do not emerge only at the national level; the regional level is affected as well. Establishing criteria for assessing the effectiveness of academic programs in promoting entrepreneurial markets thus could be irrelevant or worse, completely off-base when looking at different countries and cultures.
- The complexity of entrepreneurship as a profession represents another difficulty in assessing the effectiveness of academic programs in this field. Entrepreneurship is often considered to involve both science and art; the science has to do with business, management and functional-professional skills and thus can be taught, whereas the art includes creativity, innovation and inspiration, and there is some doubt as to whether such talents can be learned. As such, entrepreneurship programs provide only partial preparation for the entrepreneurial process, and assessing entrepreneurial success may therefore not be a valid goal.
- Finally, inherent design problems and inadequate outcome measures used to gauge student satisfaction, their attitudes toward course content and/or individual performance in entrepreneurship programs put into question the impact and effectiveness of entrepreneurship education as a whole (McMullan and Long 1987; Solomon and Fernald 1991; McMullan and Gillin 1998; Jack and Anderson 1999; Li, Zhang and Matlay 2003; Bell et al. 2004; Hytti and O'Gorman 2004).

The implications are that educational and training programs should:

- Cooperate with the business community.
- Engage successful entrepreneurs as mentors for students and potential entrepreneurs.
- Conduct needed assessments of the students and active companies.
- Recognize the global entrepreneurial labor market and create core practical entrepreneurial paradigms.
- Certify and recognize entrepreneurial programs.

■ Assess the effectiveness of the programs – by assessing the potential entrepreneurs' skills, students' satisfaction with the program and their attitudes toward its relevance, and success rates of the programs' graduates as active entrepreneurs.

AT A GLANCE 13.2   Center for Entrepreneurship, Slovenia

'Everyone has an uncultivated seed of entrepreneurship in his heart – the challenge is to share it with the mind.' – *Vision statement of the CES*

Center for Entrepreneurship (CES) is leading the evolution of entrepreneurship in education, community development and business in Slovenia. 'Our program is strongly linked to the Entrepreneurial Decision-Making Cycle: it provides consulting services to existing businesses and has evolved into a multifaceted, internationally recognized agency serving a multiplicity of stakeholders', say Martin and Cilka Bacar, the founders of CES, Slovenia.

Today, CES is recognized as a contributing partner in community and economic development throughout Slovenia and it has earned a solid reputation in the areas of: entrepreneurial counseling for business startups; community entrepreneurial and not-for-profit development; and mentoring the mentors – professional development of startups' mentors.

CES is affiliated to a budding academic college in Slovenia that focuses on entrepreneurship, and is supported by a governmental foundation; a main goal now is to deepen its partnership with the business world in Slovenia.

Underlying all of CES's programs is the belief that individual development should focus on entrepreneurial skill development as a way of assisting individuals who wish to create a meaningful career, business, or life. Today, CES operates within both the college and the community. In the college setting, entrepreneurship is developed through courses taught by CES, and through students consulting on projects and working with faculty members to commercialize their research. Priority programs involve students in venture creation, retention, and expansion in the business, not-for-profit and community contexts. CES contributes to the college's innovative strategy by establishing and enhancing partnerships *and* developing innovative programs founded on the experiences learned from CES case studies.

Within the community, CES does consulting work, i.e., business plans, market research, feasibility studies, among others. It advances professional development for the businesses themselves, and works with the not-for-profit sector on strategic planning. It contributes to the development of regional, provincial, territorial and federal educational agendas by providing resources for the development of entrepreneurial skills to other educational institutions and it contributes to strategies for local and regional community economic development.

CES has established quantitative measurements to evaluate the outputs of the various programs and activities that they manage, and the results are very promising. The Bacars say that the mission of attracting 'clients' is of prime importance, but that this is a complicated endeavor in a place like Slovenia which is in the process of balancing its economic market, because 'most entrepreneurs cannot afford our services, except for students in entrepreneurship who get these services almost free of charge; we are paid by the college and the governmental foundation.' The founders add that 'Slovenia today enjoys high levels of entrepreneurship, high investments, high rates of trade and is the richest country in Central Eastern Europe; yet people still do not acknowledge the importance of centers such as CES; they prefer to follow a "trial and error" entrepreneurial path rather than go through counseling sessions, although this route is certainly much more expensive than the costs for CES's services.'

THE ROLE OF THE ADVISORY BOARD

Board members are the resource of first resort when advice or help is needed in the classroom or in reaching out to the community. The role of the advisory board is to offer direction, advice and assistance to the new venture. Strong and proactive boards are often the driving force behind the long-term success of entrepreneurial businesses. The members of advisory boards can open doors for the entrepreneur and the business that would not have opened on their own. However, the recruitment of an advisory board should be a planned process: identifying the desired characteristics and personalities of the board members, the structure, and the level of commitment is critical.

Entrepreneurial businesses that are considering setting up an advisory board must first clarify for themselves why they are establishing the board, what they expect it to achieve and how they see its contribution to their business success. There are several possibilities for acquiring assistance from an advisory board (e.g., in marketing, managing HR, influencing the enforcement of regulations or even financial support). Entrepreneurs should determine what kind of assistance they expect and how much involvement in their business's processes – and in which topics – they are prepared to 'put up with' from the board.

Two main types of boards are most prevalent. The first is the Board of Directors which is a fiduciary body, carrying significant legal weight and liability. Its members, who are usually compensated, are the final arbiters of corporate governance in a business. The second is the Board of Advisors, which carries no fiduciary responsibility to shareholders, but simply serves as a mentoring organization for the management team.

Pearce and Shaker (1991) suggested a four-type model of advisory boards (Table 13.4), reflecting the boards' expected depth of involvement and participation in business activities (in terms of topics). Data from 500 manufacturing firms and 500 service firms revealed that the highest level of involvement in a company's financial performance is found in the participative boards, and that it is beneficial for CEOs to share power with their board of directors if they are seeking better financial performance. Prior to this, however, a detailed list of profiles for ideal candidates for an advisory board should be developed. Then, regardless of the type of board established and the relationships crafting it, a written agreement on the condition of the internal controls of the business should be fully clarified and signed along with the mutual expected involvement of the advisory board in the business (only statutory or fully proactive, for example).

Building an advisory board is complex but it does offer significant benefits. It should be managed through the following:

■ *Recruit advisors for short-term objectives.* Entrepreneurs should first focus on the short term and determine what skills, introductions and knowledge are needed to accomplish their immediate

Table 13.4 *Four-type model of advisory boards*

Topics	Higher involvement	Lower involvement
Specific	*Caretaker*, e.g., the members will be deeply involved in and responsible for human resource (HR)-related topics	*Statutory*, e.g., the members will be responsible for the legislative aspect of the business whenever the topic is relevant or requires their involvement
All	*Participative*, e.g., the members are expected to treat the business as their own and to be attentive to everything, all the time and under any circumstances. They are expected to take action and advise the CEOs on the best practices to manage the business	*Proactive*, e.g., the members are proactive but do not 'take over' the business's management; their activity is lower, although it can be applied to any topic concerning the business

business objectives. Advisors should assist in filling in the gaps for the coming months, rather than years.

■ *Advisory boards and business credibility.* Credibility is critical for entrepreneurs to attract customers, partners, key employees, financiers and other essential components to get their businesses off the ground. Picking the right advisors will help the entrepreneur establish credibility.

■ *Looking for advisors.* To find advisors who are specialists in the business's specific expertise requires some creativity; they can be reached through industry conferences, training workshops and mentoring programs, as well as by networking 'with the home field', i.e., asking relatives, friends and competitors if anyone they know has started a comparable business, talking to potential suppliers for introductions and potential advisors.

■ *Advisory boards and rewards.* There is no standard compensation scheme for advisors, because it depends on how many advisors are needed for a business, how much time they will devote and what kind of business it is in terms of complexity, innovation, uniqueness and expertise. Some advisors will ask for equity in the business in exchange for advice and introductions, others want compensation over a payment schedule (such as quarterly or annually) rather than up front, and yet others will not ask for any reward at all. Each demand for compensation should be carefully analyzed by the entrepreneur, according to a simple equity model: the value of the equity is difficult to pin down; on the other hand, limiting the reward sometimes means having unmotivated or less effective advisors.

■ *Advisors versus employees and suppliers.* It is not easy to hold advisors accountable in practice, since they are not like the employees, who receive a steady pay check (even if they are paid), nor are they like the suppliers, who bill for services rendered. Most advisors have income from other sources and will treat their 'job' as member of the advisory board as a part-time hobby or casual business interest. Since they are usually not fiscally responsible in the same way as a company officer or director, they can easily walk away if the position does not meet their expectations.

■ *Setting term limits.* Much like board members have term limits, advisory board roles should also have limited terms, such as twelve or twenty-four months. It is awkward and may even be potentially damaging to a business's reputation to kick an advisor out if he or she is not performing. Setting term limits allows the transition to happen naturally.

GOING PUBLIC

As the business, and subsequently its financial growth cycle, develops, the initial public offering appears to be critical, since the 'conventional' funding providers (i.e., banks, investors, private equity funds or personal savings) will finance only part of the business's monetary needs. This is the equity gap problem faced by many entrepreneurial SMEs; it is mostly recognized in the business's early stage, also known as the early-stage equity gap, since private investors cannot yet identify the business's strategic focus as it relates to them. One emerging means of financing in these stages is going public, especially when a business needs additional capital (Norton and Tenenbaum 1993; Deeds, Decarolis and Coombs 1997; Carpentier and Suret 2006; Janney and Folta 2006).

The benefits of going public include: the business may become more widely known; its image may improve; access to capital will increase, since the entrepreneurs may be able to contact more potential investors; obtaining future financing becomes easier if investor interest in the company grows enough to sustain a secondary trading market in its securities; controlling shareholders, such as the company's officers or directors, may have a ready market for their shares, which means that they can more easily sell their interests at retirement, or for diversification, for instance; the business may be able to attract and retain more highly qualified personnel.

Concurrently, new obligations arise: the entrepreneur must keep shareholders informed of the business's operations, financial condition, and management, all of which entails additional costs and new legal obligations. Loss of some flexibility in managing the business's affairs is another aspect of going public, especially when shareholders and their representatives must approve the business's actions (McConaughy, Dhatt and Kim 1995; Florin 2003).

NETWORKING

What does it involve?

The value of networks as an integral part of entrepreneurial success and their role in the emergence and early growth of a venture are widely acknowledged. People are more likely to hear and personalize messages, and thus change their attitudes and behaviors, if they believe that the messenger is similar to them and faces the same concerns and pressures – networking is based on this approach. Networks have therefore become quite popular in policy-making programs due to the belief that they can foster enhanced competitiveness and rejuvenation in their participants, and because a significant number of practitioners today seem to be working in such networks in order to develop and strengthen their enterprises.

Many private companies, as well as government institutions, have developed networking programs for entrepreneurs. The main purposes of these programs are to actively promote and encourage venture creation through self-sustainable assistance; that is, the network members help each other by sharing either their own experiences as entrepreneurs or their expertise (counselors, IT managers, communications experts, accountants, lawyers, etc.). Moreover, networks, especially local ones, enhance the development of job opportunities in the community by encouraging established businesses to expand locally and by attracting new industries to the area.

Networking is based on a 'peer assistance' approach, in which entrepreneurs feel free to ask the members of their networks questions, even those exposing their ignorance in certain areas. Entrepreneurs usually express their problems and dilemmas better in front of their peers – other entrepreneurs – than in front of professionals and, most important, they better understand their peers' suggestions, as they are clear and simple and are not fraught with professional jargon or tools. Moreover, it is a 'give-and-take' process, and thus entrepreneurs who cannot afford any supportive assistance can benefit from their network's experiences and suggestions free of charge. People attached to networks often hear the question 'How can I help you?' and know that the people asking it are more than happy to supply answers, by sharing their experiences and expertise in a 'givers-gain' approach. These elements can improve entrepreneurs' performance as well as their businesses' performance at many different levels. In addition to the potential for improving firm performance when participating in a network, members may meet other members who are their competitors, and profit from getting to know them better and establishing relationships with them that are founded in trust and honesty.

Networking is the backbone of referrals and sales development through the 'word-of-mouth' method. Testimonials from clients on the network about the quality of an entrepreneur's products and services constitute a most important type of informal advertising and are the building blocks of a business's evolving reputation.

Entrepreneurs entering into networking programs should proactively establish their own high-quality network, as networks have a tendency, by their sheer nature, to expand and include different people that will not cater to one's specific needs and demands.

Questions that give the other members in the network the opportunity to tell their story include: 'How did you get started in the business?', 'What do you enjoy most about what you do?', 'Were there any activities or plans for which you did not reach the desired goals?' (Conway and Steward 1998; Human and Provan 2000; Ahlstrom-Soderling 2003).

Networking to get referrals

Many entrepreneurs join business networking groups in order to gain visibility and obtain referrals. Surprisingly, in these times of high technology and immense possibilities in communication, entrepreneurs find it more difficult than in the past to obtain clients. One major reason for this is today's 'restless culture' – clients want 'quick, effective and to-the-point' solutions, and therefore a good conversation or a deep acquaintance may be considered exhausting and a waste of time by the potential clients; it may even prevent them from turning to such 'exhausting entrepreneurs'. As creating and maintaining business relationships and networking is a 'life-or-death' endeavor for entrepreneurial businesses, while active and potential clients are restless and disloyal, formal networking groups have flourished as a viable alternative for obtaining referrals.

As already noted, effective networking through such groups can lead to word-of-mouth advertisement which, in turn, often translates into the exchange of referrals. The two most important advantages of word-of-mouth advertisement are that it has a very high success rate and it is cost effective, mostly in the long term: although there is no guarantee that the favor of passing a referral to one of the groups' members will be immediately returned, the 'talking about you' process activates and stimulates visibility, which in the long run may bring in more clients.

Active and potential entrepreneurs acknowledge the benefit of visibility and credibility and join formal groups for this purpose. Joining groups for networking also requires taking a proactive stance: the member needs to set out the requirements for potential referrals. For example, an occupational therapist joining a networking group should establish the requirements for his or her potential clients in order to enhance the best potential fit between his or her expertise and the potential clients' needs; some will ask the members of the networking group to assist them in locating clients with memory-loss problems, others are experts in assigning exercises to improve the daily activities of persons with coordination problems, while yet others will prefer to work with children facing difficulties. In order to define the potential clients, entrepreneurs should be able to clarify their main activities and expertise.

The following steps are recommended to achieve the desired benefits from networking:

- Clearly state the nature of your business, its products, services, your expertise and your team's expertise. Clarify what makes you different from the competitors.
- Define who your 'preferred customer' is, and your main niche.
- Form relationships with people in the networking group that may seem unrelated to the services you provide, i.e., do not restrict yourself to 'functional' relationships. Referrals may appear indirectly from many sources.
- Allow relationships to mature.
- Build trust; your next referrals will be your active clients.

Entrepreneurs may benefit from such programs.[4]

CASE STUDY 13.1　Let's Net, China

Olee Seto is the leading franchisor in China of the international company Let's Net. Seto was born and raised in China, in a traditional family with very clear values and goals: a Chinese man should find a stable position in a big corporation. For years, talented people in China have shown a preference for working at established companies rather than face the risks of entrepreneurship; they then stay at the same workplace for life, remaining loyal and committed to their boss. Throughout China's history, orthodoxy rather than innovation has been the standard, and launching a company is neither recognized nor culturally accepted. Moreover, higher education has never been related to success in the workforce, and neither Seto's parents nor his brothers, relatives, or friends considered higher education to be an essential asset. Seto, who was a very curious child and very successful at school, wanted to both acquire higher education and launch his own business, desires which were considered highly rebellious, and so he kept them a secret.

Upon completing high school, Seto applied – in secret – to several universities in and outside of China, and was accepted by all of them. Because he was so embarrassed about abandoning his family's values, but at the same time very enthusiastic about proceeding with his studies, he decided to move to Boston, Massachusetts, where he was able to get a grant and start his studies. At first, Seto's family and relatives would not speak to him, as they felt deceived; but after a while, he found a way to make them believe in his choices and decisions and to support him.

Seto successfully completed his university studies and got several job offers from American employers. For a time, he worked at a British bank in Boston and established many effective contacts with English and American business people; he got promotions very easily and was approved to attend a very prestigious and highly selective banking course. However, at about the same time, an opportunity arose via one of his contacts and he decided to leave his promising job at the bank to launch a business, backed by his contact's investment. It was a virtual business, providing designing and internet solutions for SMEs. His vision – which was highly innovative at the time – was to be a pioneering business providing USB outsourcing services to India. The business started with many expectations; however, it did not achieve its planned goals, in terms of either financial results or penetration of the Indian market, and after two years, Seto stepped down as CEO of his own business and became a counseling partner instead. Sales rates remained unsatisfactory however, and after a while he decided to terminate his partnership in the business.

He sold it, and today it is still operational under the management of its other owners. Seto obtained many contacts through his business, most of them with business people in India, but also some in America and Britain, which he maintained even after leaving the business.

For about two years, Seto worked from home in Boston as a self-employed businessman in internet-related services; his clients were the same businesses and people he had maintained contact with from his former business, and he had many projects and earned good money. He continued to get job offers from employers who knew him or had heard of his qualifications. Although things seemed to be on the right track, Seto felt he was doing 'more of the same', and he began looking for new challenges.

During this time, he met one of his former university professors who encouraged him to apply to the MBA program in Boston. He told Seto that he stood a very good chance of being approved for the program, and Seto loved the idea. The following academic year, Seto returned to school in Boston to study for his MBA. There, he got to know a group of other students, one of whom was always rushing off to meetings. When Seto asked him about this, his colleague told him that he had launched a business and was attending meetings organized by a company for entrepreneurs that assists them in meeting with other business people, discussing mutual interests and substantially increasing referrals. Seto was curious about this company and decided to join his friend at one of these meetings.

'When I first attended the Let's Net meeting, I could not believe it – everybody cared so much about each other; and when one of them told the others he or she had more clients this week thanks to the group's activity, people would start clapping and wish him or her luck. Such an outpouring of support seemed almost unreal in our cynical business world,' gushes Seto. 'My colleague introduced me to the participants, most of them professionals and business owners. The meeting was very well structured and efficient, and the atmosphere was great.'

He decided to join the company as a permanent member and steadily attended its weekly meetings for three years; Seto encouraged his acquaintances – the ones from his former business and the job at the bank – to join the company. Seto's group was constantly expanding due to his contacts. 'I loved the networking activity and decided to join another company that had the same vision but was managed somewhat differently; and I expanded their groups as well. I got many clients from these networks, and was about to turn my self-employment work into a "real" business – but I felt that there was something missing', confesses Seto.

'I knew Let's Net had groups in many places around the world, and I was sure there was a franchisor operating their groups in China. However, when I attempted to locate this franchisor, I discovered that there was no representative for Let's Net in China. I was very surprised, and I felt that this was the opportunity I had been hoping for. I had already achieved top grades in computers and engineering and an MBA from MIT, I had earned good money from my projects, and had many acquaintances and a very good reputation in Boston – I was also very unsure of how my family would treat me if I returned to China – but I could not resist this opportunity. I took the risk and decided to launch Let's Net in China', says Seto. 'It was an undiscovered and yet so desperately needed niche there.'

The decision to launch a Let's Net group in China followed a meeting with the founder and chairman of the international Let's Net. 'The meeting was more philosophical than practical', says Seto. 'The founder did not try to convince me to launch Let's Net in China, it was more of a meeting on viewpoints, values and beliefs; he said that the decision should be entirely mine, as launching and managing Let's Net groups involved a great deal of work and dedication', says Seto. 'I was concerned about launching groups in China because of the relatively traditional culture there, but the meeting with the founder was a turning point for me,' affirms Seto.

'I was aware of the risks I was taking, although I strongly believed that the wind of change was there and that China was in a period of economic transformation. The window of opportunity was now!' exclaims Seto.

In August 2002, Seto signed a franchising contract and launched the first Let's Net group in China. 'It was a typical startup; as the leading person, you face exactly the same issues; fundamental questions arise, such as how to attract your clients, which are the best or most promising niches, and how to "sell" the new concept . . .', states Seto. He recruited two employees who were key figures in his franchise startup to assist him. Aside from these two recruits, Seto worked alone: 'I do not have the luxury to delegate, yet . . .', he says. Meanwhile, he translated the English material into Chinese, trained his employees, dedicated his time to marketing, ran the accounting, among other things. 'It is all at the ground level, we work very closely according to our business plan's goals, trying to constantly assess our activities, processes and success rate, and amending our next steps accordingly. We are also using lots of intuition, open-minded thinking and flexibility to make it work.' According to Seto, 'Networking in an orthodox culture in terms of entrepreneurship is a challenge; but there are some encouraging results and we believe that networking is working is China too!' he exclaims.

'My next planned steps are to initiate a mentorship program and I am in the process of developing different strategies to meet this challenge,' says Seto.

QUESTIONS FOR DISCUSSION

1   Identify Olee Seto's use of networking throughout his career; in what did his networks assist him?
2   Explain the relationships between networking and entrepreneurship in both traditional and modern cultures.
3   What makes networking multinational?
4   What are the 'core' skills or techniques needed for entrepreneurs to make their networking effective?
5   What would you suggest that Seto do next in order to attract more Chinese entrepreneurs to the Let's Net groups?
6   What are the strengths and weaknesses (actual or potential) of using networking in your business?

MERGERS AND ACQUISITIONS

Mergers or acquisitions, like joint ventures or strategic alliances, play a key role in consolidating businesses aimed at continual growth, and are recognized as the most common types of successful exit for venture investments. A merger is a combination of two companies to form a new one, while an acquisition is the purchase of one company by another with no new company being formed. In the case of both mergers and acquisitions, the venture firm receives stock or cash from the acquiring company and the venture investor distributes the proceeds from the sale to its limited partners.

From the entrepreneur's point of view, merging with a larger company or being acquired at the right time to capture the value that has been created through the venture is a clever solution. However, mergers or acquisitions are complicated transactions, and entrepreneurs should examine the process very carefully. For example, they should look at ways in which value can be enhanced, and anticipate risks that could serve to erode that value; they also need to work for transactions that will provide flexibility for future bolt-on acquisitions – being alert to options that might make it easier in the future to spin off a division that may not be part of the company's core strategy (Hornsby, Kuratko and Montagno 1999; Andreotti 2004; DePamphilis 2007).

Mergers and acquisitions should also be made on the basis of trust and reliability; even during the negotiation period (which may take a very long time), the relationship should not be harmed; the processes undergone by the parties involved in the merger or acquisition are complicated and long, and initial transition or post-merger integration demand a relationship based on trust for the complete success of the new entity (the merged or acquired business).

SUMMARY

This chapter discusses the management of rapid growth and sustainability in entrepreneurial businesses. These aspects require different and unique managerial practices that characterize the established stages of the business, including managing people, projects, growth strategies, competitive strategies and international opportunities toward a continuous competitive advantage. The role of entrepreneurs in achieving these goals is to seek out or create positive and beneficial relationships with key stakeholders, employees and suppliers, and to maintain effective networks to keep the 'business's wheels' in motion and to continually present a competitive advantage. The managerial expertise at these stages relies on three strategic driving forces: intellectual capital, the business's continual and rapid capacity for adaptive change, and use of the most up-to-date technologies and processes at the business level.

Education and non-academic training programs play major roles in sustaining the intellectual capital by transferring knowledge, teaching problem diagnosis and opportunity exploitation, and developing core skills, among others. The most popular themes covered by these programs facilitate achievement of the business's needs in the rapid growth stages, such as financing, marketing, creativity and innovation.

The business's continual and rapid capacity for adaptive change can be maintained by choosing the appropriate harvest strategy, i.e., going public, being acquired, selling out or merging. In addition, advisory board members are a good resource for help in that they offer direction, advice and assistance to the new venture.

Networking, acquired by companies that develop networking programs for entrepreneurs, also promotes and encourages venture creation through self-sustainable assistance, and enhances the development of job opportunities in the community by encouraging established businesses to expand locally and by attracting new industries to the area.

At the same time, the most up-to-date technologies and processes at the business level may be reached by either educational programs or by mergers and acquisitions which play a key role in consolidating businesses aimed at continual growth, and are recognized as the most common types of successful exit for venture investments.

NOTES

1 At www.oecd.org/document/21/0,2340,en_2649_33956792_35292309_1_1_1_1,00.html.
2 See Drexel University, Philadelphia's technological university; MSN in Innovation and Intra/Entrepreneurship in Advanced Nursing Practice, a program for the graduate nursing student who seeks to reinvent and innovate in nursing practice in a variety of roles, as clinician, educator, administrator, clinical scientist or in the business environment of health care, www.drexel.com/online-degrees/nursing-degrees/msn-innov/index.aspx.
3 See W3C Incubator Activity, emotion incubator, www.w3.org/2005/Incubator/emotion/.
4 BNI, www.bni.com/; Ecademy, www.ecademy.com/; ENET, www.boston-enet.org/; Travel & Network International, http://travelandnetwork.com/; European Professional Women's Network, www.europeanpwn.net/; Business Owners' Idea Café, www.businessownersideacafe.com/; Managers for Managers (M4M), www.managers4managers.eu/; Linkedin, www.linkedin.com/.

REFERENCES

Ahlstrom-Soderling, R. (2003) 'SME strategic business networks seen as learning organizations', *Journal of Small Business and Enterprise Development*, 10: 444–54.

Andreotti, A. (2004) 'Globalisation and corporation internalisation: a critical viewpoint', *International Journal of Entrepreneurship and Innovation Management*, 4: 360–72.

Bell, J., Callaghan, I., Demick, D. and Scharf, F. (2004) 'Internationalising entrepreneurship education', *Journal of International Entrepreneurship*, 2: 109–24.

Birdthistle, N., Hynes, B. and Fleming, P. (2007) 'Enterprise education programmes in secondary schools in Ireland; a multi-stakeholder perspective', *Education and Training*, 49: 265–76.

Blackburn, R.A. and Smallbone, D. (2008) 'Researching small firms and entrepreneurship in the U.K.: developments and distinctiveness', *Entrepreneurship Theory and Practice*, 32: 267–88.

Blumentritt, T., Kickul, J. and Gundry, L.K. (2005) 'Building an inclusive entrepreneurial culture: effects of employee involvement on venture performance and innovation', *International Journal of Entrepreneurship and Innovation*, 6: 77–84.

Bouwen, R. and Steyaert, C. (1990) 'Construing organizational texture in young entrepreneurial firms', *Journal of Management Studies*, 27: 637–49.

Brush, C.G., Manolova, T.S. and Edelman, L.F. (2008) 'Separated by a common language? Entrepreneurship research across the Atlantic', *Entrepreneurship Theory and Practice*, 32: 249–66.

Burton, R.M. and Obel, B. (2004) *Strategic Organizational Diagnosis and Design: The Dynamics of Fit*, Boston, MA: Kluwer Academic.

Carpentier, C. and Suret, J. (2006) 'Bypassing the financial growth cycle: evidence from capital pool companies', *Journal of Business Venturing*, 21: 45–73.

Cherwitz, R. and Darwin, T. (2005) 'Crisis as opportunity: an entrepreneurial approach to higher education productivity', in J.E. Miller and J. Groccia (eds) *On Becoming a Productive University: Strategies for Reducing Costs and Increasing Quality in Higher Education*, Bolton, MA: Anker Publishing, 58–68.

Chia, R. (1996) 'Teaching paradigm shifting in management education: university business schools and the entrepreneurial imagination', *Journal of Management Studies*, 33: 409–28.

Conway, S. and Steward, F. (1998) 'Networks and interfaces in environmental innovation: a comparative study in the UK and Germany', *Journal of High Technology Management Research*, 9: 239–53.

Cooper, A.C. (1981) 'Strategic management: new ventures and small business', *Long Range Planning*, 14: 39–45.

Corbetta, G., Huse, M. and Ravasi, D. (2004) *Crossroads of Entrepreneurship Research*, Boston, MA: Kluwer Academic.

Dana, L.P. (1992) 'Entrepreneurial education in Europe', *Journal of Education for Business*, 68: 74–8.

Davidsson, P. (2004) 'A general theory of entrepreneurship: the individual–opportunity nexus', *International Small Business Journal*, 22: 206–9.

Deeds, D.L., Decarolis, D. and Coombs, J.E. (1997) 'The impact of firm-specific capabilities on the amount of capital raised in an initial public offering: evidence from the biotechnology industry', *Journal of Business Venturing*, 12: 31–46.

DePamphilis, D. (2007) *Mergers, Acquisitions, and other Restructuring Activities*, 4th edn, London: Academic Press.

Drucker, P.F. (1985) 'The discipline of innovation', *Harvard Business Review*, 63: 67–72.

Dushnitsky, G. and Lenox, M.J. (2005) 'When do incumbents learn from entrepreneurial ventures? Corporate venture capital and investing firm innovation rates', *Research Policy*, 34: 615–39.

Florin, J. (2003) 'Substituting bonding for monitoring in technology-intensive ventures going public? A two-edged sword', *Journal of High Technology Management Research*, 14: 231–43.

Gartner, W.B. and Vesper, K.H. (1994) 'Experiments in entrepreneurship education: successes and failures', *Journal of Business Venturing*, 9: 179–87.

Habbershon, T.G. (2006) 'Commentary: a framework for managing the familiness and agency advantages in family firms', *Entrepreneurship Theory and Practice*, 30: 879–86.

Hay, M., Verdin, P. and Williamson, P. (1993) 'Successful new ventures: lessons for entrepreneurs and investors', *Long Range Planning*, 26: 31–42.

Heinonen, J. (2007) 'An entrepreneurial-directed approach to teaching corporate entrepreneurship at university level', *Education and Training*, 49: 310–24.

Henry, C., Hill, F. and Leitch, C. (2005a) 'Entrepreneurship education and training: can entrepreneurship be taught?' Part I, *Education and Training*, 47: 98–111.

Henry, C., Hill, F. and Leitch, C. (2005b) 'Entrepreneurship education and training: can entrepreneurship be taught?' Part II, *Education and Training*, 47: 158–69.

Hjorth, D. (2008) 'Nordic entrepreneurship research', *Entrepreneurship Theory and Practice*, 32: 313–38.

Hornsby, J.S., Kuratko, D.F. and Montagno, R.V. (1999) 'Perception of internal factors for corporate entrepreneurship: a comparison of Canadian and US mergers', *Entrepreneurship Theory and Practice*, 24: 9–24.

Human, S.E. and Provan, K.G. (2000) 'Legitimacy building in the evolution of small firm mutilateral networks: a comparative study of success and demise', *Administrative Science Quarterly*, 45: 327–68.

Hytti, U. and O'Gorman, C. (2004) 'What is "enterprise education"? An analysis of the objectives and methods of enterprise education programmes in four European countries', *Education and Training*, 46: 11–23.

Jack, S.L. and Anderson, A.R. (1999) 'Entrepreneurship education within the enterprise culture: producing reflective practitioners', *International Journal of Entrepreneurial Behaviour and Research*, 5: 110–25.

Janney, J.J. and Folta, T.B. (2006) 'Moderating effects of investor experience on the signaling value of private equity placements', *Journal of Business Venturing*, 21: 27–44.

Jokioinen, I. and Suomala, P. (2006) 'Concepts to products; lessons learned from industrial success stories', *European Journal of Innovation Management*, 9: 370–95.

Kariv, D. (2008) 'Managerial performance and business success: gender differences in Canadian and Israeli entrepreneurs', *Journal of Enterprising Communities: People and Places in the Global Economy* (JEC), 2: 300–31.

Katz, J.A. (1991) 'The institution and infrastructure of entrepreneurship', *Entrepreneurship Theory and Practice*, 15: 85–102.

Lafuente, A. and Salas, V. (1989) 'Types of entrepreneurs and firms: the case of new Spanish firms', *Strategic Management Journal*, 10: 17–30.

Lasch, F. and Yami, S. (2008) 'The nature and focus of entrepreneurship research in France over the last decade: a French touch?', *Entrepreneurship Theory and Practice*, 32: 339–60.

Lerner, M., Menahem, G. and Hisrich, R.D. (2005) 'Does government matter? The impact of occupational retraining, gender and ethnicity on immigrants' incorporation', *Journal of Small Business and Enterprise Development*, 12: 192–210.

Li, J., Zhang, Y. and Matlay, H. (2003) 'Entrepreneurship education in China', *Education and Training*, 45: 495–505.

Matlay, H. and Westhead, P. (2005) 'Virtual teams and the rise of e-entrepreneurship in Europe', *International Small Business Journal*, 23: 279–302.

McConaughy, D.L., Dhatt, M.S. and Kim, Y.H. (1995) 'Agency costs, market discipline and market timing: evidence from post-IPO operating performance', *Entrepreneurship Theory and Practice*, 20: 43–57.

McGrath, R.G. and Keil, T. (2007) 'The value captor's process: getting the most out of your new business ventures', *Harvard Business Review*, 85: 128–36.

McMullan, W.E. and Gillin, L.M. (1998) 'Industrial viewpoint – entrepreneurship education: developing technological start-up entreprenuers: a case study of a graduate entreprenuership programme at Swinburne University', *Technovation*, 18: 275–86.

McMullan, W.E. and Long, W.A. (1987) 'Entrepreneurship education in the nineties', *Journal of Business Venturing*, 2: 261–75.

Morris, M.H. (1998) 'From the editor: What is microenterprise development?', *Journal of Developmental Entrepreneurship*, 3: v–viii.

Neves, J.C. (2005) 'The value of financial freedom and ownership in opportunities of entrepreneurial harvest', *International Journal of Entrepreneurship and Innovation Management*, 5: 469–82.

Norton, E. and Tenenbaum, B.H. (1993) 'Specialization versus diversification as a venture capital investment strategy', *Journal of Business Venturing*, 8: 431–42.

Pearce, J.A. and Shaker, Z.A. (1991) 'The relative power of CEOs and board of directors: associations with corporate performance', *Strategic Management Journal*, 12: 135–53.

Pittaway, L. and Cope, J. (2007) 'Entrepreneurship education', *International Small Business Journal*, 25: 479–510.

Reynolds, P.L. and Lancaster, G. (2006) 'A scheme to increase profitability in entrepreneurial SMEs', *Journal of Small Business and Enterprise Development*, 13: 395–410.

Robinson, R.B. and Pearce, J.A. (1986) 'Product life-cycle considerations and the nature of strategic activities in entrepreneurial firms', *Journal of Business Venturing*, 1: 207–24.

Sadler-Smith, E., Hampson, Y., Chaston, I. and Badger, B. (2003) 'Managerial behavior, entrepreneurial style, and small firm performance', *Journal of Small Business Management*, 41: 47–67.

Schmude, J., Welter, F. and Heumann, S. (2008) 'Entrepreneurship research in Germany', *Entrepreneurship Theory and Practice*, 32: 289–311.

Siegel, R., Siegel, E. and MacMillan, I.C. (1993) 'Characteristics distinguishing high-growth ventures', *Journal of Business Venturing*, 8: 169–80.

Solomon, G.T. and Fernald, L.W. (1991) 'Trends in small business management and entrepreneurship education in the United States', *Entrepreneurship Theory and Practice*, 15: 25–39.

Terpstra, D.E. and Olson, P.D. (1993) 'Entrepreneurial start-up and growth: a classification of problems', *Entrepreneurship Theory and Practice*, 17: 5–20.

Van Stel, A., Carree, M. and Thurik, R. (2005) 'The effect of entrepreneurial activity on national economic growth', *Small Business Economics*, 24: 311–21.

Part III

The output-oriented perspective in the entrepreneurial realm

Chapter 14

Evaluating and measuring the firm's success

OBJECTIVES

After studying this chapter you will be able to:

- Distinguish between summative and formative business evaluations and identify the measures of each evaluation method.
- Identify the key elements of an entrepreneurial business in order to list the measures that evaluations need to address.
- Be proficient in the different processes and means for evaluation and fit them to the different measures of the key elements of success.
- Distinguish between the different models for evaluation of a new venture's effectiveness and success and consequently develop programs to maintain the strong elements and minimize the appearance or effect of the weak ones.
- Recognize the output versus process measures that should be addressed in evaluating the business's success.
- Explain the process of re-evaluation of programs that have been designed according to previous evaluation procedures, and design and then activate new programs in line with the findings raised in the re-evaluation procedure.

MEASURES AND DEFINITIONS

Researchers investigating the sources of a successful entrepreneurial firm's performance have focused mainly on the output measures, such as profitability, reputation, growth in number of employees, growth in number of clients, and innovation and diversification of products, services and clients. Some other researchers stress the importance of process-oriented measures, such as the process of managing and stimulating innovation, creativity and sustainable competitive advantage, which basically rely on valid emergent contingency management, as well as robust strategic management.

As demonstrated in this book, developing a new business is a challenging endeavor – which most entrepreneurs consider exciting and innovative. Yet it also presents many difficult challenges, which call for an ongoing evaluation of the business's cost-effectiveness and profitability at each stage of development. Such assessments are not only required for entrepreneurial firms; established companies face similar challenges when venturing into new markets with various innovative products, technologies or services; and they also need to convince customers of their credibility in providing satisfactory products or services. In this sense, the need for an assessment of business outputs is inherent to any firm, and it should therefore be treated not as an additional cost, but as a standard one (Kuratko, Montagno and Hornsby 1990; Berg et al. 2004; Abor and Biekpe 2006; Garman and Phillips 2006; Voisey et al. 2006).

The evaluations can be summative or formative (Phillips 1991): the ones performed before implementing an activity (e.g., development of a new product, crafting new professional teams, implementing a marketing strategy) are formative and are aimed at obtaining information based on lessons from past experiences in order to support the business design and ensure its quality, including evaluating the objectives to be met, risks linked to these objectives, feasibility of alternative options, and necessary indicators for their evaluation.

Another way of performing a formative evaluation is during or close to the end of the implementation of an activity; it is then intended to draw lessons from the first stages of the activity process and to adjust the contents of the ongoing activity in relation to realities in the field and/or contextual developments. Information gathered from such an evaluation can improve the activity processes and outcomes along the way.

A summative evaluation is performed after completion of a process and is mainly concerned with checking achieved impacts, identifying unexpected impacts and assessing the sustainability of the intervention's benefits.

Each of these evaluation practices can help in monitoring the existing level of the business's activities and consequently redirecting the development process of this activity and decisions regarding the allocation of resources. The evaluation results (when positive) can be disseminated to attract clients, investors and suppliers.

MAIN FACTORS IN EVALUATING BUSINESS PERFORMANCE

Entrepreneurs perceive high business performance as the key element in their entrepreneurial success and associate it with the ability to generate a wide range of business profits, including creating wealth, attracting resources, recruiting the best employees and sustaining the business for a longer time (Venkatraman and Ramanujam 1987; Chandler and Hanks 1994; VanderWerf 1994). To aim the business's processes toward such success, entrepreneurs should identify the elements that induce their business's success, then assess their evolution through the business stages. Evaluation thus consists of decision-making support systems that support and improve managerial decision-making outcomes related to their business by obtaining the most updated, objective information on the measures being assessed.

The term evaluation typically represents a judgment, which determines whether the procedures activated in the business should receive the resources to mature to the next business stage, or be modified or even omitted. Many entrepreneurs neglect the evaluation process: sometimes they are so enamored with their concepts and activities that they avoid any judgmental or negative evaluation of their business which will subsequently require adjustments and modifications that they are not willing to make; some perceive the evaluation process as a costly procedure and do not find the resources to invest in it; yet others do not foresee the benefits of the evaluation outcomes, as they are known to be long term and indirect. However, evaluation clarifies and deepens the culture of performance standardization; it provides an effective monitoring system and it is the right platform to develop appropriate action plans as consequences of its results. Studies show that lack of objective evaluation of the business, unrealistic prediction of the market's trends and development, weak financial knowledge, or lack of knowledge of legal issues all lead to business failure (Benbasat and Nault 1990; Eining and Dorr 1991; Basu and Blanning 1994; Ye and Johnson 1995; Wilson and McDonald 1996; Benbasat and Zmud 1999; Arnott and Pervan 2005).

There are numerous studies addressing different indicators as success factors of entrepreneurial businesses:

- *Financial data and information.* To measure performance, many researchers use determinants of the business's financial ratios, such as net profit margin, return on equity or return on assets; others use financial profitability or productivity ratios to assess firm performance (Venkatraman and Ramanujam 1987; Chandler and Hanks 1994; VanderWerf 1994; Youndt et al. 1996; Lau 1997; Santos-Requejo and Gonzalez-Benito 2000; De Toni 2001; Cainelli et al. 2004). Such indicators encompass potential pitfalls as the financial statements from small entrepreneurial businesses may be unaudited, and therefore unreliable; accounting information may be altered by accounting norms or management decisions; valuable intangible assets that impact firm competitiveness are mainly omitted from the equation and the business's success relative to its competitors is for the most part ignored (Sapienza, Smith and Gannon 1988; Eccles 1991; Salas 1992; Cuervo 1993; Kaplan and Norton 1993; Alonso and Barcenilla 1999; McGahan 1999; Camisón 2001).
- *Issues related to business strategy.* Issues such as availability of external finances, the business's ability to attract investments and support innovation, efficient asset utilization, and strategic market orientation are all indicators that are directly linked with performance, through provision of liquidity that is necessary to facilitate firm performance potential and strong financial performance (Kohli and Jaworski 1990; Narver and Slater 1990; Pelham and Wilson 1996; Winn 1997; Becchetti and Giovanni 2002).
- *Strategic relationships and meaningful networks.* These can provide the business with competitive information that can lead to improved financial performance; businesses with larger networks are better positioned to acquire the needed information and resources (Green and Brown 1997; Brüder and Preisendörfer 1998; Soh 2003).
- *Human resources on firm performance.* Human capital is a critical factor influencing firm performance: the quality and diversity of ideas among management have an impact on performance. Human capital is an important factor in assessing the investment potential of the firm due to the impact of human capital on financial performance (Brush and Chaganti 1998; Chandler and Hanks 1998; West and Meyer 1998; Watson, Stewart and BarNir 2003).
- *New product innovation.* High R&D spending has an important effect on financial performance. Innovation increases the firm's productivity and innovating businesses have been found to have higher productivity and sales growth than non-innovating firms (Chaney, Devinney and Winer 1991; Hall 1993; Regev 1998).
- *Resource availability.* The business's resources (physical capital, human capital, and organizational resources) and capabilities are pivotal in a competitive environment. Derived from the resource-based theory, businesses aim at becoming heterogeneous and difficult to imitate in resources and capabilities; therefore, many attempts are made to effectively utilize the resources in conjunction with different business strategies to improve performance (Wernerfelt 1984; Barney 1991; Connor 1991; Rumelt 1991).

From a more practical perspective, an evaluation checklist should be applied, including indicators related to the business's basic feasibility, competitive advantages, buyer decisions, marketing orientation, production considerations, staffing decisions, control considerations, and financing requirements. Several models have been studied to identify the main areas in which to evaluate new ventures: (1) marketing and sales; (2) operations; (3) research, development, and engineering; (4) financial management; (5) general management and administration; (6) personnel management, and (7) legal and tax aspects (Vesper 1990; Reynolds and Miller 1992; Pratt 1999). The model should be modified to the business's specific environment and needs, but it should not be neglected as it is an important component in the business's evaluation. Such an evaluation should preferably be based on monitoring the progress of both the processes and the indicators that lead to business success. In addition, when conducting a performance evaluation, two types of performance standards should be addressed: external and internal. External problems include customer contact, market knowledge, market planning, location, pricing, product issues, competitors, and expansion; internal problems include adequate capital, cash flow, facilities and equipment, inventory control, human resources, leadership, organizational structure, and accounting systems. Accordingly, external and internal performance standards are those processes and tools applied to cope with these problems. Another classification identifies external standards as those determined by the organization, including sales quotas, production rates, or a dress code, while internal standards are those referring to the individual's personal values and beliefs regarding how the business processes should be performed; some studies claim that internal, perceptual measures are highly correlated with external, objective measures and have the advantage of facilitating comparisons among businesses in different industries (Cardy and Dobbins 1991; Murphy and Cleveland 1995).

Entrepreneurs should apply both qualitative and quantitative variables to measure their business's performance. Table 14.1 lists output measures that should be addressed in the firm's evaluation. Table 14.2 lists process-oriented measures to be addressed in the firm's evaluation.

RE-EVALUATIONS

In his writings, Michael Porter established the significance of information in business success. In *Knowledge and Special Libraries*, Porter and Millar stress that 'it is hard to underestimate the strategic significance of new information technology . . . every company must understand the broad effects and implications of new technology and how it can create substantial and sustainable competitive advantage' (Matarazzo and Connolly 1999). The business's activities and practices should be evaluated through an ongoing process, preferably by inherent systems or experts who have been engaged for an evaluation of the business indicators. This enables the entrepreneur to be in control and redesign or redirect the business's resources according to the results he or she obtains. For example, a business developing computer games for advancing children's motor skills is in the more advanced stages of the software R&D; it is allocating a significant amount of resources to marketing and R&D to attract parents and educators, as new target groups for its newly developed products. It is critical to develop a formative evaluation survey that can indicate whether the resource allocation is worthwhile; such an evaluation at advanced stages of R&D – but not when the process is already completed – provides flexibility and adaptability; results indicating that such products will not sell or already exist in the market, or will be very expensive to develop and sell, provide the entrepreneur with crucial information for decisions on if and how to proceed with the R&D/marketing. Such an evaluation could definitely save the business a lot of money at this stage, rather than completing the process and then discovering that the products do not sell.

Table 14.1 *Output measures that should be addressed in the firm's evaluation*

Measure	Evaluation
Active customers	Number of active customers and annual growth in number of customers Diversification of segments of active customers Customer satisfaction and positive relationships with customers Do the active customers stream sales and revenues? Effective management of relationships with active customers and maintenance of those relationships
Potential customers	Number and diversification of segments of potential customers approached Number of potential customers targeted from active customers Effectiveness of marketing (rates of success)
Actual suppliers	Transfer of information by suppliers (functions of product development, procurement of materials from vendors, movement of materials between facilities, product manufacturing, distribution of finished goods to customers) Effectiveness of supply chain Supplier satisfaction with the business relationship Business satisfaction with the supplier relationships Sustainability of relationships with suppliers
Potential suppliers	Effectiveness of suppliers' forecasting of clients' demand for services Networking by suppliers After-market support for sustainability
Profitability	Valuation of the business Sales rates Positive cash flows Positive returns on investments Attainment of further future financial resources when needed Well-managed costs and expenses Positive relationship with investors, funds or other resource allocations Responsible management of resources to bring a fair return on the investment Resources that allow the company to acquire the future resources/information/skills, etc. needed to create and grow a new business
Reputation	Effectively demonstrating to the market that the firm can be trusted to fulfill its obligations to those who have entrusted it with capital Demonstrating that the firm is sustainable Demonstrating a focus on top-line growth activities which will lead to new sources of revenue
Employees	Number of employees; growth in number of employees More specialized employees More division of specialization
Products and/or services	Number of products and/or services; annual growth in number of products and/or services Growth in diversification of products and/or services High-quality products and/or services Active quality assurance process Balanced stock-owning rates Rational and effective distribution process

Table 14.2 *Process-oriented measures to be addressed in the firm's evaluation*

Ongoing processes
- Ensuring that the products for which payment has been received are delivered within the promised timeframe, are built according to the promised specifications, and are safe for use
- The product/service goes beyond customer expectations
- Generating buy-in of customers who are taking a chance on new products and services
- Developing and sustaining normative features of the customer relationship when pursuing new markets
- Customer feedback on a regular basis

Creativity and innovation
- Managing creative teams
- Encouraging innovative ideas
- Supporting and managing creativity and innovation through an open-oriented management; employee feedback; employee involvement in managerial and strategic decisions, etc.

Human resources (HR): employee recruitment, assessment, and training
- Well-structured HR process
- Recruiting using relevant and competitive measures; are the measures visible?
- Effective links between employee assessments and employee promotions at work, training, personal development, and more

Marketing: potential customers
- Effective marketing process
- Linkage between marketing and successful/unsuccessful incidents, situations or sales

Processes and products or services which have already been evaluated in previous stages of the business should be re-evaluated at the more advanced stages, either over time or with respect to changes in the business or its environment (e.g., contracting with new suppliers; recruiting a flow of employees to a project; economic changes occurring in the region; a competitor is now offering the same products/services, etc.), because dynamic, fluctuating markets and turbulent times lead to many changes in clients' tastes and needs.

Entrepreneurs should be attentive to changes in customers' tastes, needs and demands for the short-term sales, but also to their views and perspectives for long-term sales. Personal computers (PCs), for example, were perceived by customers and analysts as unnecessary systems when the PC pioneers founded their ventures; but evaluation surveys showed, after a time, a dramatic transformation in the customers' and potential customers' tastes regarding PCs. Only re-evaluations of such tastes and needs could reveal these changes.

Customer loyalty is also an issue to be assessed and reassessed. Studies have shown tremendous changes in customer loyalty to products, services, brand names or trademarks over the years. Criteria to trace customers' loyalty are erratic: they fluctuate from lower prices to best quality, professional service, accessible location, or 'just because my friend purchased it'. Continual re-evaluation of customers' tastes and criteria for loyalty are essential.

A product's strengths and weaknesses should be re-evaluated over time to determine the likelihood of its commercial success before and during the process of committing capital to developing and marketing it. Businesses such as Ikea, Best Buy or Home Depot, which based their strengths, at least in part, on 'producing high-quality products at a low cost . . . to make lives fun and easy or to help consumers create the home of their dreams whether they want to do it themselves or have it done for them' need to ensure that these remain their strengths over time. The business's asset lies in nourishing its product/service strengths, making evaluations of product quality, business processes or customer feedback on purchased products necessary. Good evaluation results may also secure a development loan by increasing credibility with banks, as well as encouraging an inventor to pursue his or her invention with a business plan and patent; poor results, on the other hand, warn the entrepreneur/inventor to reconsider proceeding with product development.

Opportunities should also be re-evaluated over time; in fact they should be re-evaluated at each stage of their development. In the case of inventions, prospective new products or services, the first formal evaluation may involve a feasibility analysis, which addresses the question of whether the proposed combination of resources can be applied, add value and achieve financial success. However, with time, business information needs change and opportunities should then be re-evaluated to determine whether they are still contributing to the business's goals and matching each of its stage's needs. Opportunities that do not fit the subsequent stage of development or implementation may be revised or even aborted.

Accordingly, the allocation of business resources should be re-evaluated in an ongoing process; such re-evaluation results may lead to useful revisions of business concepts or activities and minimize potential pitfalls. Sometimes, entrepreneurs lack the objectivity to determine that their resources are being directed to non-profitable paths: they need to execute a formal, inherent procedure to obtain results. An Israeli plastic manufacturer started to produce new, colorful and decorative bathroom equipment and accessories; as he reached the manufacturing stage and incorporated the new mix of colors and patterns into the process and the materials, the business's quality manager recommended stopping the process at once because it involved major manufacturing pitfalls. The new process was costly and the entrepreneur lacked objectivity as he adored the product's concept, and he was therefore unwilling to follow this recommendation and proceeded with the process. He based his decision on very encouraging results from old research he had conducted on the process several years earlier. The business went bankrupt because all of its products were of very low quality due to the poor manufacturing process. A re-evaluation of the process, rather than depending on the initial evaluation's results, would have avoided this.

A business's resources, capital and assets should be continually re-evaluated to determine the worth of the business property, plant and equipment, the innovation quality, the level of technology in the business, the expertise in the business, the human capital and the workers' efficiency and productivity.

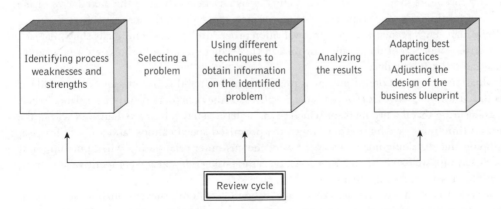

Figure 14.1 *Basic model of a business evaluation*

TOPICS AND TOOLS

- *Technological tools.* IT; technology-based instruments, software and organizational computing; electronic communication.
- *Surveys.* Client satisfaction surveys; customer preferences; employee satisfaction surveys, visibility (i.e., what the clients know about the business and the services it provides).
- *Analyses — reports analysis and observation analysis:*
  - *Reports analysis.* Return on investement (ROI); costs, sales, profitability, trends in growth or decline (number of clients, sales rates, loyal clients versus instant clients, etc.); cost effectiveness; supply chain management.
  - *Observation analysis.* Customer relationship management; service level; employee efficacy; employee performance.
  - *Quality test.* Product quality tests; process quality tests; business activities (e.g., meetings, association between employee feedback and business productivity); department quality (e.g., administration, financing, marketing).
  - *Modeling of business processes.* Documentation benefits; design benefits, i.e., understanding the current business processes, generation of new possibilities and a means of planning for project implementation; use benefits, i.e., visual representation of processes, supporting the iterative development process of systems and time efficiency.

SUMMARY

Studies in entrepreneurship and strategic management reveal that most entrepreneurs report their main goal as reaching long-term 'business success', referring mainly to creating wealth, attracting investors and recruiting the best employees. All of the other objectives are the by-products that enable achieving this success (e.g., developing innovative products, enlarging product diversity, providing the best services, etc.). Fewer entrepreneurs, however, link sustainable success with a continual evaluation of their business's outputs and processes.

The term 'evaluation' may be associated, among some individuals, to a judgmental ranking procedure in school or at university, and might even have a negative connotation; yet in entrepreneurial terms it is a decision-making support system that exposes relevant information on whether the procedures activated in the business are in line with the business's objectives, and if the entrepreneurs should support these activities by advancing them to the next stages of the business, i.e. allocating more capital and other resources to support them.

While many entrepreneurs neglect the evaluation procedure, studies continually show that lack of objective evaluation of the business or unrealistic prediction of the business vis-à-vis market trends lead to business failure.

Evaluations can focus on output measures, such as profitability, reputation, active and/or potential customers, active and/or potential suppliers, or they can focus on process-related issues, such as ensuring that the products for which payment has been received are delivered within the promised timeframe, are built according to the promised specifications, and are safe for use, developing and sustaining normative features of the customer relationship when pursuing new markets, having a well-structured HR process, recruiting using relevant and competitive measures, and visible measures, among others.

Tools for evaluations are diverse, and include technological tools, surveys, analyses such as cost analyses, analyses of the trends in growth or decline, and quality tests of the products, processes, business procedures and regulations.

CASE STUDY 14.1   Kidos, UK and India

Lindsay McDonald was employed as a writer for a local children's magazine in California for over ten years, where she wrote mainly children's stories, anecdotes and poetry. In her last year at the magazine, she became somewhat bored with her job and felt unchallenged. She therefore got a Bachelor's degree in American Literature, and her plan was to quit her job, take a short trip to India, relocate in Boston and proceed to her Master's degree at a college there. On her tour in India, she met a British business woman in the library in Bangalore, Erica, who told her about a nine-month-old publishing house she had launched in Bangalore: it was a publishing house for children's books, founded with two goals in mind – to turn original book writing into a more accessible process for individuals in India and to advance reading of local anecdotes and stories among the children in India. Erica told McDonald that this was her fourth business; the others had been in different areas, different stages and in different locations: a marketing firm in London, an advertising firm in the Netherlands and a real-estate firm in Slovenia. They all went well, especially the one in London. Erica told McDonald that with her partners, they had engaged local managers for each of their businesses yet monitored them very closely and on a regular basis through the internet; for example, they surveyed the existing customers' satisfaction every month, and undertook potential customer surveys once every three months; they engaged professional quality managers to monitor the perceived quality of their marketing and advertising services once a month and assessed their employees' productivity daily, including a formal evaluation procedure once every six months. Erica was in charge of the survey results and wrote all the reports; Don, one of the partners, was in charge of 'translating' the results into action plans; Jimmy and Petula, the other two business partners in London and the Netherlands, respectively, were in charge of accurately monitoring implementation of the action plans by interviewing the employees, their managers, the customers and the directors on productivity measures they had all developed to screen their businesses.

Erica told McDonald that they had information on everything in the businesses, e.g., the number of active customers and annual growth in number of customers; customer satisfaction; diversification of segments of active customers; the number of potential customers targeted from active customers; effectiveness of marketing according to rates of success; number of services; annual growth in number of services; growth in diversification of services, among other things.

All partners met all local managers in London once a month where they presented the survey results, analyzed changes, discussed the circumstances and potential pitfalls, and asked for feedback and updates, while the partners shared their own feedback, demands and insights with the local managers. The partners were very attentive to the managers' feedback and were flexible in changing and uttering concepts, and in changing processes or even employees to advance their businesses.

They had replaced seven local managers in ten years and reworked their mission statement and goals in all three businesses many times over based on evaluation results. Erica was convinced that the success of the businesses was the outcome of their very well-structured and well-managed evaluation process. The marketing business was increasing very rapidly and provided very large revenues; the advertising business was stable and also provided very large revenues, while the situation with the real-estate business was still vague; it was a nascent business in a country in transition and things were not yet established; they had not found investors as the business results were not yet appealing; at this point Jimmy and Petula recommended replacing the local manager. However, Erica could see from their reports that the Slovene clientele was interested in their services and she was convinced that they were on the right path. This was not the case with the publishing house in India. Erica was sole owner: the others did not believe in its potential, and they were unwilling to invest in it as they had some personal doubts as to Erica's decision to move to India after falling in love with an Indian man whom they felt she hardly knew. She therefore invested her personal savings in the business in Bangalore. Erica was a single mother and for many years had devoted her time to her family and businesses; it was true that she had drastically altered her life when she decided to move with her four children from London to India, to be with an Indian man she had met some months before. She was fascinated by the Indian culture, stories, way of life, and she let her inspiration be affected and fueled by the atmosphere in India. She launched her business in Bangalore because the man she had fallen for was unemployed and she thought that he might eventually run the business; therefore, she managed the business by herself; she had no intention of moving elsewhere, she wanted to stay with him; most of all she was fascinated by and a great advocate of the business's mission statement, so she did not hire any local manager to run it: she wanted to shape its unique character with her own ideas. Yet, Erica was not satisfied with the business's results: it was not turning a profit, she did not cut salaries from it and its activities were slow and unpredictable; she was on the verge of deciding to sell the business and move back to London; her partners were pressuring her to abandon her new way of life and 'get back to her recent life'; she faced many difficulties in her personal life in India: her chidren had not yet adjusted to the Indian culture and business was slow. Erica and McDonald had a very long conversation at the library, in which Erica shared her difficulties in managing a dual-culture family in a foreign country. During their conversation, Erica decided to give her life in Bangalore one 'last chance' and offered that McDonald stay in Bangalore and manage the business. McDonald was very inspired by Erica's story and her devotion to the businesses, her family and the man she loved, and she decided to accept the offer. She started by using a reaching-out strategy: she needed to get an idea of the Indian population in Bangalore's major perceptions of children's books and original writing. Lindsay decided to start by collecting data; she was most interested in people's mental images of what it means to write a children's book. She had the results of initial research Erica had conducted on the potential of the business, but she decided to re-evaluate the whole business's idea and concepts. She printed a one-page evaluation sheet and translated it into many languages; it included three children's drawings and five sentences that she asked people to read and then express their associative remarks; she located people from all walks of life: the local market, the library, her residential neighborhood, Erica's children's teachers. McDonald used her experience as a former writer for a children's magazine to gather information on the business via different, creative evaluation methods. She figured out that this was not a business that should be developed from scratch; it was an active business that should be boosted. Building on Erica's and her partners' successful strategies, McDonald monitored the customers' interests in original writings frequently and outlined different action plans for marketing, advertising and financing. In a few months, not only did her frequent evaluations of the interests in her business have positive effects on potential clients, but a local investor was interested in investing in the publishing house. The situation in Erica's personal life worsened and she moved back to London with her four children after two years in Bangalore. She sold a large part of the business to McDonald and the investor; she did not want to have any association to any business in India, although the business was profitable and was attracting many investors. McDonald and the investor launched several publishing houses in India and after five years they became a chain.

QUESTIONS FOR DISCUSSION

1   Identify the evaluation procedures, tools and practices Erica and her partners executed in their businesses in London, the Netherlands and Slovenia.
2   Assess the strategies taken by the partners to monitor their businesses; what are their strengths and what are their weaknesses? Explain.
3   Can you associate the evaluation procedures followed in these businesses and their success? Explain.
4   What evaluation processes did Erica undertake for Kidos? What were the sources for her different evaluation conduct in these businesses?
5   What evaluation processes did Lindsay McDonald follow for Kidos? What was her innovation?
6   Advise McDonald on how to proceed with the business's evaluation once this chain has spread all over India. Do you think she needs to adapt the model undertaken by Erica and her partners? Explain your opinion.

REFERENCES

Abor, J. and Biekpe, N. (2006) 'SMEs' access to debt finance: a comparison of white-owned and female-owned businesses in Ghana', *International Journal of Entrepreneurship and Innovation*, 7: 105–12.

Alonso, J.A. and Barcenilla, S. (1999) 'Retorno a la competitividad: nuevos desarrollos', *Revista Vasca de Economía*, 44: 43–56.

Arnott, D. and Pervan, G. (2005) 'A critical analysis of decision support systems research', *Journal of Information Technology*, 20: 67.

Barney, J.B. (1991) 'Firm resources and sustained competitive advantage', *Journal of Management*, 17: 99–120.

Basu, A. and Blanning, R.W. (1994) 'Metagraphs: a tool for modelling decision support systems', *Management Science*, 40: 1579–600.

Becchetti, L. and Giovanni, T. (2002) 'The determinants of growth for small and medium sized firms: the role of the availability of external finance', *Small Business Economics*, 19: 291–306.

Benbasat, I. and Nault, B. (1990) 'An evaluation of empirical research in managerial support systems', *Decision Support Systems*, 6: 203–26.

Benbasat, I. and Zmud, R.W. (1999) 'Empirical research in information systems: the question of relevance', *MIS Quarterly*, 23: 3–16.

Berg, P., Pihlajamaa, J., Nummi, J., Leinonen, M. and Leppo, V. (2004) 'Measurement of the quality and maturity of the innovation process: methodology and case of a medium-sized Finnish company', *International Journal of Entrepreneurship and Innovation Management*, 4: 373–82.

Brüder, J. and Preisendörfer, P. (1998) 'Network support and the success of newly founded business', *Small Business Economics*, 10: 213–25.

Brush, C. and Chaganti, R. (1998) 'Businesses without glamour? An analysis of resources on performance by size and age in small service and retail firms', *Journal of Business Venturing*, 14: 233–57.

Cainelli, G., Evangelista, R., Savona, R. and Savona, M. (2004) 'The impact of innovation on economic performance in services', *Service Industries Journal*, 24: 116.

Camisón, Z. (2001) 'La investigación sobre la pyme y su competitividad. Balance de la cuestión desde las perspectivas narrativa y meta-analítica', *Papeles de Economía Española*, 89/90: 43–86.

Cardy, R.L. and Dobbins, G.H. (1991) *Performance Appraisal: Alternative Perspectives*, Cincinnati, OH: South Western.

Chandler, G. and Hanks, S. (1994) 'Market attractiveness, resource-based capabilities, ventures strategies, and venture performance', *Journal of Business Venturing*, 9: 331–49.

Chandler, G. and Hanks, S. (1998) 'An examination of the substitutability of founders' human and financial capital in emerging business ventures', *Journal of Business Venturing*, 13: 353–69.

Chaney, P., Devinney, T. and Winer, R. (1991) 'The impact of new product introduction on the market value of fims', *Journal of Business*, 64: 573–610.

Connor, K. (1991) 'A historical comparison of resource-based theory and five schools of thought within industrial organization economics: do we have a new theory of the firm?', *Journal of Management*, 17: 121–54.

Cuervo, A. (1993) 'El papel de la empresa en la competitividad', *Papeles de Economía*, 56: 362–78.

De Toni, S. (2001) 'Performance measurement systems: models, characteristics and measures', *International Journal of Operations and Production Management*, 21: 46.

Durand, R. and Coeurderoy, R. (2001) 'Age, order of entry, strategic orientation, and organizational performance', *Journal of Business Venturing*, 16: 471–94.

Eccles, R. (1991) 'The performance measurement manifesto', *Harvard Business Review*, January/February: 131–37.

Eining, M.M. and Dorr, P.B. (1991) 'The impact of expert system usage on experiential learning in an auditing setting', *Journal of Information Systems*, spring: 1–16.

Garman, A.N. and Phillips, F.S. (2006) 'Assessing founders to predict venture success: lessons from psychologists and venture capital firms', *International Journal of Public Administration*, 29: 525–32.

Green, P. and Brown, T. (1997) 'Resource needs and the dynamic capitalism typology', *Journal of Business Venturing*, 12: 161–74.

Hall, R. (1993) 'A framework linking intangible resources and capabilities to sustainable competitive advantage', *Strategic Management Journal*, 14: 607–18.

Kaplan, R. and Norton, D. (1993) 'Evaluación de resultados: algo más que números', *Harvard-Deusto Business Review*, 55: 18–25.

Kohli, A.K. and Jaworski, B.J. (1990) 'Market orientation: the construct, research propositions, and managerial implications', *Journal of Marketing*, 54: 1–19.

Kuratko, D.F., Montagno, R.V. and Hornsby, J.S. (1990) 'Developing an intrapreneurial assessment instrument for an effective corporate entrepreneurial environment', *Strategic Management Journal*, 11: 49–58.

Lau, R. (1997) 'Operational characteristics of highly competitive manufacturing firms', *Production and Inventory Management Journal*, 38: 17–23.

Matarazzo, J.M. and Connolly, S.D. (1999) *Knowledge and Special Libraries*, Boston, MA: Butterworth-Heinemann.

McGahan, A. (1999) 'Competition, strategy and business performance', *California Management Review*, 41: 74–102.

Murphy, K.R. and Cleveland, J.N. (1995) *Understanding Performance Appraisal: Social, Organizational and Goal-oriented Perspectives*, Thousand Oaks, CA: Sage.

Narver, J.C. and Slater, S.F. (1990) 'The effect of a market orientation on business profitability', *Journal of Marketing*, 54: 20–35.

Pelham, A.M. and Wilson, D.T. (1996) 'A longitudinal study of the impact of market structure, firm structure strategy and market orientation culture on dimensions of small-firm performance', *Academy of Marketing Science Journal*, winter: 27–43.

Phillips, J.J. (1991) *Handbook of Training Evaluation and Measurement Methods*, 2nd edn, Houston, TX: Gulf.

Pratt, S.E. (1999) *Pratt's Guide to Venture Capital Sources 1999*, 23rd edn, Wellesley Hills, MA: Capital Publishing.

Regev, H. (1998) 'Innovation, skilled labour, technology and performance in Israeli industrial firms', *Economics of Innovation and New Technologies*, 5: 301–23.

Reynolds, P.D. and Miller, B. (1992) 'New firm gestation: conception, birth, and implications for research', *Journal of Business Venturing*, 7: 405–17.

Rumelt, R.P. (1991) 'How much does industry matter?', *Strategic Management Journal*, 12: 167–85.

Salas, F. (1992) *Aspectos micro-organizativos de la competitividad*, Fundación Empresa Pública, Documento de Trabajo, 92–105.

Santos-Requejo, L. and Gonzalez-Benito, O. (2000) 'Economic success factors in Spanish small retail businesses: an analysis based on sector-relative definitions', *Small Business Economics*, 15: 209–22.

Sapienza, H., Smith, K. and Gannon, M. (1988) 'Using subjective evaluations of organizational performance in small business research', *American Journal of Small Business*, 13: 45–53.

Soh, P. (2003) 'The role of networking alliances in information acquisition and its implications for new product performance', *Journal of Business Venturing*, 18: 727–44.

VanderWerf, P. (1994) 'Determinants of new ventures' objectives', in *Frontiers of Entrepreneurship Research*, Wellesley, MA: Babson College.

Venkatraman, N. and Ramanujam, V. (1987) 'Measurement of business economic performance: an examination of method convergence', *Journal of Management*, 13: 109–22.

Vesper, K.H. (1990) *New Venture Strategies*, 2nd edn, Englewood Cliffs, NJ: Prentice-Hall.

Voisey, P., Gornall, L., Jones, P. and Thomas, B. (2006) 'The measurement of success in a business incubation project', *Journal of Small Business and Enterprise Development*, 13: 454–68.

Watson, W., Stewart, W. and BarNir, A. (2003) 'The effects of human capital, organizational demography, and interpersonal processes of venture partner perceptions of firm profit and growth', *Journal of Business Venturing*, 19: 145–64.

Wernerfelt, B. (1984) 'A resource-based view of the firm', *Strategic Management Journal*, 5: 171–80.

West, G., III and Meyer, G. (1998) 'To agree or not to agree? Consensus and performance in new venturing', *Journal of Business Venturing*, 13: 395–422.

Wilson, H.N. and McDonald, M.H.B. (1996) 'Computer aided marketing planning: the experience of early adopters', *Journal of Marketing Management*, 12: 391–416.

Winn, J. (1997) 'Asset productivity turnaround: the growth/efficiency challenge', *Journal of Management Studies*, 34: 585–600.

Ye, R. and Johnson, P. (1995) 'The impact of explanation facilities on user acceptance of expert systems advice', *MIS Quarterly*, 19: 157–72.

Youndt, M., Snell, S., Dean, J. and Lepak, D. (1996) 'Human resource management, manufacturing strategy, and firm performance', *Academy of Management Journal*, 39: 836–66.

Chapter 15

The entrepreneurial avenues

OBJECTIVES

After studying this chapter you will be able to:

■ Expand the scope of your existing knowledge on the alternatives in entrepreneurial paths, based on the entrepreneur's needs and vision.

■ Identify the variety of entrepreneurial avenues, distinguish between them and recognizing the pros and cons of each avenue to either choose or advise others on the alternatives in entrepreneurship.

■ Merge creativity and outside-the-box thinking in exploiting and/or creating entrepreneurial avenues to achieve business growth and self-realization.

■ Recognize that when encountering difficulties and constraints in the business, there are different entrepreneurial avenues which, by some alteration of the original business or path, may provide higher success and self-realization.

■ Identify the demographic, ecological and sociocultural characteristics of entrepreneurs that affect their choices of entrepreneurial avenues in order to facilitate the fit between the person and the business characteristics.

■ Further explore the entrepreneurial avenues and their chances of success.

FINDING YOUR ENTREPRENEURIAL WAY

To achieve growth, business development and self-fulfillment, as well as a sense of accomplishment and self-realization, a wider diversity of entrepreneurial avenues should be acknowledged by the entrepreneur. Any one individual may choose different paths in entrepreneurship, merge several avenues or 'create' a tailor-made path that fits his or her expectations regarding business growth and self-realization.

Entrepreneurs are characterized as possessing relatively restless, nonconformist and non-conventional spirit and conduct, and a single-path career may repel them from entrepreneurship, as well as dampen their free spirit and independent attitude. However, by acknowledging that there are several options for entrepreneurship, and that all maintain the characteristics of innovation, creativity, individualism and free spirit, better performance and a stronger feeling of self-realization may be achieved.

Individuals wishing to engage in entrepreneurial activities should understand that there is no single entrepreneurial type that guarantees success: they need to find the most beneficial type of entrepreneurship for them – that best fits their needs, goals and personality.

SELF-EMPLOYMENT

Self-employment has become an increasingly important form of entrepreneurship in modern economies, complementary to classical entrepreneurship yet distinct. In fact, entrepreneurs must go through a phase of self-employment in order to actually launch their ventures. Although it is one of the oldest features of entrepreneurship, the concept of self-employment is still fraught with ambiguity. According to labor-force classifications, self-employment is a separate relational contracting with the firm, distinguished from employed persons who are related to their firms through a 'nexus of contracts'. The main activities that frequently characterize self-employed individuals take place in the 'informal economy': part- or full-time vocations (i.e., involving home production) closely related to hobbies, or services in a unique niche of expertise.

The self-employed work freely, and have a certain degree of command over their resources and capital ownership; however, the differences between self-employed individuals and entrepreneurs lie mainly in their personal characteristics; for example, self-employed individuals are not necessarily innovators, creative, cunning, or prone to insight or resourcefulness. Nevertheless, the situations and the environmental constraints faced by the self-employed are akin to those faced by entrepreneurs, for example, obstacles encountered in access to financial capital, liquidity constraints, and sales and marketing difficulties. Overcoming these obstacles and managing the business toward growth and success certainly require specific competence in leadership, strategic management, and effective teamwork. The self-employed are considered tough, down-to-earth, pragmatic people, sensible to the market's needs, sometimes driven by a need for independence and sometimes by the necessity to escape un- or underemployment[1] (Greene 2002; Singh and DeNoble 2003a, 2003b; Rosti and Chelli 2005; Arenius and Kovalainen 2006; Ngwenya 2007).

Best practice:

- Acquire managerial and leadership skills.
- Obtain business tools for running a business.
- Deepen daily management know-how with respect to maintaining a business.
- Train and learn how to manage a business toward success and growth (courses, evening classes at local colleges, books).
- Make temporary or permanent mergers with other self-employed individuals having corresponding expertise or whose clientele may be complementary.

FRANCHISING

Franchising is another entrepreneurial opportunity path to business growth, and it is known as a common and popular way for entrepreneurs to establish their own businesses quickly, relatively easily and with less risk. Franchising is the granting of a license by one person (the franchisor) to another (the franchisee), which entitles the franchisee to trade under the trademark/trade name of the franchisor and to make use of an entire package, comprising all the elements necessary to establish a previously untrained person in the business who will run it with continual assistance on a predetermined basis. This format offers the advantages of business ownership under an established brand name and existing operating standards; and this relationship is less risky than starting an independent business from scratch.

Franchisor

The business outlet is owned and operated by the franchisee; however, the franchisor retains control over the way in which products and services are marketed and sold, and controls the quality and standards of the business. The franchisor usually receives an initial fee from the franchisee, payable at the outset, together with ongoing management service fees – usually based on a percentage of annual turnover or mark-ups on supplies. In return, the franchisor has an obligation to support the franchise network, notably with training, product development, advertising, promotional activities and with a range of specialist management services. Moreover, franchisors need to train franchisees in how to operate the business and they need to provide very detailed operating manuals. Franchisors generally provide some kind of support as well, from ongoing training to administrative and technical support.

Franchisee

The franchisee's responsibility is to create a clear goal-oriented business plan defining the financial and quality business goals, and to set up measurable indicators of 'business success' in light of the specific franchise opportunities. It should be a win–win relationship, as both parties are interested in achieving the business goals, although in potentially different ways. Franchisors often have proven systems and a demonstrated track record for overcoming some challenges faced by business owners; nevertheless, it should be the franchisee's responsibility to proactively search for these systems and dig deeper by asking questions that will advance the business's success (Norton 1988; Falbe, Dandridge and Kumar 1999; Tuunanen and Hyrsky 2001; Spinelli 2007).

The Entrepreneurs.com website has established a checklist[2] of 100 questions that may assist in determining an entrepreneur's suitability to becoming a franchisee.

A number of websites provide some information on franchising.[3]

Best practice:

- Franchisors and franchisees must be very clear in setting a goal-oriented business strategy with goals that have been accepted – and preferably crafted – by both sides. A profound understanding of the franchisee's abilities and the business's capacity to achieve these goals should be discussed and planned out.
- The franchisor and franchisees must consider themselves business partners and support each other accordingly (via the franchise network, counseling, advertising, promotional activities, administrative and technical support, among other things).
- Franchisors and franchisees must create a wide-open line of communication to achieve a win–win situation.

TECHNOPRENEURS

In the new world of high technology, entrepreneurship has taken on new meaning, especially in today's fast-paced competitive environment when firms face the need to be increasingly nimble and adaptive. While often able to establish a certain level of performance based upon existing technologies, firms are also often left flat-footed in the face of emerging, novel technologies. In order to gain a competitive advantage in the technological economy, sophisticated knowledge and expertise with a standard of performance that is state-of-the-art in the high-tech arena should be implemented by entrepreneurs. Technopreneurship emerged from this new technological reality, which has spurred the establishment of complex, strategic businesses in order to survive and grow in the ever-changing technological realm.

Moreover, this new 'gung-ho' environment has encouraged the merger of academic-technological and entrepreneurial-business worlds. Being both a scientist and an entrepreneur in the technological arena has become a prevalent phenomenon. Faculty entrepreneurs are considered more productive researchers, in effect, 'star scientists', while academic entrepreneurs are thought to provide more to their startups by possessing up-to-date information and professional knowledge on new innovations of products and processes as well as on technological developments. Technopreneurship, the technological/scientific combination of the academic world and entrepreneurship, has evolved into a very profitable area in entrepreneurship.

The facilities provided by academic universities to technopreneurs, such as laboratories, research assistants, incubators and many other necessary resources, are considered a valuable strategic foundation for their businesses' success. Additionally, academia–entrepreneurship relationships ease the technopreneur's access to contacts and to establishing links with companies, through the well-known university–industry relationship, and this may be useful for both business purposes and the exploitation of new ideas.

Technopreneurship holds a unique niche in that it represents that feature of entrepreneurship that advances creativity by overcoming the conventional mental blocks and playing with the imagination and possibilities. The technopreneur is actually viewed as someone who brings together research talent, venture capital, new business concepts and management skills to create commercially successful technological innovations or, alternatively, to effectively leverage innovations through the application of technology.

Technopreneurs may come up with brilliant, innovative ideas that can rake in profits if their solutions are marketed well enough; however, they lack the facet of business management that spans solution development to marketing and even the outlining of plans on how to make a profit (Jones-Evans 1996; Zucker, Darby and Torero 2002; Oakey 2003; Lo, Liou and Yuan 2005).

Several websites provide information for technopreneurs.[4]

Best practice:

- Technological abilities and skills, in and of themselves, do not guarantee success in business: search for the training provided by the public and private sectors to improve competency in strategic business-oriented thinking and business management.
- Keep constantly professionally updated and elevate the level of technological know-how, but also be aware of the current and future shortages of skilled labor in the industry and adjust to them.
- Seek assistance in identifying these niches of shortage in the industry.
- Most important, look for source-based firms and institutions for technology transfer in order to turn technopreneurship into an ongoing process.

- Transfer creative, innovate, breakthrough thinking by teaching students and potential entrepreneurs.

SERIAL ENTREPRENEURS

Serial entrepreneurs are individuals who have been involved over the years in more than one venture, have sold and/or closed down a business in which they had an ownership stake, and currently have an ownership stake in a different independent business that is either a new business that they founded, a purchased business, or an inherited business. Entrepreneurs of this type are considered adept at taking companies from their startup point to a valuable, saleable business.

Correspondingly, portfolio entrepreneurs are individuals who currently have minority or majority ownership stakes in two or more independent businesses that are either new, purchased, and/or inherited. These entrepreneurs are regarded as skillful in managing several successful companies at a time, and thus of possessing the ability to split their control and focus on several different, active projects simultaneously.

Both types of entrepreneurs, also referred to in several studies as 'habitual entrepreneurs', are characterized as passionate individuals who flourish around the 'action' involved in encountering multiple and different projects. They are risk-takers, profit-makers, visionaries, and very easily bored; boredom is actually one of the prime factors leading them to start new businesses. They dislike the daily management of their running businesses while they are keen on meeting the challenges of fresh startups – outlining the vision, raising funds and drawing up business plans.

There is multiple evidence-based data showing that these types of entrepreneurs are successful in terms of business survival and growth. Being in perpetual motion contributes a great deal to their entrepreneurial-related experience, which assists them in overcoming the various obstacles they will encounter on their next project, in making strategic decisions along with decisions of the 'here and now' type, and especially in establishing relevant and meaningful networking for investments and investors.

The advantages of entering into 'habitual entrepreneurship' lie in launching a business connected (by the owner) to already well-established social capital, i.e., contacts and ties that are trustworthy, significant and reliable. This facilitates the launching and management of the business in many aspects, including information flow, and the marketing and funding processes. Founders with an established network with investors are more likely to receive funding for their businesses. Moreover, serial or portfolio entrepreneurs sometimes obtain financial capital, and this not only assists in building up the forthcoming funding process, but also allows personal seed funding for a while. As a result, these entrepreneurs face a significantly less stressed negotiation process with investors, and can wait for the 'right' time in order to obtain higher pre-money valuation of the business, choose the time to sell ('exit') and maximize the value they get out of the business while ensuring its success after they let it go (Westhead and Wright 1998a, 1998b; Rae 2004; Westhead, Ucbasaran and Wright 2005; Westhead et al. 2005).

Best practice:

- Build up and strengthen links and networks for the development of new businesses.
- Be aware of difficulties encountered throughout long business experience and avoid these difficulties in future businesses.
- Construct win–win situations with inexperienced entrepreneurs in transferring knowledge, by teaching them or being a model for them, while in turn being hands-on and current on the feelings, attitudes and obstacles faced by young entrepreneurs in the market.

CASE STUDY 15.1   Serial entrepreneur, Romania

Aurel Bogoescu's first memory from his childhood in Galatz, Romania, is of when he was around six or seven years old and his sister would not talk to him; he knew what he had done but he could not understand what was wrong with it. He adored his big sister Helena, and he was miserable in the face of her anger toward him. Helena had been knitting, but the sweater she was making – and that he had unraveled – was only half-knitted anyway and he was sure he saw her starting on a different sweater. When he looked at the second-hand skates he had bought with the money from the second-hand wool he had sold Bianca, his neighbor, he was convinced he had done the right thing; instead of having an unfinished sweater at home, they had skates. He told Helena that she could have them whenever she wanted – but she was still very angry at him. Today, Bogoescu is a multi-millionaire, owning several companies, 'each one of them my "baby"' he says, and investing in many other businesses. 'I have a trade-off spirit which emerged at the age of six but this is my natural behavior, thinking and aspiration; this is how I still act today', says Bogoescu.

At the age of sixteen, Bogoescu and two of his friends initiated a 'summer school' during the vacation; summer schools were not popular at that time in Romania and the concept was difficult to sell. However, Bogoescu was convinced that this was a real need: Romanian women worked very hard and he knew first-hand that his mother always had a hard time finding arrangements for his brother during school vacations. Some neighbors who knew the Bogoescus let their children spend their vacation with Bogoescu and his friends; and Bogoescu invested all of the money they had in new toys and games for the children. His friends were very angry: they wanted their money back and they threatened to beat him up, but Bogoescu promised them that their next payment would be doubled. He was wrong. During the next vacation, there was such a demand for the summer school that they 'hired' two girl-friends, and the money they got back was five times (!) their initial investment. Bogoescu saved his money in some governmental stocks and then at the age of eighteen he began to 'trade' with them in the stock market. By the age of nineteen, he had more money in the bank than his parents. Bogoescu spent most of this money on his studies and lodging in Bucharest, eventually getting his law degree. During his studies, Bogoescu launched his first business. He had been telling his friends at the university about his trading in the stock market and realized that no one understood anything about it. Bogoescu convinced a professor of finance at the university to launch a counseling business for the stock market; the professor was concerned about the risks and was not sure he was allowed to have a private business while holding a university position, so they decided to establish 'written counseling'; Bogoescu was the 'marketing' person and was the first to meet face-to-face with the clients; the clients' needs were identified and these were written down for the specialist, i.e., the professor. The business was going very well, but after two years the professor decided to quit. Meanwhile, Bogoescu had found a way to ease the students' load by photocopying the books they had to read; the machine was very far away, and Bogoescu, armed with a list of client orders, would borrow the books from the library, travel to the only shop with a photocopy machine and make the needed copies. Again, it was an innovative concept and many students used his services. However, while the demand for his services increased, his costs also increased: he was not allowed to take out more than four books at a time from the library, and the frequent travel costs to the shop made the business unprofitable.

He therefore used the money that he had earned and his savings from his previous businesses to buy a photocopy machine. Such an item was very expensive at that time, costing nearly as much as a car, but Bogoescu calculated its return of cost by the end of his studies. Bogoescu located the machine in his rented room and the business grew. However, one day the renter 'discovered' the machine and would not let Bogoescu use it: he threatened to evict him. Bogoescu decided to sell the machine. He sought, and found, the 'right' student, and convinced him to buy the machine. Bogoescu asked for double its price 'because of its potential'. In fact, he had found a very rich young man who needed cash because his family had cut him off as a punishment for bad grades at school. 'I was looking for someone desperate for this machine but who still had some money to buy it,' says Bogoescu. The man 'took over' the photocopy business and it was a great success.

Having completed his studies, Bogoescu decided to practice law in France, as his university had relations with a French university. Bogoescu practiced in a law firm in Toulouse, specializing in industrial property, i.e., protection of patents of invention, trademarks, commercial or service marks, among others. Bogoescu's stay motivated him to turn to the high-tech world; he still had money in the stock market and was excited by an invention in eye-surgery nanotechnology that one of the law firm's clients was developing. Bogoescu invested in this project and became a partner. He was not allowed to continue practicing at the law firm due to conflict of interest and he dropped out of the program. The French partner never completed the technology. However, Bogoescu managed to sell the business to another company dealing in nanotechnology R&D, which showed a great deal of interest and bought the business at a very good price; this company did manage to develop the technology and had tremendous success in France. Bogoescu felt that he had missed this opportunity and this 'failure' drove him to his next business. He returned to Romania, determined to succeed this time; he was offered a senior position in a company but rejected any corporate position. 'I was looking for needs, gaps and demands. I asked people what had changed in the years I had been in France – what they needed. Democracy was in its infancy in Romania and people did not know how to deal with it; they did not know what they needed', recalls Bogoescu. He believed that construction would be the next budding sector and launched a construction business. He hired immigrants who had moved to Romania to lower labor costs and started some construction work for a new neighborhood. When the business achieved its balance point, Bogoescu launched a rental agency for real estate in Bucharest which was extremely successful. He analyzed the potential in selling apartments to investors who were interested in real estate in Romania and led both of his businesses toward this niche. The businesses flourished. Bogoescu then invested in a music website and in a pharmacological development. Today, he continues to search for investments and new ideas for future businesses.

QUESTIONS FOR DISCUSSION

1   What are Aurel Bogoescu's main serial-entrepreneurial characteristics?
2   What advantages and disadvantages has Bogoescu encountered over the years due to these characteristics?
3   Do you find serial entrepreneurs superficial, unable to deepen a project? Is this a disadvantage?

4   How did Bogoescu exploit opportunities?

5   What do you think motivated Bogoescu to launch businesses? Did the same motivation underlie each of his businesses?

6   Can you explain Bogoescu's success?

MULTIPLE ENTREPRENEURS

The 'multipreneur' is the entrepreneur who starts multiple firms simultaneously, is fully involved in his or her businesses, especially financially, but who may have different roles in those businesses – investor, CEO, or exclusive involvement in specific areas (e.g., finance, R&D, marketing, etc.).

This form of entrepreneurship requires individuals to be able to organize resources, manage their businesses, and simultaneously forecast the risks for their business enterprises. The motivation to concurrently invest in several entrepreneurial activities is both financial and non-financial: financially, there are expectations of rapid growth and returns to the investment, as well as reinvesting financial, human and social capital back into further entrepreneurial activities. During the first entrepreneurial business experience, the entrepreneur may discover that the non-pecuniary benefits of entrepreneurship make it more attractive than returning to regular employment and this motivates him or her to launch several businesses.

Moreover, like the 'habitual entrepreneur', most multipreneurs are characterized as restless individuals who tend to be uninterested in doing 'more of the same' when managing their own businesses. They need continuous challenges and innovative experiments. Being active in different ventures which are at different stages is challenging and stimulating for them. A challenging multipreneurial activity might appear as follows: being involved in the development of a prototype at the seed stage of one venture; engaged in achieving market penetration in another business whose product has proven manufacturability and is selling; and at the same time, being involved in export marketing in a third business which is at the more advanced, mezzanine stage, with all systems really working and the potential for a major success becoming apparent (Barton 2000; Pasanen 2003; Ucbasaran, Westhead and Wright 2006).

Best practice:

- Find the time and energy to launch and run another firm(s); this is not a trivial process that 'comes and goes by itself': it involves other people, money, goals and desires, and should be treated accordingly.
- Learn from experience with the first firm, which is likely to condition the level of the anticipated financial rewards relative to the personal inputs involved.
- Determine the importance attributed to the expected non-financial returns relative to the time, money and energy involved in this form of entrepreneurship.

SPIN-OFFS

Spin-offs have attracted attention as a very successful form of new business creation. Policy-makers see spin-offs as particularly fertile innovators in an economy, as the sub- or newly formed business is a separate, albeit complementary entity relative to the parent business, yet controlled and managed by the same owner(s). This form of entrepreneurship therefore promotes the market by supplying jobs, intensifying employment, implementing innovation and potential dynamics through manufacturing and selling while, at the same time, a social-industrial peace is sustained in the labor

281

market. Spin-offs may compete with their parent business(es) or be totally independent, but either way they will still positively influence profitability for the owner. Competitors' conflicts, manipulations or any other provocative industrial actions which are manifested from time to time at the labor market level are not relevant in the spin-off realm.

Spin-offs have the advantage of acquiring growth and success more easily, enjoying more comfortable access to markets, customers and suppliers, and having a very deep, valuable knowledge of and familiarity with the parent business's products, services, and future plans which do not enhance the effective cooperation between these businesses; it also avoids the errors that occur in businesses in the first stages of constructing their relationship and adapting to each other's norms and values.

Several types of spin-offs are active in the market: (1) corporate spin-offs – when a division of a company or organization becomes an independent business; (2) government spin-offs – involving civilian goods which are the result of military or governmental research; (3) research spin-offs – new companies based on the findings of research teams at research institutions. The spin-offs which emerge from these research centers stand out with their above-average survival rate: this success is not only due to their innovative scientific-technological approach, but also to business development and research-policy support, a startup-friendly environment and the fact that they are a vital ingredient in a techno-professional university-based research environment which helps these emerging companies succeed. Such spin-offs are regarded as an ideal way of providing business and industry on impulse and creating highly qualified jobs (Scheutz 1986; Shane 2004; Tubke, De Toledo Saavedra and Gonzalez 2004).

Best practice:

- The most important criterion for a successful spin-off is to fit the spin-off product to the parent business's long-term strategy.
- Essential to success is the spin-off startup team's familiarization of the core products and services of the parent business.
- Manage a continual process of innovation in spin-offs while protecting the spin-off and parent business.

CASE STUDY 15.2 Spin-offs at Tremcar, USA and Canada

Tremcar's President, Jacques Tremblay, had established his fourth spin-off and he was looking for a manager for his plant; for the first time, he could not choose an employee from his Iberville (30 km south of Montreal) plant; instead, he was trying to assess the potential of employees at his Champlain plant, located some 50 km south of Montreal, in New York State (one hour's drive from his main plant in Iberville).

The first spin-off experience: handing over the service function

When Tremblay bought Tremcar in 1987, it employed thirty people and had annual sales of less than US$3 million. He soon realized that steel tanker production and maintenance were highly specialized activities that were learned mainly through experience.

In the next five years, the firm's growth was virtually exponential, and it quickly outgrew its premises. In 1993, to provide the additional space now needed by his company, Tremblay purchased a repair shop in Saint-Athanase (a small village located close to Tremcar's main premises) and appointed employee Louis Hébert to run it. All Tremcar's tanker repair and after-sales service activities were transferred to the new premises. Eight months later, he sold the repair service to Hébert and another employee, both of whom had been with Tremcar for many years.

Tremblay sold all of his shares in the subsidiary to his two employees, taking steps to transfer ownership, drawing up a business plan, asking his own lawyers to prepare the sales contract, and even financing the equipment purchase himself. He regarded this as an investment that would pay off in a few years' time. The transaction was completed quickly, and the transfer of power went off without a hitch.

The new firm, Citernes Hébert & Dugas, was named after its new owners, and inherited all of Tremcar's after-sales service activities along with its spare-parts sales service for Eastern Canada.

The following year, Hébert's partner withdrew and Tremblay offered to buy up his half of the firm's shares. The new shareholders' agreement was fairly straightforward, and the financial ties between Hébert and Tremblay merely strengthened their partnership. Trust was a significant element in the tacit agreement between the two men. The relationship between the two firms remained basically unchanged.

Meetings did, however, become more frequent, and the 'new' partner was able to offer extensive business management advice. For example, the Citernes Hébert employees were offered training by Tremcar's managers and engineering service. Technical advice was also available.

Citernes Hébert was, and still is, of great strategic importance to Tremcar. Over the years, Citernes Hébert's customer base has grown, and the parent company now accounts for only 25 percent of its turnover. However, the ties between the two companies go far beyond figures. Each is dependent on the other, and each has a strong interest in the other's success. In 2000, Citernes Hébert had approximately ten employees, mostly welder-mechanics.

Tremblay regards this first spin-off experience as having been extremely positive.

The second spin-off experience: improving the supply system

Tremcar grew very quickly, to the extent that its three assembly shops sometimes found it difficult to obtain components.

Tremcar's products had earned a reputation in the United States, as well as in Québec and across Canada. He was well aware that to conquer a market he had to offer reliable after-sales service. In 1999, the firm's sales in the United States were concentrated in the border states, because the American market was still largely dominated by Midwestern manufacturers. He wanted to move into the more southerly states, and signed subcontracting agreements with two service centers in Illinois and Wisconsin.

Tremcar's suppliers could not always offer the desired quality at the right price and at the right time, and it became increasingly difficult to increase production. To overcome this problem, Tremblay issued calls for bids for some components. Raynald Ostiguy was usually the lowest bidder.

Ostiguy joined Tremcar as a welder in 1991. According to Tremblay, he had always displayed leadership, dynamism and creativity; and Tremcar's president offered him a partnership arrangement that would involve building a specialized components manufacturing unit able to supply the three assembly shops.

Ostiguy had always wanted his own business and was immediately interested in the project. In April 1996, he became General Manager of Raynox, as well as a minority shareholder, with 20 percent of the firm's stocks. Again, Tremblay financed all of the equipment purchase and installation costs.

This second spin-off turned out to be more complicated than the first. This time, it did not just involve transferring a client list: a factory had to be built, the components production line had to be moved, and new staff had to be trained. Negotiations lasted several months. The new firm's goals, the shareholders' agreement and the details of the partners' relationship were negotiated simply, man to man. Throughout the preparatory period, a number of people, including the local industrial commissioner and the mayor of Saint-Césaire, a nearby village, offered their help in identifying the new premises, which were finally acquired in April 1996. Production began in May of that year.

Initially, Raynox manufactured only two products, and had two employees; by 2000, however, it had more than forty employees and was able to manufacture more than 5,000 different parts. Tremcar's rapid growth had a direct impact on Raynox, which had no choice but to keep up with its principal client's production pace.

Because Raynox is of such strategic importance to Tremcar, the partners have agreed to limit the development of its external client base. Close ties have been forged not only between the two firms, but between the two partners as well.

The third spin-off experience: expanding the service to other areas

In 1993, when he was extending his markets, Tremblay entered into a majority partnership with a Toronto competitor. He closed the factory but maintained its after-sales service department, which served Western Canada. Managing at a distance was difficult, and the management style of the previous owner, who was appointed to manage the new subsidiary, turned out to be incompatible with Tremcar's style and culture. The service provided by the Toronto firm was unsatisfactory, and the number of complaints increased. Tremblay decided to buy up all of the firm's shares and look for a new manager. After several unsuccessful contacts in Ontario, he approached Jean-Claude Robillard.

Robillard had been with Tremcar for twenty years, and his career path was very similar to that of Hébert, who knew the area well. Robillard was given half the shares in the new firm, to be known as JC Tanks & Repair. Tremcar's president financed all equipment purchases.

The two shareholders agreed on the services to be provided and the responsibilities of each party. Robillard also continued as Tremcar's representative in that area. In return, Tremblay made Tremcar's entire administrative and technical expertise available to his new manager and partner, but was unable to visit the new company as often as he had done for Hébert's company, now Hébert and Son. Nevertheless, the trust remained strong, despite the distance.

In the space of a few years, Tremcar's contribution to the Toronto firm's turnover fell to about 25 percent of its total turnover – a level similar to that for Hébert and Son. However, JC Tanks & Repair faces a very different market dynamic from its Saint-Athanase counterpart, since it has much larger customer volume and more competitors. Even so, the firm, with its eight employees, has carved itself a niche in the sector.

ACKNOWLEDGMENT

This case study was contributed by Caroline Mireault, Danielle Luc and Louis Jacques Filion, Rogers-J.-A. Bombardier Chair of Entrepreneurship, HEC Montréal, Canada.

QUESTIONS FOR DISCUSSION

1   What are the differences between the spin-offs in terms of opportunity exploitation and management? Explain.
2   What are the core topics represented in all of Jacques Tremblay's spin-offs? Explain these similarities.
3   What were the conditions that prompted the creation of the spin-offs? Was it 'luck' or planned and strategic management?
4   What are Jacques Tremblay's main characteristics that could initially indicate that he would become a creator of multiple spin-offs?
5   What is the concentration strategy underlying the spin-off process in a company?
6   Analyze how a partnership between an employer and an employee can be developed into the creation of a spin-off; do you consider this a 'recommended formula'? Explain the strengths and weaknesses of such a process.
7   What are the main benefits of the spin-off process, for the source company and for the spin-off?

BORN-GLOBAL ENTREPRENEURS

The born-global entrepreneur is a new breed of entrepreneur, represented by individuals who are the ambitious antithesis to the 'stay-at-home' type, those who are looking to sell their products around the world from 'day one'. This phenomenon is relatively rare as it involves greater risks and greater complexity than the 'usual' entrepreneurial type. The reasons for the increasing prevalence of born-global entrepreneurs are complex; the known models of many successful newer industries that have never been strongly segmented into domestic markets probably have a positive influence on the orientation toward internationalization. In addition, the continuous acceleration of consumer demand for various and highly differentiated products is deemed to have great potential for the capture of even the unexpected customers all over the world, where large international competitors are unwilling or unable to respond to those demands. The rapid drop in the cost of long-distance communication and the widespread availability of the internet make developing a presence in a geographically distant market possible and commonplace. Hence more diverse entrepreneurial opportunities emerge; knowledge-sharing between businesses develops, as do production possibilities, sales and distribution systems. Together, these enable value production in new and innovative ways.

To guarantee success for born-global entrepreneurial businesses, a carefully planned and systematic utilization of the various e-networking and international business and entrepreneurial websites is recommended.

285

Figure 15.1 shows the necessary stages which born-global entrepreneurs should consider in their internationalization process (Bell, McNaughton and Young 2001; Bell et al. 2003; Oviatt and McDougall 2005; Rialp et al. 2005; Freeman and Cavusgil 2007).

Best practices:

- Think 'big' but acquire cross-cultural awareness and understanding.
- Acquire a high level of expertise in speaking several languages, especially English; in addition to the language, understand the culture, habits, manners and main market values.
- Thoroughly study the destination markets, i.e., the level of purchase affordability, market saturation point, the process of production, among others.
- Establish stable, trustworthy and widespread networks prior to launching ventures.
- Use 'global knowledge'; for example, the use of 'networking-oriented' websites may generate two different advantages: first, collecting formal and informal information on the destination's regulations; second, being part of groups of people around the world with mutual interests and sometimes identical experiences, who are usually keen to assist one another.

ENTREPRENEURS IN FAMILY BUSINESSES

A common form of entrepreneurship is the family business, where family members are involved, actively and financially, in the business, and the business succession is mostly an internal, family process. The business is considered an asset that will bring value to the family in providing ongoing employment and earnings, sustainability of the family tradition and maintenance of family union. Family members have a powerful sense of mission accomplishment; they are usually the beneficiaries of tough on-the-job training in the business from early adolescence as well as superb academic educations. Their intensive meetings (family celebrations, holidays, etc.) facilitate positive communication 'across the dinner table' and this may promote a general atmosphere that is

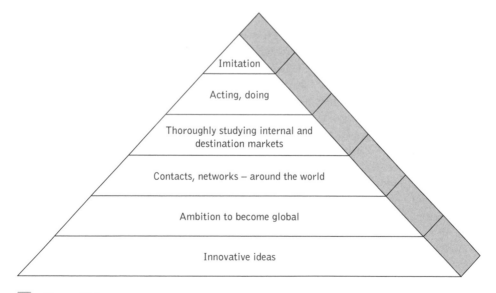

Figure 15.1 *The born-global model*

conducive to cultivating ideas and decisions as well as acquiring the necessary feedback on their business and work.

At the market level, the observable advantages of family businesses are in turning to a key source of funding for new startups and spin-offs that create employment and promote economic and technological progress. Ford, duPont, Marriott, and W.R. Grace are only a few examples of family businesses in today's market. Nevertheless, the advantages attributed to family businesses may be shadowed by the many unique problems encountered by family members when they are part of a family business; it is said that family businesses can 'unleash some disastrous demons'. Moreover, only one in three family businesses succeeds in making it from the first to the second generation. Difficulties in separating bottom-line calculations from family emotions, the case of recruiting and firing 'workers' (i.e., family members) from the business on a professional basis, the succession dilemmas, generation conflicts, inter and intra conflicts (of nuclear family versus other family members, or of members with biological ties versus ties through marriage), and decision-making processes, among others, are leading factors in the demise of family businesses. The combination of business and family affects the quality of family life, especially when families become excessively associated with their business, and suggesting a sale, for example, is akin to announcing a death in the family (Brockhaus 1994; Shepherd and Zacharakis 2000; Hall, Melin and Nordqvist 2001; Heck 2004; Dyer and Mortensen 2005).

Best practice:

- Family businesses will succeed only by emphasizing their very unique characteristics: cherish, maintain and manage this uniqueness. In some families, uniqueness comes from knowing each other very well, in others, it is loyalty and commitment to the business, and in still others, the business is a symbol of tradition and inheritance.
- The benefits of being a family (e.g., loyalty, communication) should be the guiding beacon for family businesses.
- Set very strict, non-emotional rules to guarantee success and growth in the family business, i.e., having a clear mission keeps the family members focused and reduces over-sentimentalized communication; recruitment and career ladders should be well established (e.g., family members are entitled to a job in the family business only if their performance matches the business's needs, etc).
- Make an effort to place a number of non-family members in key management positions.
- Plan succession early on, in an orderly and open way.
- Estate planning is critical, i.e., the task of transitioning financial assets and managing federal estate tax obligations.
- Most important, outside counseling is helpful, as opposed to 'keeping internal matters within the family'.

WOMEN ENTREPRENEURS

Academic research is continuously providing empirical evidence for the gender-based difficulties faced by women trying to establish and maintain a business, probably as a result of several factors, such as inflexible childcare facilities and difficulties in reconciling business and family obligations, women's initial choices of business type and sector, lack of contacts and access to goal-oriented networking, and gender discrimination in acquiring financial support. Along with these difficulties, many women choose entrepreneurship as a path to escape unemployment or under-employment, especially while attempting to return to the market following the birth of a child, or as a path that enables combining family and work responsibilities and still controlling time and task priorities. Statistical figures based on numerous academic studies show that female entrepreneurship is higher than male entrepreneurship among homemakers, people who transform their hobbies into businesses, those who run a business as a sideline to their other employment, and individuals who treat their entrepreneurial ventures as a realization of an old dream. Ayla Demirbat,[5] a woman entrepreneur from Turkey, is the owner of a small business for embroidery, lacework and traditional handcrafting for dowries. She is cited at a women entrepreneurs' website as saying: 'I started my business in the field that I loved. I think that dedication to work is an important factor for success'; Judy Rosenberg, owner of the Boston bakery chain Rosie's Bakery,[6] started her business on a whim on Valentine's Day, and for the first few months she worked from her home kitchen, dragging hundred-pound bags of flour up to her second-floor apartment and baking her goods; she went on instinct and passion rather than business smarts and faced 'ups and downs'. Many women entrepreneurs tell their stories by addressing the realization of their home-hobby dream in launching their ventures. Today, it is well known that these differences between the genders, in both their motivation to start a business and their perceptions of what ownership entails, impact upon how their businesses grow and how they are able to benefit from business support. In fact, the dilemma of whether to dedicate unique support for women entrepreneurs is encountered among both men and women entrepreneurs; supporters of gender-based assistance programs claim that such programs are very relevant to women in typifying and handling their unique perceptions, attitudes, motivations and constraints, while supporters of the generic assistance programs weigh in against gender-based programs which reinforce the already existing inequality of men and women in entrepreneurship. By supporting only women, these programs limit their ability to actually cope with the difficulties they encounter; moreover, specific programs are established for relatively weak or powerless groups which seem to need support, and this should not be the message for women in entrepreneurship (Stevenson 1990; Buttner 1993; Gerrard, Schoch and Cunningham 2003; Heilbrunn 2004; Godwin, Stevens and Brenner 2006; Manolova et al. 2007).

A number of websites provide information for women entrepreneurs.[7]

Best practice:

- Establish relevant and trustworthy networks.
- Go through training and counseling.
- Take part in associations where women can learn from other businesswomen, decipher their key success factors and follow in their footsteps.
- Seek assistance in anything that can help in establishing the business, e.g., help at home or help in the business.

AT A GLANCE 15.1   Torsten LLP, a women's law firm, Sweden

Agnes Torsten is a forty-three-year-old lawyer who manages a unique law office committed to the mission of non-discrimination on the basis of gender, race, national origin, religion, age, sexual orientation, or disability. Additionally, Torsten is involved in the human rights movement in Sweden; she founded the movement for female participation in politics; she initiated the establishment of an active committee in one of the government bureaus on anti-discriminatory employment practices with respect to individuals' sexual orientation; she is an active columnist on women's issues and a member of several international committees for women's rights.

Torsten is the founder of Torsten LLP, which is a law firm employing mostly women lawyers and administrators, as well as a few men. The firm's focus is on women's rights and its mission is in advancing any woman, in any case and under any circumstances. Torsten and her team are strong supporters of the American 'No Glass Ceiling' initiative. Torsten LLP provides advice and representation free of charge to women who cannot afford it. 'Many women still experience gender bias difficulties in the practice of law, while men perceive these barriers as having been broken down; but this is not the case: female lawyers consistently report receiving fewer opportunities to enter big companies or to advance within their companies. There is a clear sex-based bias against women lawyers, and we are here to make a change. This is our social mission, rather than advertising or a business mission', says Torsten.

As such, Torsten LLP's organization is based on equal opportunity, and all decisions related to HR personnel are based solely on the individual's qualifications and productivity. For example, more than 55 percent of Torsten LLP associates are women and one is an immigrant; more than half of Torsten LLP board members are women, some are minorities and one is a disabled man; 80 percent of the group leaders in the firm's practice are female or minorities and more that 80 percent of the firm's administrative leaders are female, some of an advanced age; all of the firm's office managers are women, including immigrants and older individuals; and half of Torsten LLP shareholders are women. Torsten LLP does not discriminate on any basis, including gender, in its recruitment or career-path determinations; and the standards for joining and promotion at Torsten LLP are openly presented to all.

In addition, Torsten and her team are very involved in community activities, and they personally visit the Women's Centers in disadvantaged neighborhoods to offer assistance – mostly free of charge. Torsten is also involved in politics, and assists other women in their entry into politics or high-status jobs and positions by representing them, professionally advising them and providing services that complement their advancement. Torsten also places a heavy emphasis on immigration, and her immigration department comprises women professionals who are fluent in various foreign languages including Spanish, French, Russian, Korean, Chinese and more. Some of the lawyers are immigrants, as Torsten is a strong supporter of providing ethnic immigrants with equal employment opportunities.

Torsten LLP's internal structuring is also unique. Although Torsten has never been married and has never given birth, she is very sensitive to maternity issues; now, after adopting a baby girl from Columbia, she is even more dedicated to these topics. She encourages her employees to bring their children in after school: there is a wonderful daycare center in the building that she launched specifically for this purpose; working hours are flexible and working from home is encouraged. Additionally, employees are encouraged to recommend their relatives and friends as applicants for jobs at the firm. Torsten explains that 'since most of our day is spent in the office, why not spend it with our loved ones?'

Torsten LLP is a very successful law firm, which has many offices in Sweden and two that were launched in two other Scandinavian countries. Torsten believes in her vision. She says,

'I have always been considered different; so I took the risk in establishing a "different" organizational atmosphere and a different environment for groups that need it.'

Mompreneurs. A distinct and budding feature of women entrepreneurship is mompreneurship; broadly, it addresses mothers who have entrepreneurial ambitions but either do not want, or are unable to go out and launch a business. Mompreneurship is much more than mothers launching home-based businesses; these are mothers who use their maternal intincts and motherhood capabilities to launch and develop an entrepreneurial business. Many mothers report a feeling of sacrificing the quality of their involvement with their families when they go out to work, and therefore avoid taking a job. Yet, some of them experience frustration, dissatisfaction and a feeling of missing out on the self-actualization that can come from having a job. Mompreneurship is thus a suitable alternative, especially because these mothers are not going into entrepreneurship just to make some money; mothers have critical entrepreneurial skills such as patience, vigor and persistence, and they know how to prioritize and master schedules (Monosoff 2005); this set of skills characterizes entrepreneurial capabilities and can be successfully transformed into the initiation and management of an entrepreneurial business. There are still very limited studies and empirical cases written on this interesting phenomenon, but there are some websites that address topics related to mompreneurship.[8]

ENTREPRENEURSHIP FOR PEOPLE WITH DISABILITIES

Many disabled people have already created opportunities for themselves through entrepreneurship. In fact, according to the US Census Bureau, people with disabilities are nearly twice as likely to be self-employed as the general population, 14.7 percent compared to 8 percent in the United States. The benefits of entrepreneurship for these individuals lie mostly in their independence and in the opportunity to make their own business decisions, the ability to set their own pace and schedule, and the avoidance of prejudice and stereotypes that are sometimes found in the recruiting process, resulting in unemployment or underemployment. The reduction in transportation problems when a business is home-based is a critical benefit as well.

People with disabilities often confront barriers when attempting to start entrepreneurial ventures, especially in accessing the capital needed to start a business, because they lack satisfactory credit or assets to use as collateral for a loan. In some cases, they may not have the information or resources required to develop a business plan, an effective route to economic independence for their clients, and more. Yet, through creative thinking and leveraging of existing resources, disabled people are helping to break down these barriers via partnerships, learning, or creating their entrepreneurial businesses in areas in which they have a competitive advantage over non-disabled entrepreneurs, for example: selling disabled accessories and aids, developing computer-related accessories for disabled users, or employing other people with disabilities in their businesses. Tran Hoang Yen from Vietnam, a disabled woman, runs her own shop and has become a successful entrepreneur, employing seventeen disadvantaged young people – more than half of whom are women with disabilities – in her small sewing shop (Baez and Abolafia 2002; Lemon and Lemon 2003; Maes and Basu 2005; Rogoff 2007).

There are associations and websites that provide information for entrepreneurs with disabilities.[9]

Best practice:

- Proactiveness and determination to enter entrepreneurship are beneficial in the long run.
- Potential entrepreneurs should apply to the numerous associations and societies that assist specific populations in specialized financing and business counseling, training and mentoring to support small and medium-sized businesses, education options, and relevant contacts.
- Partnership may be a beneficial entrepreneurial way for people with disabilities to break into the market with their businesses and to ease the management responsibilities (for example, when there is a need to travel).
- Recruit other people with disabilities, giving these people a chance and relevant experience.
- Adopt a diversified business attitude: employees, clients and suppliers of different genders, races and disabilities, among others, are welcome in your business.
- Be a role model for potential entrepreneurs with disabilities.

SOCIAL ENTREPRENEURS

Social entrepreneurs are 'changemakers' – individuals with innovative solutions to society's most pressing social problems, offering new ideas for wide-scale change rather than leaving societal needs to the government or business sectors. These entrepreneurs re-invent themselves as social entrepreneurs by combining the passion of a social mission with an image of businesslike discipline, innovation, and determination. In the face of the global phenomenon of new philanthropic reality, new for-profit businesses are competing with non-profit organizations to serve global and community needs, and funders and donors are demanding more accountability. An increasing number of non-profit businesses are beginning to appreciate the increased revenue and effectiveness that can come from adopting for-profit business approaches.

Social entrepreneurs are both visionaries and the ultimate realists: they are restless people who 'want to change the world', concerned with the practical implementation of their vision above all else. They act as agents of change for society, seizing opportunities, identifying global problems and improving systems, inventing new approaches, and creating solutions, all to change society for the better. A deep unwavering belief in their innate capacity to contribute meaningfully to economic and social development and a passion to make that happen, drive social entrepreneurs to manage their ventures towards social change. They typically measure their success in terms of the impact they have on society; however, although seeking primarily to generate social value rather than profits, they manage their ventures in a business-oriented, practical fashion, often using market principles and forces. Data, both quantitative and qualitative, are their key tools, guiding continuous feedback and improvement.

One very well-recognized example of social entrepreneurship is the rock band U2's social activity. A clothing company founded by Irish rocker and humanitarian Bono and his wife has partnered with college students in Ohio on a business project that they expect to expand to other campuses around the world.[10] Students at Miami University's Center for Social Entrepreneurship buy blank cotton T-shirts made in Africa and resell the shirts to other organizations. The students make some profit, while providing a market to help build trade and employment in Africa. Bono, the front man for U2, has gained international attention with his efforts to assist developing countries, especially Africa. He and his wife, Ali Hewson, founded Edun Apparel in 2005 to produce clothing in developing countries, providing increased trade and jobs to those areas (Barendsen and Gardner 2004; Bornstein 2004; Dean and McMullen 2007; Shaw and Carter 2007).

Ashoka,[11] Schwab,[12] Heroes[13] and many other institutions support social entrepreneurs at the launch stage, by providing them with a living stipend that allows them to focus full-time on building their institutions, spreading their ideas, and networking with global support networks of their peers and partnerships with professional consultants.

Best practice:

- To encourage social entrepreneurship, academic institutions should incorporate 'learning by doing' and 'learning by experience' models in their entrepreneurship programs, along with leadership studies and business-oriented approaches to social entrepreneurship.
- Students and active entrepreneurs wishing to contribute to society may join social entrepreneurship groups and contact social entrepreneurship networks and forums.
- Seek strategic partners.
- Some institutions provide strategic advisory and counseling assistance, and assist in 'real-time research', backing the entrepreneur with the needed skills, building some possible scenarios and providing the research tools to achieve the planned research goals.

AT A GLANCE 15.2   SOCIAL ENTREPRENEURSHIP, DUBAI

Ryan Chopra, from Dubai, is the successor of a chain of hotels in the United Arab Emirates, headquartered in Dubai City. Chopra manages some of the hotels and is the person in charge of social entrepreneurship. Chopra is thirty years old, multilingual and highly educated: most of his childhood was spent in the UK where he and his brothers attended highly qualified private schools; he then completed his studies at the army academy and went on to complete studies in financing at a prestigious university in the UK.

Chopra returned to Dubai with his wife Julie, an English teacher by profession, and together they founded a non-profit organization whose main mission was to set up schools to teach computer skills to low-income communities in Dubai. The rationale was that learning these skills would enable residents from these areas to move into society's mainstream and improve their prospects. Julie used her expertise in teaching to establish a well-structured educational plan for children and adults; they then used specialists, educational program developers in computers, and crafted an inclusive annual program. State-of-the-art computers were purchased for the program and the selected locations for the schools were first renovated and modified according to specific guidelines: Julie believes that 'for a full understanding and adaptation of educational material, the setting should be friendly and comfortable'. The floors were covered with special rugs; ergonomic furniture was chosen; the rooms were decorated, and a familiar, warm and welcoming environment was established. The pilot was run in a highly non-advanced, poor community and the first wave of participants consisted of adolescents from twelve to nineteen years of age. Teachers and psychologists were hired to be involved in the transfer of knowledge, which was headed by Julie. The results were better than expected; for example, the web course was planned for ten sessions but more than 80 percent of the participants acquired the web techniques in seven sessions; all (!) participants passed the final exam, and word-processing skills were also acquired very quickly. The second wave, consisting of adults, was also successful, although not to the same extent. Julie decided to purchase more computers and have some of the participants take them home to practice their skills. The pilot was very successful and the Chopras extended the project to other communities, all having the same characteristics in terms of socioeconomic status. More than 60,000 people – adults and children – have received computer training in these programs in Dubai; and the Chopras plan to broaden the project's scope to training these people in job-related skills – without sacrificing quality or losing sight of its original objectives. There are different types of entrepreneurial avenues (e.g., serial entrepreneurship, multiple entrepreneurship, franchising, mompreneurship), each having unique goals and practices. These avenues allow more individuals to engage in entrepreneurship by either including more individuals who currently work in non-entrepreneurial businesses or minimizing entrepreneur drop-out from entrepreneurial paths, by simply proposing a different avenue in entrepreneurship.

Like any entrepreneurial way, each avenue requires innovation, creativity, opportunity exploitation or exploration; and like any other entrepreneurial business, each avenue is potentially a leading, sustainable business. The innovation in developing such avenues in the entrepreneurial realm is in allowing the flexibility that many entrepreneurs need, with each avenue focusing on unique factors (flexibility in location, sector, number of businesses, roles in the different businesses, etc.) and using different practices (e.g., owner, manager, investor, counselor, professional counsultant, mixed roles) to accomplish it; in this way, entrepreneurs may find the path best suited to their needs. For example, individuals who identify their strength in initiation while their weakness is in administrative tasks may switch from 'classical' entreprenership (i.e., launching a business, managing it for a long time) to multipreneurship or managing spin-offs; women entrepreneurs who become mothers may switch to mompreneurship rather than dropping out of entrepreneurship entirely.

Different programs are being developed for the different avenues of entrepreneurship to facilitate the entrepreneur's route and attract potential entrepreneurs.

NOTES

1 NASE, National Association for Self-employed, www.nase.org/.
2 Entrepreneur.com, www.entrepreneur.com/franchises/buyingafranchise/franchisebasics/article7 0494.html.
3 British Franchise Association, www.british-franchise.org/; Citylocal UK, www.citylocal.co.uk/; Entreprenurs.com, www.entrepreneur.com/franchises/index.html; Franchise Classroom, www.bus.lsu.edu/ei/franchiseclass/pages/ForBook/title.html; Franchise.com, www.franchise.com/; Franchise Gator, www.franchisegator.com/; Franchise Opportunities, www.franchiseopportunities.com/; IFA, www.franchise.org/.
4 EDB Singapore, www.edb.gov.sg/edb/sg/en_uk/index.html; Emboss Technopreneurs, www.emboss-tech.com/vision.html; Israel Chief Scientist (OCS) of the Ministry of Industry Trade and Labor, www.moit.gov.il/NR/exeres/111E3D45-56E4-4752-BD27-F544B171B19A.htm; MSC Global Technopreneurs Network (MGTN), www.technopreneurdevelopment.net.my/cms/; Technopreneurs' Association of Malaysia (TeAM), www.team.net.my.
5 Women Entrepreneurs – Turkey, www.unece.org/operact/gallery/tr/tr-gal.htm.

6 Women Entrepreneurs, WEinc., www.we-inc.org/2071-500.2071-041505Z.html.
7 AFAEMME, Association of Organizations of Mediterranean Businesswomen, www.afaemme.org; BPW Danube Net – Business and Professional Women (BPW), www.bpw-europe.org, www.bpw-international.org; FEM, Female Europeans of Medium and Small Enterprises, www.fem-pme.com; FemStart, www.femstart.eu/; Plateforme Entreprendre au féminin (Women Entrepreneurs' platform), entreprendre-au-feminin.net; PROWESS, Promoting Women's Enterprise Support Services, www.prowess.org.uk; ProWomEn, Promotion of Women Entrepreneurship, www.pro women-eu.net; WENETT, Women Innovators for Europe, www.wenett.eu/; Women into the Network (WIN), networkingwomen.co.uk.
8 At www.themompreneur.com/; www.entrepreneur.com/mompreneur.
9 Alberta Centre on Entrepreneurship and Disabilities, www.ucalgary.ca/~aced/; CCDS at www.disabilitystudies.ca/vol2no1.htm; Disability.gov, www.disability.gov; HalfthePlanet.com, www.halftheplanet.com; NEWD, the Network for Entrepreneurs with Disabilities of Nova Scotia, www.entrepreneurdisability.org; ODEP, US Department of Commerce, Office of Disability Employment Policy, and SBSES, the Small Business and Self Employment Service, www.dol.gov/dol/odep/; SEDA, www.seda.org.za/content.asp?subId=266; the Abilities Fund, www.abilities fund.org; the Disabled Businesspersons' Association, www.disabledbusiness.com/; Western Economic Diversification Canada, Entrepreneurs with Disabilities Program, www.wd.gc.ca/eng/finance/programs/EDP.html.
10 At www.u2france.com/spip.php?article9889.
11 Ashoka Innovators for the Public, www.ashoka.org/social_entrepreneur.
12 The Schwab Foundation for Social Entrepreneurship, www.schwabfound.org/.
13 Heroes, www.pbs.org/opb/thenewheroes/whatis/.

REFERENCES

Arenius, P. and Kovalainen, A. (2006) 'Similarities and differences across the factors associated with women's self-employment preference in the Nordic countries', *International Small Business Journal*, 24: 31–59.

Baez, B. and Abolafia, M.Y. (2002) 'Bureaucratic entrepreneurship and institutional change: a sense-making approach', *Journal of Public Administration Research and Theory*, 12: 525–52.

Barendsen, L. and Gardner, H. (2004) 'Is the social entrepreneur a new type of leader?', *Leader to Leader*, 34: 43–50.

Barton, H.H. (2000) 'Does entrepreneurship pay? An empirical analysis of the returns to self-employment', *Journal of Political Economy*, 108: 604–31.

Bell, J., McNaughton, R. and Young, S. (2001) '"Born-again global" firms: an extension to the "born global" phenomenon', *Journal of International Management*, 7: 173–89.

Bell, J., McNaughton, R., Young, S. and Crick, D. (2003) 'Towards an integrative model of small firm internationalisation', *Journal of International Entrepreneurship*, 1: 339–62.

Bornstein, D. (2004) *How to Change the World: Social Entrepreneurs and the Power of New Ideas*, New York: Oxford University Press.

Brockhaus, R.H. (1994) 'Entrepreneurship and family business research: comparisons', *Entrepreneurship Theory and Practice*, 19: 25–38.

Buttner, E.H. (1993) 'Female entrepreneurs: how far have they come?', *Business Horizons*, 36: 59–65.

Dean, T.J. and McMullen, J.S. (2007) 'Toward a theory of sustainable entrepreneurship: reducing environmental degradation through entrepreneurial action', *Journal of Business Venturing*, 22: 50–76.

Dyer, W.G. and Mortensen, S.P. (2005) 'Entrepreneurship and family business in a hostile environment: the case of Lithuania', *Family Business Review*, 18: 247–58.

Falbe, C.M., Dandridge, T.C. and Kumar, A. (1999) 'The effect of organizational context on entrepreneurial strategies in franchising', *Journal of Business Venturing*, 14: 125–40.

Freeman, S. and Cavusgil, S.T. (2007) 'Toward a typology of commitment states among managers of born-global firms: a study of accelerated internationalization', *Journal of International Marketing*, 15: 1–40.

Gerrard, P., Schoch, H. and Cunningham, J.B. (2003) 'Values and skills of female entrepreneurs in Vietnam: an exploratory study', *Asia Pacific Business Review*, 10: 139–59.

Godwin, L.N., Stevens, C.E. and Brenner, N.L. (2006) 'Forced to play by the rules? Theorizing how mixed-sex founding teams benefit women entrepreneurs in male-dominated contexts', *Entrepreneurship Theory and Practice*, 30: 623–42.

Greene, F.J. (2002) 'An investigation into enterprise support for younger people, 1975–2000', *International Small Business Journal*, 20: 315–36.

Hall, A., Melin, L. and Nordqvist, M. (2001) 'Entrepreneurship as radical change in the family business: exploring the role of cultural patterns', *Family Business Review*, 14: 193–208.

Heck, R.Z. (2004) 'A commentary on "Entrepreneurship in family versus non-family firms: a resource-based analysis of the effect of organizational culture"', *Entrepreneurship Theory and Practice*, 28: 383–9.

Heilbrunn, S. (2004) 'Impact of gender on difficulties faced by entrepreneurs', *International Journal of Entrepreneurship and Innovation*, 5: 159–65.

Jones-Evans, D. (1996) 'Technical entrepreneurship, strategy and experience', *International Small Business Journal*, 14: 15–39.

Lemon, C. and Lemon, J. (2003) 'Community-based cooperative ventures for adults with intellectual disabilities', *Canadian Geographer*, 47: 414–28.

Lo, T., Liou, S. and Yuan, B. (2005) 'Organisation innovation and entrepreneurship: the role of the national laboratories in promoting industrial development', *International Journal of Technology Management*, 30: 67–84.

Maes, J. and Basu, M. (2005) 'Building economic self-reliance: trickle-up's microenterprise seed capital for the extreme poor in rural India', *Journal of Microfinance*, 7: 71–99.

Manolova, T.S., Carter, N.M., Manev, I.M. and Gyoshev, B.S. (2007) 'The differential effect of men and women entrepreneurs' human capital and networking on growth expectancies in Bulgaria', *Entrepreneurship Theory and Practice*, 31: 407–26.

Monosoff, T. (2005) *The Mom Inventor's Handbook: How to Turn your Great Idea into the Next Big Thing*, 1st edn, New York: McGraw-Hill.

Ngwenya, T.I. (2007) 'The integration of business with entrepreneurship as a subject to enhance entrepreneurial competency', *Business Review*, 7: 305–9.

Norton, S.W. (1988) 'Franchising, brand name capital, and the entrepreneurial capacity problem', *Strategic Management Journal*, 9: 105–14.

Oakey, R.P. (2003) 'Technical entrepreneurship in high technology small firms: some observations on the implications for management', *Technovation*, 23: 679–88.

Oviatt, M. and McDougall, P.P. (2005) 'Defining international entrepreneurship and modeling the speed of internationalization', *Entrepreneurship Theory and Practice*, 29: 537–53.

Pasanen, M. (2003) 'Multiple entrepreneurship among successful SMEs in peripheral locations', *Journal of Small Business and Enterprise Development*, 10: 418–25.

Rae, D. (2004) 'Practical theories from entrepreneurs' stories: discursive approaches to entrepreneurial learning', *Journal of Small Business and Enterprise Development*, 11: 195–202.

Rialp, A., Rialp, J., Urbano, D. and Vaillant, Y. (2005) 'The born-global phenomenon: a comparative case study research', *Journal of International Entrepreneurship*, 3: 133–71.

Rogoff, E.G. (2007) 'Opportunities for entrepreneurship in later life', *Generations*, 31: 90–5.

Rosti, L. and Chelli, F. (2005) 'Gender discrimination, entrepreneurial talent and self-employment', *Small Business Economics*, 24: 131–42.

Scheutz, C. (1986) 'Critical events for Swedish entrepreneurs in entrepreneurial spin-offs', *Technovation*, 5: 169–82.

Shane, S. (2004) *Academic Entrepreneurship: University Spin-offs and Wealth Creation*, Northampton, MA: Edward Elgar.

Shaw, E. and Carter, S. (2007) 'Social entrepreneurship; theoretical antecedents and empirical analysis of entrepreneurial processes and outcomes', *Journal of Small Business and Enterprise Development*, 14: 418–34.

Shepherd, D.A. and Zacharakis, A. (2000) 'Structuring family business succession: an analysis of the future leader's decision making', *Entrepreneurship Theory and Practice*, 24: 25–39.

Singh, G. and DeNoble, A. (2003a) 'Views on self-employment and personality: an exploratory study', *Journal of Developmental Entrepreneurship*, 8: 265–81.

Singh, G. and DeNoble, A. (2003b) 'Early retirees as the next generation of entrepreneurs', *Entrepreneurship Theory and Practice*, 27: 207–26.

Spinelli, S. (2007) 'Franchises without borders', *Business Strategy Review*, 18: 50–2.

Stevenson, L. (1990) 'Some methodological problems associated with researching women entrepreneurs', *Journal of Business Ethics*, 9: 439–46.

Tubke, A., De Toledo Saavedra, P.A. and Gonzalez, J. (2004) 'Towards a first spin-off typology and a new concept for corporate spin-off research', *International Journal of Technology Transfer and Commercialisation*, 3: 263–90.

Tuunanen, M. and Hyrsky, K. (2001) 'Entrepreneurial paradoxes in business format franchising: an empirical survey of Finnish franchisees', *International Small Business Journal*, 19: 47–62.

Ucbasaran, D., Westhead, P. and Wright, M. (2006) *Habitual Entrepreneurs*, Aldershot: Edward Elgar.

Westhead, P. and Wright, M. (1998a) 'Novice, portfolio, and serial founders in rural and urban areas', *Entrepreneurship Theory and Practice*, 22: 63–100.

Westhead, P. and Wright, M. (1998b) 'Novice, portfolio, and serial founders: are the different?', *Journal of Business Venturing*, 13: 173–204.

Westhead, P., Ucbasaran, D. and Wright, M. (2005) 'Experience and cognition: do novice, serial and portfolio entrepreneurs differ?', *International Small Business Journal*, 23: 72–98.

Westhead, P., Ucbasaran, D., Wright, M. and Binks, M. (2005) 'Novice, serial and portfolio entrepreneur behaviour and contributions', *Small Business Economics*, 25: 109–32.

Zucker, G.L., Darby, M.R. and Torero, M. (2002) 'Labor mobility from academe to commerce', *Journal of Labor Economics*, 20: 629–60.

Chapter 16

The reshaping of today's entrepreneurial activities

OBJECTIVES

After studying this chapter you will be able to:

- See today's entrepreneur through a holistic overview, as exploiting and spawning opportunities, creating economic and social prosperity within societies and doing things that make a difference. They are today's agents of change.
- Explain the different environment-related elements that influence the entrepreneurial action and their impact on the profile of today's entrepreneur.
- Recognize the support and drive that the labor market offers individuals to attract them to entrepreneurship, including a change in psychological contracts, probing for and enhancing creativity and innovation in the market, and conceiving of entrepreneurship as the choice of a successful path rather than a trash bin for the unemployed.
- Sympathize more easily with entrepreneurs and the entrepreneurial course, and look at this path as a desirable one that induces success and self-accomplishment and enables flexibility, work–life balance and combining interests in the entrepreneurial path.

In the past, owners of business ventures were concerned with profitability, survival and sustainability. The entrepreneurs of today want much more than that. They aspire to grow and to lead, to be unique, and to acquire or develop expertise in specific domains; they seek unexploited niches. Beyond expressing their creative ideas, they want to make a difference. Bolton and Thompson (2004) define today's entrepreneurs as far different from their 'traditional' predecessors. They:

- See opportunities and bring them to fruition.
- Create economic and social prosperity within societies.
- Do things that make a difference.
- Are agents of change.

Entrepreneurial action – the launching and running of a venture – is the end result of the entrepreneur's tangible and intangible *resources*, perceived opportunities in accordance with *market* conditions and demands, general *values* and attitudes toward entrepreneurship, and the entrepreneur's own *personal values* (Thompson 2004a, b).

Different and multifaceted aspects of the environment – societal, cultural and economic – all affect the profile of today's 'typical' entrepreneur. Figure 16.2 and the discussion that follows it address these effects.

CHANGING EMPLOYMENT STRUCTURES

The once pervasive view that entrepreneurship is the 'garbage can for unemployed people' has either vanished or is in the process of vanishing all over the world. In its place, a wide-ranging social acceptance of entrepreneurship, as both a career and an economically desirable national asset, is emerging, and it is even being promoted by government and educational institutions in a steadily increasing number of countries. Entrepreneurship has become a preferred career path for individuals with different occupations, educational levels and degrees of employability.

Its social legitimacy and wide public acceptance have led entrepreneurship to become a specialized field in educational, professional and government programs, and academic programs have been, and continue to be, designed by all of these interested bodies. In addition, not only do academic institutions and labor and industrial Ministries support active entrepreneurs, they also actively encourage potential ones. More recently, attempts have been made to identify entrepreneurial traits or competencies in individuals that may enable them to turn to successful careers as entrepreneurs, even among students in the lower grades at school (O'Donoghue and Townshend 2005).

THE CHANGING PSYCHOLOGICAL CONTRACT

The mutual expectations of employees and employers, which is one of the main components of the psychological contract, have changed dramatically over the years, and some researchers consider the totality of the changes a radical metamorphosis. Entrepreneurship and the psychological contract

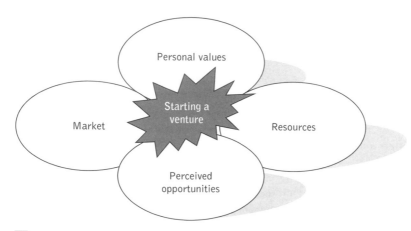

Figure 16.1 *Elements that influence entrepreneurial action*

Source: Modified from Timmons et al. (1987); Krueger (1998, 2000)

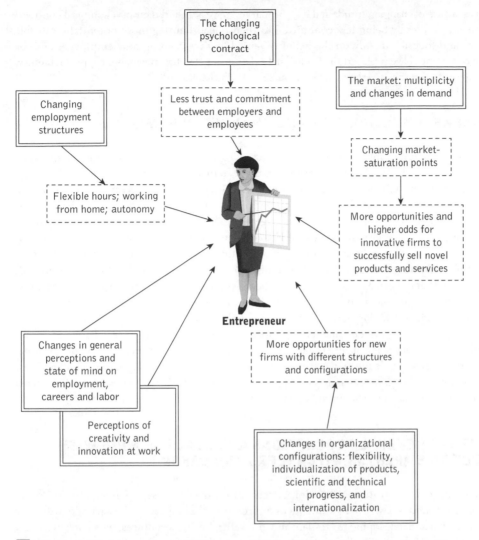

Figure 16.2 *From macro to micro: aspects of the environment that shape the entrepreneur of today*

have mutual and interconnected effects, with each causing the other to change and to expand. Job insecurity, one of the major components of the psychological contract, was once widely considered to be the threat of unemployment, and therefore loss of livelihood, and even social rejection. Today, neither the employer, be it an individual or an organization, nor the employee, are fully committed to the other, and 'having a job' has more recently undergone a virtual transmutation into the now common and more acceptable 'employment state'. However, when entrepreneurial opportunities exist, and are beneficial and highly evaluated, job insecurity is no longer an existential threat and, as a result, different psychological contracts between employees and employers have been emerging. From the employees' standpoint, quitting an active job is simpler and less life-threatening than in the past; commitment to employers or corporations has become minimal while the demands that labor has imposed upon management in the corporate market have increased exponentially.

Employers, aware of changing trends in the labor market, have adjusted their psychological contracts with their employees by being less committed to them: head-hunting more potentially valuable employees and focusing mainly on the benefits gained from recruiting new employees and/or releasing older ones have replaced the traditional relations of stability, permanence, predictability, loyalty and mutual respect (Argyris 1960; Rousseau 1995; Kickul 2001).

THE MARKET: MULTIPLICITY AND CHANGES IN DEMAND

A major danger that entrepreneurs face when launching and running a venture is the market's saturation level, which occurs when there is a limited demand for, or an oversupply of specific new products or services and/or the consumers' purchasing power decreases.[1] The points of saturation in today's markets, however, are continually changing, a fact that can be a major advantage for potential entrepreneurs as it increases business opportunities. Such opportunities can be the result of one or several concurrent changes in the market: increasing demand from new customers; readiness to purchase almost any new product and/or service; constantly changing tastes; the obsolescence of loyalty to old and familiar products or trademarks; dissatisfaction with existing products and services, and demands for both better quality and greater variety. The most important and potent change of all, however, in both developed and developing nations, is increasingly greater purchasing power, with more people being more willing and more able than in the past to pay for new products and services. Today's consumers no longer seek basic necessities and durable wares; they want products and services related to comfort and convenience, sensual gratification, and an up-scale lifestyle, for example, cell-phones, laptops, plasma-screen televisions, traveling in style and comfort, spas and physical fitness venues, and so on (Treacy and Wiersema 1993; De Castro, Balkin and Shepherd 2008).

CHANGES IN GENERAL PERCEPTIONS AND STATE OF MIND WITH RESPECT TO EMPLOYMENT, CAREERS AND LABOR

The idea of a process of 'creative destruction', a term introduced by Joseph Schumpeter in 1942,[2] is even more relevant today. Among other ideas, it presents what appears to be a paradoxical view – that by creating and developing up-to-date and innovative business ventures, new entrepreneurs dislodge and even replace the traditional businesses, especially those unable to adapt their products or services to the changing technologies and market demands. Since operating new businesses, especially small- and medium-sized enterprises (SMEs), is a relatively low-cost matter compared to the running of large enterprises, and considering that the adaptability of SMEs to changing market demands is comparatively higher, it is rather simple for new entrepreneurial businesses and SMEs to gain access to and enter the market. New entrepreneurs exploit opportunities which enterprises that are already settled in the marketplace do not readily identify. Moreover, and somewhat ironically, these opportunities are the result of the ongoing processes developed by those same active enterprises, i.e., technological development, marketing, R&D, scientific discoveries, etc. In this sense, not only do the existing businesses develop processes that promote and propel their own irrelevance in the labor market, they also pave the way for new entrepreneurs to enter it. As a result, attitudes toward both active, traditional businesses and new SMEs have changed: compared to SMEs, the traditional businesses are considered rigid, bureaucratic and cumbersome, institutions that preserve seniority-based pay and long-term employment practices and disregard creditability in recruiting or promoting their employees. Entrepreneurial businesses, on the other hand, such as SMEs, are perceived as flexible and adaptable, with recruitment and promotion practices based on the employment of highly qualified and talented personnel and professionals, among others. One of the results of this view is that employment in entrepreneurial businesses is now perceived as preferable to employment in traditional companies (Bowen and Hisrich 1986; Katz 1992; Douglas and Shepherd 2002).

PERCEPTIONS OF CREATIVITY AND INNOVATION AT WORK

Resourceful entrepreneurs transform the advantages they find into opportunities, and the opportunities they find into advantages. To do either or both of these requires the ability to see operable innovations; that is, to have a fresh way of looking at things. It also requires the entrepreneurs' persistent and proactive search for all of the expertise related to the proposed product or service. They must also search for reliable and relevant information on the development and trends of the targeted market, and on the tastes and demands of the potential consumers. This is of immense importance because the emergence of a new idea is not automatically an applicable innovation, nor can every applicable innovation be transformed into a successful entrepreneurial business. The immediate utility and necessity of the product or service, or the anticipation of its future utility, should first be established.

The entrepreneur of today is not only a creative inventor, but also the salesperson that will have to personally promote his or her innovative ideas, or directly oversee the agent entrusted with this important phase. Since people are generally resistant to change, entrepreneurs who create new ideas have to engage in an ongoing process of promoting their ideas by convincing others of their value (Aldrich and Fiol 1994; Lindsay 2005a, b; Kropp, Lindsay and Shoham 2006).

CHANGES IN ORGANIZATIONAL CONFIGURATIONS

Changes in organizational configurations, such as flexible hours and individualization of products, and in scientific and technical progress and internationalization, have created myriad opportunities for entrepreneurial firms. These, more than anything else, have had an impact on restructuring the relationship of today's entrepreneurs vis-à-vis both their clients and changing tastes and demands. Far from the situation that prevailed until the late twentieth century, when the craftsmen or suppliers were the authorities in their areas of expertise, and the demand for their merchandise or services was nearly irrelevant for their survival, today's entrepreneurs have to be extremely adaptive, sometimes even drastically changing – or even abandoning – one or more dominant aspects of their entrepreneurial business in order to survive.

Although today's organizational configurations are characterized by high levels of flexibility, galloping scientific and technical progress, the development of different products and marketing strategies, and internationalization, there is also a world of product individualization or production *artisan*-ization which virtually repudiates the impersonal and non-varying mass-produced goods. There is an increased awareness of a growing market for personalized attention, which has led many entrepreneurs to concentrate on very specific areas of expertise, and to develop tailor-made or one-of-a-kind products or services. Artisan manufacture[3] is developing rapidly in the entrepreneurial market, in crafting technological solutions, in various areas of construction, in the worlds of design and lifestyle, and more.

One very successful and well-known company that has demonstrated adaptability and success in the context of the reshaped entrepreneur's profile is Ben & Jerry's. In 1978, its founders, Ben

Cohen and Jerry Greenfield, opened a shop selling homemade ice-cream cones, in a renovated gas station in downtown Burlington, Vermont; in 1985 they turned their business into a small plant manufacturing their own very special, high-quality, homemade ice-cream. As their business developed and expanded, with more manufacturing plants being established in various other places, Ben and Jerry realized that they were losing both their original direct, personal contact with their clients and the reputation that went along with it. In 1986, Ben and Jerry decided to recreate their original 'goodwill' (the value of a business in patronage, reputation, etc. above and beyond its tangible assets) by opening the doors of their new Waterbury plant to the public and offering tours of the ice-cream-making operations.[4] As they made this transformation, the company's founders, the original entrepreneurs of a small ice-cream shop, also continued to change. They adapted their original local, community-oriented, social-responsibility approach of sharing goodwill, good times, and good ice-cream through a variety of events, to plain good business practices, but in such a way that they could continue to uphold their underlying belief in actively recognizing 'the central role that business plays in society by initiating innovative ways to improve the quality of life locally, nationally and internationally'. Along with this, they continue to develop new ice-cream flavors and new packaging designs, and to open new business areas, such as the shooting of a film. Ben & Jerry's has become a successful, internationally recognized and highly respected ice-cream company, whose products are manufactured and sold in tens of countries around the world. Central to Ben & Jerry's 'mission' is their belief that 'three parts – Product mission, Economic mission and Social mission – must thrive equally in a manner that commands deep respect for individuals in and outside the company and supports the communities of which they are a part' (Chakravarthy and Gargiulo 1998).

SUMMARY

It seems as if everything has become more complex in our modern world: the rapid, changing demands of the environment and the corresponding changes in the perceptions, significance and meaning of 'work' and 'employment' relative to 'free time'; the changes in psychological contracts in the employment realm, or changing career preferences – these, among other examples, confront entrepreneurs with new challenges in the entrepreneurial arena. As such, today's entrepreneurs must be more attentive to their environments and ultra-updated on the changes occurring around them, but should also listen very carefully to their own needs and desires, and endeavor to craft their own balanced match between their desires and environmental constraints. For example, when entrepreneurs see an opportunity to spin-off but the economic situation is in flux, rather than disregard their desire to spin-off and become unfulfilled and frustrated, they should look for different ways to achieve their desires: partnering and spinning-off, locating investors, or consulting with professionals on how to spin-off in fluctuating economic times, among others. Entrepreneurs must continually analyze the changes in the environment, psychological contracts, the market, organization, and general perceptions, to enable a re-evaluation of their own desires and goals and to be in a position to reconstruct alternative routes to achieve them.

Many entrepreneurs are currently or will be employers in the future, and they should therefore acknowledge the changes in perceptions and psychological contracts in order to craft effective, fulfilling relationships with their own employees. Acknowledging the changes in the environment encompasses admitting and recognizing that such changes exist and that they expose entrepreneurs to demanding, vague and unexpected situations with their employees; but the more entrepreneurs are willing to acknowledge these changes, the more realistic their expectations will be in relation to both their employees and their own desires.

CASE STUDY 16.1   DOLCE SUBJECT-ORIENTED TOURS, UK

Dolce Subject-oriented Tours is a unique company offering one-of-a-kind subject-oriented journeys in different parts of the world. It was founded by Louise van Harrison in 2005. The original and exclusive services Dolce provides include individually tailored, expertly guided, luxury-level tours for small groups, each accompanied by a tour host who specializes in the specific area of the clients' interest; e.g., a historian, archeologist, musicologist, or someone specializing in mysticism, fashion, or art, among others.

The strategy that Dolce has developed is unique: van Harrison interviews the members of the group wishing to travel with Dolce's guidance, studies the group's preferences, and matches a guide to the group. The guide, alone or together with the group, plans the group's tour, according to their general preferences. These can be anything from visits to small and colorful villages, stays at exotic beaches, or adventure travel; some groups ask to follow a path described in a particular book or film or, as in one case, a couple's fiftieth anniversary was celebrated by their children and grandchildren, who presented the couple with the gift of a trip that followed the path of their lives, for which they provided the information. Each tour is unique; the guide accompanies the group from the planning stage through the entire tour. All decisions are made – and signed upon – by all group members prior to the tour.

Dolce specializes in gastronomic adventure tours, allowing the travelers to experience the finest and most authentic foods and wines of a region, in that region's most prestigious restaurants and wineries, as selected in collaboration with Dolce's gastronomy specialists. Tours may be planned around special interests, such as manufacturers of uniquely flavored honeys in one specific area, or of organic olive oils in another.

Van Harrison and her team hand-pick their service providers and visit them regularly, before, during and after the actual tours, in order to ensure quality and consistency. At present, she employs six trained team members, as well as about twenty specialists in different areas, with whom she has special outsourcing contracts. Although she manages tours for people from more than ten places in the world, most of her clients are from Great Britain, Italy, and the United States.

Managing such a unique and exclusive business is not a simple matter, and targeting the wealthier people in the UK means employing specific strategies. Van Harrison says that such people 'are mostly busy people, who like to maintain their privacy, and offering them a unique tour may cross the very delicate line of that privacy. Marketing your services may turn into invading their private space; it may reveal too much about the preferences, resources and even the persons they prefer to travel with. Besides, these people have seen almost everything and finding their unique point of interest is – an art.' She adds some other important wisdom she has acquired: 'Keeping a constant eye on the strategic planning of the tour and seeing if it needs amending or updating, whilst also constantly looking at the market and the environment within which you operate to make sure the plan is still relevant, these things are vital. Once you are sure you are heading in the right direction, ensure that your mix of finance and resources is optimal to achieve the desired results.'

Innovative and original services are difficult to maintain, particularly those targeted to satisfy such a specific market: 'The competitive market is very demanding, things change often on a daily basis, so you have to keep monitoring all aspects to ensure that your organization remains "fit" for business,' she adds. 'New opportunities can arise at any time – often through my satisfied clients. In a unique business like this, one has to be alert and notice what is going on in the field, examine it laterally, and evaluate it all to see how both you and your clients can benefit from it. It's a tough assignment, but I love every moment in my work,' van Harrison concludes.

QUESTIONS FOR DISCUSSION

1 What are Dolce's main strengths, and how do they enable the company to meet changing consumption dynamics?
2 What were the main risks van Harrison took by launching Dolce?
3 What kind of psychological contract has van Harrison created vis-à-vis her clients, and how does she maintain it?
4 At what level are changes in organizational configurations exemplified in van Harrison and in her company?
5 How does van Harrison decipher her clients' preferences, and how does she maintain their satisfaction with her service?
6 What do you think are the odds that Dolce can survive as a unique, luxury-level business? Which goals would you suggest that van Harrison set for the near future of her business? Explain.

NOTES

1 Market saturation occurs mostly due to an oversupply of similar or complementary products or services, or a decrease in clients' purchasing power.
2 The term was developed by Joseph Schumpeter in his work *Capitalism, Socialism and Democracy* (1942) to denote a 'process of industrial mutation that incessantly revolutionizes the economic structure from within, incessantly destroying the old one, incessantly creating a new one'. Creative destruction occurs when something new destroys the relevance of something that already exists.
3 See *Artisan Creative*, www.artisancreative.com/company/index.shtml.
4 See Ben & Jerry's, www.benjerry.com/our_company/research_library/timeline/index.cfm.

REFERENCES

Aldrich, H.E. and Fiol, M. (1994) 'Fools rush in? The institutional context of industry creation', *Academy of Management Review*, 19: 645–70.
Argyris, C. (1960) *Understanding Organizational Behavior*, Homewood, IL: Dorsey Press.
Bolton, B. and Thompson, J.L. (2004) *Entrepreneurs: Talent, Temperament, Technique*, London: Elsevier.

Bowen, D.D. and Hisrich, R.D. (1986) 'The female entrepreneur: a career development perspective', *Academy of Management Review*, 11: 393–407.

Chakravarthy, B.S. and Gargiulo, M. (1998) 'Maintaining leadership legitimacy in the transition to new organizational forms', *Journal of Management Studies*, 35: 437–56.

De Castro, J., Balkin, D.B. and Shepherd, D.A. (2008) 'Can entrepreneurial firms benefit from product piracy?', *Journal of Business Venturing*, 23: 75–90.

Douglas, E. and Shepherd, D. (2002) 'Self-employment as a career choice: attitudes, entrepreneurial intentions, and utility maximization', *Entrepreneurial Theory and Practice*, 26: 81–90.

Katz, A. (1992) 'A psychosocial cognitive model of employment status choice', *Entrepreneurship Theory and Practice*, 17: 29–37.

Kickul, J. (2001). 'Promises made, promises broken: an exploration of employee attraction and retention practices in small businesses', *Journal of Small Business Management*, 39: 320–35.

Kropp, F., Lindsay, N.J. and Shoham, A. (2006) 'Entrepreneurial, market, and learning orientations and entrepreneurial business venture performance for South African firms', *International Marketing Review*, 23: 504–23.

Krueger, N. (1998) 'Encouraging the identification of environmental opportunities', *Journal of Organizational Change Management*, 11: 174–83.

Krueger, N. (2000) 'The cognitive infrastructure of opportunity emergence', *Entrepreneurship Theory and Practice*, 24: 5–23.

Lindsay, N.J. (2005a) 'Venture capitalist entrepreneurial orientations', in A. Lockett, D. Ucbasaran and J. Butler (eds) *Research in Entrepreneurship and Management*, 5, 223–37.

Lindsay, N.J. (2005b) 'Toward a cultural model of indigenous entrepreneurial attitude', *Academy of Marketing Sciences Review*, 5: 1–17.

O'Donoghue, D. and Townshend, I.J. (2005) 'Diversification, specialization, convergence and divergence of sectoral employment structures in the British urban system, 1991–2001', *Regional Studies*, 39: 585–602.

Rousseau, D.M. (1995) *Psychological Contracts in Organizations: Understanding Written and Unwritten Agreements*, Thousand Oaks, CA: Sage.

Schumpeter, J.A. (1942) 'The process of creative destruction', in *Capitalism, Socialism and Democracy*, New York: Harper Torchbooks.

Thompson, J.L. (2004a) 'The facets of the entrepreneur: identifying entrepreneurial potential', *Management Decision*, 42: 243–58.

Thompson, J.L. (2004b) 'Innovation through people', *Management Decision*, 42: 1082–94.

Timmons, J.A., Muzyka, D.F., Stevenson, H.H. and Bygrave, W.D. (1987) 'Opportunity recognition: the core of entrepreneurship', in *Frontiers of Entrepreneurship Research*, Wellesley, MA: Babson College.

Treacy, M. and Wiersema, F. (1993) 'Customer intimacy and other value disciplines', *Harvard Business Review*, 71: 84–94.

Conclusion

In this book the entrepreneurial procees has been presented from both evolutionary and contemporary perspectives, i.e., a developmental overview of the steps potential and active entrepreneurs need to follow to design their entrepreneurial business is incorporated with wide-ranging, international examples and case studies reflecting the core activities most relevant to entrepreneurs. This book aims to illustrate the entrepreneurial path through the changing environments and the demanding challenges entrepreneurs meet, and to discuss the means, tools and insights that can be proactively crafted by them to achieve success in their businesses and in other relevant spheres of their lives. The main message throughout this book, demonstrated at every step of this exciting journey, is proactiveness: 'If you dream about it – go for it.' The book encourages budding entrepreneurs to reach out, attempt, seek, ask for advice and assistance, and make their dreams come true. Specifically, by designing their own entrepreneurial route and environment, their dreams can become their future as well as that of mankind.

SUCCESS AND SELF-ACTUALIZATION

The famous dancer Baryshnikov was once quoted as saying: 'I do not try to dance better than anyone else. I only try to dance better than myself.' This quotation embodies the meaning of self-actualization – a psychological state of mind that brings people to higher levels of well-being, contentment and happiness, and stimulates their motivation to create, invent and produce. As such, it is very relevant to entrepreneurship. The interfacial relationship between creation, initiation or invention and an internal feeling of self-actualization is precious and should be maintained. However, there is no one, main way of achieving this; rather, there are several types of entrepreneurs, grouped on the basis of their psychological characteristics, who started their businesses within different frameworks and developed their ventures with different motivations.

It is therefore one of the entrepreneur's missions to define what it means for him or her to experience these 'peaks', this feeling of all-encompassing success: such a definition makes it possible to redefine the business's goals such that they will best match the entrepreneur's definition of self-actualization (Chang and MacMillan 1991; Miner 1997, 2000; Van de Ven et al. 1999; Alsaaty 2006; Galloway and Mochrie 2006; Gray, Foster and Howard 2006).

One tool for this purpose might be a self-feedback process conducted every six to twelve months; to conduct such a process, the model in Figure 17.1 might be applied.

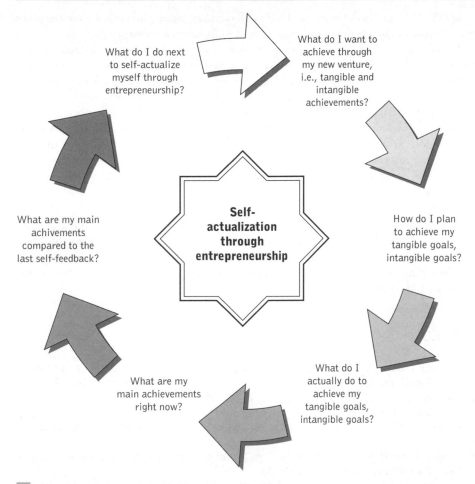

Figure 17.1 of the circular self-feedback model reads (clockwise from top):

- What do I want to achieve through my new venture, i.e., tangible and intangible achievements?
- How do I plan to achieve my tangible goals, intangible goals?
- What do I actually do to achieve my tangible goals, intangible goals?
- What are my main achievements right now?
- What are my main achivements compared to the last self-feedback?
- What do I do next to self-actualize myself through entrepreneurship?

Center: **Self-actualization through entrepreneurship**

Figure 17.1 *A self-feedback model*

Another practical tool for entrepreneurs would be to list their personal strengths as they see them, their goals or dreams in the different spheres of their lives, and then their business goals. Such a categorization might enable them to analyze the 'connecting points' – where their strengths, dreams and business goals come together. These are the places where self-actualization is cultivated and these places should be defined, acknowledged and proactively sustained.

A different means would be to list the benefits and drawbacks in being an entrepreneur, as perceived by the entrepreneur according to his or her own experience; then, rather than focusing on the benefits, the entrepreneur focuses on the drawbacks and determines how to turn them into opportunities. For example, a drawback such as 'financial instability' may be turned into an opportunity via either a perceptional switch; that is, rather than treating it as a threat it means that the entrepreneur must be hands-on with his or her financial state, and this is a significant and valuable opportunity to learn more about his or her business and the environment, or a practical switch, by employing an expert or taking courses aimed at teaching financial management of entrepreneurial businesses.

Entrepreneurial success is never guaranteed, even in the case of the most promising, innovative entrepreneurial businesses or those having already cooperated with investors. Founders of, for example, General Motors, Ford, Goodyear, Heinz and Hershey, among others, failed to the point of bankruptcy before finding their success, even when developing innovative products. Henry Ford explained this as follows: 'Life is a series of experiences, each of which makes us stronger even though it is hard to realize this. For the world was built to develop character, and we must learn that the setbacks and griefs which we endure help us in our marching onward.' The key to success lies in not being discouraged by failures, being capable of learning from those failures, restarting the whole entrepreneurial process by bouncing back from setbacks, and most important, being persistent in striving toward accomplishing a vision. When entrepreneurship is a fulfilling, satisfying and enthusiastic process where entrepreneurs find it exciting and are passionate to work on their innovations, neither internal nor external difficulties will prevent them from proceeding with their entrepreneurial course. Much of entrepreneurial success depends on the entrepreneur's motivation, will and determination to succeed.

Some consider entrepreneurship a meaningful experience, others a way of life, but when individuals are brimming with innovative ideas and are passionate to implement them, it is no longer a matter of wishful thinking, it is reality. For those experiencing a continual internal flame, this book's message is based on the notion of Pierre de Coubertin, founder of the modern Olympic Games: 'The most important thing . . . is not winning but taking part; the essential thing in life is not conquering but fighting well.'

REFERENCES

Alsaaty, F.M. (2006) 'Case study: a young entrepreneur going global', *Business Review*, 6: 178–85.

Chang, W. and MacMillan, I.C. (1991) 'A review of entrepreneurial development in the People's Republic of China', *Journal of Business Venturing*, 6: 375–9.

Galloway, L. and Mochrie, R. (2006) 'Entrepreneurial motivation, orientation and realization in rural economies: a study of rural Scotland', *International Journal of Entrepreneurship and Innovation*, 7: 173–83.

Gray, K.R., Foster, H. and Howard, M. (2006) 'Motivations of Moroccans to be entrepreneurs', *Journal of Developmental Entrepreneurship*, 11: 297–318.

Miner, J.B. (1997) 'The expanded horizon for achieving entrepreneurial success', *Organizational Dynamics*, 25: 54–67.

Miner, J.B. (2000) 'Testing a psychological typology of entrepreneurship using business founders', *Journal of Applied Behavioral Science*, 36: 43–69.

Van de Ven, A., Polley, D.E., Garud, R. and Venkataraman, S. (1999) *The Innovation Journey*, New York: Oxford University Press.

Index